## Get the eBook FREE!

(PDF, ePub, Kindle, and liveBook all included)

We believe that once you buy a book from us, you should be able to read it in any format we have available. To get electronic versions of this book at no additional cost to you, purchase and then register this book at the Manning website.

Go to https://www.manning.com/freebook and follow the instructions to complete your pBook registration.

That's it!
Thanks from Manning!

*Learn PowerShell in a Month of Lunches, Fourth Edition*

# Learn PowerShell in a Month of Lunches

## FOURTH EDITION

### COVERS WINDOWS, LINUX, AND MACOS

JAMES PETTY, TRAVIS PLUNK,
TYLER LEONHARDT, DON JONES, JEFFERY HICKS

FOREWORD BY DON JONES

MANNING
SHELTER ISLAND

Manning Publications Co.
20 Baldwin Road
PO Box 761
Shelter Island, NY 11964

| | |
|---|---|
| Development editor: | Frances Lefkowitz |
| Technical development editor: | Mike Shepard |
| Review editor: | Aleks Dragosavljević |
| Production editor: | Deirdre Hiam |
| Copy editor: | Carrie Andrews |
| Proofreader: | Katie Tennant |
| Technical proofreader: | Shawn Bolan |
| Typesetter: | Gordan Salinovic |
| Cover designer: | Leslie Haimes |

ISBN 9781617296963
Printed in the United States of America

# brief contents

# contents

# *foreword*

Sitting down to write this foreword, my first thought was, "Wow, there's a lot to unpack here." My own time with PowerShell started in 2005, about a year before the shell was unleashed at TechEd Barcelona 2006. *Learn Windows PowerShell in a Month of Lunches*, the progenitor of this book, was far from my first PowerShell tome. Jeff Hicks and I wrote three editions of *Windows PowerShell: TFM* with SAPIEN Technologies first. After those, I actually made a decision, if you can imagine it, to not write any more PowerShell books! But I quickly came to realize that the existing selection of PowerShell books—well over a dozen by then—was missing a major audience need. The books of the time were teaching PowerShell as a programming language, aiming for the fairly large audience of VBScript coders that existed at the time. But PowerShell itself was aiming for a far larger and broader audience: nonprogrammers.

That's when I took the narratives I'd been using in live PowerShell classes and started constructing a new book: one that wouldn't head directly to control-of-flow statements by chapter 3, and one that would really focus on a best-fit sequence of teaching to make learning PowerShell as easy as possible. I wanted to make, and keep, a promise: give me an hour a day for a month, and I'll make you functionally useful in PowerShell.

Month of Lunches, as a book series, had a bit of a rough road. Book publishers operate on razor-thin margins, and launching a new series consumes a lot of resources. A different publisher originally decided to give the series a shot but backed out at the last minute. Manning—in what I hope has been a fantastic decision for them—stepped up and said, "Let's do it." We developed a new cover art concept that was a radical departure from the company's norm, showing how willing they were to think creatively about this new series.

*Learn Windows PowerShell in a Month of Lunches* was a solid hit, becoming one of the best-selling PowerShell books in the world. It's been translated into a number of different languages, and for many people it was their first exposure to PowerShell. I've heard from thousands of people how the book helped them break into the world of PowerShell. For many, it was their first PowerShell learning experience. For most, it wasn't their last, but I'm proud that so many people trusted Jeff and me to get them started.

When Microsoft finally made PowerShell open source (!!!!) and cross-platform (!!!!!!!), we knew it would be time for a new Month of Lunches book—one that addressed PowerShell instead of just Windows PowerShell.

But by that point, Jeff and I were a little burned out on writing. My own career was moving in a different direction—I'd accepted a VP role at my company, and I knew I'd be hard pressed to keep up with PowerShell's rapidly changing and expanding world. My final book, *Shell of an Idea: The Untold History of PowerShell,* was in many ways a love letter to the community and product team that had been supporters and friends for more than a decade. It told the stories of how PowerShell only barely managed to come to life, and I knew as I wrote it that I wouldn't have the time to write any more about PowerShell's future.

That's why I'm so glad that the authors of this volume stepped in. The PowerShell community in general is full of incredibly generous people, always willing to answer a question and help you out. "Stepping away," for me, also meant stepping away from PowerShell.org, the website I cofounded, and the nonprofit that backed it. It meant stepping away from PowerShell + DevOps Global Summit, a conference I first financed on my American Express card. But the PowerShell community stepped up as they almost always do: new people agreed to keep the organization not only going, but also *growing.* James Petty, one of this book's coauthors, is one of those folks, and I'm forever grateful to him and his team for keeping the community spirit alive.

This book largely builds on the narrative that I created for the first Month of Lunches title and that Jeff Hicks and I refined through three editions—along with *Learn PowerShell Scripting in a Month of Lunches,* a book that's as relevant today as it was when we first wrote it. But this book breaks out of the Windows operating system and treats PowerShell as a true global citizen: you'll find examples applicable whether you're running PowerShell on Windows, Linux, or macOS—a huge undertaking for these authors, given the stark differences between those operating systems.

I remain incredibly grateful to the PowerShell community. They've made me feel welcomed, appreciated, and valuable—something I hope everyone can experience at some point. It's a community I encourage you to explore, via PowerShell.org or the many other volunteer-driven websites, GitHub repos, Twitter accounts, and other outlets. You'll be glad you did.

Finally, I want you to know that your investment of time in PowerShell will create impressive returns. PowerShell is almost unique among software in that it didn't seek to reinvent anything. Instead, it simply wanted to take all the chaotic, crazy, powerful stuff that was already in the world and make it more consistent and easier to use. PowerShell respects Linux, for example, by not trying to impose a Microsoft worldview on that operating system. Instead, PowerShell simply makes everything Linux already is just a little easier to operate.

I hope your PowerShell journey, whether it's just beginning or you're well into it, will prove as fruitful and satisfying as mine has been. I hope you'll show the authors of this book your support, because they've labored mightily to bring this into your hands. And I hope you'll take your newfound knowledge and find ways to share it with others who are just beginning *their* journey. Regardless of what's already been said or written about PowerShell, *your* take on it will prove to be the one that helps *someone* have the "aha!" moment that launches their own PowerShell success.

—DON JONES

# *preface*

Never in a million years would I have thought that one day I would be asked to help write any tech book, much less the fourth edition of *Learn PowerShell in a Month of Lunches*—the very book that started me on my journey many years ago.

When I heard that Travis Plunk and Tyler Leonhardt had signed on with Manning to write the fourth edition of the successful book, I thought, *Who better to write the next edition than two of the people on the PowerShell team?* To preserve the winning style of Don Jones and Jeffery Hicks from the earlier versions, Tyler and Travis would work from their original chapters. Because PowerShell was now available on Linux and macOS, however, this book would focus on those two operating systems and showcase the open source/cross-platform abilities of PowerShell 7. And the book would be called *Learn PowerShell in a Month of Lunches* rather than *Learn Windows PowerShell in a Month of Lunches*, which was the title of the first, second, and third editions of the classic book. Excited to see the expanded and updated version, I purchased the MEAP and was reading the chapters as they were released.

Fast-forward a year. PowerShell 7 was released. Also, readers and early reviewers of the book made it clear that Windows is still the OS where most admins spend their time, so they wanted the fourth edition to include Windows as well as Linux and macOS. So I was brought on board to finish up the book and update it to cover the latest version of PowerShell and the Windows OS. I took what Tyler and Travis had started and kept the project going, making sure that all three operating systems were represented. The book did end up being a little Windows heavy, but that's to be expected, as, again, PowerShell still has more functionality on Windows. I came from the corporate environment, using PowerShell daily to support Windows servers.

It has been an amazing journey for me to come full circle, from reading the first book to helping write this edition. Whether you are just getting started with Power-Shell or are a seasoned admin looking for the latest tips and tricks, I hope you enjoy this book.

—JAMES PETTY

# *acknowledgments*

I offer a huge thank-you to my wife, Kacie, for supporting me during this project. I also thank Don Gannon-Jones for his support, mentorship, and encouragement to join this project. This has been an amazing journey for me to come full circle from reading Don's first Month of Lunches book on PowerShell to helping write this edition.

I would also like to thank the staff at Manning: Deirdre Hiam, my project editor; Carrie Andrews, my copyeditor; Katie Tennant, my proofreader; and Shawn Bolan, my technical proofer.

To all the reviewers: Aldo Solis Zenteno, Birnou Sebarte, Brad Hysmith, Bruce Bergman, Foster Haines, Giuliano Latini, James Matlock, Jan Vinterberg, Jane Noesgaard Larsen, Jean-Sebastien Gervais, Kamesh Ganesan, Marcel van den Brink, Max Almonte, Michel Klomp, Oliver Korten, Paul Love, Peter Brown, Ranjit Sahai, Ray Booysen, Richard Michaels, Roman Levchenko, Shawn Bolan, Simon Seyag, Stefan Turalski, Stephen Goodman, Thein Than Htun, and Vincent Delcoigne, thank you. Your suggestions helped to make this a better book.

# *about this book*

We are glad you have decided to join us in a month-long journey! A month seems like a long time, but it will be worth it, we promise.

### *Who should read this book*

This book is for a wide range of audiences; however, the primary audience is those who are just getting started with PowerShell. Job functions may include help desk or server administrators.

Most of the preliminary information you will need is covered in chapter 1, but here are a few things we should mention up front. First, we strongly suggest that you follow along with the examples in the book. For the optimal experience, we suggest you run everything on a virtual machine. We have done our best to make sure the examples are cross-platform, but as you will see, there are a few chapters that are Windows specific.

Second, be prepared to read this book from start to finish, covering each chapter in order. Again, this is something we'll explain in more detail in chapter 1, but the idea is that each chapter introduces a few new things that you will need in subsequent chapters. You really shouldn't try to push through the whole book—stick with the one-chapter-per-day approach. The human brain can only absorb so much information at once, and by taking on PowerShell in small chunks, you'll actually learn it a lot faster and more thoroughly.

### About the code

This book contains a lot of code snippets. Most of them are short, so you should be able to type them easily. In fact, we recommend that you do type them, because doing so will help reinforce an essential PowerShell skill: accurate typing! Longer code snippets are given in listings and are available for download from the book's web page on the publisher's website at www.manning.com/books/learn-powershell-in-a-month-of-lunches.

That said, you should be aware of a few conventions. Code always appears in a special font, just as in this example:

```
Get-CimInstance -class Win32_OperatingSystem
➥ -computerName SRV-01
```

That example also illustrates the line-continuation character used in this book. It indicates that those two lines should be typed as a single line in PowerShell. In other words, don't press Enter or Return after `Win32_OperatingSystem`—keep right on typing. PowerShell allows for long lines, but the pages of this book can hold only so much.

Sometimes code is also **in bold** to highlight code that has changed from previous steps in the chapter, such as when a new feature adds to an existing line of code. And sometimes you'll also see that code font within the text itself, such as when we write `Get-Command`. That just lets you know that you're looking at a command, parameter, or other element that you would type within the shell.

Fourth, you'll see an element that we'll bring up again in several chapters: the backtick character (`` ` ``). Here's an example:

```
Invoke-Command -scriptblock { Get-ChildItem } `
  -computerName SRV-01,localhost,DC02
```

The character at the end of the first line isn't a stray bit of ink—it's a real character that you would type. On a US keyboard, the backtick (or grave accent) is usually near the upper left, under the Esc key, on the same key as the tilde character (~). When you see the backtick in a code listing, type it exactly as is. Furthermore, when it appears at the end of a line—as in the preceding example—make sure that it's the last character on that line. If you allow any spaces or tabs to appear after it, the backtick won't work correctly, and neither will the code example.

You can get executable snippets of code from the liveBook (online) version of this book at https://livebook.manning.com/book/learn-powershell-in-a-month-of-lunches. The complete code for the examples in the book is available for download from the Manning website at www.manning.com/books/learn-powershell-in-a-month-of-lunches, and from GitHub at https://github.com/psjamesp/Learn-PowerShell-in-a-Month-of-Lunches-4th-Edition.

### liveBook discussion forum

Purchase of *Learn PowerShell in a Month of Lunches, Fourth Edition*, includes free access to liveBook, Manning's online reading platform. Using liveBook's exclusive discussion features, you can attach comments to the book globally or to specific sections or paragraphs. It's a snap to make notes for yourself, ask and answer technical questions, and receive help from the authors and other users. To access the forum, go to https://livebook .manning.com/book/learn-powershell-in-a-month-of-lunches/discussion. You can also learn more about Manning's forums and the rules of conduct at https://livebook .manning.com/discussion.

Manning's commitment to our readers is to provide a venue where a meaningful dialogue between readers and between readers and authors can take place. It is not a commitment to any specific amount of participation on the part of the authors, whose contribution to the forum remains voluntary (and unpaid). We encourage you to ask them some challenging questions lest their interest stray! The forum and the archives of previous discussions will be accessible from the publisher's website as long as the book is in print.

# about the authors

JAMES PETTY is the president and CEO of the DevOps Collective, which runs Power-Shell.org, and is also a Microsoft Cloud and Datacenter MVP. He organizes the Power-Shell + DevOps Global Summit held each April and the DevOps + Automation Summit held in the fall, and he has helped facilitate multiple PowerShell Saturdays around the United States. A contributing author to *The PowerShell Conference Book*, volume 1, he is also cofounder of the Chattanooga PowerShell user group and the cochair for Power-Shell on the River, a two-day PowerShell conference hosted in Chattanooga, Tennessee.

TRAVIS PLUNK has been a software engineer on various PowerShell teams since 2013 and at Microsoft since 1999. He was involved in open sourcing PowerShell and moved the core PowerShell engine over shortly after PowerShell was made open source.

TYLER LEONHARD has been a software engineer on the PowerShell team for about 2 years and at Microsoft for almost 3. He is a core maintainer of the PowerShell extension for VS Code and is also active on social media (Twitter, Twitch streams, LinkedIn) as a member of the PowerShell team.

JEFFERY HICKS is an IT veteran with 30+ years of experience, much of it spent as an IT infrastructure consultant specializing in Microsoft server technologies, emphasizing automation and efficiency. He is a multiyear recipient of the Microsoft MVP Award. He works today as an independent author, teacher, and consultant. Jeff has taught about PowerShell and the benefits of automation to IT Pros worldwide. He has authored and coauthored several books, writes for numerous online sites and print publications, is a Pluralsight author, and is a frequent speaker at technology conferences and user groups. You can keep up with Jeff on Twitter (http://twitter.com/JeffHicks). You'll find his online work at https://jdhitsolutions.com/blog and https://jeffhicks.substack.com.

# *Before you begin* 1

PowerShell just turned 15 years old (on November 14, 2021). It's hard to believe it's been around this long, but there is still a large number of IT folks who haven't used it yet. We get it—there is only so much time in the day, and you are already familiar with doing things the way you always have. Or maybe your cybersecurity officer will not let you turn on PowerShell because it can only be used by the bad guys. Either way, we are glad you could join us on our adventure. We have been using Power-Shell for a long time. In fact, two of us, James and Tyler, actually learned Power-Shell from earlier editions of this very book.

There was a huge shift in the industry around 2009 when a new concept was realized about PowerShell. It isn't a scripting language, nor is it a programming language, so the way we teach PowerShell needed to change as well. PowerShell is actually a command-line shell where you run command-line utilities. Like all good shells, it has scripting capabilities, but you don't have to use them, and you certainly don't have to *start* with them.

The previous editions of this book were the result of that culture shift, and we keep that same mindset here today. It's the best that we've yet devised to teach Power-Shell to someone who might not have a scripting background (although it certainly doesn't hurt if you do). But before we jump into the instruction, let's set the stage for you.

## 1.1 Why you can no longer afford to ignore PowerShell

Batch. KiXtart. VBScript. Let's face it, PowerShell isn't exactly Microsoft's (or anyone else's) first effort at providing automation capabilities to Windows administrators. We think it's valuable to understand why you should care about PowerShell—when you do, the time you commit to learning PowerShell will pay off. Let's start by considering what life was like before PowerShell came along and look at some of the advantages of using this shell.

### 1.1.1   *Life without PowerShell*

Windows administrators have always been happy to click around in the graphical user interface (GUI) to accomplish their chores. After all, the GUI is largely the whole point of Windows—the operating system isn't called *Text*, after all. GUIs are great because they enable you to discover what you can do. Do you remember the first time you opened Active Directory Users and Computers? Maybe you hovered over icons and read tooltips, pulled down menus, and right-clicked things, all to see what was available. GUIs make learning a tool easier. Unfortunately, GUIs have zero return on that investment. If it takes you 5 minutes to create a new user in Active Directory (and assuming you're filling in a lot of the fields, that's a reasonable estimate), you'll never get any faster than that. One hundred users will take 500 minutes—there's no way, short of learning to type and click faster, to make the process go any quicker.

Microsoft has tried to deal with that problem a bit haphazardly, and VBScript was probably its most successful attempt. It might have taken you an hour to write a VBScript that could import new users from a CSV file, but after you'd invested that hour, creating users in the future would take only a few seconds. The problem with VBScript is that Microsoft didn't make a wholehearted effort in supporting it. Microsoft had to remember to make things VBScript accessible, and when developers forgot (or didn't have time), you were stuck. Want to change the IP address of a network adapter by using VBScript? Okay, you can. Want to check its link speed? You can't, because nobody remembered to hook that up in a way that VBScript could get to. Sorry. Jeffrey Snover, the architect of Windows PowerShell, calls this *the last mile*. You can do a lot with VBScript (and other, similar technologies), but it tends to let you down at some point, never getting you through that last mile to the finish line.

Windows PowerShell is an express attempt on Microsoft's part to do a better job and to get you through the last mile. And it's been a successful attempt so far. Dozens of product groups within Microsoft have adopted PowerShell, an extensive ecosystem of third parties depends on it, and a global community of experts and enthusiasts are pushing the PowerShell envelope every day.

### 1.1.2   *Life with PowerShell*

Microsoft's goal for Windows PowerShell is to build 100% of a product's administrative functionality in PowerShell. Microsoft continues to build GUI consoles, but those consoles are executing PowerShell commands behind the scenes. This approach forces the company to make sure that every possible thing you can do with the product is accessible through PowerShell. If you need to automate a repetitive task or create a process that the GUI doesn't enable well, you can drop into PowerShell and take full control for yourself.

Several Microsoft products have already adopted this approach over the years, including Exchange, SharePoint, System Center products, Microsoft 365, Azure, and let's not forget Windows Admin Center. Non-Microsoft products, including Amazon Web Services (AWS) and VMware, have taken a keen interest in PowerShell as well.

Windows Server 2012, which was where PowerShell v3 was introduced, and higher are almost completely managed from PowerShell—or by a GUI sitting atop PowerShell. That's why you can't afford to ignore PowerShell: Over the last few years, PowerShell has become the basis for more and more administration. It's already become the foundation for numerous higher-level technologies, including Desired State Configuration (DSC) and much more. PowerShell is everywhere!

Ask yourself this question: If I were in charge of a team of IT administrators (and perhaps you are), who would I want in my senior, higher-paying positions? Administrators who need several minutes to click their way through a GUI each time they need to perform a task, or ones who can perform tasks in a few seconds after automating them? We already know the answer from almost every other part of the IT world. Ask a Cisco administrator, or an AS/400 operator, or a UNIX administrator. The answer is, "I'd rather have the person who can run things more efficiently from the command line." Going forward, the Windows world will start to split into two groups: administrators who can use PowerShell and those who can't. Our favorite quote from Don Gannon-Jones at Microsoft's TechEd 2010 conference is, "Your choice is *Learn PowerShell*, or *Would you like fries with that?*" We are glad you decided to make the plunge and learn PowerShell with us!

## 1.2 Windows, Linux, and macOS, oh my

In mid-2016, Microsoft made the unprecedented decision to open source PowerShell Version 6 (then known as PowerShell Core). At the same time, it released versions of PowerShell—without the *Windows* attached—for macOS and numerous Linux builds. Amazing! Now the same object-centric shell is available on many operating systems and can be evolved and improved by a worldwide community. So for this edition of the book, we have done our best to demonstrate the multiplatform use of PowerShell and included examples for macOS and Linux environments as well. We still feel that PowerShell's biggest audience will be Windows users, but we also want to make sure you understand how it works on other operating systems.

We have done our best to make everything in this book cross-platform compatible. However, as of the writing of this book, there are just over 200 commands available for Linux and macOS, so not everything we wanted to show you will work. With that in mind, we want to call out chapters 19 and 20 in particular, as they are 100% Windows focused.

## 1.3 Is this book for you?

This book doesn't try to be all things to all people. Microsoft's PowerShell team loosely defines three audiences who use PowerShell:

- Administrators (regardless of OS) who primarily run commands and consume tools written by others

- Administrators (regardless of OS) who combine commands and tools into more-complex processes, and perhaps package those as tools that less-experienced administrators can use
- Administrators (regardless of OS) and developers who create reusable tools and applications

This book is designed primarily for the first audience. We think it's valuable for anyone, even a developer, to understand how PowerShell is used to run commands. After all, if you're going to create your own tools and commands, you should know the patterns that PowerShell uses, as they allow you to make tools and commands that work as well as they can within PowerShell.

If you're interested in creating scripts to automate complex processes, such as new user provisioning, then you'll see how to do that by the end of this book. You'll even see how to get started on creating your own commands that other administrators can use. But this book won't probe the depths of everything that PowerShell can possibly do. Our goal is to get you using PowerShell and being effective with it in a production environment.

We'll also show you a couple of ways to use PowerShell to connect to external management technologies; remoting and interacting with Common Information Model (CIM) classes and regular expressions are two examples that come quickly to mind. For the most part, we're going to introduce only those technologies and focus on how PowerShell connects to them. Those topics deserve their own books (and have them), so we concentrate solely on the PowerShell side of things. We'll provide suggestions for further exploration if you'd like to pursue those technologies on your own. In short, this book isn't meant to be the last thing you use to learn about PowerShell, but instead is designed to be a great first step.

## 1.4    How to use this book

The idea behind this book is that you'll read one chapter each day. You don't have to read it during lunch, but each chapter should take you only about 40 minutes to read, giving you an extra 20 minutes to gobble down the rest of your sandwich and practice what the chapter showed you.

### 1.4.1    The chapters

Of the chapters in this book, chapters 2 through 26 contain the main content, giving you 25 days' worth of lunches to look forward to. You can expect to complete the main content of the book in about a month. Try to stick with that schedule as much as possible, and don't feel the need to read extra chapters in a given day. It's more important that you spend some time practicing what each chapter shows you, because using PowerShell will help cement what you've learned. Not every chapter requires a full hour, so sometimes you'll be able to spend additional time practicing (and eating lunch) before you have to get back to work. We find that a lot of people learn more quickly when they stick with just one chapter a day, because it gives your brain time to mull over the new ideas and gives you time to practice them on your own. Don't rush it, and you may find yourself moving more quickly than you thought possible. Chapter 27 provides ideas for where to go next on your PowerShell journey. Finally, we include the appendix, "PowerShell cheat sheet," which is a compilation of all the "gotchas" we mention throughout the body of the book; use this as a reference when you want to find something but you can't remember where to look.

### 1.4.2 Hands-on labs

Most of the main content chapters include a short lab for you to complete. You'll be given instructions, and perhaps a hint or two. The answers for these labs appear at the end of each chapter. But try your best to complete each lab without looking at the answers.

### 1.4.3 Supplementary materials

We have one video made with this book in mind: Tyler's "How to navigate the help system in PowerShell"; it's in Manning's free content center (http://mng.bz/enYP).

 We also suggest PowerShell.org, run by James, and its YouTube channel, YouTube .com/powershellorg, which contains a ton of video content. You'll find recorded sessions from the PowerShell + DevOps Global Summit events, online community webinars, and a lot more. All free!

### 1.4.4 Further exploration

A few chapters in this book only skim the surface of some cool technologies, and we end those chapters with suggestions for exploring those technologies on your own. We point out additional resources, including free stuff that you can use to expand your skill set as the need arises.

### 1.4.5 Above and beyond

As we learned PowerShell, we often wanted to go off on a tangent and explore why something worked the way it did. We didn't learn many extra practical skills that way, but we did gain a deeper understanding of what PowerShell is and how it works. We've included some of that tangential information throughout the book in sections labeled "Above and beyond." None of those will take you more than a couple of minutes or so to read, but if you're the type of person who likes to know why something works the way it does, they can provide some fun additional facts. If you feel those sections might distract you from the practical stuff, ignore them on your first read-through. You can always come back and explore them later, after you've mastered the chapter's main material.

## 1.5   *Setting up your lab environment*

You're going to be doing a lot of practicing in PowerShell throughout this book, and you'll want to have a lab environment to work in. Please don't practice in your company's production environment.

   All you'll need to run most of the examples in this book—and to complete all of the labs—is a copy of Windows that has PowerShell 7.1 or later installed. We suggest Windows 10 or later, or Windows Server 2016 or later, both of which come with PowerShell v5.1. If you're going to play with PowerShell, you'll have to invest in a version of Windows that has it. For most of the labs, we included additional instructions for your Linux environment.

> **NOTE**   You have to download and install PowerShell 7 separately, as it runs side by side with Windows PowerShell 5.1, which comes preinstalled. However, most of these labs will run in Windows PowerShell. Instructions on how to install PowerShell 7 can be found at http://mng.bz/p2R2.

We will also be using Visual Studio Code (VS Code) with the latest stable release of the PowerShell extension, which can be installed from the marketplace. If you're using a non-Windows build of PowerShell, you'll have fewer options to worry about. Just get the right build for your version of macOS or Linux (or whatever) from http://github .com/PowerShell/PowerShell, and you should be good to go. Keep in mind, however, that a lot of the *functionality* we'll be using in our examples is unique to Windows. For example, you can't get a list of services on Linux, because Linux doesn't have services (it has daemons, which are similar), but we will do our best to use examples that are cross-platform (such as Get-Process).

> **TIP**   You should be able to accomplish everything in this book with a single computer running PowerShell, although some stuff gets more interesting if you have two or three computers, all in the same domain, to play with.

## 1.6   *Installing PowerShell*

If you don't have PowerShell 7 installed right now, it's okay. We'll go over how to do that in the next chapter. If you want to check the latest available version of PowerShell or download it, go to https://docs.microsoft.com/en-us/powershell. This official PowerShell home page has links to the latest releases and how to install them.

> **TIP**   You should check your version of PowerShell: open the PowerShell console, type $PSVersionTable, and press Enter.

Before you go any further, take a few minutes to customize PowerShell. If you're using the text-based console host, we strongly recommend that you change the default console font to the Lucida fixed-width font. The default font makes it difficult to distinguish some of the special punctuation characters that PowerShell uses. Follow these steps to customize the font:

1 Click the control box (that's the PowerShell icon in the upper left of the console window) and select Properties from the menu.

2 In the dialog box that appears, browse through the various tabs to change the font, window colors, window size and position, and so forth.

**TIP** Make sure that both the window size and screen buffer have the same width values.

Your changes will apply to the default console, meaning they'll stick around when you open new windows. Of course, all of this applies only to Windows: On non-Windows operating systems, you'll usually install PowerShell, open your operating system's command line (e.g., a Bash shell), and run `powershell`. Your console window will determine your colors, screen layout, and so on, so adjust to suit your preferences.

## 1.7 Contacting us

We're passionate about helping folks like you learn Windows PowerShell, and we try to provide as many resources as we can. We also appreciate your feedback, because that helps us come up with ideas for new resources that we can add to the site and ways to improve future editions of this book. On Twitter, you can reach Travis at @TravisPlunk, Tyler at @TylerLeonhardt, and James at @PsJamesP. We also hang out in the forums of https://forums.powershell.org if you have PowerShell questions. Another wonderful place for more resources is https://powershell.org, which includes free e-books, in-person conferences, free webinars, and tons more. James helps run the organization, and we can't recommend it highly enough as a place to continue your PowerShell education after you've finished this book.

## 1.8 Being immediately effective with PowerShell

*Immediately effective* is a phrase we've made our primary goal for this entire book. As much as possible, each chapter focuses on something that you could use in a real production environment, right away. That means we sometimes gloss over some details in the beginning, but when necessary we promise to circle back and cover those details at the right time. In many cases, we had to choose between hitting you with 20 pages of theory first, or diving right in and accomplishing something without explaining all the nuances, caveats, and details. When those choices came along, we almost always chose to dive right in, with the goal of making you *immediately effective*. But all of those important details and nuances are still explained later in the book.

Okay, that's enough background. It's time to start being immediately effective. Your first lunch lesson awaits.

# Meet PowerShell

This chapter is all about getting you situated and helping you to decide which Power-Shell interface you'll use (yes, you have a choice). If you've used PowerShell before, this material might seem redundant, so feel free to *skim* this chapter—you might still find some tidbits here and there that'll help you down the line.

Also, this chapter applies exclusively to PowerShell on Windows, macOS, and Ubuntu 18.04. Other Linux distributions have a similar setup, but they will not be covered in this chapter. For those other installation instructions, you can get them right from PowerShell's GitHub page at https://github.com/PowerShell/PowerShell#.

---

**Useful terms**

We should define a few terms that we will use quite a bit in this chapter.

*PowerShell*—Refers to the 7.x version that you have installed.

*Shell*—A shell is basically an application that can accept text-based commands and is commonly used to interact with your computer or other machines via a script or interactive experience like a terminal. Examples of shells include Bash, fish, or PowerShell.

*Terminal*—A terminal is an application that can run a shell application within it so that a user can interact with the shell in a visual way. Terminals are shell agnostic, so you can run any shell in any terminal you'd like.

*Windows PowerShell*—Refers to PowerShell 5.1 that comes preinstalled on your Windows 10 device.

---

## *2.1*    *PowerShell on Windows*

PowerShell has come preinstalled on Windows PCs since Windows 7 (and Server 2008). It is important to note that the process name for PowerShell 7 has changed on Windows. It is no longer `powershell.exe` but `pwsh.exe`. PowerShell 7 is a side-by-side installation, meaning that Windows PowerShell (5.1) is still installed by default (hence why the process name had to change).

Let's install PowerShell 7 first. There are multiple ways to install this (e.g., from the Microsoft Store, winget, Chocolatey), so you can choose any method you like, but for this book we are going with the straightforward approach, which is to download the MSI from the PowerShell GitHub repo: PowerShell/PowerShell. Make sure you download the stable release, as this is the latest GA (general availability) release from the PowerShell team (figure 2.1).

:≡   README.md

## Get PowerShell

You can download and install a PowerShell package for any of the following platforms.

| Supported Platform | Download (LTS) | Downloads (stable) | Downloads (preview) | How to Install |
|---|---|---|---|---|
| Windows (x64) | .msi | .msi  ←——— | .msi | Instructions |
| Windows (x86) | .msi | .msi | .msi | Instructions |
| Ubuntu 20.04 | .deb | .deb | .deb | Instructions |
| Ubuntu 18.04 | .deb | .deb | .deb | Instructions |
| Ubuntu 16.04 | .deb | .deb | .deb | Instructions |
| Debian 9 | .deb | .deb | .deb | Instructions |
| Debian 10 | .deb | .deb | .deb | Instructions |
| Debian 11 | .deb | .deb | .deb | |
| CentOS 7 | .rpm | .rpm | .rpm | Instructions |
| CentOS 8 | .rpm | .rpm | .rpm | |
| Red Hat Enterprise Linux 7 | .rpm | .rpm | .rpm | Instructions |
| openSUSE 42.3 | .rpm | .rpm | .rpm | Instructions |
| Fedora 30 | .rpm | .rpm | .rpm | Instructions |
| macOS 10.13+ (x64) | .pkg | .pkg | .pkg | Instructions |
| macOS 10.13+ (arm64) | .pkg | .pkg | .pkg | Instructions |
| Docker | | | | Instructions |

Figure 2.1   **This shows the different installs available for PowerShell, with the MSI pointed out for Windows installation.**

Walk through the MSI wizard, accept the defaults, and then you are done. There are several ways to launch PowerShell (figure 2.2). After it is installed, you can search for it in the task bar. This is also a great time to point out that the icons have changed a little bit as well.

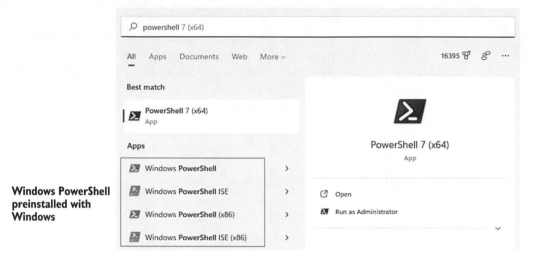

**Windows PowerShell preinstalled with Windows**

**Figure 2.2   Start menu on Windows 10 showing the side-by-side installation for PowerShell 7 and PowerShell 5.1**

If you click the PowerShell 7 icon (we suggest you make it a task bar icon as well), this will launch the PowerShell console. If you are familiar with Windows PowerShell, you will see a noticeable difference in the way it looks. That is because the background color is black and not blue. For the purposes of this book, we have changed our console colors so that they are easier to read.

The PowerShell console application is your only option when you're running PowerShell on a server that doesn't have a GUI shell installed:

- The console application is tiny. It loads fast and doesn't use much memory.
- It doesn't require any more .NET Framework stuff than PowerShell itself needs.
- You can set the colors to green text on a black background and pretend you're working on a 1970s-era mainframe.

If you decide to use the console application, we have a few suggestions for configuring it. You can make all of these configurations by clicking the window's upper-left-corner control box and selecting Properties. The resulting dialog box is shown in figure 2.3. This looks slightly different in Windows 10, as it's gained some new options, but the gist is the same.

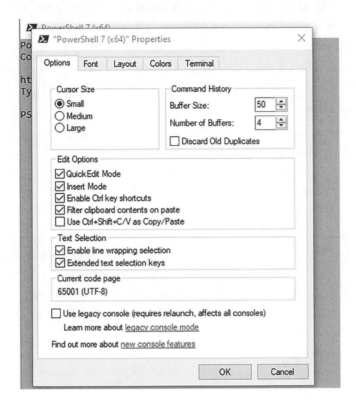

**Figure 2.3   Configuring the console application's properties**

On the Options tab, you can increase the size of the Command History Buffer Size. This buffer enables the console to remember which commands you've typed and lets you recall them by using the up and down arrows on your keyboard.

On the Font tab, pick something a bit larger than the default 12-point font. Please. We don't care if you have 20/10 vision; jack up the font size a bit. PowerShell needs you to be able to quickly distinguish between a lot of similar-looking characters—such as ' (an apostrophe or a single quote) and ` (a backtick or a grave accent)—and a tiny font doesn't help.

On the Layout tab, set both width sizes to the same number and make sure the resulting window fits on your screen. Failing to do this can result in a horizontal scrollbar at the bottom of the window, which can lead to some PowerShell output appearing wrapped off the right side of the window, where you'll never see it. We've had students spend half an hour running commands, thinking they were producing no output at all, when in fact the output was scrolled off to the right. Annoying.

Finally, on the Colors tab, don't go nuts. Keep things high contrast and easy to read. And if you really want to, you can set the colors to match your Windows Power-Shell terminal.

One point to keep in mind: this console application isn't PowerShell; it's merely the means by which you interact with PowerShell.

> **NOTE** We will not be using Windows PowerShell or the ISE for any part of our journey together. The ISE does not support PowerShell 7. We will instead be using Visual Studio Code, which is covered a little later in the chapter.

## 2.2 PowerShell on macOS

If you're using a Mac, this section is for you. We'll talk about how to install and run PowerShell specifically on macOS. This book assumes that you know how to open Terminal—macOS's default Terminal application. You can use a different terminal on macOS if you have it, but we'll stick with the default one for this book. Okay, let's install PowerShell!

### 2.2.1 Installation on macOS

Today, PowerShell does not come included with macOS. Maybe one day that will happen, but until then, we have to install it ourselves. Thankfully, it's easy to install and there are many ways to do it. We'll cover the easiest way to install PowerShell for macOS, which is via Homebrew—the preferred package manager for macOS. Homebrew provides the ability to install PowerShell via a terminal without a single click of our mouse.

> **NOTE** Homebrew also doesn't come with macOS, so if you don't have it already, you can head over to Homebrew's website (https://brew.sh) for instructions on how to install it. Go ahead and get it. We'll wait for you to get back!

Once you have Homebrew installed and ready to go, you can install PowerShell. All you need is an instance of `Terminal`, so go ahead and open that on your Mac. Leveraging Homebrew, you will install PowerShell in one command:

```
brew cask install powershell
```

Type that command into `Terminal` and press ENTER. You will then see Homebrew install PowerShell (figure 2.4).

You're all set! Let's run it. What do we run? Great question. To run PowerShell, all you do is run the command `pwsh`, which will start PowerShell in your terminal. You should see the following output:

```
~ pwsh
PowerShell 7.1.3
Copyright (c) Microsoft Corporation. All rights reserved.

https://aka.ms/pscore6-docs
Type 'help' to get help.

PS /Users/steve>
```

```
==> Satisfying dependencies

All Formula dependencies satisfied.

==>Downloading
https://github.com/PowerShell/PowerShell/releases/download/v7.1.3/powershell-
7.1.3-osx-x64.pkg

==> Verifying SHA-256 checksum for Cask 'powershell'.

==> Installing Cask powershell

==> Running installer for powershell; your password may be necessary.

==> Package installers may write to any location; options such as --appdir are
ignored.

installer: Package name is PowerShell - 7.1.3

installer: Installing at base path /

installer: The install was successful.
```

powershell was successfully installed!

**Figure 2.4  Homebrew installing PowerShell**

We now have PowerShell running in the Terminal app on macOS! Well done. This is one of the main ways to interact with PowerShell on macOS. We'll go over the other main way in a bit, but first we need to address those of you who are using Linux as your operating system.

## 2.3  *PowerShell on Linux (Ubuntu 18.04)*

This is the part where we tell you that PowerShell is so awesome that it's able to run on an incredibly long list of Linux distributions. This is also the part where we tell you that if we went through the installation of every one of those distributions, our publisher would wonder why the book turned into one million pages. We're going to run through how to install PowerShell on Ubuntu 18.04, since it was the latest LTS version at the time of writing. If you're using a machine that runs something else, fear not! All the documentation on how to install PowerShell on all the different supported Linux distributions can be found in the PowerShell docs article on specifically this topic: http://mng.bz/YgnK.

All right, now on to the installation. We should also mention . . . this book assumes that you know how to open the Terminal application on Ubuntu 18.04. You can use any terminal for these steps, but we'll stick to the default one.

### 2.3.1   *Installation on Ubuntu 18.04*

Ubuntu 18.04 ships with Canonical's own package manager, called `snap`. This gives us a single command installation of PowerShell. First, go ahead and open up an instance of Terminal and type the following command:

```
snap install powershell --classic
```

Once you do that, press ENTER to run it. You may be asked to put in your password, and if so, go ahead and put that in. This is because `snap` needs to be run as `root` to install PowerShell. The output you see should look like this:

```
PowerShell 7.1.3 from Microsoft PowerShell√ installed
```

> **NOTE**   We are adding `--classic` to the command because PowerShell is considered a "classic snap package." Classic snaps remove the restrictions on snap packages, allowing PowerShell to fully interact with the operating system.

You're all set! Let's run it. What do we run? Great question. To run PowerShell, all you have to do is run the command `pwsh`, which will start PowerShell in your terminal. You should see the following output:

```
~ pwsh
PowerShell 7.1.3
Copyright (c) Microsoft Corporation. All rights reserved.

https://aka.ms/pscore6-docs
Type 'help' to get help.

PS /Users/tyleonha>
```

We now have PowerShell running in Terminal on Ubuntu 18.04! Well done. This is one of the main ways to interact with PowerShell on Ubuntu 18.04. Now that we've got it working in the terminal, let's get the other PowerShell interface working.

## 2.4   *Visual Studio Code and the PowerShell extension*

Wait! Don't run away yet. We know it sounds like we're asking you to get that application that all your C# developer friends use, but it's just not true! Let us explain.

Microsoft offers two products with very similar names that are completely different (the saying "There are two hard problems in tech: cache invalidation, naming things, and off-by-1 errors" is true). The first product is one you might have heard of: Visual Studio. It's a full-featured integrated development environment (IDE). It's typically used by C# and F# developers. Visual Studio Code, on the other hand, is a completely different application. It's a lightweight text editor that has some resemblance to other text editors like Sublime Text or Notepad++, except that it has some added features to enhance the experience.

One of the added features is extensibility. People can author extensions for Visual Studio Code and put them on the Visual Studio Code's marketplace for other folks to consume. The PowerShell team offers an extension for PowerShell on the marketplace, and with it comes a whole bunch of nice features that will help you along your journey of learning PowerShell. Visual Studio Code with the PowerShell extension is the recommended editing experience for PowerShell, and just like PowerShell itself, they're open source and work cross-platform. You can find the source code at these locations:

- Visual Studio Code—https://github.com/Microsoft/vscode
- PowerShell extension—https://github.com/PowerShell/vscode-powershell

This is also a great opportunity for us to say that if you do have any issues with those products, open an issue on their respective GitHub pages. That's the best way to give feedback and report problems. All right, let's get into the installation steps.

**NOTE** Visual Studio Code and the PowerShell extension will be more valuable in later chapters when you learn to write scripts. You'll get there. We promise.

## What about the PowerShell ISE?

If you already know a thing or two about PowerShell and are familiar with the PowerShell ISE, you might be wondering why it's not being mentioned. The PowerShell ISE does not work with PowerShell and is in support mode only, meaning that it will only receive security-related updates. The team's focus has moved to Visual Studio Code with the PowerShell extension.

### 2.4.1 Installing Visual Studio Code and the PowerShell extension

If you've gotten this far, you've already installed PowerShell on your operating system. To install Visual Studio Code, you can use the same steps. For Windows, macOS, or Linux, go to https://code.visualstudio.com/Download and download and run the installer (figure 2.5).

- To add the PowerShell extension, launch VS Code and go to the marketplace.
- Search for PowerShell and click Install.

For those of you who prefer the command line, you can also install VS Code and the PowerShell Extension via the terminal:

- macOS: Open `Terminal` and run `brew cask install vscode`.
- Ubuntu 18.04: Open `Terminal` and run `snap install code --classic`.

**Figure 2.5   This shows the logo for the extensions and the Install button for the PowerShell 7 extension in VS Code.**

You're getting the hang of this! If you've done this correctly, running the `code` command in the terminal should open an instance of Visual Studio Code. If it doesn't work, close all of your terminal windows, open a new one, and try running the `code` command again. Once that's installed, you need to install the PowerShell extension. Since we like typing in the world of PowerShell, let's install the extension in a single command. You can install extensions by using the `code` command like so:

```
code --install-extension ms-vscode.powershell
```

Which gives you the following output:

```
~ code --install-extension ms-vscode.powershell
Installing extensions...
Installing extension 'ms-vscode.powershell' v2019.9.0..
Extension 'ms-vscode.powershell' v2019.9.0 was successfully installed.
```

Let's look at the checklist:

```
PowerShell installed ✔
Visual Studio Code installed ✔
PowerShell extension installed ✔
```

We're ready to see what this all has to offer. If you haven't already, go ahead and open Visual Studio Code by running the `code` command in your terminal.

### 2.4.2   *Getting familiar with Visual Studio Code*

From here on, the experiences will be the same regardless of what OS you are running. Here we have Visual Studio Code. It might look daunting at first, but with a little bit of practice, you'll be able to harness its power to help you write some awesome PowerShell scripts. With Visual Studio Code open, we should get it ready to work with PowerShell. Start by clicking on the little PowerShell stencil icon on the left side next to the other crazy-looking icons. It's highlighted in figure 2.6.

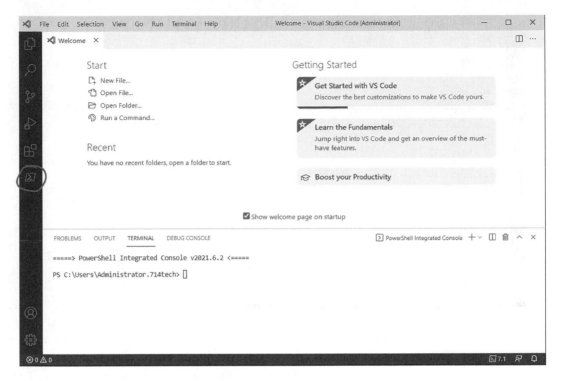

**Figure 2.6   Visual Studio Code startup screen**

After clicking on the PowerShell icon, a couple of things pop up. Let's go over what we see (figure 2.7):

- *Command Explorer*(A)—A list of commands that are available for you to run. When you hover over one, it gives you a few different actions. You can hide this by clicking on the PowerShell icon again.
- *Script editor pane*(B)—We won't be using this until the end of the book, but this is where your scripts will appear in different tabs.
- *Integrated Console*(C)—This is where the magic happens. This is PowerShell. You can run commands here just like you did in the PowerShell running in the Terminal application.

In the top right of the Integrated Console, we see a few different actions. Let's start from the right side. First we see an "x" icon. This will hide the Integrated Console and the whole terminal pane. If you ever want to bring it back, press Ctrl+`. After that you have the caret (^) icon. This will hide the script pane and maximize the terminal pane. Then we have trash can icon. This *kills terminals*. Repeat after us: "I PROMISE TO NEVER EVER EVER KILL THE POWERSHELL INTEGRATED CONSOLE." The Integrated Console is the heart of the PowerShell extension and all its features, and if you kill it, then the extension will stop working—so, please, don't trash the Integrated Console.

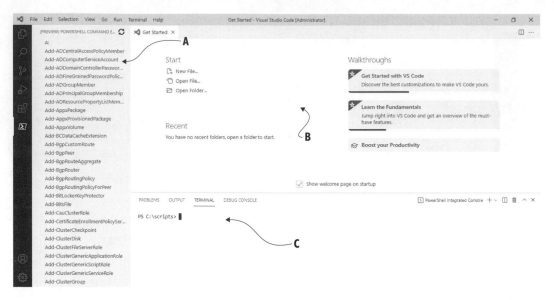

**Figure 2.7   Visual Studio Code with the PowerShell extension breakdown**

Next we have the split terminal button and the plus sign button. These buttons spawn additional terminals that can be seen in the drop-down next to them. It's important to note that Visual Studio Code picks Bash as default for these terminals since Bash is installed by default. You can easily configure this in your settings, but we can come back to that later. In the meantime, if you open a Bash terminal in Visual Studio Code, you can type pwsh just as you did in the Terminal application, and you get PowerShell.

---

**PowerShell Integrated Console vs. a normal terminal?**

As we touched on before, the PowerShell Integrated Console is the heart of the PowerShell extension. Where do you think the commands in the Command Explorer came from? Yep, that's right—the Integrated Console. There is a plethora of features to explore in the extension that depend on the Integrated Console, but just know that there's only one of them. Any other terminal that is spawned, even if it's running PowerShell, is not "integrated." Remember: Don't delete the Integrated Console.

---

The Visual Studio Code experience with PowerShell is heavily catered toward writing PowerShell scripts and modules, while the PowerShell in a Terminal application is an experience more for running through a few quick commands or long-running tasks. They both serve their purpose, and we'll see more of them throughout the book.

### 2.4.3   *Customizing Visual Studio Code and the PowerShell extension*

Like we said earlier, extensibility is a big deal to Visual Studio Code. As such, it's very easy to customize Visual Studio Code and the PowerShell extension to your liking. We'll go through a few things you can do—some useful, others just for fun!

First, let's start with Visual Studio Code's Settings page. We'll be able to configure just about anything we want. Go to File > Preferences > Settings to open the Settings page (figure 2.8). From here you can search for anything you'd like in the search box, or just scroll through everything. There's a lot to configure! If you're curious what settings the PowerShell extension provides, all you have to do is search for `powershell`, and you'll see them all.

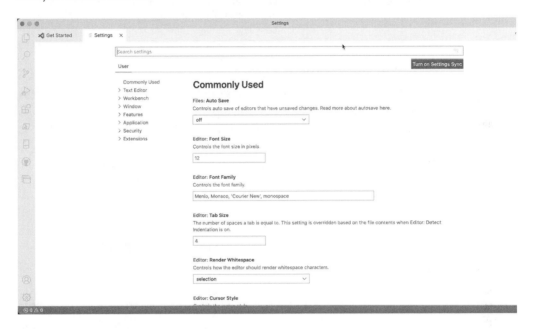

**Figure 2.8   Visual Studio Code's Settings page. We've outlined where to see the JSON version of the settings.**

You might notice that we outlined a button in this screenshot. If you click on this, you'll get a JavaScript Object Notation (JSON) representation of the settings that you have set. If you're not already familiar with JSON, don't worry. You can use the regular setting window to do just about everything the JSON view can do.

Table 2.1 shows a list of commonly used settings that you can paste right into the search box and configure to your liking.

**Table 2.1   Recommended settings**

| Setting | Description |
| --- | --- |
| Tab Completion | The Tab Completion setting helps replicate the experience you get from PowerShell in the regular terminal. You'll learn more about this concept later, but you might find this setting useful. |
| Terminal.Integrated.Shell.Windows<br>Terminal.Integrated.Shell.OSX<br>Terminal.Integrated.Shell.Linux | If you remember earlier in this chapter, when we press the "+" sign in the terminal part of Visual Studio Code, it opened Bash. This is because the default terminal on macOS and Linux is Bash. You can change this to PowerShell by changing this setting to `pwsh`. |
| Files.Default Language | When you open a new file in Visual Studio Code, it assumes that it is plain text. You can change this behavior by changing the Default Language setting. Changing this to `powershell` will ensure that new files will be PowerShell files and will give you all the Power-Shell extension features. |

Another thing you can change about Visual Studio Code is the color theme. The default dark theme is nice, but you have a plethora of options out there if you'd like to go digging for the theme that fits you perfectly. It's easy to change—all we have to do is open the Command Palette. To do this, press CMD+SHIFT+P on macOS or CTRL+SHIFT+P on Windows/Linux (alternatively, you can press F1 on either platform).

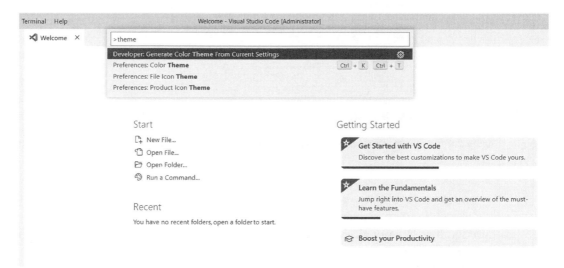

**Figure 2.9   Visual Studio Code's Command Palette. Search for actions you want to take.**

The Command Palette (figure 2.9) is one of the most useful features of Visual Studio Code, as it allows you to search for actions that you can take. The action we want to take is "changing the color theme," so let's just search for theme in the Command Palette.

You should see an option called Preferences: Color Theme—click that. This gives you a list of theme choices that you have available (figure 2.10). Use the arrow keys to go through the themes; you'll notice the theme of Visual Studio Code gets updated automatically, so you can see what you're getting into before you commit.

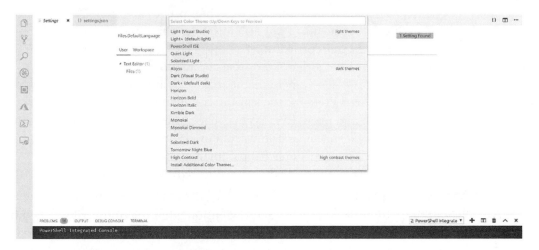

**Figure 2.10   Theme selection in Visual Studio Code**

Most in the list are default themes that come with Visual Studio Code; however, the PowerShell ISE theme comes with the PowerShell extension. You can search for more cool themes on the extension marketplace (we personally like the Horizon theme, but that's just us!) by choosing the Install Additional Color Themes item in the list.

> **TRY IT NOW**   For the remainder of this book, we'll assume you're using Visual Studio Code with the PowerShell extension and not some other scripting editor when you need to write or examine a script. Go ahead and configure the settings and your color theme to your liking if you so choose. If you decide to use PowerShell in a Terminal application instead, you'll be fine—most everything in the book will still work. We'll let you know if something is console-only or editor-only.

## 2.5   *It's typing class all over again*

PowerShell is a command-line interface, and that means you'll do a lot of typing. Typing leaves room for errors—typos. Fortunately, both PowerShell applications provide ways to help minimize typos.

> **TRY IT NOW**   The following examples are impossible to illustrate in a book, but they're cool to see in action. Consider following along in your own copy of the shell.

The console application supports tab completion in four areas:

- Type `Get-P` and press Tab a few times. You'll notice a list of possible completions. As you type more, this list will get smaller, and when PowerShell can guess that it must be a certain command, it will complete it for you.
- Type `Dir`, then a space, then /, and then press Tab. PowerShell shows you the files and folders that you can drill into from this directory.
- Type `Get-Proc` and press Tab. Then type a space and a hyphen (-). Start pressing Tab to see PowerShell's possible completions for this parameter. You could also type part of a parameter name (e.g., `-E`), and press Tab twice to see matching parameters. Press Esc to clear the command line.
- Type `New-I` and press Tab. Type a space, then `-I`, and press Tab again. Type another space and press Tab twice. PowerShell shows the legal values for that parameter. This works only for parameters that have a predefined set of allowable values (the set is called an *enumeration*). Again, press Esc to clear the command line; you don't want to run that command yet.

Visual Studio Code with the PowerShell extension offers the editor pane something like, and better than, tab completion: IntelliSense. This feature operates in all four of the same situations that we showed you for tab completion, except that you get a cool little pop-up menu, like the one shown in figure 2.11. Use your arrow keys to scroll up or down and find the item you want, press Tab or Enter to select it, and then keep typing.

CAUTION    It's *very, very, very, very, very* important to be *very, very, very, very* accurate when you're typing in PowerShell. In some cases, a single misplaced space, quotation mark, or even carriage return can make everything fail. If you're getting errors, double- and triple-check what you've typed.

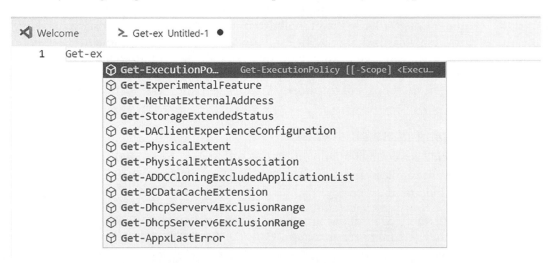

**Figure 2.11   IntelliSense works like tab completion in Visual Studio Code with the PowerShell extension. It also shows you information about the item you're completing if it's available.**

## 2.6     *What version is this?*

With PowerShell, there's an easy way to check your version. Type `$PSVersionTable` and press Enter:

```
PS /Users/steve> $PSVersionTable
Name                          Value
----                          -----
PSVersion                     7.1.3
PSEdition                     Core
GitCommitId                   7.1.3
OS                            Linux 4.18.0-20-generic #21~18.04.1-Ubuntu…
Platform                      Unix
WSManStackVersion             3.0
SerializationVersion          1.1.0.1
PSCompatibleVersions          {1.0, 2.0, 3.0, 4.0…}
PSRemotingProtocolVersion     2.3
```

You'll immediately see the version number for every PowerShell-related piece of technology, including PowerShell itself. If this doesn't work, or if it doesn't indicate 7.0 or later for `PSVersion`, you're not using the right version of PowerShell for this book. Refer to earlier sections in this chapter (2.2, 2.3, and 2.4, depending on your OS) for instructions on getting the most current version of PowerShell.

> **TRY IT NOW**   Don't wait any longer to start using PowerShell. Start by checking your version number to ensure it's at least 7.1. If it isn't, don't go any further until you've installed at least v7.1.

## 2.7     *Lab*

Because this is the book's first lab, we'll take a moment to describe how these are supposed to work. For each lab, we give you a few tasks that you can try to complete on your own. Sometimes we provide a hint or two to get you going in the right direction. From there, you're on your own.

We absolutely guarantee that everything you need to know to complete every lab is either in that same chapter or covered in a previous chapter (and the previously covered information is the stuff for which we're most likely to give you a hint). We're not saying the answer is in plain sight; most often, a chapter teaches you how to discover something on your own, and you have to go through that discovery process to find the answer. It might seem frustrating, but forcing yourself to do it will absolutely make you more successful with PowerShell in the long run. We promise.

Keep in mind that you can find sample answers at the end of each chapter. Our answers might not exactly match yours, and that will become increasingly true as we move on to more complex material. You'll often find that PowerShell offers a half dozen or more ways to accomplish almost anything. We'll show you the way we use the most, but if you come up with something different, you're not wrong. Any way that gets the job done is correct.

**NOTE**  For this lab, you can complete it on any machine running Windows 10, macOS, or Linux as long as you have PowerShell 7.1 or higher installed.

We'll start easy: we just want you to get both the console and Visual Studio Code with the PowerShell extension set up to meet your needs. Follow these five steps:

1 If you haven't downloaded and installed everything, go do that.
2 Configure the font and text size in your Terminal application (you may have to dig around for this!) and in Visual Studio Code (hint hint . . . it's a setting!).
3 In Visual Studio Code, maximize the Console pane; remove or leave the Commands Explorer at your discretion.
4 In both applications, type a single quote (') and a backtick (`) and make sure you can easily tell the difference. On a US keyboard (at least), a backtick is on the same key as the tilde (~) character, under the Esc key.
5 Also type parentheses ( ), square brackets [ ], angle brackets < >, and curly brackets {} to make sure the font and size you've selected display well, so that all of these symbols are immediately distinguishable. If there's some visual confusion about which is which, change fonts or select a bigger font size.

We've already walked you through how to accomplish most of these steps, so you don't have any answers to check for this lab, other than to be sure you've completed all five of the steps.

# Using the help system

In chapter 1, we mentioned that discoverability is a key feature that makes graphical user interfaces (GUIs) easier to learn and use and that command-line interfaces (CLIs) like PowerShell are often more difficult because they lack those discoverability features. In fact, PowerShell has fantastic discoverability features—but they're not that obvious. One of the main discoverability features is its help system.

## 3.1 The help system: How you discover commands

Bear with us for a minute as we climb up on a soapbox and preach to you. We work in an industry that doesn't place a lot of emphasis on reading, although we do have an acronym that we cleverly pass along to users when we wish *they* would *read the friendly manual*—RTFM. Most administrators tend to dive right in, relying on things like tooltips, context menus, and so forth—those *GUI* discoverability tools—to figure out how to do something. That's how we often work, and we imagine you do the same thing. But let's be clear about one point:

> If you aren't willing to read PowerShell's help files, you won't be effective with PowerShell. You won't learn how to use it; you won't learn how to administer other services like Azure, AWS, Microsoft 365, and so on, with it; and you might as well stick with the GUI.

That's about as clear as we can be. It's a blunt statement, but it's absolutely true. Imagine trying to figure out Azure Virtual Machines, or any other administrative portal, without the help of tooltips, menus, and context menus. Trying to learn to use PowerShell without taking the time to read and understand the help files is the same thing. It's like trying to assemble that do-it-yourself furniture from the department store without reading the manual. Your experience will be frustrating, confusing, and ineffective. So why do it?

If you need to perform a task and don't know what command to use, the help system is how you'll find that command. Start with the help system before going to your favorite search engine.

If you run a command and get an error, the help system is what will show you how to properly run the command so you don't get errors. If you want to link multiple commands together to perform a complex task, the help system is where you'll find out how each command is able to connect to others. You don't need to search for examples on Google or Bing; you need to learn how to use the commands themselves so that you can create your own examples and solutions.

We realize our preaching is a little heavy handed, but 90% of the problems we see users struggling with in forums could be solved if those folks would find a few minutes to sit back, take some deep breaths, and read the help. And then read this chapter, which is all about helping you understand the help you're reading in PowerShell.

From here on out, we encourage you to read the help for several more reasons:

- Although we show many commands in our examples, we almost never expose the complete functionality, options, and capabilities of each command to make understanding the concept easier to grasp. You should read the help for each and every command we show you so that you'll be familiar with the additional actions each command can accomplish.
- In the labs, we may give you a hint about which command to use for a task, but we won't give you hints about the syntax. You'll need to use the help system to discover that syntax on your own in order to complete the labs.
- We promise you that mastering the help system is the key to becoming a Power-Shell expert. No, you won't find every little detail in there, and a lot of super-advanced material isn't documented in the help system, but in terms of being an effective day-to-day administrator, you need to master the help system. This book will make that system understandable, and it will teach you the concepts that the help skips over, but it'll do this only in conjunction with the built-in help.

Stepping off the soapbox now.

### Command vs. cmdlet

PowerShell contains many types of executable commands. Some are called *cmdlets* (we will cover cmdlets in the next chapter), some are called *functions*, and so on. Collectively, they're all *commands*, and the help system works with all of them. A cmdlet is something unique to PowerShell, and many of the commands you run will be cmdlets. But we'll try to consistently use *command* whenever we're talking about the more general class of executable utility.

## *3.2*  *Updatable help*

You may be surprised the first time you fire up help in PowerShell, because, well, there isn't much there. But wait, we can explain.

Microsoft included a new feature beginning with PowerShell v3 called *updatable help*. PowerShell can download updated, corrected, and expanded help right from the internet. Initially when you ask for help on a command, you get an abbreviated, auto-generated version of help, along with a message on how to update the help files, which may look like the following:

```
PS /User/travisp> help Get-Process
NAME
    Get-Process

SYNTAX
    Get-Process [[-Name] <string[]>] [-Module] [-FileVersionInfo]
    [<CommonParameters>]

    Get-Process [[-Name] <string[]>] -IncludeUserName [<CommonParameters>]

    Get-Process -Id <int[]> -IncludeUserName [<CommonParameters>]

    Get-Process -Id <int[]> [-Module] [-FileVersionInfo] [<CommonParameters>]

    Get-Process -InputObject <Process[]> [-Module] [-FileVersionInfo]
    [<CommonParameters>]

    Get-Process -InputObject <Process[]> -IncludeUserName
    ➥ [<CommonParameters>]


ALIASES
    gps


REMARKS
    Get-Help cannot find the Help files for this cmdlet on this computer. It
    is displaying only partial help.
        -- To download and install Help files for the module that includes
    this cmdlet, use Update-Help.
        -- To view the Help topic for this cmdlet online, type: "Get-Help
    Get-Process -Online" or
            go to https://go.microsoft.com/fwlink/?LinkID=113324.
```

> **TIP**  It's impossible to miss the fact that you don't have local help installed. The first time you ask for help, PowerShell will prompt you to update the help content.

Updating PowerShell's help should be your first task. In Windows PowerShell, you were required to update help as "Administrator" or the equivalent of "root." In Power-Shell 6 and higher, you can now update help as the current user. Open PowerShell and run `Update-Help`, and you'll be good to go in a few minutes.

**TIP**   If you are not running the `en-us` culture, you may have to specify `-UICulture en-US` to get `Update-Help` to work.

It's important to get in the habit of updating the help every month or so. PowerShell can even download updated help for non-Microsoft commands, provided the commands' modules are located in the proper spot and that they've been coded to include the online location for updated help (modules are how commands are added to PowerShell, and they are explained in chapter 7).

Do you have computers that aren't connected to the internet? No problem: go to one that's connected, and use `Save-Help` to get a local copy of the help. Put it on a file server or somewhere that's accessible to the rest of your network. Then run `Update-Help` with its `-Source` parameter, pointing it to the downloaded copy of the help. That'll let any computer on your network grab the updated help from that central spot, rather than from the internet.

> **Help is open sourced**
>
> Microsoft's PowerShell help files are open source materials that are available at https://github.com/MicrosoftDocs/PowerShell-Docs. This can be a good place to see the latest source, which might not yet be compiled into help files that PowerShell can download and display.

## 3.3   *Asking for help*

PowerShell provides a cmdlet, `Get-Help`, that accesses the help system. You may see examples (especially on the internet) that show people using the `Help` keyword instead. The `Help` keyword isn't a native cmdlet at all; it is a *function*, which is a wrapper around the core `Get-Help` cmdlet.

> **Help on macOS/Linux**
>
> The help files, when viewed on macOS and Linux, are displayed using the operating system's traditional *man* (manual) feature, which usually "takes over" the screen to display the help, returning you to your normal screen when you're finished.

`Help` works much like the base `Get-Help`, but it pipes the `Help` output to `less`, allowing you to have a nice paged view instead of seeing all the help scroll by at once. Running `Help Get-Content` and `Get-Help Get-Content` produces the same results, but the former has a page-at-a-time display. You could run `Get-Help Get-Content | less` to produce that paged display, but that requires a lot more typing. We typically use only `Help`, but we want you to understand that some trickery is going on under the hood.

By the way, sometimes that paginated display can be annoying, because you have the information you need, but it still wants you to press the spacebar to display the remaining information. If you encounter this, press q to cancel the command and return to the shell prompt. When using less, q always means *quit*.

The help system has two main goals: to help you find commands to perform specific tasks and to help you learn how to use those commands after you've found them.

## 3.4    *Using help to find commands*

Technically speaking, the help system has no idea what commands are present in the shell. All it knows is what help topics are available, and it's possible for commands to not have a help file, in which case the help system won't know that the commands exist. Fortunately, Microsoft ships a help topic for nearly every cmdlet it produces, which means you usually won't find a difference. In addition, the help system can access information that isn't related to a specific cmdlet, including background concepts and other general information.

Like most commands, Get-Help (and, therefore, Help) has several parameters. One of those—perhaps the most important one—is -Name. This parameter specifies the name of the help topic you'd like to access, and it's a positional parameter, so you don't have to type -Name; you can just provide the name you're looking for. It also accepts wildcards, which makes the help system useful for discovering commands.

For example, suppose you want to do something with events on .NET objects. You don't know what commands might be available, and you decide to search for help topics that cover events. You might run either of these two commands:

```
Help *event*
Help *object*
```

The first command returns a list like the following on your computer:

```
Name                         Category   ModuleName

Get-Event                    Cmdlet     Microsoft.PowerShell.Utility
Get-EventSubscriber          Cmdlet     Microsoft.PowerShell.Utility
New-Event                    Cmdlet     Microsoft.PowerShell.Utility
Register-EngineEvent         Cmdlet     Microsoft.PowerShell.Utility
Register-ObjectEvent         Cmdlet     Microsoft.PowerShell.Utility
Remove-Event                 Cmdlet     Microsoft.PowerShell.Utility
Unregister-Event             Cmdlet     Microsoft.PowerShell.Utility
Wait-Event                   Cmdlet     Microsoft.PowerShell.Utility
```

**NOTE**    After you have installed some modules from other sources, you may notice that the command help list includes commands (and functions) from modules such as Az.EventGrid and Az.EventHub. The help system displays all of these even though you haven't loaded those modules into memory yet, which helps you discover commands on your computer that you might otherwise have overlooked. It'll discover commands from any modules that are installed in the proper location, which we'll discuss in chapter 7.

Many of the cmdlets in the previous list seem to have something to do with events. In your environment, you may also have additional commands that are unrelated or you may have "about" topics, which provide background information (discussed in detail in section 3.6). When you are using the help system to find a PowerShell command, try to search using the broadest term possible—*event* or *object* as opposed to *objectevent*—because you'll get the most results possible.

When you have a cmdlet that you think will do the job (Register-ObjectEvent looks like a good candidate for what you're after in the example), you can ask for help on that specific topic:

```
Help Register-ObjectEvent
```

Don't forget about tab completion! As a reminder, it lets you type a portion of a command name and press Tab, and the shell completes what you've typed with the closest match. You can continue pressing Tab to get a list of alternative matches.

> **TRY IT NOW**  Type Help Register- and press Tab. This will match a few commands and not complete. On a Windows machine, when you press Tab a second time, it will keep scrolling through the available commands. On a non-Windows machine, if you press Tab, a second tab will display a list of the available commands.

You can also use wildcards with Help—mainly the * wildcard, which stands in for zero or more characters. If PowerShell finds only one match to whatever you've typed, it won't display a list of topics for that one item. Instead, it'll display the content for that item.

> **TRY IT NOW**  Run Help Get-EventS*, and you should see the help file for Get-EventSubscriber, rather than a list of matching help topics.

If you've been following along in the shell, you should now be looking at the help file for Get-EventSubscriber. This file, called the *summary help*, is meant to be a short description of the command and a reminder of the syntax. This information is useful when you need to quickly refresh your memory of a command's usage, and it's where we'll begin interpreting the help file itself.

### Above and beyond

Sometimes we want to share information that, although nice, isn't essential to your understanding of the shell. We put that information into an "Above and beyond" sidebar, like this one. If you skip these, you'll be fine; if you read them, you'll often learn about an alternative way of doing something or get additional insight into PowerShell.

We mentioned that the Help command doesn't search for cmdlets; it searches for help topics. Because every cmdlet has a help file, we could say that this search retrieves the same results. But you can also directly search for cmdlets by using the Get-Command cmdlet (or its alias, gcm).

Like the `Help` cmdlet, `Get-Command` accepts wildcards—so you can, for example, run `gcm *get*` to see all of the commands that contain *get* in their name. For better or worse, that list will include not only cmdlets, but also external commands such as `wget`, which may not be useful.

A better approach is to use the `-Noun` or `-Verb` parameters. Because only command names have nouns and verbs, the results will be limited to cmdlets. `Get-Command -Noun *event*` returns a list of cmdlets dealing with events; `Get-Command -Verb Get` returns all cmdlets capable of retrieving things. You can also use the `-CommandType` parameter, specifying a type of cmdlet: `Get-Command *event* -Type cmdlet` shows a list of all cmdlets that include *event* in their names, and the list won't include any external applications or commands.

## 3.5 *Interpreting the help*

PowerShell's cmdlet help files have a particular set of conventions. Learning to understand what you're looking at is the key to extracting the maximum amount of information from these files and to learning to use the cmdlets themselves more effectively.

### 3.5.1 *Parameter sets and common parameters*

Most commands can work in a variety of ways, depending on what you need them to do. For example, here's the syntax section for the `Get-Item` help:

```
SYNTAX
    Get-Item [-Stream <String[]>] [-Credential <PSCredential>] [-Exclude
    ➥ <String[]>] [-Filter <String>] [-Force] [-Include
    <String[]>] -LiteralPath <String[]> [<CommonParameters>]

    Get-Item [-Path] <String[]> [-Stream <String[]>] [-Credential
    ➥ <PSCredential>] [-Exclude <String[]>] [-Filter <String>] [-Force]
    [-Include <String[]>] [<CommonParameters>]
```

Notice that the command in the previous syntax is listed twice, which indicates that the command supports two *parameter sets*; you can use the command in two distinct ways. Some of the parameters will be shared between the two sets. You'll notice, for example, that both parameter sets include the `-Filter` parameter. But the two parameter sets will always have at least one unique parameter that exists only in that parameter set. In this case, the first set supports `-LiteralPath`, which is not included in the second set; the second set contains the `-Path` parameter, which isn't included in the first set, but both could contain additional unshared parameters.

Here's how this works: If you use a parameter that's included in only one set, you're locked into that set and can use only additional parameters that appear within that same set. If you choose to use `-LiteralPath`, you cannot use parameters from the other set, in this case `-Path`, because it doesn't live in the first parameter set. That means `-Path` and `-LiteralPath` are *mutually exclusive*—you'll never use both of them at the same time because they live in different parameter sets.

Sometimes it's possible to run a command with only parameters that are shared between multiple sets. In those cases, the shell will usually select the first-listed parameter set. Because each parameter set implies different behavior, it's important to understand which parameter set you're running.

You'll notice that every parameter set for every PowerShell cmdlet ends with [<CommonParameters>]. This refers to a set of 11 (at the time this was written) parameters that are available on every single cmdlet, no matter how you're using that cmdlet. We'll discuss some of those common parameters later in this book, when we'll use them for a real task. Later in this chapter, though, we'll show you where to learn more about those common parameters, if you're interested.

> **NOTE**   Astute readers will by now have recognized variations in some of our examples. Readers will notice a different help layout for Get-Item depending on their version of PowerShell. You might even see a few new parameters. But the fundamentals and concepts we're explaining haven't changed. Don't get hung up on the fact that the help you see might be different from what we show in the book.

### 3.5.2  *Optional and mandatory parameters*

You don't need every single parameter in order to make a cmdlet run. PowerShell's help lists optional parameters in square brackets. For example, [-Credential <PSCredential>] indicates that the entire -Credential parameter is optional. You don't have to use it at all; the cmdlet will probably default to the current user's default credentials if you don't specify an alternative credential using this parameter. That's also why [<-Common-Parameters>] is in square brackets: you can run the command without using any of the common parameters.

Almost every cmdlet has at least one optional parameter. You may never need to use some of these parameters and may use others daily. Keep in mind that when you choose to use a parameter, you must type only enough of the parameter name so that PowerShell can unambiguously figure out which parameter you mean. For example, -F wouldn't be sufficient for -Force, because -F could also mean -Filter. But -Fo would be a legal abbreviation for -Force, because no other parameter starts with -Fo.

What if you try to run a command and forget one of the mandatory parameters? Take a look at the help for Get-Item, for example, and you'll see that the -Path parameter is mandatory. You can tell because the entire parameter—its name and its value—isn't surrounded by square brackets. This means that an optional parameter can be identified because the entire parameter and its value will be surrounded by square brackets. Try running Get-Item without specifying a file path (figure 3.1).

```
Get-Item [-Path] <System.String[]> [-Stream <System.String[]>] [-Credential
<System.Management.Automation.PSCredential>] [-Exclude <System.String[]>] [-Filter <System.String>] [-Force]
[-Include <System.String[]>] [<CommonParameters>]
```

**Figure 3.1   This is help from Get-Item showing that the path variable accepts an array of strings indicated by the square brackets [ ].**

**TRY IT NOW**   Follow along in this example by running `Get-Item` without any parameters.

PowerShell should have prompted you for the mandatory `-Path` parameter. If you type something like `~` or `./` and press Enter, the command will run correctly. You could also press Ctrl-C to abort the command.

### 3.5.3   *Positional parameters*

PowerShell's designers knew that some parameters would be used so frequently that you wouldn't want to continually type the parameter names. Those commonly used parameters are often *positional*: you can provide a value without typing the parameter's name, provided you put that value in the correct position. You can identify positional parameters in two ways: via the syntax summary or the full help.

#### FINDING POSITIONAL PARAMETERS IN THE SYNTAX SUMMARY

You'll find the first way in the syntax summary: the parameter name—only the name—will be surrounded by square brackets. For example, look at the first two parameters in the second parameter set of `Get-Item`:

```
[-Path] <String[]> [-Stream <String[]>]…[-Filter <String>]
```

The first parameter, `-Path`, isn't optional. You can tell because the entire parameter—its name and its value isn't surrounded by square brackets. But the parameter name is enclosed in square brackets, making it a positional parameter—you could provide the log name without having to type `-Path`. And because this parameter appears in the first position within the help file, you know that the log name is the first parameter you have to provide.

The second parameter, `-Stream`, is optional; both it and its value are enclosed in square brackets. Within those, `-Stream` itself is not contained in a second set of square brackets, indicating that this is not a positional parameter. If it were positional, it would look like `[[-Stream] <string[]>]`. So, you'd need to use the parameter name to provide the value.

The `-Filter` parameter (which comes later in the syntax; run `Help Get-Item` and find it for yourself) is optional, because it's entirely enclosed within square brackets. The `-Filter` name is in square brackets, which tells you that if you choose to use that parameter, you must type the parameter name (or at least a portion of it). There are some tricks to using positional parameters:

- It's okay to mix and match positional parameters with those that require their names. Positional parameters must always be in the correct positions. For example, `Get-Item ~ -Filter *` is legal: `~` will be fed to the `-Path` parameter because that value is in the first position, and `*` will go with the `-Filter` parameter because the parameter name was used.
- It's always legal to specify parameter names, and when you do so, the order in which you type them isn't important. `Get-Item -Filter * -Pa *` is legal because we've used parameter names (in the case of `-Path`, we abbreviated it).

**NOTE**   Some commands, such as Get-ChildItem, have multiple positional parameters. The first is -Path and then -Filter. If you use multiple positional parameters, don't lose track of their positions. Get-ChildItem ~ Down* will work, with ~ being attached to -Path and Down* being attached to -Filter. Get-ChildItem Down* ~ won't get anything, because ~ will be attached to -Filter, and most likely no items will match.

We'll offer a best practice: Use parameter names until you become comfortable with a particular cmdlet and get tired of typing a commonly used parameter name over and over. After that, use positional parameters to save yourself typing. When the time comes to paste a command into a text file for easier reuse, always use the full cmdlet name and type out the complete parameter name—no positional parameters and no abbreviated parameter names. Doing so makes that file easier to read and understand in the future, and because you won't have to type the parameter names repeatedly (that's why you pasted the command into a file, after all), you won't be creating extra typing work for yourself.

FINDING POSITIONAL PARAMETERS IN THE FULL HELP

We said that you can locate positional parameters in two ways. The second requires that you open the help file by using the -Full parameter of the Help command.

**TRY IT NOW**   Run Help Get-Item -Full. Remember to use the spacebar to view the help file one page at a time and to press Ctrl-C if you want to stop viewing the file before reaching the end. For now, page through the entire file, which lets you scroll back and review it all. Also, instead of -Full, try using the -Online parameter, which should work on any client computer or server with a browser. Be aware that the success of using -Online depends on the quality of the underlying help file. If the file is malformed, you might not see everything.

Page down until you see the help entry for the -Path parameter. It should look something like figure 3.2.

```
-Path <System.String[]>
    Specifies the path to an item. This cmdlet gets the item at the specified location. Wildcard characters are
    permitted. This parameter is required, but the parameter name Path is optional.

    Use a dot ('.') to specify the current location. Use the wildcard character ('*') to specify all the items in
    the current location.

    Required?                  true
    Position?                  0
    Default value              None
    Accept pipeline input?     True (ByPropertyName, ByValue)
    Accept wildcard characters? true
```

**Figure 3.2   Segment from help for Get-Item showing that the -path variable is required**

In the preceding example, you can see that this is a positional parameter, and it occurs in the first position, right after the cmdlet name, based on the 0 position index.

We always encourage students to focus on reading the full help when they're getting started with a cmdlet, rather than only the abbreviated syntax reminder. Reading the help reveals more details, including that description of the parameter's use. You can also see that this parameter does accept wildcards, which means you can provide a value like Down*. You don't need to type out the name of an item, such as the Downloads folder.

### 3.5.4 Parameter values

The help files also give you clues about the kind of input that each parameter accepts. Most parameters expect some kind of input value, which will always follow the parameter name and be separated from the parameter name by a space (not by a colon, equal sign, or any other character, although you might encounter exceptions from time to time). In the abbreviated syntax, the type of input expected is shown in angle brackets, like < >:

```
-Filter <String>
```

It's shown the same way in the full syntax:

```
-Filter <String>
    Specifies a filter in the format or language of the provider. The
    value of this parameter qualifies the Path parameter.

    The syntax of the filter, including the use of wildcard characters,
depends on the provider. Filters are more efficient than
    other parameters, because the provider applies them when the cmdlet
gets the objects rather than having PowerShell filter
    the objects after they are retrieved.

    Required?                      false
    Position?                      named
    Default value                  None
    Accept pipeline input?         False
    Accept wildcard characters?    true
```

Let's look at some common types of input:

- String—A series of letters and numbers. These can sometimes include spaces, but when they do, the entire string must be contained within quotation marks. For example, a string value such as /usr/bin doesn't need to be enclosed in quotes, but ~/book samples does, because it has that space in the middle. For now, you can use single or double quotation marks interchangeably, but it's best to stick with single quotes.
- Int, Int32, *or* Int64—An integer number (a whole number with no decimal portion).
- DateTime—Generally, a string that can be interpreted as a date based on your computer's regional settings. In the United States, that's usually something like 10-10-2010, with the month, day, and year.

We'll discuss other, more specialized types as we come to them. You'll also notice some values that have more square brackets:

```
-Path <String[]>
```

The side-by-side brackets after `String` don't indicate that something is optional. Instead, `String[]` indicates that the parameter can accept an *array*, a *collection*, or a *list* of strings. In these cases, it's always legal to provide a single value:

```
Get-Item -Path ~
```

But it's also legal to specify multiple values. A simple way to do so is to provide a comma-separated list. PowerShell treats all comma-separated lists as arrays of values:

```
Get-Item -Path ~, ~/Downloads
```

Once again, any individual value that contains a space must be enclosed in quotation marks. But the entire list doesn't get enclosed in quotation marks; it's important that only individual values be in quotes. The following is legal:

```
Get-Item -Path '~', '~/Downloads'
```

Even though neither of those values needs to be in quotation marks, it's okay to use the quotes if you want to. But the following is wrong:

```
Get-Item -Path '~, ~/Downloads'
```

In this case, the cmdlet will look for a file named `~, ~/Downloads`, which probably isn't what you want.

You can also feed a list of values to a parameter in a few other ways, including reading computer names from a file, or other cmdlets. Those techniques are a bit more complex, though, so we'll get to them in later chapters, after you learn some of the cmdlets you need to make the trick work.

Another way you can specify multiple values for a parameter (provided it's a mandatory parameter) is to not specify the parameter at all. As with all mandatory parameters, PowerShell will prompt you for the parameter value. For parameters that accept multiple values, you can type the first value and press Enter. PowerShell will then prompt for a second value, which you can type and finish by pressing Enter. Keep doing that until you're finished, and press Enter on a blank prompt to let PowerShell know you're finished. As always, you can press Ctrl-C to abort the command if you don't want to be prompted for entries.

Other parameters, referred to as *switches*, don't require any input value at all. In the abbreviated syntax, they look like the following:

```
[-Force]
```

And in the full syntax, they look like this:

```
-Force [<SwitchParameter>]
    Indicates that this cmdlet gets items that cannot otherwise be
accessed, such as hidden items. Implementation varies from
    provider to provider. For more information, see about_Providers
(../Microsoft.PowerShell.Core/About/about_Providers.md).
    Even using the Force parameter, the cmdlet cannot override security
restrictions.

    Required?                    false
    Position?                    named
    Default value                False
    Accept pipeline input?       False
    Accept wildcard characters?  false
```

The [<SwitchParameter>] part confirms that this is a switch and that it doesn't expect an input value. Switches are never positional; you always have to type the parameter name (or at least an abbreviated version of it). Switches are always optional, which gives you the choice to use them or not.

For example, Get-Item .* will not show you any files, but Get-Item .* -Force will give you a list of files starting with . because files starting with . are considered hidden, and -Force tells the command to include hidden files.

### 3.5.5 *Finding command examples*

We tend to learn by example, which is why we try to squeeze as many examples into this book as possible. PowerShell's designers know that most administrators enjoy having examples, so they built a lot of them into the help files. If you scrolled to the end of the help file for Get-Item, you probably noticed almost a dozen examples of how to use the cmdlet.

Let's look at an easier way to get to those examples, if they're all you want to see. Use the -Example parameter of the Help command, rather than the -Full parameter:

```
Help Get-Item -Example
```

**TRY IT NOW** Go ahead and pull up the examples for a cmdlet by using this new parameter.

**NOTE** Because of PowerShell's origins on Windows, many of the examples use Windows paths. You are expected to know that you can use macOS or Linux paths. In fact, PowerShell does not care if you use / or \ as the directory separator on either platform.

We love having these examples, even though some of them can be complicated. If an example looks too complicated for you, ignore it and examine the others for now. Or experiment a bit (always on a nonproduction computer) to see if you can figure out what the example does and why.

## 3.6    *Accessing "about" topics*

Earlier in this chapter, we mentioned that PowerShell's help system includes background topics as well as help for specific cmdlets. These background topics are often called "about" topics, because their filenames all start with about_. You may also recall from earlier in this chapter that all cmdlets support a set of common parameters. How do you think you could learn more about those common parameters?

> **TRY IT NOW**   Before you read ahead, see if you can list the common parameters by using the help system.

You start by using wildcards. Because the word *common* has been used repeatedly here in the book, that's probably a good keyword to start with:

```
Help *common*
```

It's such a good keyword, in fact, that it matches only one help topic: About _common _parameters. That topic displays automatically because it's the only match. Paging through the file a bit, you'll find the following list of the 11 (when this was written) common parameters:

```
-Verbose
-Debug
-WarningAction
-WarningVariable
-ErrorAction
-ErrorVariable
-OutVariable
-OutBuffer
-InformationAction
-InformationVariable
-PipelineVaribale
```

The file says that PowerShell has two additional *risk mitigation* parameters, but those aren't supported by every single cmdlet. The about topics in the help system are tremendously important, but because they're not related to a specific cmdlet, they can be easy to overlook. If you run help about* for a list of all of them, you might be surprised at how much extra documentation is hidden away inside the shell.

> **TRY IT NOW**   Run the command get-help about_* and look at all the about topics. Now run get-help about_Updateable_Help

## 3.7    *Accessing online help*

Mere human beings wrote PowerShell's help files, which means they're not error free. In addition to updating the help files (which you can do by running Update-Help), Microsoft publishes help on its website. The -Online parameter of PowerShell's help command will attempt to open the web-based help—even on macOS or Linux!—for a given command:

```
Help Get-Item -Online
```

The Microsoft Docs website hosts the help, and it's often more up to date than what's installed with PowerShell itself. If you think you've spotted an error in an example or in the syntax, try viewing the online version of the help. Not every single cmdlet in the universe has online help; it's up to each product team (such as the Azure compute team, which provides VM functionality, Azure Storage team, and so forth) to provide that help. But when it's available, it's a nice companion to what's built in.

We like the online help because it lets us read the text in one window (the web browser, where the help is also nicely formatted) as we're typing in PowerShell.

It's important for us to point out that the PowerShell team at Microsoft has open sourced all of their help files as of April 2016. Anyone can add examples, correct errors, and generally help improve the help files. The online, open source project is at https://github.com/MicrosoftDocs/Powershell-Docs and typically includes only the documentation owned by the PowerShell team; it doesn't necessarily include documentation from other teams who are producing PowerShell commands. You can bug those teams directly about open sourcing their docs!

## 3.8 Lab

**NOTE** For this lab, you need any computer running PowerShell 7.

We hope this chapter has conveyed the importance of mastering the help system in PowerShell. Now it's time to hone your skills by completing the following tasks. Keep in mind that sample answers follow. Look for *italicized* words in these tasks, and use them as clues to complete the tasks:

1 Run `Update-Help`, and ensure that it completes without errors so that you have a copy of the help on your local computer. You need an internet connection.

2 Can you find any cmdlets capable of converting other cmdlets' output into *HTML*?

3 Are there any cmdlets that can redirect output into a *file*?

4 How many cmdlets are available for working with *processes*? (Hint: Remember that cmdlets all use a singular noun.)

5 What cmdlet might you use to *set* to a PowerShell breakpoint? (Hint: PowerShell-specific nouns are often prefixed with *PS*.)

6 You've learned that aliases are nicknames for cmdlets. What cmdlets are available to create, modify, export, or import *aliases*?

7 Is there a way to keep a *transcript* of everything you type in the shell, and save that transcript to a text file?

8 Getting all processes can be overwhelming. How can you get processes by the name of the process?

9 Is there a way to tell `Get-Process` to tell you the user who started the process?

10 Is there a way to run a *command* on a remote host? (Hint: *Invoke* is the verb for running something now.)

11  Examine the help file for the `Out-File` cmdlet. The files created by this cmdlet default to a width of how many characters? Is there a parameter that would enable you to change that width?

12  By default, `Out-File` overwrites any existing file that has the same filename as what you specify. Is there a parameter that would prevent the cmdlet from overwriting an existing file?

13  How could you see a list of all *aliases* defined in PowerShell?

14  Using both an alias and abbreviated parameter names, what is the shortest command line you could type to retrieve a list of *commands* with the word *process* in the name?

15  How many cmdlets are available that can deal with generic objects? (Hint: Remember to use a singular noun like *object* rather than a plural one like *objects*.)

16  This chapter briefly mentioned *arrays*. What help topic could tell you more about them?

## 3.9   Lab answers

1  `Update-Help`

Or if you run it more than once in a single day, use the following:

```
Update-Help -force
```

2  `help html`

Or you could try using the `Get-Command`:

```
Get-Command -Noun html
```

3  `Get-Command -Noun file,printer`

4  `Get-Command -Noun process`

or

```
Help *Process
```

5  `Get-Command -Verb set -Noun psbreakpoint`

Or if you aren't sure about the noun, use a wildcard:

```
help *breakpoint
```

or

```
help *break*
```

6  `help *alias`

or

```
Get-Command -Noun alias
```

7  `help transcript`

8  `help Get-Process -Parameter Name`

9  `help Get-Process -Parameter IncludeUserName`

10  The command to execute over SSH is

```
help Invoke-Command -Parameter hostname
```

Or the command to execute over the legacy Windows protocol is

```
help Invoke-Command -Parameter computername
```

11  `Help Out-File -Full`

or

```
Help Out-File -Parameter Width
```

should show you 80 characters as the default for the PowerShell console. You would use this parameter to change it as well.

12  If you run `Help Out-File -Full` and look at parameters, you should see `-NoClobber`.

13  `Get-Alias`

14  `Gcm -na *process*`

15  `Get-Command -Noun object`

16  `help about_arrays`

Or you could use wildcards:

```
help *array*
```

# *Running commands* 4

When you start looking at PowerShell examples on the internet, it's easy to get the impression that PowerShell is some kind of .NET–based scripting or programming language. Our fellow Microsoft most valuable professional (MVP) award recipients, and hundreds of other PowerShell users, are pretty serious geeks who like to dig deep into the shell to see what we can make it do. But almost all of us began right where this chapter starts: running commands. That's what you'll be doing in this chapter: not scripting, not programming, but running commands and command-line utilities.

## 4.1 *Let's talk security*

Okay, it's time to talk about the elephant in the room. PowerShell is great, and PowerShell is awesome. But the bad guys like PowerShell just as much as we do. Securing your production environment is at the top of everyone's priority list. By now, you're probably starting to get a feel for how powerful PowerShell can be—and you're wondering whether all that power might be a security problem. It *might* be. Our goal in this section is to help you understand exactly how PowerShell can impact security in your environment and how to configure PowerShell to provide exactly the balance of security and power you require.

First and foremost, PowerShell doesn't apply any additional layers of permissions on anything it touches. PowerShell enables you to do only what you already have permission to do. If you can't create new users in Active Directory by using the graphical console, you won't be able to do so in PowerShell either. PowerShell is another means of exercising whatever permissions you already have.

PowerShell is also not a way to bypass any existing permissions. Let's say you want to deploy a script to your users, and you want that script to do something that your users don't normally have permission to do. That script isn't going to work for them. If you want your users to do something, you need to give them permission to do it. PowerShell can accomplish only those things that the person running a command or script already has permission to do.

PowerShell's security system isn't designed to prevent anyone from typing in, and running, whatever commands they have permission to execute. The idea is that it's somewhat difficult to trick a user into typing a long, complicated command, so PowerShell doesn't apply any security beyond the user's existing permissions. But we know from past experience that it's easy to trick users into running a script, which might well contain malicious commands. This is why most of PowerShell's security is designed with the goal of preventing users from unintentionally running scripts. The *unintentionally* part is important: nothing in PowerShell's security is intended to prevent a determined user from running a script. The idea is to prevent users only from being *tricked* into running scripts from untrusted sources.

### 4.1.1 *Execution policy*

The first security measure PowerShell includes is an *execution policy*. This machine-wide setting governs the scripts that PowerShell will execute. The default setting on Windows 10 is Restricted. On Windows Servers, the default is `RemotedSigned` and the execution policy on non-Windows devices is not enforced. The Restricted setting on Windows 10 devices prevents scripts from being executed at all. That's right: by default, you can use PowerShell to interactively run commands, but you can't use it to run scripts. Let's pretend that you downloaded a script off the internet. If you try to run it, you'll get the following error message:

```
File C:\Scripts\Get-DiskInventory.ps1 cannot be loaded because the execution
 of scripts is disabled on this system. Please see "get-help about_signing"
 for more details.
```

View the current execution policy by running `Get-ExecutionPolicy`. You can change the execution policy in one of three ways:

- *By running the* `Set-ExecutionPolicy` *command*—This changes the setting in the `HKEY_LOCAL_MACHINE` portion of the Windows Registry and usually must be run by an administrator, because regular users don't have permission to write to that portion of the Registry.
- *By using a Group Policy Object (GPO)*—Starting with Windows Server 2008 R2, support for PowerShell-related settings is included. The PowerShell settings shown in figure 4.1 are located under Computer Configuration > Policies > Administrative Templates > Windows Components > Windows PowerShell. Figure 4.2 displays the policy setting as enabled. When configured via a GPO, the setting in the Group Policy overrides any local setting. In fact, if you try to run `Set-ExecutionPolicy`, it'll work, but a warning message will tell you that your new setting had no effect because of a Group Policy override.
- *By manually running* `PowerShell.exe` *and using its* `-ExecutionPolicy` *command-line switch*—When you run it in this fashion, the specified execution policy overrides any local setting as well as any Group Policy–defined setting. Which we can see in figure 4.1.

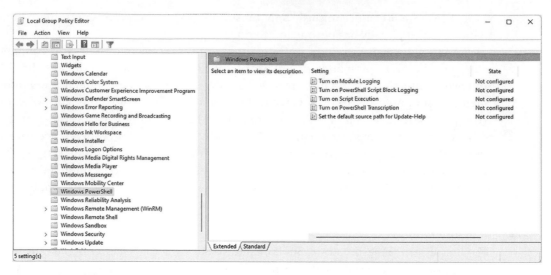

Figure 4.1    **Finding the Windows PowerShell settings in a Group Policy Object**

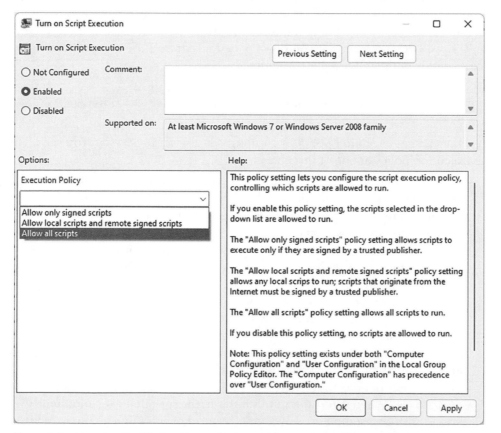

Figure 4.2    **Changing the Windows PowerShell execution policy in a Group Policy Object**

You can set the execution policy to one of five settings (note that the Group Policy Object provides access to only the middle three of the following list):

- `Restricted`—This is the default, and scripts aren't executed. The only exceptions are a few Microsoft-supplied scripts that set up PowerShell's default configuration settings. Those scripts carry a Microsoft digital signature and won't execute if modified.
- `AllSigned`—PowerShell will execute any script that has been digitally signed by using a code-signing certificate issued by a trusted certification authority (CA).
- `RemoteSigned`—PowerShell will execute any local script and will execute remote scripts if they've been digitally signed by using a code-signing certificate issued by a trusted CA. *Remote scripts* are those that exist on a remote computer, usually accessed by a Universal Naming Convention (UNC) path. Scripts marked as having come from the internet are also considered remote. Edge, Chrome, Firefox, and Outlook all mark downloads as having come from the internet.
- `Unrestricted`—All scripts will run.
- `Bypass`—This special setting is intended for use by application developers who are embedding PowerShell within their application. This setting bypasses the configured execution policy and should be used only when the hosting application is providing its own layer of script security. You're essentially telling PowerShell, "Don't worry. I have security covered."

> **Wait, what?**
>
> Did you notice that you could set the execution policy in a Group Policy Object, but also override it by using a parameter of `PowerShell.exe`? What good is a GPO-controlled setting that people can easily override? This emphasizes that the execution policy is intended to protect only *uninformed* users from *unintentionally* running *anonymous* scripts.
>
> The execution policy isn't intended to stop an informed user from doing anything intentional. It's not that kind of security setting.
>
> In fact, a smart malware coder could as easily access the .NET Framework functionality directly, without going to the trouble of using PowerShell as a middleman. Or to put it another way, if an unauthorized user has admin rights to your computer and can run arbitrary code, you're already in trouble.

Microsoft recommends that you use `RemoteSigned` when you want to run scripts and that you use it only on computers where scripts must be executed. According to Microsoft, all other computers should be left at `Restricted`. They say that `RemoteSigned` provides a good balance between security and convenience. `AllSigned` is stricter but requires all of your scripts to be digitally signed. The PowerShell community as a whole is more divided, with a range of opinions on what a good execution policy is. For now, we'll go with Microsoft's recommendation and let you explore the topic more on your own, if you wish.

> **NOTE**  Plenty of experts, including Microsoft's own "Scripting Guy," suggest using the Unrestricted setting for ExecutionPolicy. Their feeling is that the feature doesn't provide a layer of security, and you shouldn't give yourself false confidence that it's protecting you from anything.

## 4.2  *Not scripting, but running commands*

PowerShell, as its name indicates, is a *shell.* Other shells you've probably used or at least heard of include cmd.exe, Bash, Zsh, fish, and ksh. PowerShell is not only a shell but also a *scripting language*—but not in the way JavaScript or Python are.

With those languages, as with most programming languages, you sit down in front of a text editor or integrated development environment (IDE) and type a series of keywords to form a script. You save that file, and perhaps double-click it to test it. Power-Shell can work like that, but that's not necessarily the main usage pattern for PowerShell, particularly when you're getting started. With PowerShell, you type a command, add a few parameters to customize the command's behavior, press Enter, and immediately see your results.

Eventually, you'll get tired of typing the same command (and its parameters) over and over again, so you'll copy and paste it all into a text file. Give that file a .ps1 file-name extension, and you suddenly have a *PowerShell script.* Now, instead of typing the command over and over, you run that script, and it executes whatever commands are inside. It's typically far less complex than writing a program in a full programming language. In fact, it's a pattern similar to that used by UNIX administrators for years. Common UNIX/Linux shells, such as Bash, have a similar approach: run commands until you get them right, and then paste them into a text file and call it a *script.*

Don't get us wrong: You can get as complex as you need to with PowerShell. It does support the same kind of usage patterns as Python and other scripting or programming languages. PowerShell gives you access to the full underlying power of .NET Core, and we've seen PowerShell "scripts" that were practically indistinguishable from a C# program written in Visual Studio. PowerShell supports these different usage patterns because it's intended to be useful to a wide range of audiences. The point is that just because it *supports* that level of complexity doesn't mean you *have* to use it at that level, and it doesn't mean you can't be extremely effective with less complexity.

Here's an analogy. You probably drive a car. If you're like us, changing the oil is the most complex mechanical task you'll ever do with your car. We're not car geeks and can't rebuild an engine. We also can't do those cool, high-speed J-turns that you see in the movies. You'll never see us driving a car on a closed course in a car commercial. But the fact that we're not professional stunt drivers doesn't stop us from being extremely effective drivers at a less complex level. Someday we might decide to take up stunt driving for a hobby (our insurance companies will be thrilled), and at that point we'll need to learn a bit more about how our cars work, master some new skills, and so on. The option is always there for us to grow into. But for now, we're happy with what we can accomplish as normal drivers.

For now, we'll stick with being normal "PowerShell drivers," operating the shell at a lower level of complexity. Believe it or not, users at this level are the primary target audience for PowerShell, and you'll find that you can do a lot of incredible stuff without going beyond this level. All you need to do is master the ability to run commands within the shell, and you're on your way.

## 4.3 The anatomy of a command

Figure 4.3 shows the basic anatomy of a complex PowerShell command. We call this the *full-form* syntax of a command. We're showing a somewhat complex command here, so you can see all of the things that might show up.

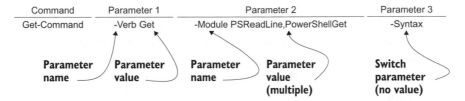

**Figure 4.3  The anatomy of a PowerShell command**

To make sure you're completely familiar with PowerShell's rules, let's cover each of the elements in the previous figure in more detail:

- The cmdlet name is `Get-Command`. PowerShell cmdlets always have this verb-noun naming format. We explain more about cmdlets in the next section.
- The first parameter name is `-Verb`, and it's being given the value `Get`. Because the value doesn't contain any spaces or punctuation, it doesn't need to be in quotation marks.
- The second parameter name is `-Module`, and it's being given two values: `PSReadLine` and `PowerShellGet`. These are in a comma-separated list, and because neither value contains spaces or punctuation, neither value needs to be inside quotation marks.
- The final parameter, `-Syntax`, is a switch parameter. That means it doesn't get a value; specifying the parameter is sufficient.
- Note that there's a mandatory space between the command name and the first parameter.
- Parameter names always start with a dash (`-`).
- There's a mandatory space after the parameter name and between the parameter's value and the next parameter name.
- There's no space between the dash (`-`) that precedes a parameter name and the parameter name itself.
- Nothing here is case sensitive.

Get used to these rules. Start being sensitive about accurate, neat typing. Paying attention to spaces and dashes and other rules will minimize the silly errors that PowerShell throws at you.

## 4.4   *The cmdlet naming convention*

First, let's discuss some terminology. As far as we know, we're the only ones who use this terminology in everyday conversation, but we do it consistently, so we may as well explain:

- A *cmdlet* is a native PowerShell command-line utility. These exist only inside PowerShell and are written in a .NET Core language such as C#. The word *cmdlet* is unique to PowerShell, so if you add it to your search keywords on your favorite search engine, the results you get back will be mainly PowerShell related. The word is pronounced *command-let.*
- A *function* can be similar to a cmdlet, but rather than being written in a .NET language, functions are written in PowerShell's own scripting language.
- An *application* is any kind of external executable, including command-line utilities such as `ping` and `ipconfig`.
- *Command* is the generic term that we use to refer to any or all of the preceding terms.

Microsoft has established a naming convention for cmdlets. That same naming convention *should* be used for functions, too, although Microsoft can't force anyone but its own employees to follow that rule.

The rule is this: Names start with a standard verb, such as `Get` or `Set` or `New` or `Pause`. You can run `Get-Verb` to see a list of approved verbs (you'll see about 100, although only about a dozen are common). After the verb is a dash, followed by a singular noun, such as `Job` or `Process` or `Item`. Developers get to make up their own nouns, so there's no *Get-Noun* cmdlet to display them all.

What's the big deal about this rule? Well, suppose we told you that there were cmdlets named `Start-Job`, `Get-Job`, `Get-Process`, `Stop-Process`, and so forth. Could you guess what command would start a new process on your machine? Could you guess what command would modify an Azure virtual machine (VM)? If you guessed `Start-Process`, you got the first one right. If you guessed `Set-VM`, you were close: it's `Set-AzVM`, and you'll find the command on Azure VMs in the Az.Compute module (we will go over modules in chapter 7). All the Azure commands use that same prefix of `Az`, followed by the noun that the command messes with. The point is that by having this consistent naming convention with a limited set of verbs, it becomes possible for you to guess at command names, and you could then use `Help` or `Get-Command`, along with wildcards, to validate your guess. It becomes easier for you to figure out the names of the commands you need, without having to run to Google or Bing every time.

> **NOTE**   Not all of the so-called verbs are really verbs. Although Microsoft officially uses the term *verb-noun naming convention,* you'll see "verbs" like `New`, `Where`, and so forth. You'll get used to it.

## 4.5  *Aliases: Nicknames for commands*

Although PowerShell command names can be nice and consistent, they can also be long. A command name such as `Remove-AzStorageTableStoredAccessPolicy` is a lot to type, even with tab completion. Although the command name is clear—looking at it, you can probably guess what it does—it's an *awful* lot to type.

That's where PowerShell aliases come in. An *alias* is nothing more than a nickname for a command. Tired of typing `Get-Process`? Try this:

```
PS /Users/james> Get-Alias -Definition "Get-Process"
Capability      Name
----------      ----
Cmdlet          gps -> Get-Process
```

Now you know that `gps` is an alias for `Get-Process`.

When using an alias, the command works in the same way. Parameters are the same; everything is the same—the command name is just shorter.

If you're staring at an alias (folks on the internet tend to use them as if we've all memorized the hundreds of built-in aliases) and can't figure out what it is, ask help:

```
PS /Users/james> help gps
NAME
    Get-Process
SYNOPSIS
    Gets the processes that are running on the local computer.
SYNTAX
    Get-Process [[-Name] <String[]>] [-FileVersionInfo] [-Module]
    [<CommonParameters>]
    Get-Process [-FileVersionInfo] -Id <Int32[]> [-Module]
    [<CommonParameters>]
    Get-Process [-FileVersionInfo] -InputObject <Process[]> [-Module]
    [<CommonParameters>]
    Get-Process -Id <Int32[]> -IncludeUserName [<CommonParameters>]
    Get-Process [[-Name] <String[]>] -IncludeUserName [<CommonParameters>]
    Get-Process -IncludeUserName -InputObject <Process[]>
    ➥ [<CommonParameters>]
```

When asked for help about an alias, the help system will always display the help for the full command, which includes the command's complete name.

---

**Above and beyond**

You can create your own aliases by using `New-Alias`, export a list of aliases by using `Export-Alias`, or even import a list of previously created aliases by using `Import-Alias`. When you create an alias, it lasts only as long as your current shell session. Once you close the window, it's gone. That's why you might want to export them, so that you can use them in another PowerShell session.

> *(continued)*
>
> We tend to avoid creating and using custom aliases, though, because they're not available to anyone but the person who made them. If someone can't look up what `xtd` does, we're creating confusion and incompatibility.
>
> And `xtd` doesn't do anything. It's a fake alias we made up.

We must point out, because PowerShell is now available on non-Windows operating systems, that its concept of *alias* is a little different from an alias in, say, Bash. In Bash, an alias can be a kind of shortcut for running a command *that includes a bunch of parameters*. PowerShell doesn't behave that way. An alias is *only* a nickname for the command name, and the alias can't include any predetermined parameters.

## 4.6  Taking shortcuts

Here's where PowerShell gets tricky. We'd love to tell you that everything we've shown you so far is the only way to do things, but we'd be lying. And, unfortunately, you're going to be out on the internet stealing (well, repurposing) other people's examples, and you'll need to know what you're looking at.

In addition to aliases, which are shorter versions of command names, you can also take *shortcuts* with parameters. You have three ways to do this, each potentially more confusing than the last.

### 4.6.1  Truncating parameter names

PowerShell doesn't force you to type out entire parameter names. As you might recall from chapter 3, instead of typing `-ComputerName`, for example, you could go with `-comp`. The rule is that you have to type enough of the name for PowerShell to be able to distinguish it. If there's the `-ComputerName` parameter, the `-Common` parameter, and the `-Composite` parameter, you'd have to type at least `-compu`, `-comm`, and `-compo`, because that's the minimum number of letters necessary to uniquely identify each.

If you must take shortcuts, this isn't a bad one to take, if you can remember to press Tab after typing that minimum-length parameter so that PowerShell can finish typing the rest of it for you.

### 4.6.2  Using parameter name aliases

Parameters can also have their own aliases, although they can be terribly difficult to find, as they aren't displayed in the help files or anyplace else convenient. For example, the `Get-Process` command has the `-ErrorAction` parameter. To discover its aliases, you run this command:

```
PS /Users/james> (get-command get-process | select -Expand
  parameters).erroraction.aliases
```

We've boldfaced the command and parameter names; replace these with whatever command and parameter you're curious about. In this case, the output reveals that -ea is an alias for -ErrorAction, so you could run this:

```
PS /Users/james> Get-Process -ea Stop
```

Tab completion will show you the -ea alias; if you typed Get-Process -e and started pressing Tab, it'd show up. But the help for the command doesn't display -ea at all, and tab completion doesn't indicate that -ea and -ErrorAction are the same thing.

> **NOTE** These are called *common parameters*. You can run the command Get-Help about_CommonParamaters to read more about them.

### 4.6.3 *Using positional parameters*

When you're looking at a command's syntax in its help file, you can spot positional parameters easily:

```
SYNTAX
    Get-ChildItem [[-Path] <string[]>] [[-Filter] <string>] [-Include
    ➥ <string[]>] [-Exclude <string[]>] [-Recurse] [-De
    pth <uint>] [-Force] [-Name] [-Attributes {ReadOnly | Hidden | System |
    ➥ Directory | Archive | Device | Normal | Tem
    porary | SparseFile | ReparsePoint | Compressed | Offline |
    ➥ NotContentIndexed | Encrypted | IntegrityStream | NoScr
    ubData}] [-FollowSymlink] [-Directory] [-File] [-Hidden] [-ReadOnly]
[-System] [<CommonParameters>]
```

Here, both -Path and -Filter are positional, and you know that because the parameter name and the accepted input is contained within square brackets. A clearer explanation is available in the full help (help Get-ChildItem -Full, in this case), which looks like this:

```
-Path <String[]>
    Specifies a path to one or more locations. Wildcards are
    permitted. The default location is the current directory (.).
    Required?                    false
    Position?                    0
    Default value                Current directory
    Accept pipeline input?       true (ByValue, ByPropertyName)
    Accept wildcard characters?  True
```

That's a clear indication that the -Path parameter is in position 0, which means it's the first parameter after the cmdlet. For positional parameters, you don't have to type the parameter name; you can provide its value in the correct position. For example:

```
PS /Users/james> Get-ChildItem /Users
    Directory: /Users
Mode            LastWriteTime      Length Name
----            -------------      ------ ----
d----        3/27/2016  11:20 AM          james
d-r--        2/18/2016   2:06 AM          Shared
```

That's the same as this:

```
PS /Users/james> Get-ChildItem -Path /Users
    Directory: /Users
Mode                 LastWriteTime     Length Name
----                 -------------     ------ ----
d-----          3/27/2019  11:20 AM           james
d-----          2/18/2019   2:06 AM           Shared
```

The problem with positional parameters is that you're taking on the responsibility of remembering what goes where. You must type all positional parameters first, in the correct order, before you can add any named (nonpositional) parameters. If you mix up the parameter order, the command fails. For simple commands such as `Dir`, which you've probably used for years, typing `-Path` feels weird, and almost nobody does it. But for more-complex commands, which might have three or four positional parameters in a row, it can be tough to remember what goes where.

For example, this is a bit difficult to read and interpret:

```
PS /Users/james> move file.txt /Users/james/
```

This version, which uses full cmdlet name and parameter names, is easier to follow:

```
PS /Users/james> move-item -Path /tmp/file.txt -Destination /Users/james/
```

This version, which puts the parameters in a different order, is allowed when you use the parameter names:

```
PS /Users/james> move -Destination /Users/james/ -Path /tmp/file.txt
```

We tend to recommend against using positional (unnamed) parameters unless you're banging out something quick and dirty at the command line. In anything that will persist, such as a PowerShell script file or a blog post, include all of the parameter names. We do that as much as possible in this book, except in a few instances where we have to shorten the command line to make it fit within the printed page.

## 4.7   *Support for external commands*

So far, all of the commands you've run in the shell (at least the ones we've suggested that you run) have been built-in cmdlets. Over 2,900 cmdlets come built into Power-Shell on your Windows machine and over 200 on your Linux or macOS machine. You can add more—products such as Azure PowerShell, AWS PowerShell, and SQL Server all come with add-ins that include hundreds of additional cmdlets.

But you're not limited to PowerShell cmdlets. You can also use the same external command-line utilities that you've probably been using for years, including `ping`, `nslookup`, `ifconfig` or `ipconfig`, and so forth. Because these aren't native Power-Shell cmdlets, you use them the same way that you always have. Go ahead and try a few old favorites right now.

It's the same story on non-Windows operating systems. You can use `grep`, `bash`, `sed`, `awk`, `ping`, and whatever other existing command-line tools you may have. They'll run normally, and PowerShell will display their results the same way that your old shell (e.g., Bash) would have.

**TRY IT NOW** Try running some external command-line utilities that you've used previously. Do they work the same? Do any of them fail?

This section illustrates an important lesson: with PowerShell, Microsoft (perhaps for the first time ever) isn't saying, "You have to start over and learn everything all over again." Instead, Microsoft is saying, "If you already know how to do something, keep doing it that way. We'll try to provide you with better and more complete tools going forward, but what you already know will still work."

In some instances, Microsoft has provided better tools than some of the existing, older ones. For example, the native `Test-Connection` cmdlet provides more options and more-flexible output than the old, external `ping` command. But if you know how to use `ping`, and it's solving whatever need you have, go right on using it. It'll work fine from within PowerShell.

All that said, we do have to deliver a harsh truth: not every external command will work flawlessly from within PowerShell, at least not without a little tweaking on your part. That's because PowerShell's parser—the bit of the shell that reads what you've typed and tries to figure out what you want the shell to do—doesn't always guess correctly. Sometimes you'll type an external command, and PowerShell will mess up, start spitting out errors, and generally not work.

For example, things can get tricky when an external command has a lot of parameters—that's where you'll see PowerShell break the most. We won't dive into the details of why it works, but here's a way to run a command that ensures that its parameters will work properly:

```
$exe = "func"
$action = "new"
$language = "powershell"
$template = "HttpTrigger"
$name = "myFunc"
& $exe $action -l $language -t $template -n $name
```

This supposes that you have an external command named `func`. (This real-life command-line utility is used to interact with Azure Functions.) If you've never used it or don't have it, that's fine; most old-school command-line utilities work the same way, so this is still a good teaching example. It accepts several parameters:

- `"new"` here is the action you want to take, and `-new`, `init`, `start`, and `logs` are the options.
- `-l` is for the language you want the function to be.
- `-t` is for the template you want to use.
- `-n` is for the name of the function.

What we've done is put all the various elements—the executable path and name, as well as all of the parameter values—into placeholders, which start with the $ character. That forces PowerShell to treat those values as single units, rather than trying to parse them to see whether any contain commands or special characters. Then we used the invocation operator (&), passing it the executable name, all of the parameters, and the parameters' values. That pattern will work for almost any command-line utility that's being grumpy about running within PowerShell.

Sound complicated? Well, here's some good news: In PowerShell v3 and later, you don't have to mess around so much. Just add two dashes and a percent symbol in front of anything, and PowerShell won't even try to parse it; it'll just pass it right to the command-line utility that you're using. To be absolutely clear, this means you won't be able to pass variables as parameter values.

Here's a quick example of what will fail:

```
PS /Users/james> $name = "MyFunctionApp"
PS /Users/james> func azure functionapp list-functions --% $name

Can't find app with name "$name"
```

We tried to run the command-line utility func to list all of our Azure functions with the name "MyFunctionApp", but if we explicitly state what we want, PowerShell will pass all the parameters to the underlying command without trying to do anything with them:

```
PS /Users/james> func new -t HttpTrigger -n --% "MyFunc"
Select a template: HttpTrigger
Function name: [HttpTrigger] Writing /Users/tyler/MyFuncApp/MyFunc/run.ps1
Writing /Users/tyler/MyFuncApp/MyFunc/function.json
The function "MyFunc" was created successfully from the "HttpTrigger"
➥ template.
PS /Users/james>
```

Hopefully this isn't something you'll need to do often.

## 4.8   *Dealing with errors*

It's inevitable that you'll see some ugly red text as you start working with PowerShell—and probably from time to time even after you're an expert-level shell user. Happens to us all. But don't let the red text stress you out. (Personally, it takes us back to high school English class and poorly written essays, so *stress* is putting it mildly.)

The alarming red text aside, PowerShell's error messages have improved greatly over the years (a lot of this has to do with the fact that the error messages are also open sourced). For example, as shown in figure 4.4, they try to show you exactly where PowerShell ran into trouble.

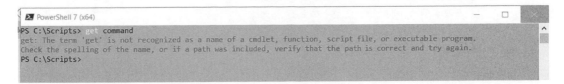

**Figure 4.4    Interpreting a PowerShell error message**

Most error messages are easy to understand. In figure 4.4, right at the beginning, it's saying, "You typed get, and I have no idea what that means." That's because we typed the command name wrong: it's supposed to be Get-Command, not Get Command. Oops. What about figure 4.5?

```
PowerShell 7 (x64)                                                    —  □  ×
PS C:\Scripts> dir C:\users\James\ \s
Get-ChildItem: Second path fragment must not be a drive or UNC name. (Parameter 'expression')
PS C:\Scripts>
```

**Figure 4.5    What's a "second path fragment"?**

The error message in figure 4.5, "Second path fragment must not be a drive or UNC name," is confusing. What second path? We didn't type a second path. We typed one path, C:\Users\James and a command-line parameter, \s. Right?

Well, no. One of the easiest ways to solve this kind of problem is to read the help and to type the command out completely. If we'd typed Get-ChildItem -Path C:\Users\james, we'd have realized that \s isn't the correct syntax. We meant -Recurse. Sometimes the error message might not seem helpful—and if it seems like you and PowerShell are speaking different languages, you are. PowerShell obviously isn't going to change its language, so you're probably the one in the wrong, and consulting the help and spelling out the entire command, parameters and all, is often the quickest way to solve the problem.

## 4.9  *Common points of confusion*

Whenever it seems appropriate, we wrap up each chapter with a brief section that covers some of the common mistakes we see. The idea is to help you see what most often confuses other administrators like yourself and to avoid those problems—or at least to be able to find a solution for them—as you start working with the shell.

### 4.9.1  *Typing cmdlet names*

First up is the typing of cmdlet names. It's always verb-noun, like Get-Content. All of these are options we'll see newcomers try, but they won't work:

- `Get Content`
- `GetContent`
- `Get=Content`
- `Get_Content`

Part of the problem comes from typos (e.g., = instead of -) and part from verbal laziness. We all pronounce the command as *Get Content*, verbally omitting the dash. But you have to type the dash.

### 4.9.2   *Typing parameters*

Parameters are also consistently written. Parameters, such as `-Recurse`, get a dash before their name. If the parameter has a value, a space will come between the parameter name and its value. You need to have spaces separating the cmdlet name from its parameters, and the parameters from each other. The following are correct:

- `123`
- `Dir -rec` (the shortened parameter name is fine)
- `New-PSDrive -name DEMO -psprovider FileSystem -root \\Server\Share`

But these examples are all incorrect:

- `Dir-rec` (no space between alias and parameter)
- `New-PSDrive -nameDEMO` (no space between parameter name and value)
- `New-PSDrive -name DEMO-psprovider FileSystem` (no space between the first parameter's value and the second parameter's name)

PowerShell isn't normally picky about upper- and lowercase, meaning that `dir` and `DIR` are the same, as are `-RECURSE` and `-recurse` and `-Recurse`. But the shell sure is picky about those spaces and dashes.

## 4.10   *Lab*

> **NOTE**   For this lab, you need PowerShell v7 or later running on Windows, macOS, or Linux.

Using what you learned in this chapter, and in the previous chapter on using the help system, complete the following tasks in PowerShell:

1  Display a list of running processes.
2  Test the connection to google.com or bing.com without using an external command like `ping`.
3  Display a list of all commands that are of the cmdlet type. (This is tricky—we've shown you `Get-Command`, but you need to read the help to find out how to narrow down the list as we've asked.)
4  Display a list of all aliases.
5  Make a new alias, so you can run `ntst` to run `netstat`  from a PowerShell prompt.

6 Display a list of processes that begin with the letter *p*. Again, read the help for the necessary command—and don't forget that the asterisk (*) is a near-universal wildcard in PowerShell.

7 Make a new folder (aka directory) using the `New-Item` cmdlet with the name of MyFolder1. Then do it again and call it MyFolder2. Use `Help` if you're not familiar with `New-Item`.

8 Remove the folders from step 7 in a single command. Use `Get-Command` to find a similar cmdlet to what we used in step 7—and don't forget that the asterisk (*) is a near-universal wildcard in PowerShell.

We hope these tasks seem straightforward to you. If so—excellent. You're taking advantage of your existing command-line skills to make PowerShell perform a few practical tasks for you. If you're new to the command-line world, these tasks are a good introduction to what you'll be doing in the rest of this book.

## 4.11 Lab answers

1 `Get-Process`

2 `Test-Connection google.com`

3 `Get-Command -Type cmdlet`

4 `Get-Alias`

5 `New-Alias -Name ntst -Value netstat`

6 `Get-Process -Name p*`

7 New-Item -Name MyFolder1 -Path c:\scripts -Type Directory;
   New-Item -Name MyFolder2 -Path c:\scripts -Type Directory

8 `Remove-item C:\Scripts\MyFolder*`

# Working with providers

One of the more potentially confusing aspects of PowerShell is its use of a *provider*. A provider gives access to specialized data stores for easier viewing and management. The data appears in a drive in PowerShell.

We warn you that some of this chapter might seem a bit remedial for you. We expect that you're familiar with the filesystem, for example, and you probably know all the commands you need to manage the filesystem from a shell. But bear with us: we're going to point things out in a specific way so that we can use your existing familiarity with the filesystem to help make the concept of providers easier to understand. Also, keep in mind that PowerShell isn't Bash. You may see some things in this chapter that look familiar, but we assure you that they're doing something quite different from what you're used to.

## 5.1 What are providers?

A PowerShell provider, or *PSProvider*, is an adapter. It's designed to take some kind of data storage, such as Windows Registry, Active Directory, or even the local filesystem, and make it look like a disk drive. You can see a list of installed PowerShell providers right within the shell:

```
PS C:\Scripts\ > Get-PSProvider
Name                  Capabilities                             Drives
----                  ------------                             ------
Alias                 ShouldProcess                            {Alias}
Environment           ShouldProcess                            {Env}
FileSystem            Filter, ShouldProcess, Credentials       {/}
Function              ShouldProcess                            {Function}
Variable              ShouldProcess                            {Variable}
```

Providers can also be added into the shell, typically along with a module, which are the two ways that PowerShell can be extended. (We'll cover those extensions later in the book.) Sometimes, enabling certain PowerShell features may create a new PSProvider. For example, you can manipulate environment variables with the `Environment` provider, which we will cover in section 5.5 and you can see here:

```
PS C:\Scripts> Get-PSProvider
Name                    Capabilities                            Drives
----                    ------------                            ------
Alias                   ShouldProcess                           {Alias}
Environment             ShouldProcess                           {Env}
FileSystem              Filter, ShouldProcess, Credentials      {/}
Function                ShouldProcess                           {Function}
Variable                ShouldProcess                           {Variable}
```

Notice that each provider has different capabilities. This is important, because it affects the ways in which you can use each provider. These are some of the common capabilities you'll see:

- `ShouldProcess`—The provider supports the use of the `-WhatIf` and `-Confirm` parameters, enabling you to "test" certain actions before committing to them.
- `Filter`—The provider supports the `-Filter` parameter on the cmdlets that manipulate providers' content.
- `Credentials`—The provider permits you to specify alternate credentials when connecting to data stores. There's a `-Credential` parameter for this.

You use a provider to create a *PSDrive*. A PSDrive uses a single provider to connect to data storage. You're creating a drive mapping, and thanks to the providers, a PSDrive is able to connect to much more than disks. Run the following command to see a list of currently connected drives:

```
PS C:\Scripts> Get-PSDrive

Name            Used (GB)       Free (GB) Provider        Root
----            ---------       --------- --------        ----
/                  159.55          306.11 FileSystem      /
Alias                                     Alias
Env                                       Environment
Function                                  Function
Variable                                  Variable
```

In the preceding list, you can see that we have one drive using the `FileSystem` provider, one using the `Env` provider, and so forth. The PSProvider adapts the data store, and the PSDrive makes it accessible. You use a set of cmdlets to see and manipulate the data exposed by each PSDrive. For the most part, the cmdlets you use with a PSDrive have the word `Item` somewhere in their noun:

```
PS C:\Scripts> Get-Command -Noun *item*
Capability      Name
----------      ----
Cmdlet          Clear-Item
Cmdlet          Clear-ItemProperty
Cmdlet          Copy-Item
Cmdlet          Copy-ItemProperty
Cmdlet          Get-ChildItem
Cmdlet          Get-Item
Cmdlet          Get-ItemProperty
Cmdlet          Invoke-Item
Cmdlet          Move-Item
Cmdlet          Move-ItemProperty
Cmdlet          New-Item
Cmdlet          New-ItemProperty
Cmdlet          Remove-Item
Cmdlet          Remove-ItemProperty
Cmdlet          Rename-Item
Cmdlet          Rename-ItemProperty
Cmdlet          Set-Item
Cmdlet          Set-ItemProperty
```

We'll use these cmdlets, and their aliases, to begin working with the providers on our system. Because it's probably the one you're most familiar with, we'll start with the filesystem—the FileSystem PSProvider.

## 5.2  *Understanding how the filesystem is organized*

The filesystem is organized around two main types of objects—folders and files. *Folders* are also a kind of container, capable of containing both files and other folders. *Files* aren't a type of container; they're more of an endpoint object.

You're probably most familiar with viewing the filesystem through Finder on macOS, the file browser on Linux, or Explorer on your Windows device (figure 5.1), where the hierarchy of drives, folders, and files is visually obvious.

PowerShell's terminology differs somewhat from that of the filesystem. Because a PSDrive might not point to a filesystem—for example, a PSDrive can be mapped to the Environment, Registry, or even an SCCM endpoint, which is obviously not a filesystem— PowerShell doesn't use the terms *file* and *folder*. Instead, it refers to these objects by the more generic term *item*. Both a file and a folder are considered items, although they're obviously different types of items. That's why the cmdlet names we showed you previously all use Item in their noun.

Items can, and often do, have properties. For example, a file item might have properties including its last write time, whether or not it's read-only, and so on. Some items, such as folders, can have *child items*, which are the items contained within that

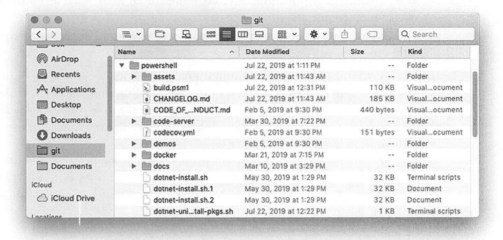

**Figure 5.1  Viewing files, folders, and drives in Finder and Windows Explorer**

item. Knowing those facts should help you make sense of the verbs and nouns in the command list we showed you earlier:

- Verbs such as `Clear`, `Copy`, `Get`, `Move`, `New`, `Remove`, `Rename`, and `Set` can all apply to items (e.g., files and folders) and to item properties (e.g., the date the item was last written or whether it's read-only).
- The `Item` noun refers to individual objects, such as files and folders.

- The `ItemProperty` noun refers to attributes of an item, such as read-only, creation time, length, and so on.
- The `ChildItem` noun refers to the items (e.g., files and subfolders) contained within an item (e.g., a folder).

Keep in mind that these cmdlets are intentionally generic, because they're meant to work with a variety of data stores. Some of the cmdlets' capabilities don't make sense in certain situations. As an example, because the `FileSystem` provider doesn't support the `Transactions` capability, none of the cmdlets' `-UseTransaction` parameters will work with items in the filesystem drives.

Some PSProviders don't support item properties. For example, the `Environment` PSProvider is what's used to make the `ENV:` drive available in PowerShell. This drive provides access to the environment variables, but as the following example shows, they don't have item properties:

```
PS C:\Scripts> Get-ItemProperty -Path Env:\PSModulePath
Get-ItemProperty : Cannot use interface. The IPropertyCmdletProvider
interface is not supported by this provider.
```

The fact that not every PSProvider is the same is perhaps what makes providers so confusing for PowerShell newcomers. You have to think about what each provider is giving you access to, and understand that even when the cmdlet knows how to do something, that doesn't mean the particular provider you're working with will support that operation.

## 5.3  *Navigating the filesystem*

Another cmdlet you need to know when working with providers is `Set-Location`. This is what you use to change the shell's current location to a different container-type item, such as a folder:

```
Linux / macOS
PS /Users/tplunk> Set-Location -Path /
PS />

Windows
PS C:\Scripts > Set-Location -Path /
PS />
```

You're probably more familiar with this command's alias, `cd`, which corresponds to the `Change Directory` command from Bash. Here we use the alias and pass the desired path as a positional parameter:

```
Linux / macOS
PS /Users/tplunk> cd /usr/bin
PS /usr/bin>

Windows
PS C:\Scripts\> cd C:\Users\tplunk
PS C:\Users\tplunk>
```

> ### Drives on non-Windows operating systems
> macOS and Linux don't use *drives* to refer to discrete attached storage devices. Instead, the entire operating system has a single root, represented by a slash (in PowerShell, a backslash is also accepted). But PowerShell still provides PSDrives in non-Windows operating systems for other providers. Try running `Get-PSDrive` to see what's available.

One of the trickier tasks in PowerShell is creating new items. For example, how do you create a new directory? Try running `New-Item` and you'll get an unexpected prompt:

```
PS C:\Users\tplunk\Documents> New-Item testFolder
Type:
```

Remember, the `New-Item` cmdlet is generic—it doesn't know you want to create a folder. It can create folders, files, and much more, but you have to tell it the type of item you want to create:

```
PS C:\Users\tplunk\Documents> New-Item testFolder -ItemType Directory


    Directory: C:\Users\tplunk\Documents

Mode                LastWriteTime         Length Name
----                -------------         ------ ----
d-----         5/26/19 11:56 AM                testFolder
```

Windows PowerShell did include a `mkdir` command, which most people think is an alias for `New-Item`. But using `mkdir` doesn't require you to specify the directory `-ItemType`. Because of the conflict with the built-in `mkdir` command, the `mkdir` function was removed in PowerShell Core for non-Windows platforms.

## 5.4  *Using wildcards and literal paths*

Most providers allow you to specify paths in two ways using the `Item` cmdlets. This section will discuss these two ways of specifying paths. The `Item` cmdlets include the `-Path` parameter, and by default that parameter accepts wildcards. Looking at the full help for `Get-ChildItem`, for example, reveals the following:

```
-Path <String[]>
    Specifies a path to one or more locations. Wildcards are
      permitted. The default location is the current directory (.).
    Required?                    false
    Position?                    1
    Default value                Current directory
    Accept pipeline input?       true (ByValue, ByPropertyName)
    Accept wildcard characters?  True
```

The * wildcard stands in for zero or more characters, whereas the ? wildcard stands in for any single character. You've doubtless used this time and time again, probably with the Dir alias for Get-ChildItem:

```
PS C:\Scripts > dir y*


    Directory: C:\Scripts

Mode                LastWriteTime         Length Name
----                -------------         ------ ----
--r---         5/4/19 12:03 AM           70192 yaa
--r---         5/4/19 12:02 AM           18288 yacc
--r---         5/4/19 12:03 AM           17808 yes
```

In Linux and macOS, most of these wildcards are allowed as part of the names of items in the filesystem as well as in most other stores. In the Environment, for example, you'll find a few values with names that include ?. This presents a problem: When you use * or ? in a path, is PowerShell supposed to treat it as a wildcard character or as a literal character? If you look for items named variable?, do you want the item with variable? as its name, or do you want ? treated as a wildcard, giving you items such as variable7 and variable8 instead?

PowerShell's solution is to provide an alternate -LiteralPath parameter. This parameter doesn't accept wildcards:

```
-LiteralPath <String[]>
    Specifies a path to one or more locations. Unlike the Path
    parameter, the value of the LiteralPath parameter is used exactly
    as it is typed. No characters are interpreted as wildcards. If
    the path includes escape characters, enclose it in single
    quotation marks. Single quotation marks tell PowerShell
    not to interpret any characters as escape sequences.
    Required?                    true
    Position?                    named
    Default value
    Accept pipeline input?       true (ByValue, ByPropertyName)
    Accept wildcard characters?  False
```

When you want * and ? taken literally, you use -LiteralPath instead of the -Path parameter. Note that -LiteralPath isn't positional; if you plan to use it, you have to type -LiteralPath. If you provide a path in the first position (such as y* in our first example), it'll be interpreted as being for the -Path parameter. Wildcards are also treated as such.

## 5.5   *Working with other providers*

One of the best ways to get a feel for these other providers, and how the various item cmdlets work, is to play with a PSDrive that isn't the filesystem. Of the providers built into PowerShell, the Environment is probably the best example to work with (in part because it's available on every system).

We will create an environment variable. Note that we are using an Ubuntu terminal for this exercise, but you can follow along just the same regardlessly if you are on a
Windows or macOS machine (the wonders of cross-platform). Start by listing all environment variables:

```
PS /Users/tplunk> Get-ChildItem env:*

Name                         Value
----                         -----
XPC_FLAGS                    0x0
LANG                         en_US.UTF-8
TERM                         xterm-256color
HOME                         /Users/tplunk
USER                         tplunk
PSModulePath                 /Users/tplunk/.local/share/powershell/Modu…
HOMEBREW_EDITOR              code
PWD                          /Users/tplunk
COLORTERM                    truecolor
XPC_SERVICE_NAME             0
```

Next, set the environment variable A to the value 1:

```
PS /Users/tplunk> Set-Item -Path Env:/A -Value 1

PS /Users/tplunk> Get-ChildItem Env:/A*

Name                         Value
----                         -----
A                            1
```

### 5.5.1 Windows Registry

Another provider we can look at on a Windows machine is the Registry. Let's start by
changing to the HKEY_CURRENT_USER portion of the Registry, exposed by the HKCU:
drive:

```
PS C:\> set-location -Path hkcu:
```

> **NOTE** You may have to launch PowerShell as administrator.

Next, navigate to the right portion of the Registry:

```
PS HKCU:\> set-location -Path software
PS HKCU:\software> get-childitem
    Hive: HKEY_CURRENT_USER\software
Name                         Property
----                         --------
7-Zip                        Path64 : C:\Program Files\7-Zip\
                             Path   : C:\Program Files\7-Zip\

Adobe
Amazon
AppDataLow
```

```
AutomatedLab
BranchIO
ChangeTracker
Chromium
Clients

PS HKCU:\software> set-location microsoft
PS HKCU:\software\microsoft> Get-ChildItem
    Hive: HKEY_CURRENT_USER\software\microsoft
Name                            Property
----                            --------
Accessibility
Active Setup
ActiveMovie
ActiveSync
AppV
Assistance
AuthCookies
Avalon.Graphics
Clipboard                       ShellHotKeyUsed : 1
Common
CommsAPHost
ComPstUI
Connection Manager
CTF
Device Association Framework
DeviceDirectory                 LastUserRegistrationTimestamp : {230, 198,
    218, 150…}
Edge                            UsageStatsInSample              : 1
                                EdgeUwpDataRemoverResult        : 2
                                EdgeUwpDataRemoverResultDbh     : 1
                                EdgeUwpDataRemoverResultRoaming : 0
                                EdgeUwpDataRemoverResultData    : 1
                                EdgeUwpDataRemoverResultBackupData : 1
EdgeUpdate                      LastLogonTime-Machine : 132798161806442449
EdgeWebView                     UsageStatsInSample : 1
EventSystem
Exchange
F12
Fax
```

You're almost finished. You'll notice that we're sticking with full cmdlet names rather than using aliases to emphasize the cmdlets themselves:

```
PS HKCU:\software\microsoft> Set-Location .\Windows
PS HKCU:\software\microsoft\Windows> Get-ChildItem
    Hive: HKEY_CURRENT_USER\software\microsoft\Windows
Name                            Property
----                            --------
AssignedAccessConfiguration
CurrentVersion
```

```
DWM                               Composition                : 1
                                  ColorPrevalence            : 0
                                  ColorizationColor          : 3288334336
                                  ColorizationColorBalance   : 89
                                  ColorizationAfterglow      : 3288334336
                                  ColorizationAfterglowBalance : 10
                                  ColorizationBlurBalance    : 1
                                  EnableWindowColorization   : 0
                                  ColorizationGlassAttribute : 1
                                  AccentColor                : 4278190080
                                  EnableAeroPeek             : 1
Shell
TabletPC
Windows Error Reporting           LastRateLimitedDumpGenerationTime :
➡ 132809598562003780
Winlogon
```

Note the `EnableAeroPeek` Registry value. Let's change it to `0`:

```
PS HKCU:\software\microsoft\Windows> Set-ItemProperty -Path dwm -PSProperty
EnableAeroPeek -Value 0
```

You also could have used the `-Name` parameter instead of `-PSProperty`. Let's check it again to make sure the change "took":

```
PS HKCU:\software\microsoft\Windows> Get-ChildItem
    Hive: HKEY_CURRENT_USER\software\microsoft\Windows
Name                              Property
----                              --------
AssignedAccessConfiguration
CurrentVersion
DWM                               Composition                : 1
                                  ColorPrevalence            : 0
                                  ColorizationColor          : 3288334336
                                  ColorizationColorBalance   : 89
                                  ColorizationAfterglow      : 3288334336
                                  ColorizationAfterglowBalance : 10
                                  ColorizationBlurBalance    : 1
                                  EnableWindowColorization   : 0
                                  ColorizationGlassAttribute : 1
                                  AccentColor                : 4278190080
                                  EnableAeroPeek             : 0
Shell
TabletPC
Windows Error Reporting           LastRateLimitedDumpGenerationTime :
➡ 132809598562003780
Winlogon
```

Mission accomplished! Using these same techniques, you should be able to work with any provider that comes your way.

## 5.6    Lab

**NOTE**    For this lab, you need any computer running PowerShell v7.1 or later.

Complete the following tasks from a PowerShell prompt:

1 Create a new directory called Labs.
2 Create a zero-length file named /Labs/Test.txt (use New-Item).
3 Is it possible to use Set-Item to change the contents of /Labs/Test.txt to -TESTING? Or do you get an error? If you get an error, why?
4 Using the Environment provider, display the value of the system environment variable PATH.
5 Use help to determine what the differences are between the -Filter, -Include, and -Exclude parameters of Get-ChildItem.

## 5.7    Lab answers

1 New-Item -Path ~/Labs -ItemType Directory
2 New-Item -Path ~/labs -Name test.txt -ItemType file
3 The FileSystem provider doesn't support this action.
4 Either of these commands works:

```
Get-Item env:PATH
Dir env:PATH
```

5 -Include and -Exclude must be used with -Recurse or if you're querying a container. Filter uses the PSProvider's filter capability, which not all providers support. For example, you could use DIR -filter in the filesystem.

---

**Above and beyond**

Did you run into any issues with task 4? PowerShell on a Windows machine is case insensitive, meaning uppercase and lowercase letters don't matter. PATH is the same as path. However, in a Linux or macOS machine, capitalization matters: PATH is not the same as path.

# The pipeline: Connecting commands

*6*

In chapter 4, you learned that running commands in PowerShell is the same as running commands in any other shell: you type a cmdlet name, give it parameters, and press Enter. What makes PowerShell special isn't the way it runs commands but the way it allows multiple commands to be connected to each other in powerful, one-line sequences.

## 6.1 Connecting one command to another: Less work for you

PowerShell connects commands to each other by using a *pipeline*. The pipeline provides a way for one command to pass, or *pipe*, its output to another command, allowing that second command to have something to work with. This can be seen with the vertical bar | between two cmdlets (figure 6.1).

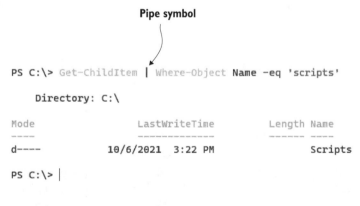

```
                            Pipe symbol



PS C:\> Get-ChildItem | Where-Object Name -eq 'scripts'

    Directory: C:\

Mode                 LastWriteTime         Length Name
----                 -------------         ------ ----
d----          10/6/2021  3:22 PM                 Scripts

PS C:\>
```

**Figure 6.1   Showing the pipe | in a command**

69

You've already seen this in action in commands such as Dir | more. You're piping the output of the Dir command into the more command; the more command takes that directory listing and displays it one page at a time. PowerShell takes that same piping concept and extends it to greater effect.

PowerShell's use of a pipeline may seem similar at first to the way UNIX and Linux shells work. Don't be fooled, though. As you'll come to realize over the next few chapters, PowerShell's pipeline implementation is much richer and more modern.

## 6.2   *Exporting to a file*

PowerShell provides several powerful ways to export data to useful formats, such as TXT, CSV, JSON, and XML (Extensible Markup Language). In your workflow, you may need to export data from Azure Active Directory or from cloud storage. In this chapter, we will go through the process of piping data. We will start by getting the data from some simple built-in commands to simplify the process, but the concept is the same.

Let's start by running a few simple commands. Then we'll learn how to join them together. Here are a few commands that we can use:

- Get-Process (or gps)
- Get-Command (or gcm)
- Get-History -count 10 (or h)

We picked these commands because they're easy and straightforward. We gave you the aliases for Get-Process and Get-Command in parentheses. For Get-History, we specified the -count parameter with a value of 10 so that we only get the last 10 history entries.

> **TRY IT NOW**   Go ahead and choose the commands you want to work with. We use Get-Process for the following examples; you can stick with one of the three we've listed, or switch between them to see the differences in the results.

What do you see? When we run Get-Process, a table with several columns of information appears on the screen (figure 6.2).

```
PS /mnt/c/Users> get-process

NPM(K)    PM(M)     WS(M)    CPU(s)       Id  SI ProcessName
------    -----     -----    ------       --  -- -----------
     0     0.00      3.53      0.08        7   6 bash
     0     0.00      0.31      0.06        1   1 init
     0     0.00      0.22      0.00        6   6 init
     0     0.00     86.54      2.68    17493   6 pwsh
```

Figure 6.2   The output of Get-Process is a table with several columns of information.

It's great to have that information on the screen, but you might want to do more with the information. For example, if you want to make charts and graphs of memory and CPU utilization, you might want to export the information into a CSV file that could be read into an application for further data manipulation.

### 6.2.1 Exporting to CSV

Exporting to a file is where the pipeline and a second command come in handy:

```
Get-Process | Export-CSV procs.CSV
```

Similar to piping `Dir` to `more`, we've piped our processes to `Export-CSV`. That second cmdlet has a mandatory positional parameter (discussed in chapter 3) that we've used to specify the output filename. Because `Export-CSV` is a native PowerShell cmdlet, it knows how to translate the output generated by `Get-Process` into a standard CSV file.

Go ahead and open the file in Visual Studio Code to see the results, as shown in figure 6.3.

```
code ./procs.CSV
```

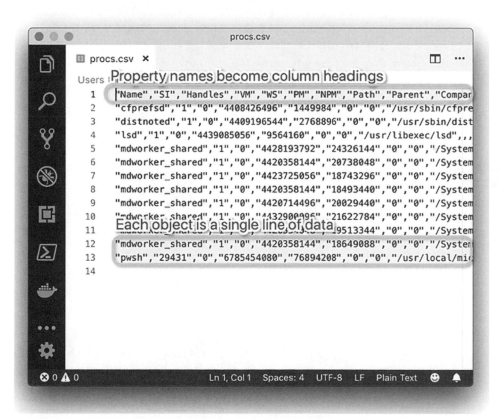

**Figure 6.3  Viewing the exported CSV file in Windows Notepad**

The first line of the file contains column headings, and the subsequent lines list the information for the various processes running on the computer. You can pipe the output of almost any `Get-` cmdlet to `Export-CSV` and get excellent results. You may also notice that the CSV file contains a great deal more information than what's typically shown on the screen. That's intentional. The shell knows it can't possibly fit all of that information on the screen, so it uses a configuration, supplied by Microsoft, to select the most important information for onscreen display. In later chapters, we'll show you how to override that configuration to display whatever you want.

Once the information is saved into a CSV file, you can easily email it to colleagues and ask them to view it from within PowerShell. To do this, they'd import the file:

```
Import-CSV procs.CSV
```

The shell would read in the CSV file and display the process information. It wouldn't be based on live information, but it would be a snapshot from the exact point in time that you created the CSV file.

### 6.2.2  *Exporting to JSON*

Let's say you want to export the process information and include the thread information. The thread information is what is called a *nested property* on the `process` object. Let's take a look (figure 6.4). Note that `Select-Object Threads` tells PowerShell to display only the `Threads` property. We will cover `Select-Object` in more depth in chapter 8.

```
PS C:\Scripts> get-process pwsh | Select-Object Threads

Threads
-------
{13980, 4212, 18832, 10772…}

PS C:\Scripts> (Get-Process -Name pwsh).threads

BasePriority           : 8
CurrentPriority        : 9
Id                     : 13980
PriorityBoostEnabled   : True
PriorityLevel          : Normal
StartAddress           : 0
ThreadState            : Wait
WaitReason             : UserRequest
IdealProcessor         :
ProcessorAffinity      :
PrivilegedProcessorTime : 00:00:00.1250000
StartTime              : 8/11/2021 10:24:38 AM
TotalProcessorTime     : 00:00:00.3125000
UserProcessorTime      : 00:00:00.1875000
Site                   :
Container              :
```

Figure 6.4  We are showing two different ways to display the `Threads` property.

If you try to export processes using `ConvertTo-CSV`, the `Threads` property will have the value `System.Diagnostics.ProcessThreadCollection`. So, we need another way to export data if we want the nested properties under the `Threads` property.

PowerShell also has a `ConvertTo-Json` cmdlet, which creates a JSON file that allows storage of these nested properties. Most languages have libraries to understand JSON. You'll also have a matching `ConvertFrom-Json` cmdlet. Both the `ConvertFrom` and `ConvertTo` cmdlets (such as `ConvertFrom-CSV` and `ConvertTo-CSV`) either produce or consume a string on the pipeline. This is the command to convert processes into JSON, using `Out-File` to save the results to a file:

```
PS C:\Scripts\> Get-Process | ConvertTo-Json | Out-File procs.json
```

You can get the data back by running the following command:

```
PS C:\Scripts\> Get-Content ./procs.json | ConvertFrom-Json
```

If you run this command, you will notice that the data is in a very different format than when you run the `Get-Process` command. We will show you how to deal with that in the next section. Figure 6.5 shows an excerpt of what the `Threads` property looks like in the exported JSON.

```
"SessionId": 30545,
"StartInfo": null,
"Threads": [
  {
    "BasePriority": 0,
    "CurrentPriority": 31,
    "Id": 48912032,
    "PriorityBoostEnabled": false,
    "PriorityLevel": null,
    "StartAddress": {
      "value": 0
    },
    "ThreadState": 3,
    "WaitReason": null,
    "PrivilegedProcessorTime": "00:00:06.0846000",
    "StartTime": null,
    "TotalProcessorTime": "00:00:32.9342000",
    "UserProcessorTime": "00:00:26.8496000",
    "Site": null,
    "Container": null
  },
  {
    "BasePriority": 0,
    "CurrentPriority": 31,
    "Id": 143200480
```

**Figure 6.5  Showing what the `Threads` property looks like in JSON format**

### 6.2.3    Exporting to XML

In the previous section, you noticed that the data returned by `ConvertFrom-Json` is displayed very differently than if you get it from the original command. This is because the objects are not of the same type (we will cover objects in chapter 8). There is a command to export data and get back the original objects.

PowerShell has an `Export-Clixml` cmdlet, which creates a generic CLI XML file that allows PowerShell to reconstruct the original objects (or something very close). `Clixml` is unique to PowerShell, and although any program is technically capable of understanding the XML it produces, it is best for when the results are being used by PowerShell. You'll also have a matching `Import-Clixml` cmdlet. Both the import and export cmdlets (such as `Import-CSV` and `Export-CSV`) expect a filename as a mandatory parameter.

> **When to use Export-Clixml**
>
> If getting the original objects is better, why not use it all the time? There are several disadvantages:
>
> - The format is often much larger.
> - The format is specific to PowerShell and can be complicated to read in other languages.
> - On Windows, PowerShell will encrypt security-related portions of the file, which means that the file can only be decrypted by the user or machine that created the file.

**TRY IT NOW** Try exporting such things as processes, or commands, to a CLIXML file. Make sure you can reimport the file, and try opening the resulting file in Visual Studio Code or another text editor on your system to see how each application displays the information.

Does PowerShell include any other import or export commands? You could find out by using the `Get-Command` cmdlet and specifying a `-Verb` parameter with either `Import` or `Export`.

**TRY IT NOW** See if PowerShell comes with any other import or export cmdlets. You may want to repeat this check after you load new commands into the shell—something you'll do in the next chapter.

### 6.2.4    Out-File

We have talked about CSV, JSON, and XML files, but what if you simply want a flat file to store your data in? Let's look at the `Out-File` command. It takes the data that is in the pipeline and directs it out to a flat file—below a text file in our example:

```
Get-ChildItem | Select-Object Name | Out-File process.txt
```

### 6.2.5   *Comparing files*

Both CSV and CLIXML files can be useful for persisting snapshots of information, sharing those snapshots with others, and reviewing those snapshots at a later time. In fact, Compare-Object has a great way of using them.

First, run help Compare-Object and read the help for this cmdlet. We want you to pay attention to three parameters in particular: -ReferenceObject, -DifferenceObject, and -Property.

Compare-Object is designed to take two sets of information and compare them to each other. For example, imagine that you run Get-Process on two computers that are sitting side by side. The computer that's configured exactly the way you want is on the left and is the *reference computer*. The computer on the right might be the same, or it might be somewhat different; this one is the *difference computer*. After running the command on each, you're staring at two tables of information, and your job is to figure out whether any differences exist between the two.

Because these are processes that you're looking at, you're always going to see differences in things like CPU and memory utilization numbers, so we'll ignore those columns. In fact, focus on the Name column, because we want to see whether the difference computer contains any additional, or any fewer, processes than the reference computer. It might take you a while to compare all of the process names from both tables, but you don't have to—that's exactly what Compare-Object will do for you. Let's say you sit down at the reference computer and run this:

```
Get-Process | Export-CliXML reference.xml
```

We prefer using CLIXML rather than CSV for comparisons like this, because CLIXML can hold more information than a flat CSV file. You then transport that XML file to the difference computer and run this command:

```
Compare-Object -Reference (Import-Clixml reference.xml)
➥-Difference (Get-Process) -Property Name
```

Because the previous step is a bit tricky, we'll explain what's happening:

- As in math, parentheses in PowerShell control the order of execution. In the previous example, they force Import-Clixml and Get-Process to run before Compare-Object runs. The output from Import-Clixml is fed to the -Reference parameter, and the output from Get-Process is fed to the -Difference parameter.

  The parameter names are -ReferenceObject and -DifferenceObject. Keep in mind that you can abbreviate parameter names by typing enough of their names for the shell to be able to figure out which one you want. In this case, -Reference and -Difference are more than enough to uniquely identify these parameters. We probably could have shortened them even further to something like -ref and -diff, and the command would still have worked.

- Rather than comparing the two complete tables, `Compare-Object` focuses on the `Name`, because we gave it the `-Property` parameter. If we hadn't, it would think that every process is different because the values of columns such as `VM`, `CPU`, and `PM` are always going to be different.
- The result is a table telling you what's different. Every process that's in the reference set but not in the difference set will have a <= indicator (which indicates that the process is present only on the left side). If a process is on the difference computer but not the reference computer, it'll have a => indicator instead. Processes that match across both sets aren't included in the `Compare-Object` output.

**TRY IT NOW**   Go ahead and try this. If you don't have two computers, start by exporting your current processes to a CLIXML file, as shown in the previous example. Then start some additional processes, another `pwsh`, such as Visual Studio Code, nano (a command-line editor), the browser, or a game. Your computer will become the difference computer (on the right), whereas the CLIXML file will still be the reference computer (on the left).

Here's the output from our test:

```
PS C:\Scripts>Compare-Object -ReferenceObject (Import-Clixml ./procs.xml)
➡ -DifferenceObject (Get-Process) -Property name

name            SideIndicator
----            -------------
nano            =>
pwsh            =>
```

This is a useful management trick. If you think of those reference CLIXML files as configuration baselines, you can compare any current computer to that baseline and get a difference report. Throughout this book, you'll discover more cmdlets that can retrieve management information, all of which can be piped into a CLIXML file to become a baseline. You can quickly build a collection of baseline files for services, processes, operating system configuration, users and groups, and much more, and then use those at any time to compare the current state of a system to that baseline.

**TRY IT NOW**   For fun, try running the `Compare-Object` command again, but leave off the `-Property` parameter entirely. See the results? Every single process is listed, because values such as `PM`, `VM`, and so forth, have all changed, even though they're the same processes. The output also isn't as useful, because it displays each process's type name and process name.

By the way, you should know that `Compare-Object` generally doesn't do well at comparing text files. Although other operating systems and shells have a `Compare-Object` command that's explicitly intended for comparing text files, PowerShell's `Compare-Object` command works differently. You'll see how differently in this chapter's lab.

**NOTE** If it seems as though you're using `Get-Process` and `Get-Command` often, well, that's on purpose. We guarantee you have access to those cmdlets because they're native to PowerShell and don't require an add-in such as Azure PowerShell or AWS Tools for PowerShell. That said, the skills you're learning apply to every cmdlet you'll ever need to run, including those that ship with Azure compute, Azure Storage, Azure Virtual Network, and Azure PowerShell module.

## 6.3 Piping to a file

Whenever you have nicely formatted output—for example, the tables generated by `Get-Command` or `Get-Process`—you may want to preserve that in a file or even on paper. Normally, cmdlet output is directed to the screen, which PowerShell refers to as the *host*, but you can change where that output goes. We've already shown you one way to do so:

```
Dir > DirectoryList.txt
```

The > character is a shortcut added to PowerShell to provide syntactic compatibility with the Bash shell. In reality, when you run that command, PowerShell does the following under the hood:

```
Dir | Out-File DirectoryList.txt
```

You can run that same command on your own, instead of using the > syntax. Why would you do so? Because `Out-File` also provides additional parameters that let you specify alternative character encodings (such as UTF-8 or Unicode), append content to an existing file, and so forth. By default, the files created by `Out-File` are 80 columns wide, which means sometimes PowerShell might alter command output to fit within 80 characters. That alteration might make the file's contents appear different than when you run the same command on the screen. Read the help file for `Out-File` to see if you can spot a parameter that would let you change the output file width to something other than 80 characters.

**TRY IT NOW** Don't look here for the answer—open up that help file and see what you can find. We guarantee you'll spot the right parameter in a few moments.

PowerShell has a variety of `Out-` cmdlets. One is called `Out-Default`, and it's the one the shell uses when you don't specify a different `Out-` cmdlet. If you run

```
Dir
```

you're technically running

```
Dir | Out-Default
```

even if you don't realize it. `Out-Default` does nothing more than direct content to `Out-Host`, which means you're running

```
Dir | Out-Default | Out-Host
```

without realizing it. `Out-Host` displays information on the screen. What other `Out-` cmdlets can you find?

> **TRY IT NOW**    Time to investigate other `Out-` cmdlets. To get started, try using the `Help` command and wildcards such as `Help Out*`. Another option is to use the `Get-Command` in the same way, such as `Get-Command Out*`. Or you could specify the `-Verb` parameter `Get-Command -Verb Out`. What did you come up with?

`Out-Null` and `Out-String` have specific uses that we won't get into right now, but you're welcome to read their help files and look at the examples included in those files.

## 6.4    *Converting to HTML*

Want to produce HTML reports? Pipe your command to `ConvertTo-Html`. This command produces well-formed, generic HTML that displays in any web browser. It's plain-looking, but you can reference a Cascading Style Sheets (CSS) file to specify more-attractive formatting if desired. Notice that this command doesn't require a filename:

```
Get-Process -Id $PID | ConvertTo-Html
```

> **TRY IT NOW**    Make sure that you run that command yourself—we want you to see what it does before you proceed.

In the PowerShell world, the verb `Export` implies that you're taking data, converting it to some other format, and saving that other format in some kind of storage, such as a file. The verb `ConvertTo` implies only a portion of that process: the conversion to a different format but not saving it into a file. When you ran the preceding command, you got a screen full of HTML, which probably wasn't what you wanted. Stop for a second; can you think of how you'd get that HTML into a text file on disk?

> **TRY IT NOW**    If you can think of a way, go ahead and try it before you read on.

This command does the trick:

```
Get-Process | ConvertTo-Html | Out-File processes.html
```

See how connecting more and more commands allows you to have increasingly powerful command lines? Each command handles a single step in the process, and the entire command line as a whole accomplishes a useful task.

PowerShell ships with other `ConvertTo-` cmdlets, including `ConvertTo-CSV` and `ConvertTo-Xml`. As with `ConvertTo-Html`, these don't create a file on disk; they translate command output into CSV or XML, respectively. You could pipe that converted output to `Out-File` to then save it to disk, although it would be shorter to use `Export-CSV` or `Export-Clixml`, because those do both the conversion and the saving.

---

**Above and beyond**

Time for a bit more useless background information, although in this case it's the answer to a question that many students often ask us: why would Microsoft provide both `Export-CSV` and `ConvertTo-CSV`, as well as two nearly identical cmdlets for XML?

In certain advanced scenarios, you might not want to save the data to a file on disk. For example, you might want to convert data to XML and then transmit it to a web service or some other destination. By having distinct `ConvertTo-` cmdlets that don't save to a file, you have the flexibility to do whatever you want.

---

## 6.5 Using cmdlets that modify the system: Killing processes

Exporting and converting aren't the only reasons you might want to connect two commands together. For example, consider—*but please don't run*—this command:

```
Get-Process | Stop-Process
```

Can you imagine what that command would do? We'll tell you: you could kill critical processes. It would retrieve every process and then start trying to end each one of them. It would get to a critical process, such as the `/usr/sbin/coreaudiod` on macOS, and your computer would no longer be able to play sound. If you're running PowerShell inside a virtual machine and want to have a little fun, go ahead and try running that command.

The point is that cmdlets with the same noun (in this case, `Process`) can often pass information among themselves. Typically, you'd specify the name of a specific process rather than trying to stop them all:

```
Get-Process -Name bash | Stop-Process
```

Jobs offer something similar: the output from `Get-Job` can be piped to cmdlets such as `Stop-Job`, `Receive-Job`, `Wait-Job`, and so forth. We will cover jobs in detail in chapter 14.

As you might expect, specific rules limit which commands can connect to each other. For example, if you look at a command sequence such as `Get-Process | New-Alias`, you probably wouldn't expect it to do anything sensible (although it might well do something nonsensical). In chapter 7, we'll dive into the rules that govern how commands can connect to each other.

We'd like you to know one more thing about cmdlets such as `Stop-Job` and `Stop-Process`. These cmdlets modify the system in some fashion, and all cmdlets that modify the system have an internally defined *impact level*. The cmdlet's creator sets this impact level, and it can't be changed. The shell has a corresponding `$Confirm-Preference` setting, which is set to `High` by default. Type the following setting name to see your shell's setting:

```
PS /Users/jsnover> $ConfirmPreference
High
```

Here's how it works: when a cmdlet's internal impact level is equal to or higher than the shell's `$ConfirmPreference` setting, the shell will automatically ask, "Are you sure?" when the cmdlet does whatever it's trying to do. If you used a virtual machine to try the crash-your-computer command we mentioned earlier, you probably were asked, "Are you sure?" for each process. When a cmdlet's internal impact level is less than the shell's `$ConfirmPreference` setting, you don't automatically get the "Are you sure?" prompt. But you can force the shell to ask you whether you're sure:

```
Get-Process | Stop-Process -Confirm
```

You just add the `-Confirm` parameter to the cmdlet. This should be supported by any cmdlet that makes some kind of change to the system, and it'll show up in the help file for the cmdlet if it's supported.

A similar parameter is `-WhatIf`. This is supported by any cmdlet that supports `-Confirm`. The `-WhatIf` parameter isn't triggered by default, but you can specify it whenever you want to:

```
PS C:\Scripts > Get-Process | Stop-Process -WhatIf
What if: Performing operation "Stop-Process" on Target "conhost (1920)
".
What if: Performing operation "Stop-Process" on Target "conhost (1960)
".
What if: Performing operation "Stop-Process" on Target "conhost (2460)
".
What if: Performing operation "Stop-Process" on Target "csrss (316)".
```

This tells you what the cmdlet would have done, without letting the cmdlet do it. It's a useful way to preview what a potentially dangerous cmdlet would have done to your computer, to make certain that you want to do that.

## 6.6    *Common points of confusion*

One common point of confusion in PowerShell revolves around the `Export-CSV` and `Export-Clixml` commands. Both commands, technically speaking, create text files. The output of either command can be viewed in Visual Studio Code, as shown in figure 6.3. But you have to admit that the text is definitely in a special kind of format—either in CSV or XML.

The confusion tends to set in when someone is asked to read these files back into the shell. Do you use `Get-Content` (or its alias `type`)? For example, suppose you do this:

```
PS C:\Scripts>Get-Process | Select-Object -First 5 | export-CSV processes.CSV
➥ -IncludeTypeInformation
```

Notice the `-IncludeTypeInformation` switch; we will come back to it later. Now, try reading that back in by using `Get-Content`:

```
PS C:\Scripts>Get-Content ./processes.CSV
#TYPE System.Diagnostics.Process
     "Name","SI","Handles","VM","WS","PM","NPM","Path","Parent","Company","CP
     U","FileVersion","ProductVersion","Description","Product","__NounName","
     SafeHandle","Handle","BasePriority","ExitCode","HasExited","StartTime","
     ExitTime","Id","MachineName","MaxWorkingSet","MinWorkingSet","Modules","
     NonpagedSystemMemorySize64","NonpagedSystemMemorySize","PagedMemorySize6
     4","PagedMemorySize","PagedSystemMemorySize64","PagedSystemMemorySize","
     PeakPagedMemorySize64","PeakPagedMemorySize","PeakWorkingSet64","PeakWor
     kingSet","PeakVirtualMemorySize64","PeakVirtualMemorySize","PriorityBoos
     tEnabled","PriorityClass","PrivateMemorySize64","PrivateMemorySize","Pro
     cessName","ProcessorAffinity","SessionId","StartInfo","Threads","HandleC
     ount","VirtualMemorySize64","VirtualMemorySize","EnableRaisingEvents","S
     tandardInput","StandardOutput","StandardError","WorkingSet64","WorkingSe
     t","SynchronizingObject","MainModule","MainWindowHandle","MainWindowTitl
     e","Responding","PrivilegedProcessorTime","TotalProcessorTime","UserProc
     essorTime","Site","Container"
""","87628","0","0","0","0","0",,,,,,,,"Process","Microsoft.Win32.SafeHandles
     .SafeProcessHandle","0","0",,"False",,,"0",".",,,,"System.Diagnostics.Pro
     cessModuleCollection","0","0","0","0","0","0","0","0","0","0","0","0","F
     alse","Normal","0","0","",,"87628",,"System.Diagnostics.ProcessThreadCol
     lection","0","0","0","False",,,,"0","0",,,"0","","True",,,,,
```

We truncated the preceding output, but there's a lot more of the same. Looks like garbage, right? You're looking at the raw CSV data. The command didn't try to interpret, or *parse*, the data at all. Contrast that with the results of `Import-CSV`:

```
PS C:\Scripts>Import-CSV ./processes.CSV
NPM(K)     PM(M)      WS(M)      CPU(s)       Id  SI ProcessName
------     -----      -----      ------       --  -- -----------
     0      0.00       0.00        0.00        0 …28
     0      0.00       0.00        0.00        1   1
     0      0.00       0.00        0.00       43  43
     0      0.00       0.00        0.00       44  44
     0      0.00       0.00        0.00       47  47
```

Much nicer, right? The `Import-` cmdlets pay attention to what's in the file, attempt to interpret it, and create a display that looks more like the output of the original command (`Get-Process`, in this case). To do this with `Export-CSV`, you must use the `-IncludeTypeInformation` switch. Typically, then, if you create a file with `Export-CSV`, you read it by using `Import-CSV`. If you create it by using `Export-Clixml`, you generally read it by using `Import-Clixml`. By using these commands in pairs, you get better results. Use `Get-Content` only when you're reading in a text file and don't want PowerShell attempting to parse the data—that is, when you want to work with the raw text.

## 6.7    Lab

We've kept this chapter's text slightly shorter because some of the examples probably took you a bit longer to complete and because we want you to spend more time completing the following hands-on exercises. If you haven't already completed all of the "Try it now" tasks in this chapter, we strongly recommend that you do so before tackling these tasks:

1  Create two similar, but different, text files. Try comparing them by using `Compare-Object`. Run something like this: `Compare-Object -Reference (Get-Content File1.txt) -Difference (Get-Content File2.txt)`. If the files have only one line of text that's different, the command should work.

2  What happens if you run `Get-Command | Export-CSV commands.CSV | Out-File` from the console? Why does that happen?

3  Apart from getting one or more jobs and piping them to `Stop-Job`, what other means does `Stop-Job` provide for you to specify the job or jobs you want to stop? Is it possible to stop a job without using `Get-Job` at all?

4  What if you want to create a pipe-delimited file instead of a CSV file? You'd still use the `Export-CSV` command, but what parameters would you specify?

5  How do you include the type information in the # comment line at the top of an exported CSV file?

6  `Export-Clixml` and `Export-CSV` both modify the system because they can create and overwrite files. What parameter would prevent them from overwriting an existing file? What parameter would ask whether you were sure before proceeding to write the output file?

7  The operating system maintains several regional settings, which include a default list separator. On US systems, that separator is a comma. How can you tell `Export-CSV` to use the system's default separator rather than a comma?

## 6.8    Lab answers

1  ```
PS C:\Scripts > "I am the walrus" | Out-File file1.txt

PS C:\Scripts > "I'm a believer" | Out-File file2.txt
PS C:\Scripts > $f1 = Get-Content .\file1.txt
PS C:\Scripts > $f2 = Get-Content .\file2.txt
PS C:\Scripts > Compare-Object $f1 $f2
InputObject                      SideIndicator
-----------                      -------------
I'm a believer                   =>
I am the walrus                  <=
```
```

2  If you don't specify a filename with `Out-File`, you'll get an error. But even if you do, `Out-File` won't do anything because the file is created by `Export-CSV`.

3  `Stop-Job` can accept one or more job names as parameter values for the –Name parameter. For example, you could run this:

```
Stop-job jobName
```

4  `get-Command | Export-CSV commands.CSV -Delimiter "|"`

5  Use the –IncludeTypeInformation parameter with `Export-CSV`.

6  `Get-Command | Export-CSV services.CSV –NoClobber`
   `Get-Command | Export-CSV services.CSV -Confirm`

7  `Get-Command | Export-CSV services.CSV -UseCulture`

# *Adding commands*

One of PowerShell's primary strengths is its extensibility. As Microsoft continues to invest in PowerShell, it develops more and more commands for products such as Azure compute (Virtual Machines), Azure SQL, Azure Virtual Network, Azure DNS, and so on. You typically manage these through the Azure portal. We will discuss how to install the Azure PowerShell modules later in this chapter.

## 7.1 How one shell can do everything

How can one shell do everything? Let's think about your smartphone. How do you add functionality to your phone without upgrading the operating system? You install an app.

When you install an app, it can add widgets or even add commands you can say to the voice assistant. Adding commands to the voice assistant is probably the most like the extension model of PowerShell. PowerShell provides ways of adding commands that you can use.

So, let's say you installed an app called Ride Share. The app might add a voice command that lets you say, "Book me a ride to work with Ride Share." The phone finds your work address and sends the command to the app.

PowerShell works in a similar way. PowerShell calls its extensions *modules*. There are no widgets, but commands can be added. We will cover how to install modules later in the next section.

## 7.2 Extensions: Finding and installing modules

Before PowerShell 6.0, there were two kinds of extensions: modules and snap-ins. PowerShell v6 and newer support one type of extension called a *module*. Modules are designed to be more self-contained and easier to distribute.

Microsoft introduced a module called PowerShellGet, which makes it easier to search for, download, install, and update modules from online repositories. Power-ShellGet is a lot like the package managers Linux admins love so much—rpm, yum, apt-get, and so on. Microsoft even runs an online *gallery*, or repository, called Power-Shell Gallery (http://powershellgallery.com).

> **WARNING** *Microsoft runs* doesn't mean *Microsoft produces, verifies, and endorses.* The PowerShell Gallery contains community-contributed code, and you should use due caution before running someone else's code in your environment.

You can search for modules like most search engines at https://powershellgallery .com/. The module for Azure is called *Az*. Figure 7.1 shows an example of searching for that module.

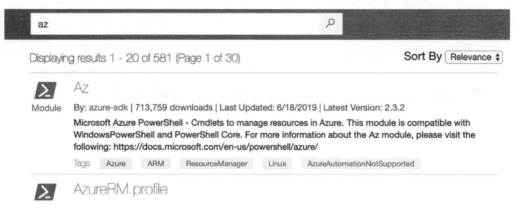

**Figure 7.1  Showing the search for Az in the PowerShell Gallery**

If you click the Az module name, it will take you to more detail about the module. Under Package Details > PSEditions, you can check if the author has tested the module with PowerShell Core (figure 7.2).

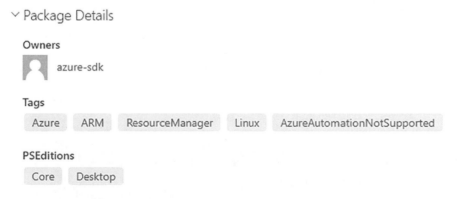

**Figure 7.2  Showing that the module is Core compatible**

Then look under Installation Options (figure 7.3).

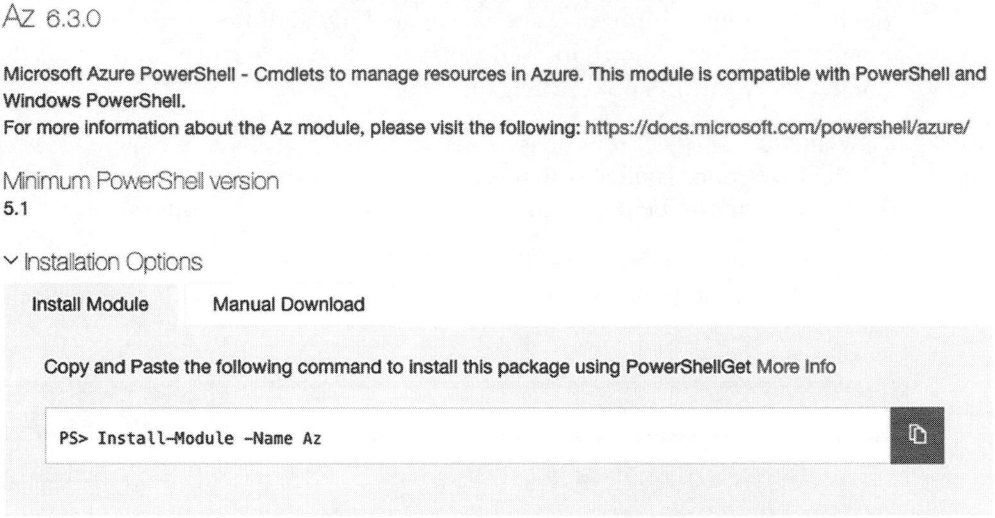

Az 6.3.0

Microsoft Azure PowerShell - Cmdlets to manage resources in Azure. This module is compatible with PowerShell and
Windows PowerShell.
For more information about the Az module, please visit the following: https://docs.microsoft.com/powershell/azure/

Minimum PowerShell version
5.1

⌄ Installation Options

| Install Module | Manual Download |
|---|---|

Copy and Paste the following command to install this package using PowerShellGet More Info

```
PS> Install-Module -Name Az
```

Figure 7.3   **Showing installation command available via the PowerShell Gallery**

Notice it says that at least PowerShell 5.1 is required to run the module, and it gives
instructions on how to install the module. If we run the command `Install-Module`
`-Name Az`, we can see what happens:

```
PS C:\Scripts> Install-Module az

Untrusted repository
You are installing the modules from an untrusted repository. If you trust
    this
repository, change its InstallationPolicy value by running the Set-
    PSRepository
 cmdlet. Are you sure you want to install the modules from 'PSGallery'?
[Y] Yes  [A] Yes to All  [N] No  [L] No to All  [S] Suspend  [?] Help
(default is "N"):y
```

It prompts you asking if you trust installing from the gallery, and if you say yes, then it
installs the module. You can run the `Get-Module` command to verify it installed the
module, but the `-ListAvailable` parameter is required because the module is not
loaded:

```
PS C:\Scripts> Get-Module az -ListAvailable


    Directory:
    C:\Users\Tyler\Documents\powershell\Modules

ModuleType Version    Name
---------- -------    ----
Script     6.3.0      Az
```

The path and version will vary for you, but the output should be similar.

---

**More about getting modules from the internet**

The PowerShellGet module allows installing modules from http://PowerShellGallery .com. Using PowerShellGet is easy and can even be fun:

- Run `Register-PSRepository` to add the URL of a repository. http:// PowerShellGallery.com is usually set up by default, but it's even possible to set up your own "gallery" internally for private use, and you'd use `Register-PSRepository` to point to it.
- Use `Find-Module` to find modules in repositories. You can use wildcards (*) in names, specify tags, and have many other choices for narrowing the search results.
- Use `Install-Module` to download and install a module after you've found it.
- Use `Update-Module` to make sure your local copy of a module is the latest version, and if it isn't, download and install the latest.

PowerShellGet includes several other commands (http://PowerShellGallery.com links to the documentation), but these are the ones you'll start out using. For example, try installing the Azure PowerShell module, or Jeff Hicks's PSScriptTools module from the PowerShell Gallery.

---

## 7.3 *Extensions: Finding and adding modules*

PowerShell automatically looks in a certain set of paths to find modules. The `PSModule-Path` environment variable defines the paths where PowerShell expects modules to live:

```
PS /Users/Tyler> (Get-Content Env:/PSModulePath) -split ':'
C/Users/Tyler.local/share/powershell/Modules
/usr/local/share/powershell/Modules
/usr/local/microsoft/powershell/7/Modules
```

> **TRY IT NOW**  The preceding command was run on a macOS device. Run the command `(Get-Content Env:/PSModulePath) -split ':'` and see what the results are for you. Note that they will be different, depending on what OS you are using.

As you can see in this example, there are three default locations: one in the folder where PowerShell is installed, where system modules live; one in the local/share/ folder, where you can put modules shared by all users; and one in the .local folder, where you can add any personal modules. If you're running even later versions of PowerShell, you might see additional locations that Microsoft is now using. You can also add a module from any other location, provided you know its full path. On your Windows machine, you will see a similar layout where modules are installed:

```
$env:PSModulePath -split ';'

C:\Users\Administrator\Documents\PowerShell\7\Modules
C:\Program Files\WindowsPowerShell\Modules
C:\Windows\system32\PowerShell\7\Modules
```

The path is important in PowerShell. If you have modules located elsewhere, you should add their paths to the `PSModulePath` environment variable. You can do this in your profile with the following command (we'll cover how to set up a profile later in this chapter):

```
PS C:\Scripts> $env:PSModulePath += [System.IO.Path]::PathSeparator +
➥ 'C:\Scripts/myModules'
```

> **NOTE** There are a few things that we have not mentioned yet in the preceding example. But that's okay. We promise we will get to them.

Why is the `PSModulePath` so important? Because with it, PowerShell can automatically locate all of the modules on your computer. After it finds your modules, PowerShell *autodiscovers* them. It will look to you as if all of your modules are loaded all of the time. Ask for help on a module, and you'll get it, without having to load it. Run any command you've found, and PowerShell will automatically load the module containing that command. PowerShell's `Update-Help` command also uses `PSModulePath` to discover what modules you have, and then it seeks updated help files for each one.

For example, run `Get-Module | Remove-Module` to remove any loaded modules. This will remove almost all commands from the current session, so if you try this, close and reopen PowerShell. Then run the following command (your results may differ slightly, depending on your OS and what modules you have installed):

```
PS C:\Scripts> help *storaget*
    Name                                        Category ModuleName

    Get-AzStorageTable                          Cmdlet   Az.Storage
    Get-AzStorageTableStoredAccessPolicy        Cmdlet   Az.Storage
    New-AzStorageTable                          Cmdlet   Az.Storage
    New-AzStorageTableSASToken                  Cmdlet   Az.Storage
    New-AzStorageTableStoredAccessPolicy        Cmdlet   Az.Storage
    Remove-AzStorageTable                       Cmdlet   Az.Storage
    Remove-AzStorageTableStoredAccessPolicy     Cmdlet   Az.Storage
    Set-AzStorageTableStoredAccessPolicy        Cmdlet   Az.Storage
```

As you can see, PowerShell discovers several commands (of the `Cmdlet` variety) that have the word `storage` in their name (I used `storaget` to simplify the results in the example). You can then ask for help on one of these, even though you haven't loaded the module:

```
PS C:\Scripts> Get-Help Get-AzStorageTable
    NAME
    Get-AzStorageTable
```

```
SYNOPSIS
    Lists the storage tables.

SYNTAX
    Get-AzStorageTable [[-Name] <System.String>] [-Context
<Microsoft.Azure.Commands.Common.Authentication.Abstractions.IStorageContext>]
➡ [-DefaultProfile

<Microsoft.Azure.Commands.Common.Authentication.Abstractions.Core
➡ .IAzureContextContainer>] [<CommonParameters]
```

If you want to, you can even run the command, and PowerShell will make sure the module is loaded for you. This autodiscovery and autoloading functionality is useful, helping you to find and use commands that aren't even present in the shell when you start.

PowerShell's module autodiscovery enables the shell to complete command names (using Tab in the console or IntelliSense in the Visual Studio Code), display help, and run commands, even for modules you haven't explicitly loaded into memory. These features make it worth the effort to keep PSModulePath as lean as possible (i.e., don't put a lot of different locations in it) and keep your modules up to date.

What if a module isn't located in one of the paths referenced by PSModulePath? You'd need to run Import-Module and specify the complete path to the module, such as C:\Scripts/myModules/myModule.

Modules can also add PowerShell providers. Running Get-PSProvider will get you a list of providers:

```
PS /Users/James> get-psprovider

Name                 Capabilities                    Drives
----                 ------------                    ------
Alias                ShouldProcess                   {Alias}
Environment          ShouldProcess                   {Env}
FileSystem           Filter, ShouldProcess, Crede... {/, Temp}
Function             ShouldProcess                   {Function}
Variable             ShouldProcess                   {Variable}
```

### Installing Google Cloud commands

Installing and adding the Google Cloud commands is a little different because they break a rule—they require input the first time you try to use the module. You install their commands at first just like other modules: Install-Module -Name Google-Cloud. But if you try to find the commands, it will fail. So, you need to run Import-Module GoogleCloud -Force. The -Force is in case PowerShell thinks the module is loaded; it will try to reload it. Now the module will prompt you to finish the installation (assuming it is still designed the same as it was when we wrote this book). Now we'll run the commands to deal with Google Cloud SQL instances.

```
(continued)
PS C:\Scripts> Get-Command -Name *-gcSqlinstance

CommandType      Name
-----------      ----
Cmdlet           Add-GcSqlInstance
Cmdlet           ConvertTo-GcSqlInstance
Cmdlet           Export-GcSqlInstance
Cmdlet           Get-GcSqlInstance
Cmdlet           Import-GcSqlInstance
Cmdlet           Remove-GcSqlInstance
Cmdlet           Restart-GcSqlInstance
Cmdlet           Update-GcSqlInstance
```

## 7.4   *Command conflicts and removing extensions*

Take a close look at the commands we added for both Google Cloud SQL instances and Azure Table storage. Notice anything special about the commands' names?

Most PowerShell extensions—Amazon Web Services being a notable exception—add a short prefix to the noun portion of their command names. Get-GcSqlInstance, for example, or Get-AzStorageTable. These prefixes may seem awkward, but they're designed to prevent command conflicts.

For example, suppose you load two modules that each contain a Get-User cmdlet. With two commands having the same name and being loaded at the same time, which one will PowerShell execute when you run Get-User? The last one loaded, as it turns out. But the other command with the same name isn't inaccessible. To specifically run either command, you have to use a somewhat awkward naming convention that requires both the module name and the command name. If one Get-User comes from a module called MyCoolPowerShellModule, you have to run this:

```
MyCoolPowerShellModule\Get-User
```

That's a lot of typing, and it's why Microsoft suggests adding a product-specific prefix, such as Az or Gc, to the noun of each command. Adding prefixes helps prevent a conflict and helps make commands easier to identify and use.

**NOTE**   The Amazon Web Services module does not use a prefix.

If you do wind up with a conflict, you can always remove one of the conflicting modules. Run Remove-Module, along with the module name, to unload a module.

**NOTE**   Add your own prefix to any module when you import the module. Import-Module ModuleName -Prefix MyPrefix will change Get-Original-CmdLet to Get-MyPrefixOriginalCommand.

## 7.5 **Playing with a new module**

Let's put your newfound knowledge to use. We want you to follow along with the commands we present in this section. More important, we want you to follow the process and the thinking that we'll explain, because this is how we teach ourselves to use new commands without rushing out and buying a new book for every product and feature that we run across. In the lab for this chapter, we'll have you repeat this same process on your own, to learn a more in-depth task.

Our goal is to compress a file on our computer into a zip archive. We have no idea whether PowerShell can even do this, so we start by asking the help system for a clue:

```
PS C:\Scripts> help *-archive
Name                         Category  Module
----                         --------  ------
Compress-Archive             Function  Microsoft.PowerShell.Arc...
```

Aha! As you can see, we have an entire `Microsoft.PowerShell.Archive` (the full name was truncated) module on our computer. The previous list shows the `Compress-Archive` command, but we're curious about what other commands are available. To find out, we manually load the module and list its commands:

```
PS C:\Scripts> get-command -Module Microsoft.PowerShell.Archive


CommandType      Name
-----------      ----
Function         Compress-Archive
Function         Expand-Archive
```

> **NOTE** We could have asked for help on `Compress-Archive` or even run the command directly. PowerShell would have loaded the Microsoft.PowerShell .Archive module for us in the background. But because we're exploring, this approach lets us view the module's complete list of commands.

This list of commands looks more or less the same as the earlier list. Fine, let's see what the `Compress-Archive` command looks like:

```
PS C:\Scripts> Get-Help Compress-Archive

NAME
    Compress-Archive

SYNTAX
    Compress-Archive [-Path] <string[]> [-DestinationPath]
    <string> [-CompressionLevel {Optimal | NoCompression |
    Fastest}] [-PassThru] [-WhatIf] [-Confirm]
    [<CommonParameters>]
```

Seems straightforward, and only -Path and -DestinationPath are mandatory parameters. Let's try creating a file and compressing it with the command:

```
PS C:\Scripts> 'test lunch' | Out-File chapter7.txt
PS C:\Scripts> Compress-Archive -Path .\chapter7.txt -DestinationPath
➥  .\chapter7.zip
```

Okay, no news is usually good news. Still, it'd be nice to see that the command did something. Let's try this instead:

```
PS C:\Scripts> Compress-Archive -Path .\chapter7.txt -DestinationPath
    .\chapter7.zip -Force -Verbose
VERBOSE: Preparing to compress...
VERBOSE: Performing the operation "Compress-Archive" on target
➥  "C:\Scripts\chapter7.txt".
VERBOSE: Adding 'C:\Scripts/chapter7.txt'.
```

The -Verbose switch is available for all cmdlets and functions, although not all of these commands do anything with it. In this case, we get a message indicating what's happening, which tells us the command did run. The -Force switch for this command says to overwrite the zip file we created the first time.

## 7.6   *Common points of confusion*

PowerShell newcomers frequently do one thing incorrectly when they start working with modules: they don't read the help. Specifically, they don't use the -Example or -Full switches when asking for help.

Frankly, looking at built-in examples is the best way to learn how to use a command. Yes, it can be a bit daunting to scroll through a list of hundreds of commands (the Az.* modules, for example, add well over 2,000 new commands), but using Help and Get-Command with wildcards should make it easier to narrow the list to whatever noun you think you're after. From there, *read the help*!

## 7.7   *Lab*

As always, we're assuming that you have the latest version of PowerShell on a computer or virtual machine to test with:

1   Browse the PowerShell Gallery. Find a module or two that you think sounds interesting and install it.
2   Browse the available commands for the module you just downloaded.
3   Use the commands from section 7.2 to find and install (if needed) the latest-version module by Microsoft for working with archives that contain the command Compress-Archive.
4   Import the module you just installed.
5   Create a Tests folder for the next step with 10 files in it, and name it ~/Test-Folder.

6 Use `Compress-Archive` to create a zip of the contents of ~/TestFolder, and name the archive `TestFolder.zip`.

7 Expand the archive to ~/TestFolder2.

8 Use `Compare-Object` and `Select-Object -ExpandProperty Name` to compare just the names of the files in the folders to verify you have the same files.

## 7.8   *Lab answers*

Here's one way to approach this:

1 `Install-Module moduleyoufound`
   - If you are on a Windows machine, we suggest the `import-excel` module.

2 `Get-Command -module moduleyoufound`
   `- Get-command -module az`

3 `Find-Module -Command Compress-Archive | Install-Module -Force`

4 `Import-Module Microsoft.PowerShell.Archive`

5 `1..10` will create a collection of the numbers between 1 and 10. If you did this another way, don't worry.
   `- New-Item ~/TestFolder -ItemType Directory`
   `- 1..10 | ForEach-Object {New-Item "~/TestFolder/$_.txt" -ItemType File -Value $_}`

6 `Compress-Archive ~/TestFolder/* -DestinationPath ~/TestFolder.zip`

7 `Expand-Archive ~/TestFolder.zip -DestinationPath ~/TestFolder2`

8 This is a possible way. Remember, `dir` is an alias for `Get-ChildItem`.

```
$reference = Get-ChildItem ~/TestFolder| Select-Object -ExpandProperty name
$difference = Get-ChildItem ~/TestFolder3| Select-Object -ExpandProperty name
Compare-Object -ReferenceObject $reference -DifferenceObject $difference
```

# Objects:
# Data by another name

We're going to do something a little different in this chapter. PowerShell's use of objects can be one of its most confusing elements, but at the same time it's also one of the shell's most critical concepts, affecting everything you do in the shell. We've tried various explanations over the years, and we've settled on a couple that each work well for distinctly different audiences. If you have programming experience and are comfortable with the concept of objects, we want you to skip to section 8.2. If you don't have a programming background and haven't programmed or scripted with objects before, start with section 8.1 and read straight through the chapter.

## 8.1    What are objects?

Take a second to run `Get-Process` in PowerShell. You should see a table with several columns, but those columns barely scratch the surface of the wealth of information available about processes. Each process object also has a machine name, a main window handle, a maximum working set size, an exit code and time, processor affinity information, and a great deal more. You'll find more than 60 pieces of information associated with a process. Why does PowerShell show so few of them?

The simple fact is that *most* of the things PowerShell can access offer more information than will comfortably fit on the screen. When you run any command, such as `Get-Process`, `Get-AzVm`, or `Get-AzStorageBlob`, PowerShell constructs—entirely in memory—a table that contains all of the information about those items. For `Get-Process`, that table consists of something like 67 columns, with one row for each process that's running on your computer. Each column contains a bit of information, such as virtual memory, CPU utilization, process name, process ID, and so on. Then PowerShell looks to see whether you've specified which of those columns you want to view. If you haven't, the shell looks up a configuration file provided by Microsoft and displays only those table columns that Microsoft thinks you want to see.

One way to see all of the columns is to use `ConvertTo-Html`:

```
Get-Process | ConvertTo-Html | Out-File processes.html
```

That cmdlet doesn't bother filtering the columns. Instead, it produces an HTML file that contains all of them. That's one way to see the entire table.

In addition to all of those columns of information, each table row has actions associated with it. Those actions include what the operating system can do to, or with, the process listed in that table row. For example, the operating system can close a process, kill it, refresh its information, or wait for the process to exit, among other things.

Anytime you run a command that produces output, that output takes the form of a table in memory. When you pipe output from one command to another, like this

```
Get-Process | ConvertTo-Html
```

the entire table is passed through the pipeline. The table isn't filtered down to a smaller number of columns until every command has run.

Now for some terminology changes. PowerShell doesn't refer to this in-memory table as a *table*. Instead, it uses these terms:

- *Object*—This is what we've been calling a *table row*. It represents a single thing, such as a single process or a single storage account.
- *Property*—This is what we called a *table column*. It represents one piece of information about an object, such as a process name, a process ID, or a VM's running status.
- *Method*—This is what we called an *action*. A method is related to a single object and makes that object do something—for example, killing a process or starting a VM.
- *Collection*—This is the entire set of objects, or what we've been calling a *table*.

If you find the following discussion on objects to be confusing, refer to this four-point list. Always imagine a *collection* of objects as being a big, in-memory table of information, with *properties* as the columns and individual *objects* as the rows (figure 8.1).

**Figure 8.1  Showing that the object (file) has multiple properties such as** `Author` **and** `FileType`

## 8.2  *Understanding why PowerShell uses objects*

One of the reasons that PowerShell uses objects to represent data is that, well, you have to represent data *somehow*, right? PowerShell could have stored that data in a format such as XML, or perhaps its creators could have decided to use plain-text tables. But they had specific reasons for not taking those routes.

The first reason is due to PowerShell's history of previously being Windows-only. Windows itself is an object-oriented operating system—or at least, most of the software that runs on Windows is object-oriented. Choosing to structure data as a set of objects is easy, because most of the operating system lends itself to those structures. As it turns out, we can apply that object-oriented mindset to other operating systems, and even other paradigms like the cloud and DevOps.

Another reason to use objects is that they ultimately make things easier on you and give you more power and flexibility. For the moment, let's pretend that PowerShell doesn't produce objects as the output of its commands. Instead, it produces simple text tables, which is what you probably thought it was doing in the first place. When you run a command such as `Get-Process`, you're getting formatted text as the output:

```
PS /Users/travis> Get-Process
Handles  NPM(K)    PM(K)      WS(K) VM(M)    CPU(s)     Id ProcessName
-------  ------    -----      ----- -----    ------     -- -----------
     39       5     1876       4340    52     11.33   1920 Code
     31       4      792       2260    22      0.00   2460 Code
     29       4      828       2284    41      0.25   3192 Code
    574      12     1864       3896    43      1.30    316 pwsh
    181      13     5892       6348    59      9.14    356 ShipIt
    306      29    13936      18312   139      4.36   1300 storeaccountd
    125      15     2528       6048    37      0.17   1756 WifiAgent
   5159    7329    85052      86436   118      1.80   1356 WifiProxy
```

What if you want to do something else with this information? Perhaps you want to make a change to all of the processes running `Code`. To do this, you have to filter the list a bit. On UNIX or Linux, you might try to use a command such as `grep` (which you *could* run in PowerShell, by the way!), telling it, "Look at this text list for me. Keep only those rows where columns 58–64 contain the characters `Code`. Delete all of the other rows." The resulting list contains only those processes you specified:

```
Handles  NPM(K)    PM(K)      WS(K) VM(M)    CPU(s)     Id ProcessName
-------  ------    -----      ----- -----    ------     -- -----------
     39       5     1876       4340    52     11.33   1920 Code
     31       4      792       2260    22      0.00   2460 Code
     29       4      828       2284    41      0.25   3192 Code
```

You then pipe that text to another command, perhaps telling it to extract the process ID from the list. "Go through this and get the characters from columns 52–56, but drop the first two (header) rows." The result might be this:

```
1920
2460
3192
```

Finally, you pipe *that* text to yet *another* command, asking it to kill the processes (or whatever else you were trying to do) represented by those ID numbers.

This is exactly how IT professionals that use `bash` work. They spend a lot of time learning how to get better at parsing text; using tools such as `grep`, `awk`, and `sed`; and becoming proficient in the use of regular expressions. Going through this learning process makes it easier for them to define the text patterns they want their computer to look for. In the old days before PowerShell was cross-platform, UNIX and Linux IT professionals would rely on scripting languages like Perl and Python, which have more batteries included in terms of text parsing. But this text-based approach does present some problems:

- You can spend more time messing around with text than doing your real job.
- If the output of a command changes—say, moving the ProcessName column to the start of the table—then you have to rewrite all of your commands, because they're all dependent on things like column positions.
- You have to become proficient in languages and tools that parse text—not because your job involves parsing text, but because parsing text is a means to an end.
- Languages like Perl and Python are solid scripting languages . . . but are not shells as well.

PowerShell's use of objects helps to remove all of that text-manipulation overhead. Because objects work like tables in memory, you don't have to tell PowerShell which text column a piece of information is located at. Instead, you tell it the column name, and PowerShell knows exactly where to go to get that data. Regardless of how you arrange the final output on the screen or in a file, the in-memory table is always the same, so you never have to rewrite your commands because a column moved. You spend a lot less time on overhead tasks and more time focusing on what you want to accomplish.

True, you do have to learn a few syntax elements that let you properly instruct PowerShell, but you have to learn a *lot* less than if you were working in a purely text-based shell.

**DON'T GET MAD** None of the preceding is intended as a dig at Bash, Perl, or Python, by the way. Every tool has pros and cons. Python is a great general-purpose programming language that has even found its way into the machine learning and artificial intelligence space—but that's not why you're reading this book. You're looking for something to up your game as an IT professional, and PowerShell is the perfect tool for it.

## 8.3  *Discovering objects: Get-Member*

If objects are like a giant table in memory, and PowerShell shows you only a portion of that table on the screen, how can you see what else you have to work with? If you're thinking that you should use the `Get-Help` command, we're glad, because we've certainly been pushing that down your throat in the previous few chapters. But unfortunately, you'd be wrong.

The help system documents only background concepts (in the form of the about topics) and command syntax. To learn more about an object, you use a different command: Get-Member. You should become comfortable using this command—so much so, that you start looking for a shorter way to type it. We'll give you that right now: the alias gm.

You can use gm after any cmdlet that normally produces output. For example, you already know that running Get-Process produces output on the screen. You can pipe it to gm:

```
Get-Process | gm
```

Whenever a cmdlet produces a collection of objects, as Get-Process does, the entire collection remains accessible until the end of the pipeline. It's not until every command has run that PowerShell filters the columns of information to be displayed and creates the final text output you see. Therefore, in the preceding example, gm has complete access to all of the process objects' properties and methods, because they haven't been filtered for display yet. gm looks at each object and constructs a list of the objects' properties and methods. It looks like this:

```
PS C:\> Get-Process | gm
   TypeName: System.Diagnostics.Process
Name                    MemberType     Definition
----                    ----------     ----------
Handles                 AliasProperty  Handles = Handlecount
Name                    AliasProperty  Name = ProcessName
NPM                     AliasProperty  NPM = NonpagedSystemMemo...
PM                      AliasProperty  PM = PagedMemorySize
VM                      AliasProperty  VM = VirtualMemorySize
WS                      AliasProperty  WS = WorkingSet
Disposed                Event          System.EventHandler Disp...
ErrorDataReceived       Event          System.Diagnostics.DataR...
Exited                  Event          System.EventHandler Exit...
OutputDataReceived      Event          System.Diagnostics.DataR...
BeginErrorReadLine      Method         System.Void BeginErrorRe...
BeginOutputReadLine     Method         System.Void BeginOutputR...
CancelErrorRead         Method         System.Void CancelErrorR...
CancelOutputRead        Method         System.Void CancelOutput...
```

We've trimmed the preceding list because it's long, but hopefully you get the idea.

> **TRY IT NOW**  Don't take our word for it. This is the perfect time to follow along and run the same commands we do, to see their complete output.

By the way, it may interest you to know that all of the properties, methods, and other things attached to an object are collectively called its *members*, as if the object itself were a country club and all of these properties and methods belonged to the club. That's where Get-Member takes its name from—it's getting a list of the objects' members. But remember, because the PowerShell convention is to use singular nouns, the cmdlet name is Get-Member, *not* Get-Members.

**IMPORTANT**   It's easy to overlook, but pay attention to the first line of output from `Get-Member`. It's `TypeName`, which is the unique name assigned to that particular type of object. It may seem unimportant now—after all, who cares what it's named? But it's going to become crucial in the next chapter.

## 8.4   *Using object attributes, or properties*

When you examine the output of `gm`, you'll notice several kinds of properties:

- `ScriptProperty`
- `Property`
- `NoteProperty`
- `AliasProperty`

### Above and beyond

Normally, objects in .NET—which is where all of PowerShell's objects come from—have only *properties*. PowerShell dynamically adds the other stuff: `ScriptProperty`, `NoteProperty`, `AliasProperty`, and so on. If you happen to look up an object type in Microsoft's documentation (you can plug the object's `TypeName` into your favorite search engine to find the docs.microsoft.com page), you won't see these extra properties.

PowerShell has an extensible type system (ETS) that's responsible for adding these last-minute properties. Why does it do this? In some cases, it's to make objects more consistent, such as adding a `Name` property to objects that natively have only something like `ProcessName` (that's what an `AliasProperty` is for). Sometimes it's to expose information that's deeply buried in the object (process objects have a few `ScriptProperties` that do this).

Once you're in PowerShell, these properties all behave the same way. But don't be surprised when they don't show up on the official documentation page: the shell adds these extras, often to make your life easier.

For your purposes, these properties are all the same. The only difference is in how the properties were originally created, but that's not something you need to worry about. To you, they're all properties, and you'll use them the same way.

A property always contains a value. For example, the value of a process object's `ID` property might be `1234`, and the `Name` property of that object might have a value of `Code`. Properties describe something about the object: its status, its ID, its name, and so on. In PowerShell, properties are often read-only, meaning you can't change the name of a service by assigning a new value to its `Name` property. But you can retrieve the name of a service by reading its `Name` property. We estimate that 90% of what you'll do in PowerShell will involve properties.

## 8.5    *Using object actions, or methods*

Many objects support one or more methods, which, as we mentioned earlier, are actions that you can direct the object to take. A process object has a `Kill` method, which terminates the process. Some methods require one or more input arguments that provide additional details for that particular action, but you won't be running into any of those this early in your PowerShell education. You may spend months or even years working with PowerShell and never need to execute a single object method. That's because many of those actions are also provided by cmdlets.

For example, if you need to terminate a process, you have three ways to do so. One way is to retrieve the object and then somehow execute its `Kill` method. Another way is to use a couple of cmdlets:

```
Get-Process -Name Code | Stop-Process
```

You can also accomplish that by using a single cmdlet:

```
Stop-Process -Name Code
```

Our focus in this book is entirely on using PowerShell cmdlets to accomplish tasks. They provide the easiest, most IT professional–centric, most task-focused way of accomplishing things. Using methods starts to edge into .NET programming, which can be more complicated and can require a lot more background information. For that reason, you'll rarely—if ever—see us execute an object method in this book. Our general philosophy at this point is, "If you can't do it with a cmdlet, go back and use the GUI." You won't feel that way for your entire career, we promise, but for now it's a good way to stay focused on the "PowerShell way" of doing things.

> **Above and beyond**
>
> You don't need to know about them at this stage in your PowerShell education, but in addition to properties and methods, objects can also have events. An *event* is an object's way of notifying you that something happened to it. A process object, for example, can trigger its `Exited` event when the process ends. You can attach your own commands to those events, so that, for example, an email is sent when a process exits. Working with events in this fashion is an advanced topic that's beyond the scope of this book.

## 8.6    *Sorting objects*

Most PowerShell cmdlets produce objects in a deterministic fashion, which means that they tend to produce objects in the same order every time you run the command. Both Azure VMs and processes, for example, are listed in alphabetical order by name. What if we want to change that?

Suppose we want to display a list of processes, with the biggest consumers of CPU at the top of the list and the smallest consumers at the bottom. We need to somehow reorder that list of objects based on the CPU property. PowerShell provides a simple cmdlet, `Sort-Object`, that does exactly that:

```
Get-Process | Sort-Object -Property CPU
```

> **TRY IT NOW** We're hoping that you'll follow along and run the commands in this chapter. We aren't pasting the output into the book because these tables are long.

That command isn't exactly what we want. It does sort on CPU, but it does so in ascending order, with the largest values at the bottom of the list. Reading the help for `Sort-Object`, we see that it has a `-Descending` parameter that should reverse the sort order. We also notice that the `-Property` parameter is positional, so we don't need to type the parameter name.

We abbreviated `-Descending` to `-desc`, and we have the result we want. The `-Property` parameter accepts multiple values (which we're sure you saw in the help file, if you looked).

In the event that two processes are using the same amount of virtual memory, we want them sorted by process ID, and the following command accomplishes that:

```
Get-Process | Sort-Object CPU,ID -desc
```

As always, a comma-separated list is the way to pass multiple values to any parameter that supports them.

## 8.7 Selecting the properties you want

Another useful cmdlet is `Select-Object`. It accepts objects from the pipeline, and you can specify the properties that you want displayed. This enables you to access properties that are normally filtered out by PowerShell's configuration rules, or to trim down the list to a few properties that interest you. This can be useful when piping objects to `ConvertTo-HTML`, because that cmdlet usually builds a table containing every property. Compare the results of these two commands:

```
Get-Process | ConvertTo-HTML | Out-File test1.html
Get-Process | Select-Object -Property Name,ID,CPU,PM | ConvertTo-Html |
➡ Out-File test2.html
```

> **TRY IT NOW** Go ahead and run each of these commands separately, and then examine the resulting HTML files in a web browser to see the differences.

Look at the help for `Select-Object` (or you can use its alias, `Select`). The `-Property` parameter is positional, which means we could shorten that last command:

```
Get-Process | Select Name,ID,CPU,PM | ConvertTo-HTML | Out-File test3.html
```

Spend some time experimenting with `Select-Object`. Try variations of the following command, which allows the output to appear on the screen:

```
Get-Process | Select Name,ID,CPU,PM
```

Try adding and removing different process object properties from that list and reviewing the results. How many properties can you specify and still get a table as the output? How many properties force PowerShell to format the output as a list rather than as a table?

---

**Above and beyond**

`Select-Object` also has `-First` and `-Last` parameters, which let you keep a subset of the objects in the pipeline. For example, `Get-Process | Select -First 10` keeps the first 10 objects. There are no criteria involved, such as keeping certain processes; it's merely grabbing the first (or last) 10.

---

**CAUTION**   People often get mixed up about two PowerShell commands: `Select-Object` and `Where-Object`, which you haven't seen yet. `Select-Object` is used to choose the properties (or columns) you want to see, and it can also select an arbitrary subset of output rows (using `-First` and `-Last`). `Where-Object` removes, or filters, objects out of the pipeline based on criteria you specify.

## 8.8   *Objects until the end*

The PowerShell pipeline always contains objects until the last command has been executed. At that time, PowerShell looks to see what objects are in the pipeline, and then looks at its various configuration files to see which properties to use to construct the onscreen display. It also decides whether that display will be a table or a list, based on internal rules and on its configuration files. (We'll explain more about those rules and configurations, and how you can modify them, in chapter 10.)

   An important fact is that the pipeline can contain many kinds of objects over the course of a single command line. For the next few examples, we're going to take a single command line and physically type it so that only one command appears on a single line of text. That'll make it a bit easier to explain what we're talking about. Here's the first one:

```
Get-Process |
Sort-Object CPU -Descending |
Out-File c:\procs.txt
```

In this example, we start by running `Get-Process`, which puts process objects into the pipeline. The next command is `Sort-Object`. That doesn't change what's in the pipeline; it changes only the order of the objects, so at the end of `Sort-Object`, the pipeline still contains processes. The last command is `Out-File`. Here, PowerShell has to produce output, so it takes whatever's in the pipeline—processes—and formats them according to its internal rule set. The results go into the specified file. Next up is a more complicated example:

```
Get-Process |
Sort-Object CPU -Descending |
Select-Object Name,ID,CPU
```

This starts off in the same way. `Get-Process` puts process objects into the pipeline. Those go to `Sort-Object`, which sorts them and puts the same process objects into the pipeline. But `Select-Object` works a bit differently. A process object always has the exact same members. In order to trim down the list of properties, `Select-Object` can't remove the properties you don't want, because the result wouldn't be a process object anymore. Instead, `Select-Object` creates a new kind of custom object called a PSObject. It copies over the properties you do want from the process, resulting in a custom object being placed into the pipeline.

> **TRY IT NOW** Try running this three-cmdlet command line, keeping in mind that you should type the whole thing on a single line. Notice how the output is different from the normal output of `Get-Process`?

When PowerShell sees that it's reached the end of the command line, it has to decide how to lay out the text output. Because there are no longer any process objects in the pipeline, PowerShell won't use the default rules and configurations that apply to process objects. Instead, it looks for rules and configurations for a PSObject, which is what the pipeline now contains. Microsoft doesn't provide any rules or configurations for PSObjects, because they're meant to be used for custom output. Instead, PowerShell takes its best guess and produces a table, on the theory that those three pieces of information probably will still fit in a table. The table isn't as nicely laid out as the normal output of `Get-Process`, though, because the shell lacks the additional configuration information needed to make a nicer-looking table.

You can use gm to see the objects that wind up in the pipeline. Remember, you can add gm after any cmdlet that produces output:

```
Get-Process | Sort-Object CPU -Descending | gm
Get-Process | Sort-Object CPU -Descending | Select Name,ID,CPU | gm
```

> **TRY IT NOW** Try running those two command lines separately, and notice the difference in the output.

Notice that, as part of the gm output, PowerShell shows you the type name for the object it sees in the pipeline. In the first case, that's a `System.Diagnostics.Process` object, but in the second case the pipeline contains a different kind of object. Those new *selected* objects contain only the three properties specified—Name, ID, and CPU—plus a couple of system-generated members.

Even gm produces objects and places them into the pipeline. After running gm, the pipeline no longer contains either process or the *selected* objects; it contains the type of object produced by gm: a `Microsoft.PowerShell.Commands.MemberDefinition`. You can prove that by piping the output of gm to gm itself:

```
Get-Process | gm | gm
```

> **TRY IT NOW**  You'll definitely want to try this, and think hard about it to make sure it makes sense to you. You start with `Get-Process`, which puts process objects into the pipeline. Those go to gm, which analyzes them and produces its own `MemberDefinition` objects. Those are then piped to gm, which analyzes them and produces output that lists the members of each `Member-Definition` object.

A key to mastering PowerShell is learning to keep track of the kind of object that's in the pipeline at any given point. While gm can help you do that, sitting back and verbally walking yourself through the command line is also a good exercise that can help clear up confusion.

## 8.9  *Common points of confusion*

Newcomers tend to make a few common mistakes as they get started with PowerShell. Most of these go away with a little experience, but we direct your attention to them with the following list, to give you a chance to catch yourself if you start heading down the wrong path.

- Remember that the PowerShell help files don't contain information on objects' properties. You'll need to pipe the objects to gm (`Get-Member`) to see a list of properties.
- Remember that you can add gm to the end of any pipeline that typically produces results. A command line such as `Get-Process -Name Code | Stop-Process` doesn't usually produce results, so tacking `| gm` onto the end won't produce anything either.
- Pay attention to neat typing. Put a space on either side of every pipeline character, because your command lines should read as `Get-Process | gm` and not `Get-Process|gm`. That spacebar key is extra large for a reason—use it.
- Remember that the pipeline can contain various types of objects at each step. Think about what type of object is in the pipeline, and focus on what the next command will do to that *type* of object.

## 8.10  *Lab*

> **NOTE**  For this lab, you need any computer running PowerShell v7 or later.

This chapter has probably covered more, and more difficult, new concepts than any chapter to this point. We hope that you were able to make sense of it all and that these exercises will help you cement what you've learned. The lab may be more challenging than previous labs, but we want you to start getting in the habit of figuring out which commands to use—and relying on `get-command` and help, rather than on us, to find the correct command. After all, that is what you'll be doing once you start working with PowerShell on the job and encountering all sorts of situations we don't address in the book. Some of these tasks draw on skills you've learned in previous chapters, to refresh your memory and keep you sharp:

1  Identify a cmdlet that produces a random number.
2  Identify a cmdlet that displays the current date and time.
3  What type of object does the cmdlet from task 2 produce? (What is the *TypeName* of the object produced by the cmdlet?)
4  Using the cmdlet from task 2 and `Select-Object`, display only the current day of the week in a table like the following (caution: the output will right-align, so make sure your PowerShell window doesn't have a horizontal scrollbar):

```
DayOfWeek
---------
   Monday
```

5  Identify a cmdlet that will show you all the times in a directory.
6  Using the cmdlet from task 5, display all the times in the directory of your choice. Then extend the expression to sort the list by the time the items were created and display only the filename(s) and the date created. Remember that the column headers shown in a command's default output aren't necessarily the real property names—you need to look up the real property names to be sure.
7  Repeat task 6, but this time sort the items by the last write time; then display the filename, creation time, and the last write time. Save this in a CSV file and an HTML file.

## 8.11  Lab answers

```
1  Get-Random
2  Get-Date
3  System.DateTime
4  Get-Date | select DayofWeek
5  Get-ChildItem
6  Get-ChildItem | Sort-Object CreationTime | Select-Object
   ➥ Name,CreationTime

7  Get-ChildItem | Sort-Object LastWritetime | Select-Object
   ➥ Name,LastWritetime,CreationTime | Export-CSV files.csv

   Get-ChildItem | Sort-Object LastWritetime | Select-Object
   ➥ Name,LastWritetime,CreationTime | Out-file files.html
```

# A practical interlude

It's time to put some of your new knowledge to work. In this chapter, we're not going to teach you anything new. Instead, we're going to walk you through a detailed example using what you've learned. This is an absolutely real-world example: We're going to set ourselves a task and then let you follow our thought processes as we figure out how to complete it. This chapter is the epitome of what this book is all about, because instead of just handing you the answer on how to do something, we're helping you realize that *you can teach yourself.*

## 9.1 Defining the task

First of all, we're assuming that you're working on any operating system running PowerShell 7.1 or higher. The example we're going to work through may very well work on earlier versions of Windows PowerShell, but we have not tested this.

In the world of DevOps, there is a specific language that almost always pops up—besides PowerShell, of course. It's a rather controversial language among IT pros and DevOps engineers—people either love it or hate it. Any guesses? If you guessed YAML, you're right! YAML stands for "YAML ain't markup language" (it's what we call a recursive acronym, when the acronym contains the acronym), and although it says that it isn't, in a lot of ways it is similar to a simple markup language—in other words, it's just a file with a certain structure to it, just like CSVs and JSON have a certain structure to them. Since we see a lot of YAML in the DevOps world, it's important that we have the tools to interact with YAML files.

## 9.2 Finding the commands

The first step in solving any task is to figure out which commands will do it for you. Your results might differ from ours, depending on what you have installed, but it's the process we're going through that's important. Because we know we want to manage some virtual machines, we'll start with *YAML* as a keyword:

```
PS C:\Scripts\ > Get-Help *YAML*
PS C:\Scripts\ >
```

Hmm. That wasn't helpful. Nothing showed up. Okay, let's try another approach—this time, we focus on commands rather than on help files:

```
PS C:\Scripts\ > get-command -noun *YAML*
PS C:\Scripts\ >
```

Okay, so there are no commands whose names contain *YAML*. Disappointing! So now we have to see what might be in the online PowerShell Gallery:

```
PS C:\Scripts\ > find-module *YAML* | format-table -auto
Version Name            Repository Description
------- ----            ---------- -----------
0.4.0   powershell-yaml PSGallery  Powershell module for serializing...
1.0.3   FXPSYaml        PSGallery  PowerShell module used to...
0.2.0   Gainz-Yaml      PSGallery  Gainz: Yaml...
0.1.0   Gz-Yaml         PSGallery  # Gz-Yaml...
```

Much more promising! So let's install that first module:

```
PS C:\Scripts\ > install-module powershell-yaml
You are installing the module(s) from an untrusted repository. If you
trust this repository, change its InstallationPolicy value by
running the Set-PSRepository cmdlet.
Are you sure you want to install software from
'https://go.microsoft.com/fwlink/?LinkID=397631&clcid=0x409'?
[Y] Yes  [A] Yes to All  [N] No  [L] No to All  [S] Suspend
[?] Help(default is "N"): y
```

Now, at this point, you do have to be careful. Although Microsoft runs PowerShell Gallery, it doesn't validate any of the code that others publish. So we did take a break in our process, review the code that we'd just installed, and made sure we were comfortable with it before we continued. It also helps that the author of this module is a fellow MVP, Boe Prox, and we trust him. Now let's see the commands we just gained:

```
PS C:\Scripts\ > get-command -module powershell-yaml | format-table -auto
CommandType Name             Version Source
----------- ----             ------- ------
Function    ConvertFrom-Yaml 0.4.0   powershell-yaml
Function    ConvertTo-Yaml   0.4.0   powershell-yaml
```

Okay, those seem straightforward. ConvertTo and ConvertFrom—sounds like all we need.

## 9.3    *Learning to use the commands*

With any luck, the author included help with their module. If you ever write a module someday, always remember that if other folks are going to use it, you should proba-bly—no, you *should*—include help so that consumers of your module know how to use it. If you didn't, it'd be like shipping a piece of IKEA furniture without the instruction manual—don't do it! There is another book called *Learn PowerShell Toolmaking in a Month of Lunches* (Manning, 2012), where two of its authors, Don Jones and Jeffery Hicks, cover how to write modules and how to put help in them—and adding help is the right thing to do. Let's see whether the author did the right thing:

```
PS C:\Scripts\ > help ConvertFrom-Yaml
NAME
    ConvertFrom-Yaml

SYNTAX
    ConvertFrom-Yaml [[-Yaml] <string>] [-AllDocuments] [-Ordered]
    ➥ [-UseMergingParser] [<CommonParameters>]



PARAMETERS
    -AllDocuments      Add-Privilege
```

Drat! No help. Well, in this instance, it's not too bad because PowerShell helps even though the author didn't write any help. PowerShell still gives you the syntax, parame-ters, output, and aliases—that's enough info for this straightforward command. So we need a sample YAML file. . . . Well, it's worth using a live example from the PowerShell GitHub repository:

https://raw.githubusercontent.com/PowerShell/PowerShell/master/.vsts-ci/templates/credscan.yml

This is the Azure Pipelines YAML file that the PowerShell team uses to run CredScan—a tool used for scanning if secrets or credentials have accidentally been added to code. The PowerShell team has it set up to run every time someone sends a pull request (aka a code change) to the PowerShell GitHub repository so that it can be caught immedi-ately. Running tasks during a pull request is a common practice called *continuous integration* (CI).

Go ahead and download that file, and let's read the file from PowerShell:

```
PS C:\Scripts\ > Get-Content -Raw /Users/travis/Downloads/credscan.yml
parameters:
  pool: 'Hosted VS2017'
  jobName: 'credscan'
  displayName: Secret Scan

jobs:
- job: ${{ parameters.jobName }}
  pool:
    name: ${{ parameters.pool }}
```

```
  displayName: ${{ parameters.displayName }}

  steps:
  - task: securedevelopmentteam.vss-secure-development-tools.build-task
    ➡ -credscan.CredScan@2
    displayName: 'Scan for Secrets'
    inputs:
      suppressionsFile: tools/credScan/suppress.json
      debugMode: false

  - task: securedevelopmentteam.vss-secure-development-tools.build-task
    ➡ -publishsecurityanalysislogs.PublishSecurityAnalysisLogs@2
    displayName: 'Publish Secret Scan Logs to Build Artifacts'
    continueOnError: true

  - task: securedevelopmentteam.vss-secure-development-tools.build-task
    ➡ -postanalysis.PostAnalysis@1
    displayName: 'Check for Failures'
    inputs:
      CredScan: true
      ToolLogsNotFoundAction: Error
```

Okay great, so we've figured out how to read in the YAML file. Next let's convert it into something a bit easier to work with:

```
PS C:\Scripts\ > Get-Content -Raw /Users/travis/Downloads/credscan.yml |
    ➡ ConvertFrom-Yaml


Name                             Value
----                             -----
parameters                       {pool, jobName, displayName}
jobs                             {${{ parameters.displayName }}}
```

Well, then. That was easy. Let's see what kind of object we have:

```
PS C:\Scripts\ > Get-Content -Raw /Users/travis/Downloads/credscan.yml |
    ➡ ConvertFrom-Yaml | gm


   TypeName: System.Collections.Hashtable
Name              MemberType         Definition
----              ----------         ----------
Add               Method             void Add(System.Object key...
Clear             Method             void Clear(), void
     IDictionary.Clear()
Clone             Method             System.Object Clone(), ...
Contains          Method             bool Contains(System.Object key)...
ContainsKey       Method             bool ContainsKey(System.Object key)
ContainsValue     Method             bool ContainsValue(System.Object...
CopyTo            Method             void CopyTo(array array, int...
Equals            Method             bool Equals(System.Object obj)
GetEnumerator     Method             System.Collections.IDictionary...
GetHashCode       Method             int GetHashCode()
```

```
GetObjectData      Method                  void GetObjectData(System.Runtim...
     GetType
       Method                  type GetType()
OnDeserialization Method                  void
     OnDeserialization(System.Object...Remove
       Method                  void Remove(System.Object key), voi... ToString
       Method                  string ToString()
Item               ParameterizedProperty System.Object Item(System.Object
                   ↪ key...
Count              Property                int Count {get;}
IsFixedSize        Property                bool IsFixedSize {get;}
IsReadOnly         Property                bool IsReadOnly {get;}
IsSynchronized     Property                bool IsSynchronized {get;}
Keys               Property                System.Collections.ICollection K...
SyncRoot           Property                System.Object SyncRoot {get;}
Values             Property                System.Collections.ICollection
     Value...
```

Okay, so it's a hash table. Hash tables are just a grab bag of stuff. You'll see them a lot throughout your PowerShell journey. These are great because they can easily be turned into other formats. Let's try to take what we got in YAML and turn it into another very important data structure in DevOps—JSON. Let's see what we have to work with:

```
PS C:\Scripts\ > Get-Help *json*

Name            Category Module                      Synopsis
----            -------- ------                      --------
ConvertFrom-Json Cmdlet   Microsoft.PowerShell.Utility...
ConvertTo-Json   Cmdlet   Microsoft.PowerShell.Utility...
Test-Json        Cmdlet   Microsoft.PowerShell.Utility...
```

Bingo, a `ConvertTo-Json` cmdlet. Let's use the pipeline to convert YAML into JSON. We'll need to use `ConvertTo-Json`'s `Depth` parameter (you can read about this from the help), which allows us to specify how deep the cmdlet should go in trying to make the JSON structure. For what we're doing, 100 is a safe bet. All right, let's bring it together:

```
PS C:\Scripts\ > Get-Content -Raw /Users/travis/Downloads/credscan.yml |
    ↪ ConvertFrom-Yaml | ConvertTo-Json -Depth 100

{
  "parameters": {
    "pool": "Hosted VS2017",
    "jobName": "credscan",
    "displayName": "Secret Scan"
  },
  "jobs": [
    {
      "job": "${{ parameters.jobName }}",
      "pool": {
        "name": "${{ parameters.pool }}"
```

```
        },
        "steps": [
          {
            "task": "securedevelopmentteam.vss-secure-development-tools.build
            ➥ -task-credscan.CredSca          "inputs": {
              "debugMode": false,
              "suppressionsFile": "tools/credScan/suppress.json"
            },
            "displayName": "Scan for Secrets"
          },
          {
nalysislogs.PublishSecurityAnalysisLogs@2",
            "continueOnError": true,
            "displayName": "Publish Secret Scan Logs to Build Artifacts"
          },
          {
            "task": "securedevelopmentteam.vss-secure-development-tools.build
            ➥ -task-postanalysis.PostAnalysis@1",
            "inputs": {
              "CredScan": true,
              "ToolLogsNotFoundAction": "Error"
            },
            "displayName": "Check for Failures"
          }
        ],
        "displayName": "${{ parameters.displayName }}"
    }
  ]
}
```

It works! We now have some JSON based on a YAML file. This is a useful exercise, as there are many different DevOps tools out in the wild that accept YAML or JSON (AutoRest, Kubernetes, to name a couple). As a result, you might prefer YAML, but your coworker prefers JSON. Now you have an easy way to share with each other by converting it this way.

Now, we freely admit that this isn't a complicated task. But the task itself isn't the point of this chapter. The point is *how we figured it out*. What did we do?

1 We started by searching the local help files for any that contained a specific keyword. When our search term didn't match a command name, PowerShell did a full search of all the help files' contents. That's useful, because if a file had even *mentioned* YAML, we'd have found it.

2 We moved on to searching for specific command names. This would help find commands *for which no help files were installed*. Ideally, commands should always have help files, but we don't live in an ideal world, so we always take this extra step.

3 Finding nothing locally, we searched PowerShell Gallery and found a promising-looking module. We installed the module and reviewed its commands.

4 Even though the module author didn't provide help, PowerShell helped us out and we were able to figure out how to run the commands to convert to and from YAML. This helps us see how the commands' data is structured and what sorts of values the commands are expecting.

5 Using the information we had gathered to that point, we were able to implement the change we wanted.

## 9.4 Tips for teaching yourself

Again, the real point of this book is to teach you how to teach yourself—and that's what this chapter illustrates. Here are a few tips:

- Don't be afraid of the help, and be sure to read the examples. We say that over and over, and it's like nobody believes us. We still see newcomers, right in front of us, secretly going to Google to find examples. What's so scary about the help files? If you're willing to read someone's blog, why not give the examples in the help files a shot first?

- Pay attention. Every bit of information on the screen is potentially important—don't mentally skip over the stuff that you're not immediately looking for. That's easy to do, but don't. Instead, look at each thing, and try to figure out what it's for and what information you can derive from it.

- Don't be afraid to fail. Hopefully you have a virtual machine that you can play in—so use it. Newcomers are constantly asking us questions like, "Hey, if I do such and such, what will happen?" to which we've started replying, "No idea—try it." Experimentation is good. In a virtual machine, the worst that can happen is you have to roll back to a snapshot, right? So give it a whirl, whatever you're working on.

- If one thing doesn't work, don't bang your head against a wall—try something else.

Everything gets easier with time, patience, and practice—but be sure that you're *thinking* along the way.

## 9.5 Lab

NOTE   For this lab, you can use any OS you prefer (try it on multiple ones if you would like), and make sure you are using PowerShell 7.1 or higher.

Now it's your turn. We're assuming that you're working in a virtual machine or other machine that is okay to mess up a little in the name of learning. Please don't do this in a production environment on a mission-critical computer!

This exercise will be about secrets management. DevOps engineers should be very familiar with this concept. The idea is simple: We have a bunch of sensitive information (passwords, connection strings, etc.) that we need to use in our commands, but we need to keep those secrets in a secure location. We also may want to share those secrets with other members on our team—and an email is not secure enough, folks!

The PowerShell team has recently been working on a module called Secrets Management to do just this. It's a generic module for interacting with any secret store that supports it. Some will be local secret stores like the macOS Keychain, and others will be cloud services like Azure Key Vault and HashiCorp Vault. Your goal is to grab this module, store a secret in your secret store of choice, and then retrieve it. If you use a cloud-based secret store, try to retrieve the secret from a different machine as the ultimate test.

## 9.6  *Lab answer*

We're sure you were expecting us to give you a full list of commands to run to complete this lab exercise. However, this entire chapter has been about figuring these things out on your own. The secrets management module is well documented. If you have been following along with us, then you will not have any problems with this lab.

# The pipeline, deeper

## 10

At this point, you've learned to be pretty effective with PowerShell's pipeline. Running commands (e.g., `Get-Process | Sort-Object VM -desc | ConvertTo-Html | Out-File procs.html`) is powerful, accomplishing in one line what used to take several lines of script. But you can do even better. In this chapter, we dig deeper into the pipeline and uncover some of its most powerful capabilities, which allow you to pass data between commands the right way with less work.

### 10.1   The pipeline: Enabling power with less typing

One of the reasons we like PowerShell so much is that it enables us to be more effective administrators without having to write complex scripts, as we used to have to do in Bash. The key to powerful one-line commands lies in the way the PowerShell pipeline works.

Let us be clear: you could skip this chapter and still be effective with PowerShell, but in most cases you'd have to resort to Bash-style scripts and programs. Although PowerShell's pipeline capabilities can be complicated, they're probably easier to learn than more-complicated programming skills. By learning to manipulate the pipeline, you can be much more effective without needing to write scripts.

The whole idea here is to get the shell to do more of your work for you, with as little typing as possible. We think you'll be surprised at how well the shell can do that!

### 10.2   How PowerShell passes data down the pipeline

Whenever you string together two commands, PowerShell has to figure out how to get the output of the first command to the input of the second command. In the upcoming examples, we refer to the first command as *Command A*. That's the command that produces something. The second command is *Command B*, which needs to accept Command A's output and then do its own thing:

```
CommandA | CommandB
```

For example, suppose you have a text file that contains one module name on each line, as shown in figure 10.1.

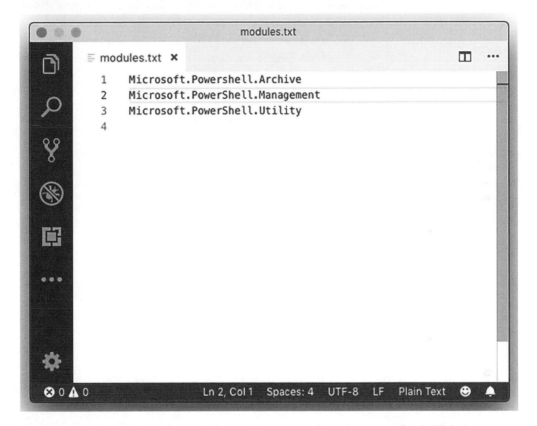

**Figure 10.1   Creating a text file containing module names, with one name per line in VS Code**

You might want to use those module names as the input to a command, telling that command which module you want it to run against. Consider this example:

```
Get-Content .\modules.txt | Get-Command
```

When Get-Content runs, it places the module names into the pipeline. PowerShell then has to decide how to get those to the Get-Command command. The trick with PowerShell is that commands can accept input only through parameters. PowerShell has to figure out which parameter of Get-Command will accept the output of Get-Content. This figuring-out process is called *pipeline parameter binding*, and it's what we cover in this chapter. PowerShell has two methods for getting the output of Get-Content onto a parameter of Get-Command. The first method the shell will try is called ByValue; if that doesn't work, it'll try ByPropertyName.

## 10.3  *Plan A: Pipeline input ByValue*

With this method of pipeline parameter binding, PowerShell looks at the type of object produced by Command A and tries to see whether any parameter of Command B can accept that type of object from the pipeline. You can determine this for yourself: First pipe the output of Command A to Get-Member to see what type of object Command A is producing. Then examine the full help of Command B (e.g., Get-Help Get-Command -Full) to see whether any parameter accepts that type of data from the pipeline ByValue. Figure 10.2 shows what you might discover.

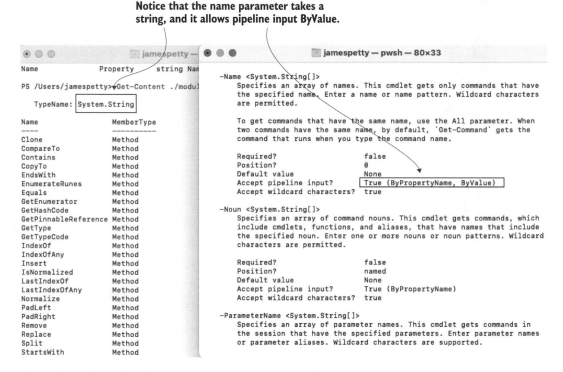

Figure 10.2    Comparing the output of Get-Content to the input parameters of Get-Command

What you'll find is that Get-Content produces objects of the type System.String (or String for short). You'll also find that Get-Command does have a parameter that accepts String from the pipeline ByValue. The problem is that it's the -Name parameter, which according to the help "specifies an array of names. This cmdlet gets only commands that have the specified name." That isn't what we want—our text file, and therefore our String objects, are module names, not command names. If we ran

```
Get-Content .\modules.txt | Get-Command
```

we'd be attempting to retrieve commands named `Microsoft.PowerShell.Archive` and so forth, which is probably not going to work.

If multiple parameters accept the same type from the pipeline, all parameters will receive the same value. Because the `-Name` parameter accepts `String` from the pipeline `ByValue`, for all practical purposes, no other parameter can do so. That dashes our hopes for trying to pipe module names from our text file to `Get-Command`.

In this case, pipeline input is working, but it isn't achieving the results we're hoping for. Let's consider a different example, where we do get the results we want. Here's the command line:

```
Get-Content ./modules.txt | Get-Module
```

Let's pipe the output of Command A to `Get-Member` and examine the full help for Command B. Figure 10.3 shows what you'll find.

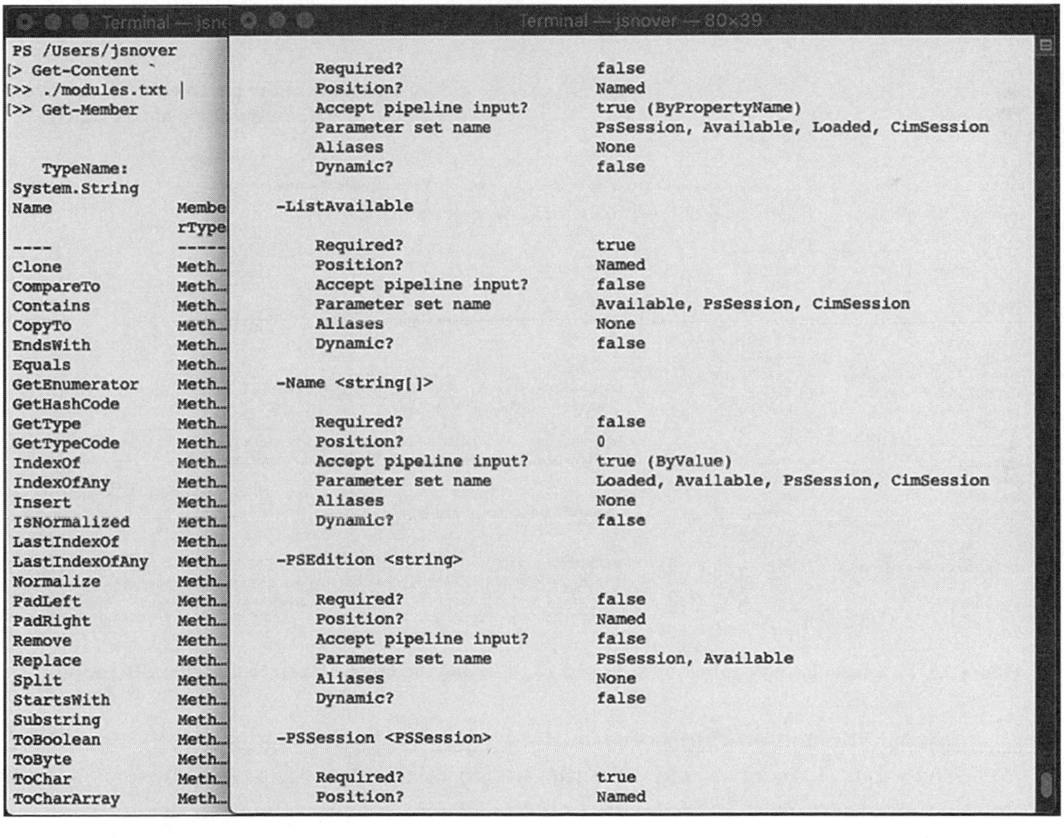

**Figure 10.3   Binding the output of `Get-Content` to a parameter of `Get-Module`**

Get-Content produces objects of the type String. Get-Module can accept those string objects from the pipeline ByValue; it does so on its -Name parameter. According to the help, that parameter "specifies names or name patterns of modules that this cmdlet gets." In other words, Command A gets one or more String objects, and Command B tries to find a module with the name in the string.

> **TIP**    For the most part, commands sharing the same noun (as Get-Process and Stop-Process do) can usually pipe to each other ByValue. Take some time to see if you can pipe the output of Get-Process to Stop-Process.

Let's cover one more example:

```
Get-ChildItem -File | Stop-Process -WhatIf
```

On the face of it, this might not seem to make any sense. But let's see this through by piping Command A's output to Get-Member and reexamining the help for Command B. Figure 10.4 shows what you should find.

**Notice that none of the parameters of Stop-Process match the FileInfo output type of Get-ChildItem.**

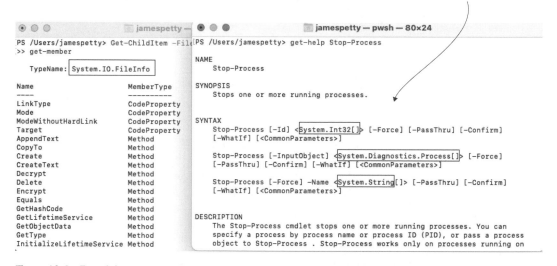

**Figure 10.4   Examining the output of Get-ChildItem and the input parameters of Stop-Process**

Get-ChildItem produces objects of the type FileInfo (technically, System.IO.FileInfo, but you can usually take the last bit of the TypeName as a shortcut). Unfortunately, there isn't a single parameter of Stop-Process that can accept a FileInfo object. The ByValue approach has failed, and PowerShell will try its backup plan: ByPropertyName.

## 10.4  *Plan B: Pipeline input ByPropertyName*

With this approach, you're still looking to attach the output of Command A to parameters of Command B. But ByPropertyName is slightly different from ByValue. With this backup method, it's possible for multiple parameters of Command B to become involved. Once again, pipe the output of Command A to Get-Member, and then look at the syntax for Command B. Figure 10.5 shows what you should find: the output of Command A has one property whose name corresponds to a parameter on Command B.

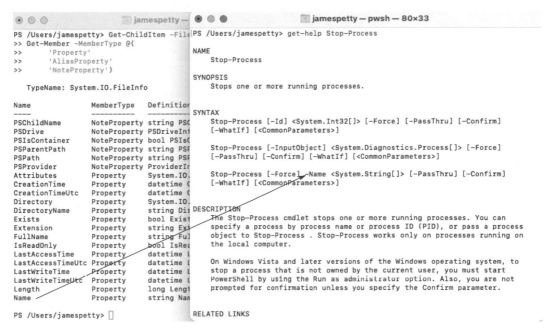

**Figure 10.5  Mapping properties to parameters**

A lot of folks overthink what's happening here, so let's be clear on how simple the shell is being: it's looking for property names that match parameter names. That's it. Because the property Name is spelled the same as the parameter -Name, the shell tries to connect the two.

But it can't do so right away; first it needs to see whether the -Name parameter will accept input from the pipeline ByPropertyName. A glance at the full help, shown in figure 10.6, is required to make this determination.

In this case, -Name does accept pipeline input ByPropertyName, so this connection works. Now, here's the trick: unlike ByValue, which involves only one parameter, ByPropertyName connects every matching property and parameter (provided each parameter has been designed to accept pipeline input ByPropertyName). In our current example, only Name and -Name match. The results? Examine figure 10.7.

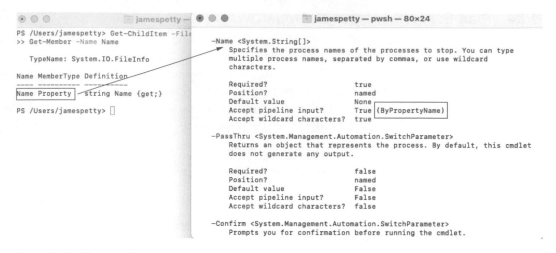

**Figure 10.6    Checking to see whether the `Stop-Process` command's `-Name` parameter accepts pipeline input `ByPropertyName`**

```
● ● ●                  Terminal — jsnover — 80×39
PS /Users/jsnover
[> Get-ChildItem -File | Stop-Process
Stop-Process : Cannot find a process with the name "chapter7.zip". Verify the pr
ocess name and call the cmdlet again.
At line:1 char:23
+ Get-ChildItem -File | Stop-Process
+                       ~~~~~~~~~~~~
+ CategoryInfo          : ObjectNotFound: (chapter7.zip:String) [Stop-Process],
ProcessCommandException
+ FullyQualifiedErrorId : NoProcessFoundForGivenName,Microsoft.PowerShell.Comman
ds.StopProcessCommand

Stop-Process : Cannot find a process with the name "computers.txt". Verify the p
rocess name and call the cmdlet again.
At line:1 char:23
+ Get-ChildItem -File | Stop-Process
+                       ~~~~~~~~~~~~
+ CategoryInfo          : ObjectNotFound: (computers.txt:String) [Stop-Process],
 ProcessCommandException
+ FullyQualifiedErrorId : NoProcessFoundForGivenName,Microsoft.PowerShell.Comman
ds.StopProcessCommand

Stop-Process : Cannot find a process with the name "module.psm1". Verify the pro
cess name and call the cmdlet again.
At line:1 char:23
+ Get-ChildItem -File | Stop-Process
+                       ~~~~~~~~~~~~
+ CategoryInfo          : ObjectNotFound: (module.psm1:String) [Stop-Process], P
rocessCommandException
+ FullyQualifiedErrorId : NoProcessFoundForGivenName,Microsoft.PowerShell.Comman
ds.StopProcessCommand

Stop-Process : Cannot find a process with the name "MonadManifesto.md". Verify t
he process name and call the cmdlet again.
At line:1 char:23
+ Get-ChildItem -File | Stop-Process
+                       ~~~~~~~~~~~~
+ CategoryInfo          : ObjectNotFound: (MonadManifesto.md:String) [Stop-Proce
ss], ProcessCommandException
```

**Figure 10.7    Attempting to pipe `Get-ChildItem` to `Stop-Process`**

We see a bunch of error messages. The problem is that filenames are usually things like chapter7.zip and computers.txt, whereas the process's executables might be things like pwsh. Stop-Process deals only with those executable names. But even though the Name property connects to the -Name parameter via the pipeline, the values inside the Name property don't make sense to the -Name parameter, which leads to the errors.

Let's look at a more successful example. Create a simple CSV file in Visual Studio Code, using the example in figure 10.8.

**Figure 10.8   Create this CSV file in Visual Studio Code.**

Save the file as aliases.txt. Now, back in the shell, try importing it, as shown in figure 10.9. You should also pipe the output of Import-Csv to Get-Member, so that you can examine the output's members.

You can clearly see that the columns from the CSV file become properties, and each data row in the CSV file becomes an object. Now, examine the help for New-Alias, as shown in figure 10.10.

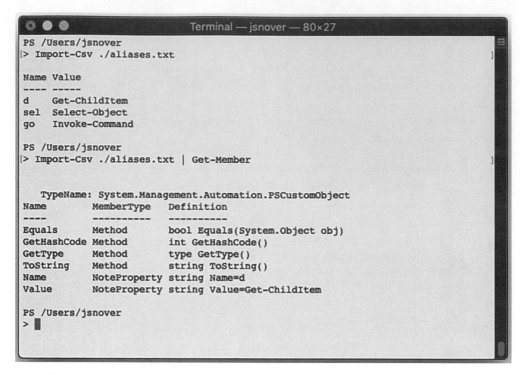

**Figure 10.9    Importing the CSV file and checking its members**

**Figure 10.10    Matching properties to parameter names**

Both properties (Name and Value) correspond to parameter names of New-Alias. Obviously, this was done on purpose—when you create the CSV file, you can name those columns anything you want. Now, check whether -Name and -Value accept pipeline input ByPropertyName, as shown in figure 10.11.

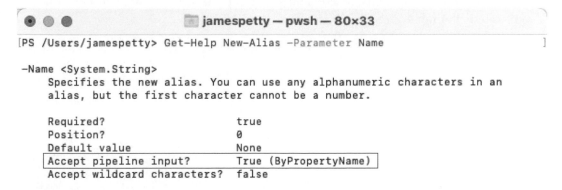

```
●  ●  ●                    jamespetty — pwsh — 80×33
[PS /Users/jamespetty> Get-Help New-Alias -Parameter Name            ]

-Name <System.String>
    Specifies the new alias. You can use any alphanumeric characters in an
    alias, but the first character cannot be a number.

    Required?                    true
    Position?                    0
    Default value                None
    Accept pipeline input?       True (ByPropertyName)
    Accept wildcard characters?  false
```

**Figure 10.11  Checking if `Name` and `Value` are parameters that accept pipeline input `ByPropertyName`**

Both parameters do, meaning this trick works. Try running the command

```
Import-Csv .\aliases.txt | New-Alias
```

The result is three new aliases, named d, sel, and go, which point to the commands Get-ChildItem, Select-Object, and Invoke-Command, respectively. This is a powerful technique for passing data from one command to another and for accomplishing complex tasks in a minimum number of commands.

## 10.5  *When things don't line up: Custom properties*

The CSV example is cool, but it's pretty easy to make property and parameter names line up when you're creating the input from scratch. Things get tougher when you're forced to deal with objects that are created for you, or data that's being produced by someone else.

For this next example, let's play with a new command: New-ADUser. It's part of the Active Directory module. You can get that module on a client computer by installing Microsoft's Remote Server Administration Tools (RSAT). But for now, don't worry about running the command; follow along with the example.

New-ADUser has parameters designed to accept information about a new Active Directory user. Here are some examples:

- -Name (mandatory)
- -samAccountName (technically not mandatory, but you have to provide it to make the account usable)
- -Department
- -City
- -Title

We could cover the others, but let's work with these. All of them accept pipeline input ByPropertyName.

For this example, you'll again assume you're getting a CSV file, but it's coming from your company's human resources or personnel department. You've given them your desired file format a dozen times, but they persist in giving you something that's close, but not quite right, as shown in figure 10.12.

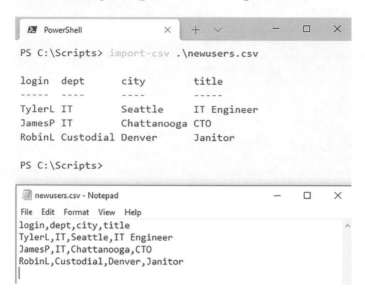

**Figure 10.12   Working with the CSV file provided by human resources**

As you can see in figure 10.12, the shell can import the CSV file fine, resulting in three objects with four properties apiece. The problem is that the dept property won't line up with the -Department parameter of New-ADUser, the login property is meaningless, and you don't have samAccountName or Name properties—both of which are required if you want to be able to run this command to create new users:

```
PS C:\> import-csv .\newusers.csv | new-aduser
```

How can you fix this? You could open the CSV file and fix it, but that's a lot of manual work over time, and the whole point of PowerShell is to reduce manual labor. Why not set up the shell to fix it instead? Look at the following example:

```
PS C:\> import-csv .\newusers.csv |
>> select-object -property *,
>>   @{name='samAccountName';expression={$_.login}},
>>   @{label='Name';expression={$_.login}},
>>   @{n='Department';e={$_.Dept}}
>>
login          : TylerL
dept           : IT
city           : Seattle
title          : IT Engineer
```

```
samAccountName : TylerL
Name           : TylerL
Department     : IT
login          : JamesP
dept           : IT
city           : Chattanooga
title          : CTO
samAccountName : JamesP
Name           : Jamesp
Department     : IT
login          : RobinL
dept           : Custodial
city           : Denver
title          : Janitor
samAccountName : RobinL
Name           : RobinL
Department     : Custodial
```

That's some pretty funky syntax, so let's break it down:

- We use `Select-Object` and its `-Property` parameter. We start by specifying the property `*`, which means "all of the existing properties." Notice that the `*` is followed by a comma, which means we're continuing the list of properties.
- We then create a hash table, which is the construct starting with `@{` and ending with `}`. Hash tables consist of one or more key-value pairs, and `Select-Object` has been programmed to look for specific keys, which we'll provide to it.
- The first key that `Select-Object` wants can be `Name`, `N`, `Label`, or `L`, and the value for that key is the name of the property we want to create. In the first hash table, we specify `samAccountName`; in the second, `Name`; and in the third, `Department`. These correspond to the parameter names of `New-ADUser`.
- The second key that `Select-Object` needs can be either `Expression` or `E`. The value for this key is a script block, contained within curly brackets `{}`. Within that script block, you use the special `$_` placeholder to refer to the existing piped-in object (the original row of data from the CSV file) followed by a period. The placeholder `$_` lets you access one property of the piped-in object, or one column of the CSV file. This specifies the contents for the new properties.

**TRY IT NOW**  Go ahead and create the CSV file that's shown in figure 10.12. Then try running the exact command we did previously—you can type it exactly as shown.

What we've done is taken the contents of the CSV file—the output of `Import-CSV`—and modified it, dynamically, in the pipeline. Our new output matches what `New-ADUser` wants to see, so we can now create new users by running this command:

```
PS C:\> import-csv .\newusers.csv |
>> select-object -property *,
>>   @{name='samAccountName';expression={$_.login}},
>>   @{label='Name';expression={$_.login}},
```

```
>>   @{n='Department';e={$_.Dept}} |
>> new-aduser
>>
```

The syntax might be a bit ugly, but the technique is incredibly powerful. It's also usable in many other places in PowerShell, and you'll see it again in upcoming chapters. You'll even see it in the examples contained in PowerShell's help files; run `Help Select -Example` and look for yourself.

## 10.6   *Working with Azure PowerShell*

We are going to assume that you have an Azure PowerShell setup for the rest of this chapter. So, let's get that working. If you don't have a subscription, you can sign up for a trial here: https://azure.microsoft.com/en-us/free/. If this link is out of date, search for Azure Free trial.

Once you have your subscription, make sure you have the Az module installed. Review chapter 7, but the command is

```
Install-Module az
```

Now that you have Az installed, run `Connect-AzAccount` and follow the instructions; currently, it has you open a browser and enter a code. It should tell you that you are connected, by printing your email, subscription name, and some other information.

If you have multiple subscriptions associated with the account, you may be connected to the wrong subscription. If so, then make sure you select the correct subscription. If your subscription name is Visual Studio Enterprise, the command would be `Select-AzSubscription -SubscriptionName 'Visual Studio Enterprise'`.

## 10.7   *Parenthetical commands*

Sometimes, no matter how hard you try, you can't make pipeline input work. For example, consider `Get-Command`. Look at the help for its `-Module` parameter, shown in figure 10.13.

Although this parameter accepts module names from the pipeline, it does it by property name. Sometimes the command might just not accept pipeline input. In this case, the method we've been discussing is easier. The following won't work:

```
Get-Content .\modules.txt | Get-Command
```

The `String` objects produced by `Get-Content` won't match the `-Module` parameter of `Get-Command`, but instead go to `-Name`. What can we do? Use parentheses:

```
PS /Users/tyler1> Get-Command -Module (Get-Content ./modules.txt)
```

Think back to high school algebra class, and you'll recall that parentheses mean "do this first." That's what PowerShell does: it runs the parenthetical command first. The results of that command—in this case, a bunch of `String` objects—are fed to the

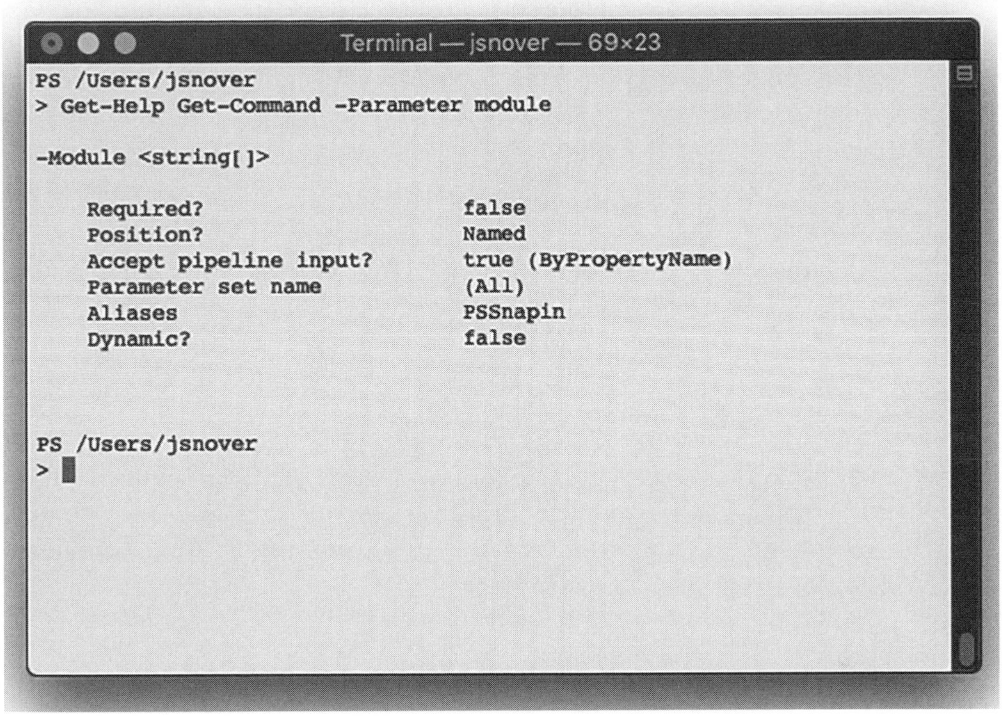

```
Terminal — jsnover — 69×23

PS /Users/jsnover
> Get-Help Get-Command -Parameter module

-Module <string[]>

    Required?                    false
    Position?                    Named
    Accept pipeline input?       true (ByPropertyName)
    Parameter set name           (All)
    Aliases                      PSSnapin
    Dynamic?                     false



PS /Users/jsnover
> ▮
```

**Figure 10.13   Reading the `Module` parameter help for `Get-Command`**

parameter. Because `-Module` happens to want a bunch of `String` objects, the command works.

> **TRY IT NOW**   Get a few module names using `Get-Module -ListAvailable` for testing this; then go ahead and try that command. Put the correct module names into your own modules.txt file.

The parenthetical command trick is powerful because it doesn't rely on pipeline parameter binding at all—it takes objects and sticks them right into the parameter. But the technique doesn't work if your parenthetical command isn't generating the exact type of object that the parameter expects, so sometimes you'll have to manipulate things a bit. Let's look at how.

## 10.8  *Extracting the value from a single property*

In section 10.7, we showed you an example of using parentheses to execute `Get-Content`, feeding its output to the parameter of another cmdlet:

```
Get-Command -Module (Get-Content ./modules.txt)
```

Let's explore another use of parentheses. There is a command to create a storage account called `New-AzStorageAccount`. Let's say you want to create a storage account and put it in a resource group that already exists in the Azure location. Rather than getting your resource group names from an existing text file, you might want to query the existing resource group names from Azure. With the Az.Storage module (which is included in the Az module we installed in section 10.6), you could query all of your resource groups in a location:

```
Get-AzResourceGroup -Location westus2
```

Could you use the same parentheses trick to feed resource group names to `New-AzStorageAccount`? For example, would the following work?

```
PS /Users/tyler1> New-AzStorageAccount -ResourceGroupName
  (Get-AzResourceGroup -Location westus2| Select-Object -First 1)
  -Name test0719 -SkuName Standard_ZRS -Location westus2
```

Sadly, it won't. Look at the help for `New-AzStorageAccount`, and you'll see that the `-ResourceGroupName` parameter expects `String` values. Note, `Select-Object -First 1` was added to get only the first resource group, as `-ResourceGroupName` takes only one string, not an array of strings.

Run this instead:

```
Get-AzResourceGroup | Get-Member
```

`Get-Member` reveals that `Get-AzResourceGroup` is producing objects of the type `PSResourceGroup`. Those aren't `String` objects, so `-ResourceGroupName` won't know what to do with them. But the `PSResourceGroup` objects do have a `ResourceGroupName` property. What you need to do is extract the values of the objects' `ResourceGroupName` properties and feed those values, which are resource group names, to the `-ResourceGroupName` parameter.

> **TIP**  This is an important fact about PowerShell, and if you're a bit lost right now, *stop* and reread the preceding paragraphs. `Get-AzResourceGroup` produces objects of the type `PSResourceGroup`; `Get-Member` proves it. The `-ResourceGroupName` parameter of `New-AzStorageAccount` can't accept a `PSResourceGroup` object; it accepts only `String` objects, as shown in its help file. Therefore, that parenthetical command won't work as written.

Once again, the `Select-Object` cmdlet can rescue you, because it includes the `-ExpandProperty` parameter, which accepts a property name. The cmdlet takes that property, extracts its values, and returns those values as the output of `Select-Object`. Consider this example:

```
Get-AzResourceGroup -Location westus2 | Select-Object -First 1
  -ExpandProperty ResourceGroupName
```

You should get a single resource group name. It can be fed to the -ResourceGroup-Name parameter of New-AzStorageAccount (or any other cmdlet that has a -ResourceGroupName parameter):

```
New-AzStorageAccount -ResourceGroupName (Get-AzResourceGroup -Location
➥ westus2 | Select-Object -First 1 -ExpandProperty ResourceGroupName)
➥ -Name downloads -SkuName Standard_LRS -Location westus2
```

> **TIP** Once again, this is an important concept. Normally, a command like Select-Object -Property Name produces objects that happen to have only the Name property, because that's all we specified. The -ComputerName parameter doesn't want some random object that has a Name property; it wants a String, which is a much simpler value. -ExpandProperty Name goes into the Name property and extracts its values, resulting in simple strings being returned from the command.

Again, this is a cool trick that makes it possible to combine an even wider variety of commands with each other, saving you typing and making PowerShell do more of the work.

Before we move on, let's cover -Property on Select-Object. Try changing the command in the parenthesis to

```
Get-AzResourceGroup -Location westus2 | Select-Object -First 1
➥ -Property ResourceGroupName
```

Now pipe it to Get-Member. It's still a PSResourceGroup. PowerShell creates a new custom object with just the properties you selected. So, -ResourceGroupName on New-AzStorageAccount still won't take this object. Let's see how PowerShell does this. Run the following:

```
(Get-AzResourceGroup -Location westus2 | Select-Object -First 1
➥ -Property ResourceGroupName).GetType().Name
```

The output is PSCustomObject. This is a wrapper type PowerShell uses to expose the properties you selected.

Let's go over what we learned. This is a powerful technique. It can be a little hard to grasp at first, but understanding that a property is kind of like a box can help. With Select-Object -Property, you're deciding what boxes you want, but you still have boxes. With Select-Object -ExpandProperty, you're extracting the contents of the box and getting rid of the box entirely. You're left with the contents.

## 10.9 *Lab*

Once again, we've covered a lot of important concepts in a short amount of time. The best way to cement your new knowledge is to put it to immediate use. We recommend doing the following tasks in order, because they build on each other to help remind you what you've learned and to help you find practical ways to use that knowledge.

To make this a bit trickier, we're going to force you to consider how to use the Az.Accounts module (which is included in the Az module we installed in section 10.6). This should work on any macOS or Ubuntu machine:

- The `Get-AzSubscription` command has the `-SubscriptionName` parameter; running `Get-AzSubscription -SubscriptionName MySubscriptionName` retrieves the subscription with the name `MySubscriptionName` from your account.
- The `Selecet-AZSubscription` command has the `-Subscription` parameter; running `Select-AzSubscription -Subscription MySubscriptionName` sets the subscription in the context that most commands in the Az.* module use to determine the subscription to use.
- The `Get-AzContext` command can be used to determine which subscription is selected.

That's all you need to know. With that in mind, complete the following tasks.

> **NOTE** You're not being asked to run these commands. This is more of a mental exercise. Instead, you're being asked whether these commands will function and why.

1  Would the following command work to retrieve a list of commands from modules that start with Microsoft.* on the current machine? Why or why not? Write an explanation, similar to the ones we provided earlier in this chapter.

```
Get-Command -Module (Get-Module -ListAvailable -Name Microsoft.* |
Select-Object -ExpandProperty name)
```

2  Would this alternative command work to retrieve the list of commands from the same modules? Why or why not? Write an explanation, similar to the ones we provided earlier in this chapter.

```
Get-Module -ListAvailable -Name Microsoft.* | Get-Command
```

3  Would this set the subscription in the Azure context? Consider if `Get-AzSubcription` retrieves multiple subscriptions.

```
Get-AzSubscription | Select-AzSubscription
```

4  Write a command that uses pipeline parameter binding to retrieve the first subscription and set that in the Azure context. Don't use parentheses.

5  Write a command that uses pipeline parameter binding to retrieve the first subscription and set that in the Azure context. Don't use pipeline input; instead, use a parenthetical command (a command in parentheses).

6  Sometimes someone forgets to add a pipeline parameter binding to a cmdlet. For example, would the following command work to set the subscription in the

Azure context? Write an explanation, similar to the ones we provided earlier in this chapter.

```
'mySubscriptionName' | Select-AzSubscription
```

## 10.10 *Lab answers*

1. This should work, because the nested `Get-Module` expression will return a collection of module names, and the `-Module` parameter can accept an array of values.

2. This won't work, because `Get-Command` doesn't accept the module parameter by value. It will accept `-Name` by value, but this is the command name, not the module object.

3. Technically this does set the subscription, but if there are multiple accounts, whichever one is processed last is the one set. It works because the first cmdlet returns a `PSAzureSubscription`, and `Select-AzSubscription` has `-SubscriptionObject`, which accepts that type from the pipeline `ByValue`.

4. `Get-AzSubscription | Select-Object -First 1 | Select-AzSubscription`

5. `Select-AzSubscription -SubscriptionObject (Get-AzSubscription | Select-Object -First 1)`

6. This will not work. The `Subscription` parameter in `Select-AzSubscription` doesn't take any pipeline binding.

## 10.11 *Further exploration*

We find that many students have difficulty embracing this pipeline-input concept, mainly because it's so abstract. Unfortunately, this stuff is also crucial to understanding the shell. Reread this chapter if you need to, rerun the example commands we've provided, and look super carefully at the output to understand how the pipeline is working. For example, why is this command's output

```
Get-Date | Select -Property DayOfWeek
```

slightly different from the following command's output?

```
Get-Date | Select -ExpandProperty DayOfWeek
```

If you're still not sure, drop us a line in the forums on https://livebook.manning.com/book/learn-powershell-in-a-month-of-lunches-linux-and-macos-edition/discussion.

# Formatting: And why it's done on the right

Let's quickly review. You know that PowerShell cmdlets produce objects and that those objects often contain more properties than PowerShell shows by default. You know how to use `gm` to get a list of all of an object's properties, and you know how to use `Select-Object` to specify the properties you want to see. Up to this point in the book, you've relied on PowerShell's default configuration and rules to determine how the final output will appear on the screen (or in a file, or in hard-copy form). In this chapter, you'll learn to override those defaults and create your own formatting for your commands' output.

## 11.1 Formatting: Making what you see prettier

We don't want to give the impression that PowerShell is a full-fledged management-reporting tool, because it isn't. But PowerShell has good capabilities for collecting information, and, with the right output, you can certainly produce reports using that information. The trick is getting the right output, and that's what formatting is all about.

On the surface, PowerShell's formatting system can seem easy to use—and for the most part that's true. But the formatting system also contains some of the trickiest "gotchas" in the entire shell, so we want to make sure you understand how it works and why it does what it does. We're not just going to show you a few new commands here; rather, we'll explain how the entire system works, how you can interact with it, and what limitations you might run into.

## 11.2 Working with the default formatting

Run our old friend `Get-Process` again, and pay special attention to the column headers. Notice that they don't exactly match the property names. Instead, each header has a specific width, alignment, and so forth. All that configuration stuff has to come from someplace, right? You'll find it in one of the .format.ps1xml files that install with PowerShell. Specifically, formatting directions for process objects are in DotNetTypes.format.ps1xml.

> **TRY IT NOW**  You definitely want to have PowerShell open so that you can follow along with what we're about to show you. This will help you understand what the formatting system is up to under the hood.

We'll begin by changing to the PowerShell installation folder, specifically, where PSReadLine is, and opening PSReadLine.format.ps1xml. PSReadLine is a PowerShell module that provides the experience when you type in a PowerShell console. It adds a bunch of fancy keyboard shortcuts and syntax highlighting, and is customizable. Be careful not to save any changes to this file. It's digitally signed, and any changes that you save—even a single carriage return or space added to the file—will break the signature and prevent PowerShell from using the file.

```
PS /Users/jamesp/> cd $pshome/Modules/PSReadLine
PS /Users/jamesp/> code PSReadLine.format.ps1xml
```

> **TIP**  You might get a warning code: The term 'code' is not recognized as a name of a cmdlet, function, script file, or executable program. To fix this, open the command palette and run the following shell command: Shell Command: Install 'code' command in PATH.

Next, find out the exact type of object returned by Get-PSReadLineKeyHandler:

```
PS /Users/jamesp/> Get-PSReadLineKeyHandler | get-member
```

Now, follow these steps:

1  Copy and paste the complete type name, Microsoft.PowerShell.KeyHandler, to the clipboard.
2  Switch over to Visual Studio Code and press Cmd-F (or Ctrl-F on Windows) to open the Search dialog.
3  In the Search dialog, paste in the type name you copied to the clipboard. Press Enter.
4  You should see Microsoft.PowerShell.KeyHandler in the file. Figure 11.1 shows what you should find.

What you're now looking at in Visual Studio Code is the set of directions that govern how a key handler is displayed by default. Scroll down, and you'll see the definition for a *table view*, which you should expect because you already know that key handlers display in a multicolumn table. You'll see the familiar column names, and if you scroll down a bit more, you'll see where the file specifies which property will display in each column. You'll see definitions for column widths and alignments too. When you're

```
C: › Program Files › PowerShell › 7 › Modules › PSReadLine ›  ☰ PSReadLine.format.ps1xml
  1   <Configuration>
  2     <ViewDefinitions>
  3       <View>
  4         <Name>PSReadLine-KeyBindings</Name>
  5         <ViewSelectedBy>
  6           <TypeName>Microsoft.PowerShell.KeyHandler</TypeName>
  7         </ViewSelectedBy>
  8         <GroupBy>
  9           <PropertyName>Group</PropertyName>
 10           <CustomControl>
 11             <CustomEntries>
 12               <CustomEntry>
 13                 <CustomItem>
 14                   <ExpressionBinding>
 15                     <ScriptBlock>
 16   $d = [Microsoft.PowerShell.KeyHandler]::GetGroupingDescription($_.Group)
 17   "{0}`n{1}" -f $d,('='*$d.Length)
 18   </ScriptBlock>
 19                   </ExpressionBinding>
 20                 </CustomItem>
 21               </CustomEntry>
 22             </CustomEntries>
 23           </CustomControl>
 24         </GroupBy>
 25         <TableControl>
 26           <TableHeaders>
 27             <TableColumnHeader>
 28               <Label>Key</Label>
 29             </TableColumnHeader>
 30             <TableColumnHeader>
 31               <Label>Function</Label>
 32             </TableColumnHeader>
 33             <TableColumnHeader>
```

**The KeyHandler type we care about and its view definition**

**Figure 11.1   Locating the key handler view in Visual Studio Code**

finished browsing, close Visual Studio Code, being careful not to save any changes that you may have accidentally made to the file, and go back to PowerShell.

> **TRY IT NOW**  You can also get this format data by running the following command. You can mess around with the object you get back, but we won't be focusing on it.

```
PS /Users/jamesp/> Get-FormatData -PowerShellVersion 7.1 -TypeName
➥ Microsoft.PowerShell.KeyHandler
```

When you run Get-PSReadLineKeyHandler, here's what happens in the shell:

1  The cmdlet places objects of the type Microsoft.PowerShell.KeyHandler into the pipeline.
2  At the end of the pipeline is an invisible cmdlet called Out-Default. It's always there, and its job is to pick up whatever objects are in the pipeline after all of your commands have run.

**3**  Out-Default passes the objects to Out-Host, because the PowerShell console is designed to use the screen (called the *host*) as its default form of output. In theory, someone could write a shell that uses files or printers as the default output instead, but nobody has (that we know of).

**4**  Most of the Out- cmdlets are incapable of working with standard objects. Instead, they're designed to work with special formatting instructions. So, when Out-Host sees that it has been handed standard objects, it passes them to the formatting system.

**5**  The formatting system looks at the type of the object and follows an internal set of formatting rules (we'll cover those in a moment). It uses those rules to produce formatting instructions, which are passed back to Out-Host.

**6**  Once Out-Host sees that it has formatting instructions, it follows those instructions to construct the onscreen display.

All of this happens whenever you manually specify an Out- cmdlet too. For example, run Get-Process | Out-File procs.txt, and Out-File will see that you've sent it some normal objects. It will pass those to the formatting system, which creates formatting instructions and passes them back to Out-File. Out-File then constructs the text file based on those instructions. So the formatting system becomes involved anytime objects need to be converted into human-readable textual output.

What rules does the formatting system follow in step 5? For the first formatting rule, the system looks to see whether the type of object it's dealing with has a predefined view. That's what you saw in PSReadLine.format.ps1xml: a predefined view for a KeyHandler object. A few other .format.ps1xml files are installed with PowerShell, and they're all loaded by default when the shell starts. You can create your own predefined views as well, although doing so is beyond the scope of this book.

The formatting system looks for predefined views that specifically target the object type it's dealing with. In this case, it's looking for the view that handles Microsoft .PowerShell.KeyHandler objects.

What if there's no predefined view? Let's find out using the System.Uri type, which doesn't have an entry in a format.ps1xml file (we promise!). Try running this:

```
[Uri]"https://github.com"
```

This is using a concept called "casting," where we say, "Hey, PowerShell, I've got this string that looks like a URI. Can you just treat it like the type System.Uri?" And PowerShell replies, "You got it!" and gives you a Uri object. You might notice we didn't have to specify System in the line that we ran. That's because PowerShell tacks on System to the front if it can't find a type just called Uri. Clever PowerShell! Anyway, the output of that is a long list of properties like so:

```
AbsolutePath   : /
AbsoluteUri    : https://github.com/
LocalPath      : /
Authority      : github.com
```

```
HostNameType    : Dns
IsDefaultPort   : True
IsFile          : False
IsLoopback      : False
PathAndQuery    : /
Segments        : {/}
IsUnc           : False
Host            : github.com
Port            : 443
Query           :
Fragment        :
Scheme          : https
OriginalString  : https://github.com
DnsSafeHost     : github.com
IdnHost         : github.com
IsAbsoluteUri   : True
UserEscaped     : False
UserInfo        :
```

The formatting is not too bad for something that doesn't have any special formatting. That's because PowerShell will look at the properties of the type and show them in a friendly view. We can control which properties we see here by introducing a format .ps1xml for this type, or we can allow the formatting system to take its next step, or what we call the *second formatting rule*: It looks to see whether anyone has declared a default display property set for that type of object. You'll find those in a different configuration file, types.ps1xml. Since we're not going to dive deep into writing our own format and types files, we're going to give you one to load in, and we'll just see how it affects the output. First, let's create and open up a new file called Uri.Types.ps1xml file in Visual Studio Code:

```
PS /Users/jamesp/> code /tmp/Uri.Types.ps1xml
```

Now, paste in the following content and save the file:

```xml
<?xml version="1.0" encoding="utf-8" ?>
<Types>
  <Type>
    <Name>System.Uri</Name>
    <Members>
      <MemberSet>
        <Name>PSStandardMembers</Name>
        <Members>
          <PropertySet>
            <Name>DefaultDisplayPropertySet</Name>
            <ReferencedProperties>
              <Name>Scheme</Name>
              <Name>Host</Name>
              <Name>Port</Name>
              <Name>AbsoluteUri</Name>
              <Name>IsFile</Name>
            </ReferencedProperties>
          </PropertySet>
        </Members>
```

```
        </Members>
      </MemberSet>
    </Members>
  </Type>
</Types>
```

Excellent, now, see the `DefaultDisplayPropertySet`? Make a note of the five properties listed there. Then go back to PowerShell and run this:

```
PS /Users/jamesp/> Update-TypeData -Path /tmp/Uri.Types.ps1xml
```

We've just loaded that Types.ps1xml file we just created. Now let's run the original line again and see what it gets us:

```
PS /Users/jamesp/> [Uri]"https://github.com"

Scheme      : https
Host        : github.com
Port        : 443
AbsoluteUri : https://github.com/
IsFile      : False
```

Do the results look familiar? They should—the properties you see are there solely because they're listed as defaults in Types.ps1xml. If the formatting system finds a default display property set, it'll use that set of properties for its next decision. If it doesn't find one, the next decision will consider all of the object's properties.

That next decision—the *third formatting rule*—is about the kind of output to create. If the formatting system displays four or fewer properties, it uses a table. If there are five or more properties, it uses a list. That's why the `System.Uri` object wasn't displayed as a table: its five properties trigger a list. The theory is that more than four properties might not fit well into an ad hoc table without truncating information.

Now you know how the default formatting works. You also know that most `Out-` cmdlets automatically trigger the formatting system so that they can get the formatting instructions they need. Next let's look at how to control that formatting system ourselves and override the defaults.

Oh, and by the way, the formatting system is why PowerShell sometimes seems to "lie." For example, run `Get-Process` and look at the column headers. See the one labeled `PM(K)`? Well that's a lie, sort of, because there's no property called `PM(K)`. There's a property called `PM`. The lesson here is that formatted column headers are just that—column headers. They aren't necessarily the same as the underlying property names. The only safe way to see property names is to use `Get-Member`.

## 11.3  *Formatting tables*

PowerShell has four formatting cmdlets, and we'll work with the three that provide the most day-to-day formatting capability (the fourth is briefly discussed in an "Above and beyond" sidebar near the end of this chapter). First up is `Format-Table`, which has an alias, `ft`.

If you read the help file for `Format-Table`, you'll notice that it has several parameters. These are some of the most useful ones, along with examples of how to use them:

- `-Property`—This parameter accepts a comma-separated list of properties that should be included in the table. These properties aren't case sensitive, but the shell will use whatever you type as the column headers, so you can get nicer-looking output by properly casing the property names (e.g., *CPU* instead of *cpu*). This parameter accepts wildcards, meaning you can specify * to include all properties in the table, or something like `c*` to include all properties starting with *c*. Notice that the shell will still display only the properties it can fit in the table, so not every property you specify may display. This parameter is positional, so you don't have to type the parameter name, provided the property list is in the first position. Try these examples (the second example from the help file for `Format-Table` is shown here):

```
Get-Process | Format-Table -Property *
Get-Process | Format-Table -Property ID,Name,Responding
Get-Process | Format-Table *
   Id Name             Responding
   -- ----             ----------
20921 XprotectService     True
 1242 WiFiVelocityAge     True
  434 WiFiAgent           True
89048 VTDecoderXPCSer     True
27019 VTDecoderXPCSer     True
  506 ViewBridgeAuxil     True
  428 usernoted           True
  407 UserEventAgent      True
  544 useractivityd       True
  710 USBAgent            True
 1244 UsageTrackingAg     True
  416 universalaccess     True
  468 TrustedPeersHel     True
  412 trustd              True
24703 transparencyd       True
 1264 TextInputMenuAg     True
38115 Telegram            True
  425 tccd                True
  504 talagent            True
 1219 SystemUIServer      True
```

- `-GroupBy`—This parameter generates a new set of column headers each time the specified property value changes. This works well only when you've first sorted the objects on that same property. An example is the best way to show how this works (this one will group Azure VMs based on whether they are running or stopped):

```
PS /Users/jamesp/> Get-AzVM -Status | Sort-Object PowerState |
➥ ft -Property Name,Location,ResourceGroupName -GroupBy PowerState

   PowerState: VM running
```

```
Name         Location  ResourceGroupName
----         --------  -----------------
MyUbuntuVM   eastus2   MYUBUNTUVM


    PowerState: VM deallocated
Name          Location  ResourceGroupName
----          --------  -----------------
MyUbuntuVM2   eastus2   MYUBUNTUVM
WinTestVM2    westus2   WINTESTVM2
```

- `-Wrap`—If the shell has to truncate information in a column, it'll end that column with ellipses (. . .) to visually indicate that information was suppressed. This parameter enables the shell to wrap information, which makes the table longer but preserves all the information you want to display. Here's an example:

```
PS /Users/jamesp/> Get-Command | Select-Object Name,Source | ft -Wrap

Name                              Source
----                              ------
Compress-Archive                  Microsoft.P
                                  owerShell.A
                                  rchive
Configuration                     PSDesiredSt
                                  ateConfigur
                                  ation
Expand-Archive                    Microsoft.P
                                  owerShell.A
                                  rchive
Expand-GitCommand                 posh-git
Find-Command                      PowerShellG
                                  et
Find-DscResource                  PowerShellG
                                  et
Find-Module                       PowerShellG
                                  et
Find-RoleCapability               PowerShellG
                                  et
```

**TRY IT NOW** You should run through all of these examples in the shell, and feel free to mix and match these techniques. Experiment to see what works and what sort of output you can create. These commands will only work if you have already connected to an Azure account and if you have existing virtual machines in Azure.

## 11.4 Formatting lists

Sometimes you need to display more information than will fit horizontally in a table, which can make a list useful. `Format-List` is the cmdlet you'll turn to, or you can use its alias, `fl`.

This cmdlet supports some of the same parameters as `Format-Table`, including `-Property`. In fact, `fl` is another way of displaying the properties of an object. Unlike gm, fl will also display the values for those properties so that you can see what kind of information each property contains:

```
Get-Verb | Fl *
...
Verb        : Remove
AliasPrefix : r
Group       : Common
Description : Deletes a resource from a container

Verb        : Rename
AliasPrefix : rn
Group       : Common
Description : Changes the name of a resource

Verb        : Reset
AliasPrefix : rs
Group       : Common
Description : Sets a resource back to its original state

Verb        : Resize
AliasPrefix : rz
Group       : Common
Description : Changes the size of a resource

Verb        : Search
AliasPrefix : sr
Group       : Common
Description : Creates a reference to a resource in a container

Verb        : Select
AliasPrefix : sc
Group       : Common
Description : Locates a resource in a container
...
```

We often use fl as an alternative way of discovering the properties of an object.

**TRY IT NOW**   Read the help for Format-List, and try experimenting with its parameters.

## 11.5   *Formatting wide lists*

The last cmdlet, Format-Wide (or its alias, fw), displays a wider, multicolumn list. It's able to display only the values of a single property, so its -Property parameter accepts only one property name, not a list, and it can't accept wildcards.

By default, Format-Wide looks for an object's Name property, because Name is a commonly used property and usually contains useful information. The display generally defaults to two columns, but a -Columns parameter can be used to specify more columns:

```
Get-Process | Format-Wide name -col 4

iTerm2         java          keyboardserv... Keychain Ci...
knowledge-ag... LastPass      LocationMenu   lockoutagent
```

```
loginwindow    lsd          Magnet        mapspushd
mdworker       mdworker_sha... mdworker_sha... mdworker_sh...
mdworker_sha... mdworker_sha... mdworker_sha... mdworker_sh...
mdworker_sha... mdworker_sha... mdworker_sha... mdwrite
media-indexer mediaremotea... Microsoft Ed... Microsoft E...
Microsoft Ed... Microsoft Ed... Microsoft Ed... Microsoft E...
Microsoft Ed... Microsoft Ed... Microsoft Ed... Microsoft E...
```

**TRY IT NOW**  Read the help for `Format-Wide`, and try experimenting with its parameters.

## 11.6   *Creating custom columns and list entries*

Flip back to the previous chapter and review section 10.5. In that section, we showed you how to use a hash table construct to add custom properties to an object. Both `Format-Table` and `Format-List` can use those same constructs to create custom table columns or custom list entries.

   You might do this to provide a column header that's different from the property name being displayed:

```
Get-AzStorageAccount | Format-Table @{name='Name';expression=
  {$_.StorageAccountName}},Location,ResourceGroupName
```

```
Name                       Location        ResourceGroupName
----                       --------        -----------------
myubuntuvmdiag             eastus2         MyUbuntuVM
ismtrainierout             westus          ismtrainierout
cs461353efc2db7x45cbxa2d westus            cloud-shell-storage...
mtnbotbmyhfk               westus          mtnbot
pssafuncapp                westus          pssafuncapp
```

**NOTE**  This will only work if an Azure connection and storage account already exists.

Or, you might put a more complex mathematical expression in place:

```
Get-Process | Format-Table Name, @{name='VM(MB)';expression={$_.VM / 1MB
➥ -as [int]}}
```

We admit, we're cheating a little bit by throwing in a bunch of stuff that we haven't talked about yet. We might as well talk about it now:

- Obviously, we're starting with `Get-Process`, a cmdlet you're more than familiar with by now. If you run `Get-Process | fl *`, you'll see that the VM property is in bytes, although that's not how the default table view displays it.
- We're telling `Format-Table` to start with the process's Name property.
- Next we're using a special hash table to create a custom column that will be labeled VM(MB). That's the first part up to the semicolon, which is a separator. The second part defines the value, or expression, for that column by taking the object's normal VM property and dividing it by 1 MB. The slash is PowerShell's

division operator, and PowerShell recognizes the shortcuts KB, MB, GB, TB, and PB as denoting kilobyte, megabyte, gigabyte, terabyte, and petabyte, respectively.

- The result of that division operation will have a decimal component that we don't want to see. The -as operator enables us to change the data type of that result from a floating-point value to, in this case, an integer value (specified by [int]). The shell will round up or down, as appropriate, when making that conversion. The result is a whole number with no fractional component:

```
Name              VM(MB)
----              ------
USBAgent            4206
useractivityd       4236
UserEventAgent      4235
usernoted           4242
ViewBridgeAuxil     4233
VTDecoderXPCSer     4234
VTDecoderXPCSer     4234
WiFiAgent           4255
WiFiVelocityAge     4232
XprotectService     4244
```

We show you this little division-and-changing trick because it can be useful in creating nicer-looking output. We won't spend much more time in this book on these operations (although we'll tell you that * is used for multiplication, and as you might expect, + and - are for addition and subtraction, respectively).

---

**Above and beyond**

Try repeating this example:

```
Get-Process |
Format-Table Name,
@{name='VM(MB)';expression={$_.VM / 1MB -as [int]}} -AutoSize
```

But this time don't type it all on one line. Type it exactly as it's shown here in the book, on three lines total. You'll notice after typing the first line, which ends with a pipe character, that PowerShell changes its prompt. That's because you ended the shell in a pipe, and the shell knows that more commands are coming. It will enter this same "waiting for you to finish" mode if you press Enter without properly closing all curly brackets, braces, quotation marks, and parentheses.

If you didn't mean to enter that extended-typing mode, press Ctrl-C to abort, and start over. In this case, you could type the second line of text and press Enter, and then type the third line and press Enter. In this mode, you'll have to press Enter one last time, on a blank line, to tell the shell you're finished. When you do so, it will execute the command as if it had been typed on a single, continuous line.

Unlike `Select-Object`, whose hash tables can accept only a `Name` and `Expression` key (although they'll also accept N, L, and `Label` for `Name`, and will accept E for `Expression`), the `Format-` commands can handle additional keys that are intended to control the visual display. These additional keys are most useful with `Format-Table`:

- `FormatString` specifies a formatting code, causing the data to be displayed according to the specified format. This is mainly useful with numeric and date data. Go to the documentation on formatting types at http://mng.bz/XWyl to review the available codes for standard numeric and date formatting and for custom numeric and date formatting.
- `Width` specifies the desired column width.
- `Alignment` specifies the desired column alignment, either `Left` or `Right`.

Using those additional keys makes it easier to achieve the previous example's results, and even to improve them:

```
Get-Process |
➡ Format-Table Name,
➡ @{name='VM(MB)';expression={$_.VM};formatstring='F2';align='right'}
➡ -AutoSize
```

Now we don't have to do the division, because PowerShell will format the number as a fixed-point value having two decimal places, and it will right-align the result.

## 11.7 Going out: To a file or to the host

Once something is formatted, you have to decide where it'll go. If a command line ends in a `Format-` cmdlet, the formatting instructions created by the `Format-` cmdlet go to `Out-Default`, which forwards them to `Out-Host`, which displays them on the screen:

```
Get-ChildItem | Format-Wide
```

You could also manually pipe the formatting instructions to `Out-Host`, which accomplishes exactly the same thing:

```
Get-ChildItem | Format-Wide | Out-Host
```

Alternatively, you can pipe formatting instructions to `Out-File` to direct formatted output to a file. As you'll read in section 11.9, only one of those two `Out-` cmdlets should ever follow a `Format-` cmdlet on the command line.

Keep in mind that `Out-File` defaults to a specific character width for output, which means a text file might look different from an onscreen display. The cmdlet has a `-Width` parameter that enables you to change the output width, if desired, to accommodate wider tables.

## 11.8   Another out: GridViews

In the old days of Windows PowerShell, there was a cmdlet that was included called `Out-GridView`, which provides another useful form of output—a graphical user interface (GUI). For PowerShell 6+, a cross-platform version of this cmdlet was created, but it exists in the PowerShell Gallery in the form of a module. You can install this cmdlet by running

```
Install-Module Microsoft.PowerShell.GraphicalTools
```

Note that `Out-GridView` isn't technically formatting; in fact, `Out-GridView` entirely bypasses the formatting subsystem. No `Format-` cmdlets are called, no formatting instructions are produced, and no text output is displayed in the console window. `Out-GridView` can't receive the output of a `Format-` cmdlet—it can receive only the regular objects output by other cmdlets.

Figure 11.2 shows what happens when we run the command `Get-Process | Out-GridView`.

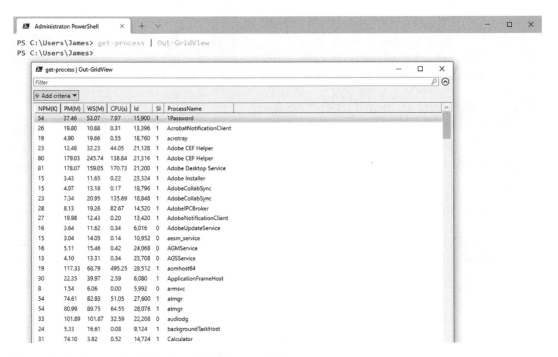

Figure 11.2   The results of the `Out-GridView` cmdlet

## 11.9   Common points of confusion

As we mentioned at the start of this chapter, the formatting system has most of the gotchas that trip up PowerShell newcomers. They tend to run across two issues, so we'll try to help you avoid them.

### 11.9.1 *Always format right*

It's incredibly important that you remember one rule from this chapter: *format right*. Your Format- cmdlet should be the last thing on the command line, with Out-File as the only exception. The reason for this rule is that the Format- cmdlets produce formatting instructions, and only an Out- cmdlet can properly consume those instructions. If a Format- cmdlet is last on the command line, the instructions will go to Out-Default (which is always at the end of the pipeline), which will forward them to Out-Host, which is happy to work with formatting instructions. Try running this command to illustrate the need for this rule:

```
Get-History | Format-Table | gm

   TypeName: Microsoft.PowerShell.Commands.Internal.Format.FormatStartData
Name                                      MemberType Definition
----                                      ---------- ----------
Equals                                    Method     bool Equals(System.Object
                                                     ↦ obj)
GetHashCode                               Method     int GetHashCode()
GetType                                   Method     type GetType()
ToString                                  Method     string ToString()
autosizeInfo                              Property
    Microsoft.PowerShell.Commands.Internal.Format.AutosizeInfo,
    ↦ System.Management.Automation, Version=7.0.0.0,...
ClassId2e4f51ef21dd47e99d3c952918aff9cd Property    string
↦ ClassId2e4f51ef21dd47e99d3c952918aff9cd {get;}
groupingEntry                             Property
    Microsoft.PowerShell.Commands.Internal.Format.GroupingEntry,
    ↦ System.Management.Automation, Version=7.0.0.0...
pageFooterEntry                           Property
    Microsoft.PowerShell.Commands.Internal.Format.PageFooterEntry,
    ↦ System.Management.Automation, Version=7.0.0...
pageHeaderEntry                           Property
    Microsoft.PowerShell.Commands.Internal.Format.PageHeaderEntry,
    ↦ System.Management.Automation, Version=7.0.0...
shapeInfo                                 Property
    Microsoft.PowerShell.Commands.Internal.Format.ShapeInfo,
    ↦ System.Management.Automation, Version=7.0.0.0, Cu...

   TypeName: Microsoft.PowerShell.Commands.Internal.Format.GroupStartData
Name                                      MemberType Definition
----                                      ---------- ----------
Equals                                    Method     bool Equals(System.Object
                                                     ↦ obj)
GetHashCode                               Method     int GetHashCode()
GetType                                   Method     type GetType()
ToString                                  Method     string ToString()
ClassId2e4f51ef21dd47e99d3c952918aff9cd Property    string
    ClassId2e4f51ef21dd47e99d3c952918aff9cd {get;}
groupingEntry                             Property
    Microsoft.PowerShell.Commands.Internal.Format.GroupingEntry,
    ↦ System.Management.Automation, Version=7.0.0.0...
```

```
shapeInfo                              Property
➥ Microsoft.PowerShell.Commands.Internal.Format.ShapeInfo,
➥ System.Management.Automation, Version=7.0.0.0, Cu...
```

You'll notice that gm isn't displaying information about your history objects because the `Format-Table` cmdlet doesn't output history objects. It consumes the history objects you pipe in, and it outputs formatting instructions—which is what gm sees and reports on. Now try this:

```
Get-History | Select-Object Id,Duration,CommandLine | Format-Table |
ConvertTo-Html | Out-File history.html
```

Go ahead and open history.html in a browser, and you'll see some crazy results. You didn't pipe history objects to `ConvertTo-Html`; you piped formatting instructions, so that's what got converted to HTML. This illustrates why a `Format-` cmdlet, if you use one, has to be either the last thing on the command line or the second-to-last, with the last cmdlet being `Out-File`.

Also know that `Out-GridView` is unusual (for an `Out-` cmdlet, at least), in that it *won't* accept formatting instructions and *will* accept only standard objects. Try these two commands to see the difference:

```
PS C:\>Get-Process | Out-GridView
PS C:\>Get-Process | Format-Table | Out-GridView
```

That's why we explicitly mentioned `Out-File` as the only cmdlet that should follow a `Format-` cmdlet (technically, `Out-Host` can also follow a `Format-` cmdlet, but there's no need because ending the command line with the `Format-` cmdlet will get the output to `Out-Host` anyway).

### 11.9.2 *One type of object at a time, please*

The next thing to avoid is putting multiple kinds of objects into the pipeline. The formatting system looks at the first object in the pipeline and uses the type of that object to determine what formatting to produce. If the pipeline contains two or more kinds of objects, the output won't always be complete or useful.

For example, run this:

```
PS /Users/jamesp/> Get-Process; Get-History

NPM(K)    PM(M)    WS(M)    CPU(s)      Id  SI ProcessName
------    -----    -----    ------      --  -- -----------
...
     0     0.00     1.74      0.25    1244   1 UsageTrackingAg
     0     0.00     0.68      0.19     710   1 USBAgent
     0     0.00     4.12      6.37     544   1 useractivityd
     0     0.00     5.44      8.00     407   1 UserEventAgent
     0     0.00     7.50      3.43     428   1 usernoted
     0     0.00     3.44      8.71     506   1 ViewBridgeAuxil
```

```
     0      0.00       5.91       0.08     27019 ...19 VTDecoderXPCSer
     0      0.00       5.92       0.07     89048 ...48 VTDecoderXPCSer
     0      0.00      10.79      50.02       434    1 WiFiAgent
     0      0.00       1.11       0.20      1242    1 WiFiVelocityAge
     0      0.00      10.28       4.30     20921 ...21 XprotectService
Id                 : 1
CommandLine        : Update-TypeData -Path /tmp/Uri.Types.ps1xml
ExecutionStatus    : Completed
StartExecutionTime : 9/21/2019 12:20:03 PM
EndExecutionTime   : 9/21/2019 12:20:03 PM
Duration           : 00:00:00.0688690

Id                 : 2
CommandLine        : Update-TypeData -Path /tmp/Uri.Types.ps1xml
ExecutionStatus    : Completed
StartExecutionTime : 9/21/2019 12:21:07 PM
EndExecutionTime   : 9/21/2019 12:21:07 PM
Duration           : 00:00:00.0125330eyp
```

That semicolon allows us to put two commands onto a single command line, without piping the output of the first cmdlet into the second one. This means both cmdlets run independently, but they put their output into the same pipeline. As you see, the output starts out fine, displaying process objects. But the output breaks down when it's time to display the history objects. Rather than producing the table you're used to, PowerShell reverts to a list. The formatting system isn't designed to take multiple kinds of objects and make the results look as attractive as possible.

What if you want to combine information drawn from two (or more) places into a single form of output? You absolutely can, and you can do so in a way that the formatting system can deal with nicely. But that's an advanced topic that we won't get to in this book.

---

**Above and beyond**

Technically, the formatting system *can* handle multiple types of objects—if you tell it how. Run Dir | gm, and you'll notice that the pipeline contains both DirectoryInfo and FileInfo objects (gm has no problem working with pipelines that contain multiple kinds of objects and will display member information for all of them.) When you run Dir by itself, the output is perfectly legible. That's because Microsoft provides a predefined custom formatting view for DirectoryInfo and FileInfo objects, and that view is handled by the Format-Custom cmdlet.

Format-Custom is mainly used to display various predefined custom views. You could technically create your own predefined custom views, but the necessary XML syntax is complicated and isn't publicly documented at this time, so custom views are limited to what Microsoft provides.

Microsoft's custom views do get a lot of usage, though. PowerShell's help information is stored as objects, for example, and the formatted help files you see on the screen are the result of feeding those objects into a custom view.

## 11.10 Lab

> **NOTE**   For this lab, you need any computer running PowerShell 7.1 or later.

See if you can complete the following tasks:

1  Display a table of processes that includes only the process names, IDs, and whether they're responding to Windows (the `Responding` property has that information). Have the table take up as little horizontal room as possible, but don't allow any information to be truncated.

2  Display a table of processes that includes the process names and IDs. Also include columns for virtual and physical memory usage, expressing those values in megabytes (MB).

3  Use `Get-Module` to get a list of loaded modules. Format the output as a table that includes, in this order, the module name and the version. The column headers must be `ModuleName` and `ModuleVersion`.

4  Use `Get-AzStorageAccount` and `Get-AzStorageContainer` to display *all* of your storage containers so that a separate table is displayed for storage containers that are accessible to the public and storage containers that are not. (Hint: Piping is your friend . . . use a `-GroupBy` parameter.)

5  Display a four-column-wide list of all directories in the home directory.

6  Create a formatted list of all .dll files in $pshome, displaying the name, version information, and file size. PowerShell uses the `Length` property, but to make it clearer, your output should show `Size`.

## 11.11 Lab answers

```
1  Get-Process | Format-Table Name,ID,Responding -Wrap
2  Get-Process | Format-Table Name,ID,
   @{l='VirtualMB';e={$_.vm/1MB}},
   @{l='PhysicalMB';e={$_.workingset/1MB}}
3  Get-Module| Format-Table @{l='ModuleName';e={$_.Name }},
   @{l='ModuleVersion';e={$_.Version}}
4  Get-AzStorageAccount | Get-AzStorageContainer | ft -GroupBy PublicAccess
5  gci ~ -Directory | format-wide –column 4
6  gci $pshome/*.dll |
   Format-List Name,VersionInfo,@{Name="Size";Expression={$_.length}}
```

## 11.12 Further exploration

This is the perfect time to experiment with the formatting system. Try using the three main `Format-` cmdlets to create different forms of output. The labs in upcoming chapters will often ask you to use specific formatting, so you might as well hone your skills with these cmdlets and start memorizing the more-often-used parameters covered in this chapter.

# Filtering
## and comparisons

Up to this point, you've been working with whatever output the shell gave you: all the processes, filesystem objects, and various Azure commands. But this type of output isn't always going to be what you want. Often you'll want to narrow down the results to a few items that specifically interest you, such as getting processes or files that match a pattern. That's what you'll learn to do in this chapter.

## 12.1 Making the shell give you just what you need

The shell offers two broad models for narrowing results, and they're both referred to as *filtering*. In the first model, you try to instruct the cmdlet that's retrieving information for you to retrieve only what you've specified. In the second model (discussed in section 12.5), which takes an iterative approach, you take everything the cmdlet gives you and use a second cmdlet to filter out the things you don't want.

Ideally, you'll use the first model, which we call *filter left*, as much as possible. It may be as simple as telling the cmdlet what you're after. For example, with Get-Process, you can tell it which process names you want:

```
Get-Process -Name p*,*s*
```

But if you want Get-Process to return only the processes with more than 1 GB of memory, regardless of their names, you can't tell the cmdlet to do that for you, because it doesn't offer any parameters to specify that information.

Similarly, if you're using the Get-ChildItem, it includes the -Path parameter, which supports wildcards. Although you could get all files and filter using Where-Object, we don't recommend it. Once again, this technique is ideal because the cmdlet has to retrieve only matching objects. We call this the *filter left*, sometimes referred to as *early filtering*, technique.

## 12.2   *Filtering left*

*Filter left* means putting your filtering criteria as far to the left, or toward the beginning, of the command line as possible. The earlier you can filter out unwanted objects, the less work the remaining cmdlets on the command line will have to do, and possibly less unnecessary information may have to be transmitted across the network to your computer.

The downside of the filter-left technique is that every single cmdlet can implement its own means of specifying filtering, and every cmdlet will have varying abilities to perform filtering. With `Get-Process`, for example, you can filter only on the `Name` or `Id` property of the processes.

When you're not able to get a cmdlet to do all the filtering you need, you can turn to a PowerShell Core cmdlet called `Where-Object` (which has the alias `where`). This uses a generic syntax, and you can use it to filter any kind of object after you've retrieved it and put it into the pipeline.

To use `Where-Object`, you need to learn how to tell the shell what you want to filter, and that involves using the shell's comparison operators.

## 12.3   *Using comparison operators*

In computers, a *comparison* always takes two objects or values and tests their relationship to one another. You might be testing whether they're equal, or whether one is greater than another, or whether one of them matches a text pattern of some kind. You indicate the kind of relationship you want to test by using a *comparison operator.* The result of the test in simple operations results in a Boolean value: `True` or `False`. Put another way, either the tested relationship is as you specified, or it isn't.

PowerShell uses the following comparison operators. Note that when comparing text strings, these aren't case sensitive; an uppercase letter is seen as equal to a lowercase letter:

- `-eq`—Equality, as in `5 -eq 5` (which is `True`) or `"hello" -eq "help"` (which is `False`)
- `-ne`—Not equal to, as in `10 -ne 5` (which is `True`) or `"help" -ne "help"` (which is `False`, because they are, in fact, equal, and we're testing to see if they're unequal)
- `-ge` *and* `-le`—Greater than or equal to, and less than or equal to, as in `10 -ge 5` (`True`) or `(Get-Date) -le '2020-12-02'` (which will depend on when you run this, and shows how dates can be compared)
- `-gt` *and* `-lt`—Greater than and less than, as in `10 -lt 10` (`False`) or `100 -gt 10` (`True`)

For string comparisons, you can also use a separate set of case-sensitive operators if needed: `-ceq`, `-cne`, `-cgt`, `-clt`, `-cge`, `-cle`.

If you want to compare more than one thing at once, you can use the logical operators -and and -or. Each takes a subexpression on either side, and we usually enclose them in parentheses to make the line easier to read:

- (5 -gt 10) -and (10 -gt 100) is False, because one or both subexpressions are False.
- (5 -gt 10) -or (10 -lt 100) is True, because at least one subexpression is True.

In addition, the logical -not operator reverses True and False. This can be useful when you're dealing with a variable or a property that already contains True or False, and you want to test for the opposite condition. For example, if you want to test whether a process isn't responding, you could do the following (you'll use $_ as a placeholder for a process object):

```
$_.Responding -eq $False
```

PowerShell defines $False and $True to represent the False and True Boolean values. Another way to write that comparison is as follows:

```
-not $_.Responding
```

Because Responding normally contains True or False, the -not reverses False to True. If the process isn't responding (meaning Responding is False), your comparison will return True, indicating that the process is "not responding." We prefer the second technique because it reads, in English, more like what we're testing for: "I want to see if the process isn't responding." You'll sometimes see the -not operator abbreviated as an exclamation mark (!).

A couple of other comparison operators are useful when you need to compare strings of text:

- -like—Accepts *, ?, and [] as wildcards, so you can compare to see if "Hello" -like "*ll*" (that would be True). The reverse is -notlike, and both are case insensitive; use -clike and -cnotlike for case-sensitive comparisons. You can find the other available wildcards in the about_Wildcards help file.
- -match—Makes a comparison between a string of text and a regular expression pattern. Its logical opposite is -notmatch, and as you might expect, -cmatch and -cnotmatch provide case-sensitive versions. Regular expressions are covered in a later chapter of this book.

The neat thing about the shell is that you can run almost all of these tests right at the command line (the exception is the one using the $_ placeholder—it won't work by itself, but you'll see where it will work in the next section).

**TRY IT NOW** Go ahead and try any—or all—of these comparisons. Type them on a line—for example, 5 -eq 5—press Enter, and see what you get.

You can find the other available comparison operators in the `about_Comparison` `_Operators` help file, and you'll learn about a few of the other ones in chapter 25.

## 12.4  *Filtering objects out of the pipeline*

Once you've written a comparison, where do you use it? Well, you can use it with the shell's generic filtering cmdlet, `Where-Object`.

For example, do you want to get rid of all processes but the ones using more than 100 MB of memory (`WorkingSet`)?

```
Get-Process | Where-Object -FilterScript {$_.WorkingSet -gt 100MB}
```

The `-FilterScript` parameter is positional, which means you'll often see this typed without it:

```
Get-Process | Where-Object {$_.WorkingSet -gt 100MB}
```

If you get used to reading that aloud, it sounds sensible: "where `WorkingSet` greater than 100 MB." Here's how it works: when you pipe objects to `Where-Object`, it examines each one of them using its filter. It places one object at a time into the `$_` placeholder and then runs the comparison to see whether it's `True` or `False`. If it's `False`, the object is dropped from the pipeline. If the comparison is `True`, the object is piped out of `Where-Object` to the next cmdlet in the pipeline. In this case, the next cmdlet is `Out-Default`, which is always at the end of the pipeline (as we discussed in chapter 11) and which kicks off the formatting process to display your output.

That `$_` placeholder is a special creature: you've seen it used before (in chapter 10), and you'll see it in one or two more contexts. You can use this placeholder only in the specific places where PowerShell looks for it, and this happens to be one of those places. As you learned in chapter 10, the period tells the shell that you're not comparing the entire object, but rather just one of its properties, `WorkingSet`.

We hope you're starting to see where `Get-Member` comes in handy. It gives you a quick and easy way to discover the properties of an object, which lets you turn around and use those properties in a comparison like this one. Always keep in mind that the column headers in PowerShell's final output don't always reflect the property names. For example, run `Get-Process`, and you'll see a column like `PM(MB)`. Run `Get-Process | Get-Member`, and you'll see that the actual property name is `PM`. That's an important distinction: always verify property names by using `Get-Member`; don't use a `Format-` cmdlet.

### Above and beyond

PowerShell v3 introduced a new "simplified" syntax for `Where-Object`. You can use it only when you're doing a single comparison; if you need to compare multiple items, you still have to use the original syntax, which is what you've seen in this section.

Folks debate whether or not this simplified syntax is helpful. It looks something like this:

```
Get-Process | where WorkingSet -gt 100MB
```

Obviously, that's a bit easier to read: it dispenses with the curly brackets {} and doesn't require the use of the awkward-looking $_ placeholder. But this new syntax doesn't mean you can forget about the old syntax, which you still need for more-complex comparisons:

```
Get-Process | Where-Object {$_.WorkingSet -gt 100MB -and $_.CPU -gt 100}
```

What's more, there are years' worth of examples out on the internet that all use the old syntax, which means you have to know it to use them. You also have to know the new syntax, because it will now start cropping up in developers' examples. Having to know two sets of syntax isn't exactly "simplified," but at least you know what's what.

## 12.5 *Using the iterative command-line model*

We want to go on a brief tangent with you now to talk about what we call the PowerShell iterative command-line model. The idea behind this model is that you don't need to construct these large, complex command lines all at once and entirely from scratch. Start small.

Let's say you want to measure the amount of virtual memory being used by the 10 most virtual-memory-hungry processes. But if PowerShell itself is one of those processes, you don't want it included in the calculation. Let's take a quick inventory of what you need to do:

1 Get processes.
2 Get rid of everything that's PowerShell.
3 Sort the processes by virtual memory.
4 Keep only the top 10 or bottom 10, depending on how you sort them.
5 Add up the virtual memory for whatever is left.

We believe you know how to do the first three steps. The fourth is accomplished using your old friend, Select-Object.

> **TRY IT NOW** Take a moment and read the help for Select-Object. Can you find any parameters that would enable you to keep only the first or last object in a collection?

We hope you found the answer. Finally, you need to add up the virtual memory. This is where you need to find a new cmdlet, probably by doing a wildcard search with Get-Command or Help. You might try the Add keyword, or the Sum keyword, or even the Measure keyword.

> **TRY IT NOW** See if you can find a command that would measure the total of a numeric property like virtual memory. Use Help or Get-Command with the * wildcard.

As you're trying these little tasks (and not reading ahead for the answer), you're making yourself into a PowerShell expert. Once you think you have the answer, you might start in on the iterative approach.

To start, you need to get processes. That's easy enough:

```
Get-Process
```

> **TRY IT NOW**   Follow along in the shell and run these commands. After each, examine the output, and see if you can predict what you need to change for the next iteration of the command.

Next, you need to filter out what you don't want. Remember, *filter left* means you want to get the filter as close to the beginning of the command line as possible. In this case, you'll use `Where-Object` to do the filtering, because you want it to be the next cmdlet in the pipeline. That's not as good as having the filtering occur on the first cmdlet, but it's better than filtering later on down the pipeline.

In the shell, press the up arrow on the keyboard to recall your last command, and then add the next command:

```
Get-Process | Where-Object { $_.Name -notlike 'pwsh*' }
```

You're not sure if it's `pwsh` or `pwsh.exe`, so you use a wildcard comparison to cover all your bases. Any process that isn't like those names will remain in the pipeline.

Run that to test it, and then press the up arrow again to add the next bit:

```
Get-Process | Where-Object { $_.Name -notlike 'pwsh*' } |
Sort-Object VM -Descending
```

Pressing Enter lets you check your work, and the up arrow lets you add the next piece of the puzzle:

```
Get-Process | Where-Object  { $_.Name -notlike 'pwsh*' } |
Sort-Object VM -Descending | Select -First 10
```

Had you sorted in the default ascending order, you would have wanted to keep the `-last 10` before adding this last bit:

```
Get-Process | Where-Object { $_.Name -notlike 'pwsh*' } |
Sort-Object VM -Descending | Select -First 10 |
Measure-Object -Property VM -Sum
```

We hope you were able to figure out at least the name of that last cmdlet, if not the exact syntax used here.

This model—running a command, examining the results, recalling it, and modifying it for another try—is what differentiates PowerShell from more traditional scripting languages. Because PowerShell is a command-line shell, you get those immediate results, as well as the ability to quickly and easily modify your command if the results aren't what you expect. You should also be seeing the power you have when you combine even the handful of cmdlets you've learned up to this point in the book.

## 12.6 Common points of confusion

Anytime we introduce `Where-Object` in a class, we usually come across two main sticking points. We tried to hit those concepts hard in the preceding discussion, but if you have any doubts, we'll clear them up now.

### 12.6.1 Filter left, please

You want your filtering criteria to go *as close to the beginning of the command line as possible.* If you can accomplish the filtering you need in the first cmdlet, do so; if not, try to filter in the second cmdlet so that the subsequent cmdlets have as little work to do as possible.

Also, try to accomplish filtering as close to the source of the data as possible. For example, if you're querying processes from a remote computer and need to use `Where-Object`—as we did in one of this chapter's examples—consider using PowerShell remoting to have the filtering occur on the remote computer, rather than bringing all of the objects to your computer and filtering them there. You'll tackle remoting in chapter 13, and we mention this idea of filtering at the source again there.

### 12.6.2 When $_ is allowed

The special `$_` placeholder is valid only in the places where PowerShell knows to look for it. When it's valid, it contains one object at a time from the ones that were piped into that cmdlet. Keep in mind that what's in the pipeline can and will change throughout the pipeline, as various cmdlets execute and produce output.

Also be careful of nested pipelines—the ones that occur inside a parenthetical command. For example, the following can be tricky to figure out:

```
Get-Process -Name (Get-Content c:\names.txt |
Where-Object -filter { $_ -notlike '*daemon' }) |
Where-Object -filter { $_.WorkingSet -gt 128KB }
```

Let's walk through that:

1  You start with `Get-Process`, but that isn't the first command that will execute. Because of the parentheses, `Get-Content` will execute first.
2  `Get-Content` is piping its output—which consists of simple `String` objects—to `Where-Object`. That `Where-Object` is inside the parentheses, and within its filter, `$_` represents the `String` objects piped in from `Get-Content`. Only those strings that don't end in *daemon* will be retained and output by `Where-Object`.
3  The output of `Where-Object` becomes the result of the parenthetical command, because `Where-Object` was the last cmdlet inside the parentheses. Therefore,

all of the names that don't end in *daemon* will be sent to the -Name parameter of Get-Process.

4  Now Get-Process executes, and the Process objects it produces will be piped to Where-Object. That instance of Where-Object will put one service at a time into its $_ placeholder, and it will keep only those services whose WorkingSet property is greater than 128KB.

Sometimes we feel like our eyes are crossing with all the braces and curly braces, periods, and parentheses, but that's how PowerShell works, and if you can train yourself to walk through the command carefully, you'll be able to figure out what it's doing.

## 12.7  Lab

Remember that Where-Object isn't the only way to filter, and it isn't even the one you should turn to first. We've kept this chapter brief to allow you more time to work on the hands-on examples. Keeping in mind the principle of *filter left*, try to accomplish the following:

1  Get the commands from the PSReadLine module.
2  Get the commands using the verb Get from the PSReadLine module.
3  Display all files under /usr/bin that are larger than 5 MB.
4  Find all modules on the PowerShell Gallery that start with PS and the author starts with Microsoft.
5  Get the files in the current directory where the LastWriteTime is in the last week. (Hint: (Get-Date).AddDays(-7) will give you the date from a week ago.)
6  Display a list of all processes running with either the name pwsh *or* the name bash.

## 12.8   Lab answers

```
1  Get-Command -Module PSReadLine
2  Get-Command Get-* -Module PSReadLine
3  Get-ChildItem /usr/bin/* | Where-Object {$_.length -gt 5MB}
4  Find-Module -Name PS* | Where-Object {$_.Author -like 'Microsoft*'}
5  Get-ChildItem | where-object LastWriteTime -ge (get-date).AddDays(-7)
6  Get-Process -Name pwsh,bash
```

## 12.9   Further exploration

Practice makes perfect, so try filtering some of the output from the cmdlets you've already learned about, such as Get-ChildItem, Get-Process, and even Get-Command. For example, you might try to filter the output of Get-Command to show only cmdlets. Or use Test-Connection to ping several computers or websites (such as google.com or facebook.com), and show the results only from computers that didn't respond. We're not suggesting that you need to use Where-Object in every case, but you should practice using it when it's appropriate.

# Remote control: One-to-one and one-to-many

# 13

Let's take a look at the `Invoke-Command` command. Notice that it has a `-ComputerName` parameter. Hmmm . . . does that mean it can run commands on other hosts too? After a bit of experimenting, you'll discover that's exactly what it does. How many other commands have the ability to connect to remote machines? While there is not a way to obtain a concrete number to answer this question, there are quite a lot.

What we've realized is that PowerShell's creators are a bit lazy—and that's a good thing. Because they didn't want to have to code a `-HostName` parameter for every single cmdlet, they created a shell-wide system called *remoting*. This system enables you to run any cmdlet on a remote computer. In fact, you can even run commands that exist on the remote computer but that don't exist on your own computer—meaning you don't always have to install every administrative cmdlet on your workstation. This remoting system is powerful, and it offers interesting administrative capabilities.

> **NOTE** Remoting is a huge, complex technology. We introduce you to it in this chapter and cover usage scenarios that you'll deal with 80% to 90% of the time. But we can't cover it all, so in the "Further exploration" section at the end of this chapter, we point you to a must-have resource that covers remoting's configuration options.

## 13.1 The idea behind remote PowerShell

Remote PowerShell works somewhat similarly to Telnet and other age-old remote-control technologies. When you run a command, it's running *on* the remote computer—only the results of that command come back to your computer.

### 13.1.1  *Remoting on Windows devices*

PowerShell uses a communications protocol called *Web Services for Management* (WSMan). WSMan operates entirely over HTTP or HTTPS (HTTP by default), making it easy to route through firewalls if necessary (because each of those protocols uses a single port to communicate). Microsoft's implementation of WSMan comes in the form of a background service, Windows Remote Management (WinRM). WinRM is installed by default on Windows 10 devices and Server 2012 and up. By default, these services are disabled but can easily be enabled individually or by group policy.

### 13.1.2  *Remoting on macOS and Linux devices*

As you can guess, WSMan and WinRM are Windows-only services. So in order for PowerShell to have remoting capabilities, the team decided that it would be best to use the industry standard Secure Shell (SSH). SSH makes it easy to route through firewalls if necessary (because that protocol uses a single port to communicate) and has been used by Linux professionals for decades. Microsoft has ported OpenSSH to Windows, so you can even use this to remote into Windows.

> ### Setting up PSRP over SSH on Windows
> You may want to set up PowerShell remoting protocol (PSRP) over SSH on any Windows machine you have PowerShell Core installed on. We won't go into the details on how to set this up, but the instructions are available in Microsoft's documentation: http://mng.bz/laPd.

### 13.1.3  *Cross-platform remoting*

You've already learned that PowerShell cmdlets all produce objects as their output. When you run a remote command, its output objects need to be put into a form that can be easily transmitted over a network. XML, it turns out, is an excellent way to do that, so PowerShell automatically *serializes* those output objects into XML. The XML is transmitted across the network and is then *deserialized* on your computer back into objects that you can work with inside PowerShell. Serialization and deserialization are really just a form of format conversion: from objects to XML (serialization), and from XML to objects (deserialization).

Why should you care how this output is returned? Because those serialized-then-deserialized objects are only snapshots, of sorts; they don't update themselves continually. For example, if you were to get the objects that represent the processes running on a remote computer, what you'd get back would be accurate for only the exact point in time at which those objects were generated. Values such as memory usage and CPU utilization won't be updated to reflect subsequent conditions. In addition, you can't tell the deserialized objects to do anything—you can't instruct one to stop itself, for example.

Those are basic limitations of remoting, but they don't stop you from doing some amazing stuff. In fact, you can tell a remote process to stop itself, but you have to be clever about it. We'll show you how later in this chapter. To make remoting work, you have two basic requirements:

- Both your computer and the one you want to send commands to must be running PowerShell v7.1 or later.
- Ideally, both computers need to be members of the same domain, or of trusted/ trusting domains. It's possible to get remoting to work outside a domain, but it's trickier, and we don't cover it in this chapter. To learn more about that scenario, open PowerShell and run `help about_remote_troubleshooting`.

**TRY IT NOW**  We hope you'll be able to follow along with some of the examples in this chapter. To participate, you'll ideally have a second test computer (or a virtual machine) that's in the same Active Directory domain as the test computer you've been using up to this point. You can run any version of Windows on that second computer, provided you have PowerShell v7.1 or later installed. If you are using two Windows devices, it will make your life a lot easier if they are part of the same domain. If you can't set up an additional computer or virtual machine, use `localhost` to create remoting connections to your current computer. You're still using remoting, but it isn't as exciting to be "remote controlling" the computer at which you're sitting.

## 13.2 Setting up PSRP over SSH

Let's spend some time getting SSH set up in your environment.

### 13.2.1 macOS and Linux

On the computer, make sure that the SSH server and client are installed. On Ubuntu, these are the instructions:

```
sudo apt install openssh-client
sudo apt install openssh-server
```

For macOS, the client is installed by default. Here is the command to enable the server:

```
sudo systemsetup -setremotelogin on
```

Next, we need to install the module that enables PSRP over SSH:

```
Install-Module EnableSSHRemoting
```

Then, run the command to enable PSRP over SSH:

```
sudo pwsh -c Enable-SSHRemoting
```

Next, you need to restart the OpenSSH service. On Ubuntu, this is the command to restart the service:

```
sudo service sshd restart
```

On macOS, this is the command:

```
sudo launchctl stop com.openssh.sshd
sudo launchctl start com.openssh.sshd
```

### 13.2.2  *Setting up SSH on Windows*

SSH can run on Windows desktops and servers as well. In fact, you can disable WinRM if you really want to (we don't suggest you do that). Most likely, if you are using SSH for remoting on a Windows device, you are either remoting to or from a Linux or macOS device.

Install the OpenSSH client and server:

```
Add-WindowsCapability -Online -Name OpenSSH.Client~~~~0.0.1.0

Add-WindowsCapability -Online -Name OpenSSH.Server~~~~0.0.1.0
```

Here is the initial configuration of the SSH server:

```
Start-Service sshd

Set-Service -Name sshd -StartupType 'Automatic'
```

Confirm the firewall rule is configured. It should be created automatically by setup:

```
Get-NetFirewallRule -Name *ssh*
```

There should be a firewall rule named `OpenSSH-Server-In-TCP`, which should be enabled. Configure and edit the sshd_config file located at `$env:ProgramData\ssh` on the target machine (figure 13.1).

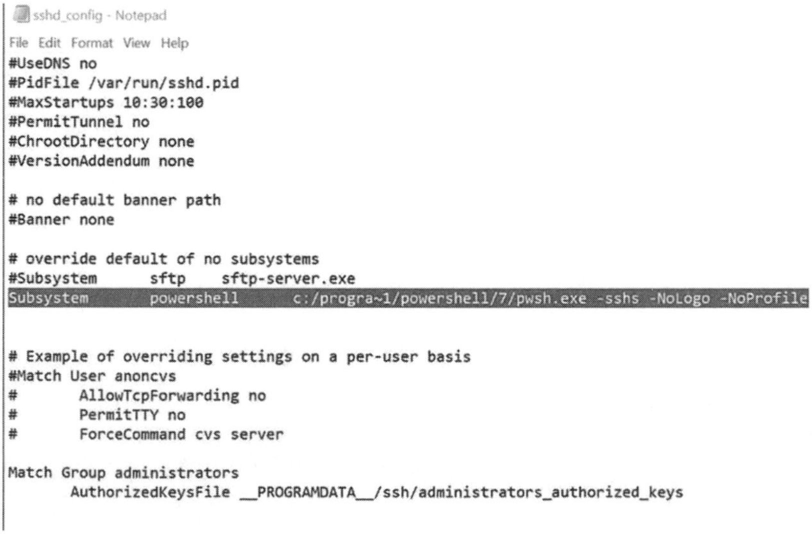

```
sshd_config - Notepad
File  Edit  Format  View  Help
#UseDNS no
#PidFile /var/run/sshd.pid
#MaxStartups 10:30:100
#PermitTunnel no
#ChrootDirectory none
#VersionAddendum none

# no default banner path
#Banner none

# override default of no subsystems
#Subsystem       sftp      sftp-server.exe
Subsystem        powershell       c:/progra~1/powershell/7/pwsh.exe -sshs -NoLogo -NoProfile


# Example of overriding settings on a per-user basis
#Match User anoncvs
#         AllowTcpForwarding no
#         PermitTTY no
#         ForceCommand cvs server

Match Group administrators
        AuthorizedKeysFile __PROGRAMDATA__/ssh/administrators_authorized_keys
```

**Figure 13.1   This is what the sshd_config file looks like with the PowerShell changes added.**

Verify that password authentication is enabled by removing the # sign:

```
PasswordAuthentication yes
```

Add the Subsystem for PowerShell. You can see that we are using the 8.3 short names for the file paths that contain spaces.

```
Subsystem powershell c:/progra~1/powershell/7/pwsh.exe -sshs -NoLogo
➥ -NoProfile
```

The 8.3 short name for the Program Files folder in Windows is usually Progra~1. However, you can use the following command to make sure:

```
Get-CimInstance Win32_Directory -Filter 'Name="C:\\Program Files"' |
➥ Select-Object EightDotThreeFileName
```

An optional enable-key authentication is

```
PubkeyAuthentication yes
```

Restart the OpenSSH service:

```
Restart-Service sshd
```

> **Be sure to secure your SSH server**
>
> You should research current standards for securing OpenSSH. At the time of writing, the basics are only to enable private-key authentication. Also, be sure to secure your private key. Here are links on how to do this for major platforms:
>
> macOS: http://mng.bz/Bxyw
>
> Ubuntu: http://mng.bz/do9g

## 13.3 PSRP over SSH overview

Let's talk about SSH, because you're going to have to configure it in order to use remoting. Once again, you need to configure PSRP over SSH—and PowerShell remoting—on only those computers that will *receive* incoming commands. In most of the environments we've worked in, the administrators have enabled remoting on every computer. Doing so gives you the ability to remote into client desktop and laptop computers in the background (meaning the users of those computers won't know you're doing so), which can be tremendously useful.

SSH allows multiple subsystems to register. This allows different protocols to work over the same port. When you enable SSH remoting, PowerShell registers as a subsystem, and incoming connections from PSRP are routed to that subsystem. Figure 13.2 illustrates how the pieces fit together.

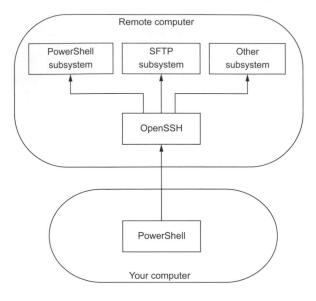

Figure 13.2   **The relationship between OpenSSH and PowerShell**

As shown, you can have dozens or even hundreds of sshd subsystems on your system. Each endpoint can point to a different application.

Figure 13.2 also illustrates the sshd *listener*. sshd acts as a listener sitting and waiting for incoming network traffic—kind of like a web server listening for incoming requests. A listener "listens" on a specific port and on a specific IP address.

> **TRY IT NOW**   Go ahead and enable remoting on your second computer (or on the first one, if that's the only one you have to work with). If you receive an error message when you enable remoting, stop and figure it out.

## 13.4   *WinRM overview*

Let's talk about WinRM, because you're going to have to configure it in order to use remoting. Once again, you need to configure WinRM—and PowerShell remoting—on only those computers that will *receive* incoming commands. In most of the environments we've worked in, the administrators have enabled remoting on every Windows-based computer (keep in mind that PowerShell and remoting are supported all the way back to Windows XP). Doing so gives you the ability to remote into client desktop and laptop computers in the background (meaning the users of those computers won't know you're doing so), which can be tremendously useful.

WinRM isn't unique to PowerShell. Microsoft is starting to use it for more and more administrative communications—even things that use other protocols today. With that in mind, Microsoft made WinRM capable of routing traffic to multiple administrative applications—not only PowerShell. WinRM acts as a dispatcher: when traffic comes in, WinRM decides which application needs to deal with that traffic. All WinRM traffic is tagged with the name of a recipient application, and those applications must register as *endpoints* with WinRM so that WinRM will listen for incoming traffic on their behalf. This means you need to not only enable WinRM, but also tell PowerShell to register as an endpoint with WinRM. Figure 13.3 illustrates how the pieces fit together.

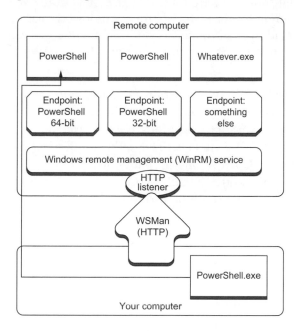

**Figure 13.3 The relationship between WinRM, WSMan, endpoints, and PowerShell**

As shown, you can have dozens or even hundreds of WinRM endpoints on your system (PowerShell calls them *session configurations*). Each endpoint can point to a different application, and you can even have endpoints that point to the same application but provide different permissions and functionality. For example, you could create a PowerShell endpoint that allows only one or two commands, and make it available to specific users in your environment. We don't dive that deep into remoting in this chapter, but we do later in the book.

Figure 13.3 also illustrates the WinRM *listener,* which in the figure is of the HTTP variety. A listener sits and waits for incoming network traffic on behalf of WinRM—kind of like a web server listening for incoming requests. A listener "listens" on a specific port and on a specific IP address, although the default listener created by `Enable-PSRemoting` listens on *all* local IP addresses.

The listener connects to the defined endpoint. One way to create an endpoint is to open a copy of PowerShell—making sure that you're running it as an administrator—and run the `Enable-PSRemoting` cmdlet. You might sometimes see references to a different cmdlet, called `Set-WSManQuickConfig`. You don't need to run that one; `Enable-PSRemoting` will call it for you, and `Enable-PSRemoting` performs a few extra steps that are necessary to get remoting up and running. All told, the cmdlet will start the WinRM service, configure it to start automatically, register PowerShell as an endpoint, and even set up a Windows Firewall exception to permit incoming WinRM traffic.

> **TRY IT NOW**   Go ahead and enable remoting on your second computer (or on the first one, if that's the only one you have to work with). Make sure you're running PowerShell as an administrator if you are on a Windows device (the Window's title bar should read Administrator). If you're not, close the shell, right-click the PowerShell icon in the Start menu, and select Run as Administrator from the context menu.

The most common error you will receive is "WinRM firewall exception will not work since one of the network connection types on this machine is set to Public." Any network connection set to `Public` can't have Windows Firewall exceptions, so when `Enable-PSRemoting` tries to create one, it fails. The only solution is to go into Windows and modify the network adapter setting so that whatever network you're on is either Work or Home. But don't do this if you're connected to a public network (e.g., a public wireless hotspot), because you'll be turning off some valuable security protections.

> **NOTE**   You don't have to worry about PowerShell remoting and public networks as much on server operating systems, because they don't have the same restrictions in the OS.

If you're not excited about having to run around to every computer to enable remoting, don't worry: you can also do it with a Group Policy Object (GPO). The necessary GPO settings are built into your domain controllers (you can download an ADM template from www.microsoft.com/en-us/download to add these GPO settings to an older domain's domain controllers). Open a GPO and look under Computer Configuration > Administrative Templates > Windows Components. Near the bottom of the list, you'll find both Remote Shell and Windows Remote Management. For now, we'll assume you'll run `Enable-PSRemoting` on those computers that you want to configure, because at this point you're probably playing around with only a virtual machine or two.

> **NOTE**   PowerShell's `about_remote_troubleshooting` help topic provides more coverage on using GPOs. Look for the "How to enable remoting in an enterprise" and "How to enable listeners by using a Group Policy" sections within that help topic.

## 13.5   *Using Enter-PSSession and Exit-PSSession for one-to-one remoting*

PowerShell uses remoting in two distinct ways. The first is one-to-one, or 1:1, remoting. The second is one-to-many, or 1:N, remoting (and you'll see it in the next section). With one-to-one remoting, you're accessing a shell prompt on a single remote computer. Any commands you run will run directly on that computer, and you'll see results in the shell window. This is vaguely similar to using SSH or Remote Desktop Connection, except you are limited to the command-line environment of Windows PowerShell. This kind of remoting also uses a *fraction* of the resources that Remote Desktop requires, so it imposes much less overhead on your servers.

Before we can connect to a remote computer, we need you to understand the difference between `-hostname` and `-computername` parameters:

- `-hostname`—Use this to use SSH.
- `-computername`—Use this to connect via WinRM.

PowerShell has no way of knowing what protocol you are trying to use, so you have to tell it. To establish a one-to-one connection with a remote computer, run the following command:

```
Enter-PSSession -HostName Ubuntu1 -UserName tyler1
Enter-PSSession -ComputerName SRV2 -UserName contoso\tyler1
```

Alternatively, you can use this syntax:

```
Enter-PSSession -HostName tyler1@Ubuntu1
```

(You need to provide the correct computer name instead of `SRV2` or `Ubuntu1`.)

Assuming that you enabled remoting on your remote computer, and you're all in the same domain, and your network is functioning correctly, you should get a connection established. PowerShell lets you know that you've succeeded by changing the shell prompt:

```
[Ubuntu1] PS /home/tyler1>
```

```
[SRV2] PS C:\>
```

The shell prompt tells you that everything you're doing is taking place on `Ubunut1` (or whichever server you connected to). You can run whatever commands you like. You can even import modules.

> **TRY IT NOW**  Try to create a remoting connection to your second computer or virtual machine. If you haven't done so, you'll also need to enable remoting on that computer before you try to connect to it. Note that you need to know the hostname or IP address.

Any command you run on the remote computer will run under the credentials you use to authenticate, so you'll be able to do anything you'd normally have permission to do. It's as if you logged into that computer's console and used its copy of Power-Shell directly.

Even if you have a PowerShell profile script on the remote computer, it won't run when you connect using remoting. We haven't fully covered profile scripts yet (they're in chapter 26), but suffice it to say, they're a batch of commands that run automatically each time you open the shell. Folks use them to automatically load shell extensions and modules and so forth. That doesn't happen when you remote into a computer, so be aware of that.

   Aside from this fairly minor caveat, you should be good to go. But wait—what do you do when you're finished running commands on the remote computer? Many PowerShell cmdlets come in pairs, with one cmdlet doing something and the other doing the opposite. In this case, if `Enter-PSSession` gets you *into* the remote computer, can you guess what would get you *out* of the remote computer? If you guessed `Exit-PSSession`, give yourself a prize. The command doesn't need any parameters; run it and your shell prompt will change back to normal, and the remote connection will close automatically.

> **TRY IT NOW**    Exit the remoting session, if you created one. We're done with it for now.

What if you forget to run `Exit-PSSession` and instead close the PowerShell window? Don't worry. PowerShell is smart enough to figure out what you did, and the remote connection will close all by itself.

   We do have one caution to offer: When you're remoting into a computer, don't run `Enter-PSSession` *from that computer* unless you fully understand what you're doing. Let's say you work on Computer A, which runs Ubuntu, and you remote into SRV2. Then, at the PowerShell prompt, you run this:

```
[Ubuntu1] PS /home/tyler1>
Enter-PSSession -computername SRV2 -UserName contsco\tyler1
```

This causes Ubuntu1 to maintain an open connection to SRV2, which can start to create a *remoting chain* that's hard to keep track of and that imposes unnecessary overhead on your servers. At times you may *have* to do this—we're thinking mainly of instances where a computer such as SRV2 sits behind a firewall and you can't access it directly, so you use SRV1 as a middleman to hop over to Server-DC4. But, as a general rule, try to avoid remote chaining. The PowerShell team has a great article on making a second hop in PowerShell Remoting at http://mng.bz/AxXe.

> **CAUTION**    Some people refer to remote chaining as *the second hop*, and it's a major PowerShell gotcha. We offer a hint: If the PowerShell prompt is displaying a computer name, then you're finished. You can't issue any more remote control commands until you exit that session and "come back" to your computer.

When you're using this one-to-one remoting, you don't need to worry about objects being serialized and deserialized. As far as you're concerned, you're typing directly on the remote computer's console. If you retrieve a process and pipe it to `Stop-Process`, it'll stop running, as you'd expect it to.

## 13.6    *Using Invoke-Command for one-to-many remoting*

The next trick—and honestly, this is one of the coolest things in PowerShell—is to send a command to *multiple remote computers at the same time*. That's right, full-scale distributed computing. Each computer will independently execute the command and send the results back to you. It's all done with the `Invoke-ScriptBlock` cmdlet, and it's called *one-to-many*, or 1:N, remoting. The command looks like this:

```
Invoke-Command -ComputerName SRV2,DC3,SRV4
-ScriptBlock { Get-Process pwsh } -UserName tyler1
```

> **TRY IT NOW**   Run this command. Substitute the name of your remote computer (or computers) and username where we put our three server names.

Everything in those curly braces `{}` gets transmitted to the remote computers—all three of them. By default, PowerShell talks to up to 32 computers at once; if you specify more than that, it will queue them up, and as one computer completes, the next one in line will begin. If you have an awesome network and powerful computers, you could raise that number by specifying the `-throttleLimit` parameter of `Invoke-Command`. Read the command's help for more information.

---

### Be careful about the punctuation

We need to further consider the syntax for a one-to-many remoting example, because in this case PowerShell's punctuation can get confusing. That confusion can make you do the wrong thing when you start constructing these command lines on your own.

Here's an example to consider:

```
Invoke-Command -HostName SRV2,DC3,SRV4
-ScriptBlock { Get-Process pwsh |
Where-Object {$_.Parent.ProcessName -like '*term*'}} -UserName
```

Two commands in this example use curly braces: `Invoke-Command` and `Where-Object`. `Where-Object` is entirely nested within the outer set of braces. The outermost set of braces encloses everything that's being sent to the remote computers for execution:

```
Get-Process pwsh  | Where-Object {$_.Parent.ProcessName -like '*term*'}
```

Following that nesting of commands can be tough, particularly in a book like this one, where the physical width of the page makes it necessary to display the command across several lines of text.

Be sure you can identify the exact command that's being sent to the remote computer and that you understand the use for each matched set of curly braces.

---

If you carefully read the help for `Invoke-Command` (see how we're continuing to push those help files?), you'll also notice a parameter that lets you specify a script file, rather than a command. That parameter lets you send an entire script from your local computer to the remote computers—meaning you can automate some complex tasks and have each computer do its own share of the work.

> **TRY IT NOW**  Make sure you can identify the -ScriptBlock parameter in the help for Invoke-Command and that you can spot the parameter that would enable you to specify a file path and name instead of a script block.

We want to circle back to the -HostName parameter we mentioned at the beginning of the chapter. When we first used Invoke-Command, we typed a comma-separated list of hostnames, as we did in the previous example. But we work with a lot of computers, and we don't want to have to type them all in every time. We keep text files for some of our common computer categories, such as web servers and domain controllers. Each text file contains one computer name per line, and that's it—no commas, no quotes, no nothing. PowerShell makes it easy for us to use those files:

```
Invoke-Command -ScriptBlock { dir }
-HostName (Get-Content webservers.txt) -UserName tylerl
```

The parentheses here force PowerShell to execute Get-Content first—the same way parentheses work in math. The results of Get-ScriptBlock are then stuck into the -HostName parameter, which works against each of the computers listed in the file.

## 13.7 *Differences between remote and local commands*

We want to explain the differences between running commands by using Invoke-Command and running those same commands locally, as well as the differences between remoting and other forms of remote connectivity. For this discussion, we'll use this command as our example:

```
Invoke-Command -HostName SRV2,DC3,SRV4
-ScriptBlock { Get-Process pwsh -UserName tylerl  |
Where-Object {$_.Parent.ProcessName -like '*term*'}}
```

### 13.7.1 *Deserialized objects*

Another caveat to keep in mind about remoting is that the objects that come back to your computer aren't fully functional. In most cases, they lack methods, because they're no longer "attached" to "live" software.

For example, run this on your local computer, and you'll notice that a System .Diagnostics.Process object has numerous methods associated with it:

```
PS > Get-Process | Get-Member


   TypeName: System.Diagnostics.Process

Name                         MemberType      Definition
```

```
----                           ----------      ----------
Handles                        AliasProperty   Handles = Handlecount
Name                           AliasProperty   Name = ProcessName
NPM                            AliasProperty   NPM = NonpagedSystemMemory...
PM                             AliasProperty   PM = PagedMemorySize64
SI                             AliasProperty   SI = SessionId
VM                             AliasProperty   VM = VirtualMemorySize64
WS                             AliasProperty   WS = WorkingSet64
Parent                         CodeProperty    System.Object Parent{get=G...
Disposed                       Event           System.EventHandler Dispos...
ErrorDataReceived              Event           System.Diagnostics.DataRec...
Exited                         Event           System.EventHandler Exited...
OutputDataReceived             Event           System.Diagnostics.DataRec...
BeginErrorReadLine             Method          void BeginErrorReadLine()
BeginOutputReadLine            Method          void BeginOutputReadLine()
CancelErrorRead                Method          void CancelErrorRead()
CancelOutputRead               Method          void CancelOutputRead()
Close                          Method          void Close()
CloseMainWindow                Method          bool CloseMainWindow()
Dispose                        Method          void Dispose(), void IDisp...
Equals                         Method          bool Equals(System.Object ...
GetHashCode                    Method          int GetHashCode()
GetLifetimeService             Method          System.Object GetLifetimeS...
GetType                        Method          type GetType()
InitializeLifetimeService      Method          System.Object InitializeLi...
Kill                           Method          void Kill(), void Kill(boo...
Refresh                        Method          void Refresh()
Start                          Method          bool Start()
ToString                       Method          string ToString()
WaitForExit                    Method          void WaitForExit(), bool W...
WaitForInputIdle               Method          bool WaitForInputIdle(), b...
__NounName                     NoteProperty    string __NounName=Process
```

## Now get some of those same objects via remoting:

```
PS > Invoke-Command {Get-Process} -HostName localhost -UserName tyler1 |
  ➥ Get-Member


    TypeName: Deserialized.System.Diagnostics.Process

Name             MemberType   Definition
----             ----------   ----------
GetType          Method       type GetType()
ToString         Method       string ToString(), string To...
Company          NoteProperty object Company=null
CPU              NoteProperty object CPU=null
Description      NoteProperty object Description=null
FileVersion      NoteProperty object FileVersion=null
Handles          NoteProperty int Handles=0
Name             NoteProperty string Name=
NPM              NoteProperty long NPM=0
Parent           NoteProperty object Parent=null
Path             NoteProperty object Path=null
```

```
PM                          NoteProperty long PM=0
Product                     NoteProperty object Product=null
ProductVersion              NoteProperty object ProductVersion=null
PSComputerName              NoteProperty string PSComputerName=localh...
PSShowComputerName          NoteProperty bool PSShowComputerName=True
RunspaceId                  NoteProperty guid RunspaceId=26297051-1cb...
SI                          NoteProperty int SI=53860
VM                          NoteProperty long VM=0
WS                          NoteProperty long WS=0
__NounName                  NoteProperty string __NounName=Process
BasePriority                Property     System.Int32 {get;set;}
Container                   Property        {get;set;}
EnableRaisingEvents         Property     System.Boolean {get;set;}
```

The methods—except the universal `ToString()` and `GetType()` methods common to all objects—are gone. This is a read-only copy of the object; you can't tell it to do things like stop, pause, resume, and so forth. So any actions you want taken as the result of your command should be included in the script block that's sent to the remote computer; that way, the objects are still live and contain all of their methods.

### 13.7.2  *Local vs. remote processing*

We'll cite our original example again:

```
Invoke-Command -HostName SRV2,DC3,SRV4
-ScriptBlock { Get-Process pwsh -UserName tyler1   |
Where-Object {$_.Parent.ProcessName -like '*term*'}}
```

Here's what happens here:

- The computers are contacted in parallel, meaning the command can complete somewhat more quickly.
- Each computer queries the records and filters them *locally*. The only data transmitted across the network is the result of that filtering, meaning that only the records we care about are transmitted.
- Before transmitting, each computer serializes its output into XML. Our computer receives that XML and deserializes it back into something that looks like objects. But they aren't real event log objects, and that might limit what we can do with them once they're on our computer.

Now, compare it to this alternative:

```
Invoke-Command -HostName SRV2,DC3,SRV4
-ScriptBlock { Get-Process pwsh } -UserName tyler1   |
Where-Object {$_.Parent.ProcessName -like '*term*'}
```

The differences are subtle. Well, we see only one difference: we moved one of those curly braces.

In the second version, only `Get-Process` is being invoked remotely. All of the results generated by `Get-Process` are serialized and sent to our computer, where they're deserialized into objects and then piped to `Where` and filtered. The second version of the command is less efficient, because a lot of unnecessary data is being transmitted across the network, and our one computer has to filter the results from three computers, rather than those three computers filtering their own results for us. The second version, then, is a bad idea.

Let's look at two versions of another command, starting with the following:

```
Invoke-Command -ComputerName SRV2
-ScriptBlock { Get-Process -name pwsh } -UserName tyler1 |
Stop-Process
```

Now let's look at the second version:

```
Invoke-Command -ComputerName SRV2
-ScriptBlock { Get-Process -name pwsh } -UserName tyler1 |
Stop-Process }
```

Once again, the only difference between these two is the placement of a curly brace. But in this example, the first version of the command won't work.

Look carefully: we're sending `Get-Process -name pwsh` to the remote computer. The remote computer retrieves the specified process, serializes it into XML, and sends it to us across the network. Our computer receives that XML, deserializes it back into an object, and pipes it to `Stop-Process`. The problem is that the deserialized XML doesn't contain enough information for our computer to realize that the process came from a *remote machine*. Instead, our computer will try to stop the `pwsh` process *running locally*, which isn't what we want at all.

The moral of the story is to always complete as much of your processing on the remote computer as possible. The only thing you should expect to do with the results of `Invoke-Command` is to display them or store them as a report, or a data file, and so forth. The second version of our command follows that advice: what's being sent to the remote computer is `Get-Process -name pwsh | Stop-Process`, so the entire command—both getting the process and stopping it—happens on the remote computer. Because `Stop-Process` doesn't normally produce any output, there won't be any objects to serialize and send to us, so we won't see anything on our local console. But the command will do what we want: stop the `pwsh` process *on the remote computer*, not on our local machine.

Whenever we use `Invoke-Command`, we always look at the commands after it. If we see commands for formatting, or for exporting data, we're fine, because it's okay to do those things with the results of `Invoke-Command`. But if `Invoke-Command` is followed by action cmdlets—ones that start, stop, set, change, or do something else—then we sit back and try to think about what we're doing. Ideally, we want all of those actions to happen on the remote computer, not on our local computer.

## 13.8  *But wait, there's more*

The previous examples have all used ad hoc remoting connections, meaning that we specified hostnames. If you're going to be reconnecting to the same computer (or computers) several times within a short period of time, you can create reusable, persistent connections to use instead. We cover that technique in chapter 18.

We should also acknowledge that not every company is going to allow PowerShell remoting to be enabled—at least, not right away. Companies with extremely restrictive security policies may, for example, have firewalls on all client and server computers, which would block the remoting connection. If your company is one of those, see whether an exception is in place for SSH or WinRM. We find that's a common exception, because administrators obviously need some remote connectivity to servers. If SSH or WinRM is allowed, then you can user PowerShell remoting over SSH.

## 13.9  *Common points of confusion*

Whenever beginners using remoting, some common problems crop up over the course of the day:

- Remoting is designed to be more or less automatically configured. If every computer involved is on the same domain, and your username is the same, things will typically work great. If not, you need to run `help about_remote_troubleshooting` and dig into the details.
- When you invoke a command, you're asking the remote computer to launch PowerShell, run your command, and then close PowerShell. The next command you invoke on that same remote computer will be starting from scratch—anything that was run in the first invocation will no longer be in effect. If you need to run a whole series of related commands, put them all into the same invocation.

## 13.10  Lab

**NOTE**    For this lab, you need a computer running PowerShell v7 or later. Ideally, you should have two computers on the same network with remoting enabled.

It's time to combine some of what you've learned about remoting with what you've learned in previous chapters. See if you can accomplish the following tasks:

1  Make a one-to-one connection with a remote computer (or with `localhost` if you have only one computer). Launch your favorite text editor. What happens?
2  Using `Invoke-Command`, retrieve a list of processes currently running from one or two remote computers (it's okay to use `localhost` twice if you have only one computer). Format the results as a wide list. (Hint: It's okay to retrieve results and have the formatting occur on your computer—don't include the `Format-` cmdlets in the commands that are invoked remotely.)
3  Use `Invoke-Command` to get a list of the top 10 processes for virtual memory (VM) usage. Target one or two remote computers, if you can; if you have only one computer, target `localhost` twice.

4 Create a text file that contains three computer names, with one name per line. It's okay to use the same computer name, or `localhost`, three times if you have access to only one computer. Then use `Invoke-Command` to retrieve the 10 newest files from the home directory (~).

5 Using `Invoke-Command`, query one or more remote computers to display the property `PSVersion` from the `$PSVersionTable` variable. (Hint: This requires you to get the property of an item.)

## 13.11 Lab answers

1 
```
Enter-PSSession Server01
[Ubuntu1] /home/tyler1> nano
```

The nano process will launch, but there won't be any interactive process either locally or remotely. In fact, run this way, the prompt won't return until the nano process ends—although an alternative command to launch it is `Start-Process nano`.

```
[SRV2] PS C:\Users\Administrator\Documents> Notepad
```

The Notepad process will launch, but there won't be any interactive process either locally or remotely. In fact, run this way, the prompt won't return until the Notepad process ends—although an alternative command to launch it is `Start-Process Notepad`.

2 
```
Invoke-Command –scriptblock {Get-Process } -HostName
➥ Server01,Server02  -UserName yourUser | Format-Wide -Column 4
```
3 
```
Invoke-Command -scriptblock {get-process | sort VM -Descending |
➥ Select-first 10} -HostName Server01,Server02 -UserN
```
4 
```
Invoke-Command -scriptblock { Cct-ChildItcm ~/* | Sort-Object
➥ -Property LastWriteTime -Descending | Select-Object -First 10}
➥ -HostName (Get-Content computers.txt) -UserName yourUser
```
5 
```
Invoke-ScriptBlock -scriptblock $ -Server01,Server02 -UserName yourUser
```

## 13.12 Further exploration

We could cover a lot more about remoting in PowerShell—enough that you'd be reading about it for *another* month of lunches. Unfortunately, some of its trickier bits aren't well documented. We suggest heading up to PowerShell.org, and more specifically to their e-book resources, where Don and fellow MVP Dr. Tobias Weltner have put together a comprehensive (and free!) *Secrets of PowerShell Remoting* mini e-book for you (see https://leanpub.com/secretsofpowershellremoting). The guide rehashes some of the basics you learned in this chapter, but it primarily focuses on detailed, step-by-step directions (with color screenshots) that show how to configure a variety of remoting scenarios. The guide also digs into some of the grittier details of the protocol and troubleshooting, and even has a short section on how to talk to information security people about remoting. The guide is updated periodically, so check back every few months to make sure you have the latest edition.

# Multitasking with background jobs

Everyone's always telling you to *multitask*, right? Why shouldn't PowerShell help you with that by doing more than one thing at a time? It turns out that PowerShell can do exactly that, particularly for longer-running tasks that might involve multiple target computers. Make sure you've read chapter 13 before you dive into this chapter, because we'll be taking those remoting concepts a step further.

> **HEADS UP** We will be using a lot of the Az cmdlets in this chapter, which does require an active Azure subscription. These are just the examples we chose to highlight.

## 14.1 Making PowerShell do multiple things at the same time

You should think of PowerShell as a single-threaded application, meaning that it can do only one thing at a time. You type a command, you press Enter, and the shell waits for that command to execute. You can't run a second command until the first command finishes.

But with its background jobs functionality, PowerShell has the ability to move a command onto a separate background thread or a separate background PowerShell process. That enables the command to run in the background as you continue to use the shell for another task. You have to make that decision before running the command; after you press Enter, you can't decide to move a long-running command into the background.

After commands are in the background, PowerShell provides mechanisms to check on their status, retrieve any results, and so forth.

## 14.2 Synchronous vs. asynchronous

Let's get some terminology out of the way first. PowerShell runs normal commands *synchronously*, meaning you press Enter and then wait for the command to complete. Moving a job into the background allows it to run *asynchronously*, meaning you can continue to use the shell for other tasks as the command completes. Let's look at some important differences between running commands in these two ways:

- When you run a command synchronously, you can respond to input requests. When you run commands in the background, there's no opportunity to see input requests—in fact, they'll stop the command from running.
- Synchronous commands produce error messages when something goes wrong. Background commands produce errors, but you won't see them immediately. You'll have to make arrangements to capture them, if necessary. (Chapter 24 discusses how you do that.)
- If you omit a required parameter on a synchronous command, PowerShell can prompt you for the missing information. On a background command, it can't, so the command will fail.
- The results of a synchronous command start displaying as soon as they become available. With a background command, you wait until the command finishes running and then retrieve the cached results.

We typically run commands synchronously to test them out and get them working properly, and run them in the background only after we know they're fully debugged and working as we expect. We follow these measures to ensure that the command will run without problems and that it will have the best chance of completing in the background. PowerShell refers to background commands as *jobs*. You can create jobs in several ways, and you can use several commands to manage them.

> **Above and beyond**
>
> Technically, the jobs we discuss in this chapter are only a few kinds of jobs you'll encounter. Jobs are an extension point for PowerShell, meaning it's possible for someone (either in Microsoft or as a third party) to create other things called jobs that look and work a bit differently than what we describe in this chapter. You may run into other kinds of jobs as you extend the shell for various purposes. We want you to understand that little detail and to know that what you're learning in this chapter applies only to the native, regular jobs that come with PowerShell.

## 14.3 Creating a process job

The first type of job we cover is perhaps the easiest: a process job. This is a command that runs in another PowerShell process on your machine in the background.

To launch one of these jobs, you use the `Start-Job` command. A `-ScriptBlock` parameter lets you specify the command (or commands) to run. PowerShell makes up a default job name (Job1, Job2, etc.), or you can specify a custom job name by using the -Name parameter. Rather than specifying a script block, you can specify the -FilePath parameter to have the job execute an entire script file full of commands. Here's a simple example:

```
PS /Users/travisp/> start-job -scriptblock { gci }
Id   Name  PSJobTypeName  State    HasMoreData  Location   Command
--   ----  -------------  -----    -----------  --------   -------
1    Job1  BackgroundJob  Running  True         localhost  gci
```

The command creates the job object, and as the previous example shows, the job begins running immediately. The job is also assigned a sequential job ID number, which is shown in the table.

The command also has a -WorkingDirectory parameter that allows you to change where your job starts on the filesystem. By default, it always starts in the home directory. Don't ever make assumptions about file paths from within a background job: use absolute paths to make sure you can refer to whatever files your job command may require, or use the -WorkingDirectory parameter. Here's an example:

```
PS /Users/travisp/> start-job -scriptblock { gci } -WorkingDirectory /tmp
Id   Name  PSJobTypeName  State    HasMoreData  Location   Command
--   ----  -------------  -----    -----------  --------   -------
3    Job3  BackgroundJob  Running  True         localhost  gci
```

Sharp-eyed readers will note that the first job we created is named Job1 and given the ID 1, but the second job is Job3 with ID 3. It turns out that every job has at least one *child job*, and the first child job (a child of Job1) is given the name Job2 and the ID 2. We'll get to child jobs later in this chapter.

Here's something to keep in mind: although process jobs run locally, they do require PowerShell remoting to be enabled, which we covered in chapter 13.

## 14.4 Creating a thread job

There's a second type of job that ships as part of PowerShell that we'd like to talk about. It's called a *thread job*. Rather than running in a totally different PowerShell process, a thread job will spin up another thread in the *same* process. Here's an example:

```
PS /Users/travisp/> start-threadjob -scriptblock { gci }
Id   Name  PSJobTypeName  State    HasMoreData  Location    Command
--   ----  -------------  -----    -----------  --------    -------
1    Job1  ThreadJob      Running  False        PowerShell  gci
```

Looks very similar to the previous job output, huh? Only two differences—the PSJob-TypeName, which is ThreadJob, and the Location, which is PowerShell. This tells us that this job ran within the process that we're currently using, but in a different thread.

Since the overhead of spinning up a new thread is drastically faster than spinning up a new process, thread jobs are fantastic for short-term scripts and commands that you want to start fast and run in the background. Inversely, you can use process jobs for long-running scripts on your machine.

> **HEADS UP** Although thread jobs start faster, keep in mind that one process can only have so many threads running at the same time before it starts to slow down. PowerShell baked in a "throttle limit" of 10 to help prevent you from bogging down PowerShell too much. This means that only 10 thread jobs can run at the same time. If you want to up the limit, you can. Just specify the `-ThrottleLimit` parameter and pass in the new limit you want to use. You'll eventually start seeing diminishing returns if you start 50, 100, 200 thread jobs at a time. Keep that in mind.

## 14.5 *Remoting, as a job*

Let's review the final technique you can use to create a new job: PowerShell's remoting capabilities, which you learned about in chapter 13. There's an important difference: whatever command you specify in the `-scriptblock` (or `-command`, which is an alias for the same parameter) will be transmitted in parallel to each computer you specify. Up to 32 computers can be contacted at once (unless you modify the `-throttleLimit` parameter to allow more or fewer), so if you specify more than 32 computer names, only the first 32 will start. The rest will start after the first set begins to finish, and the top-level job will show a completed status after all of the computers finish.

Unlike the other two ways to start a job, this technique requires you to have Power-Shell v6 or higher installed on each target computer and remoting over SSH to be enabled in PowerShell on each target computer. Because the command physically executes on each remote computer, you're distributing the computing workload, which can help improve performance for complex or long-running commands. The results come back to your computer and are stored with the job until you're ready to review them.

In the following example, you'll also see the `-JobName` parameter that lets you specify a job name other than the boring default:

```
PS C:\> invoke-command -command { get-process }
-hostname (get-content .\allservers.txt )
-asjob -jobname MyRemoteJob
WARNING: column "Command" does not fit into the display and was removed.
Id          Name            State     HasMoreData    Location
--          ----            -----     -----------    --------
8           MyRemoteJob     Running   True           server-r2,lo...
```

## 14.6 *Jobs in the wild*

We wanted to use this section to show an example of a PowerShell module that exposes its own PSJobs so you can look out for this pattern in your PowerShell journey. Let's take the command `New-AzVm`, for example:

```
PS /Users/travisp/> gcm New-AzVM -Syntax

New-AzVM -Name <string> -Credential <pscredential> [-ResourceGroupName
    <string>] [-Location <string>] [-Zone <string[]>] [-VirtualNetworkName
    <string>] [-AddressPrefix <string>] [-SubnetName <string>] [-
    SubnetAddressPrefix <string>] [-PublicIpAddressName <string>] [-
    DomainNameLabel <string>] [-AllocationMethod <string>] [-
    SecurityGroupName <string>] [-OpenPorts <int[]>] [-Image <string>] [-
    Size <string>] [-AvailabilitySetName <string>] [-SystemAssignedIdentity]
    [-UserAssignedIdentity <string>] [-AsJob] [-DataDiskSizeInGb <int[]>] [-
    EnableUltraSSD] [-ProximityPlacementGroup <string>] [-HostId <string>]
    [-DefaultProfile <IAzureContextContainer>] [-WhatIf] [-Confirm]
    [<CommonParameters>]

New-AzVM [-ResourceGroupName] <string> [-Location] <string> [-VM]
    <PSVirtualMachine> [[-Zone] <string[]>] [-DisableBginfoExtension] [-Tag
    <hashtable>] [-LicenseType <string>] [-AsJob] [-DefaultProfile
    <IAzureContextContainer>] [-WhatIf] [-Confirm] [<CommonParameters>]

New-AzVM -Name <string> -DiskFile <string> [-ResourceGroupName <string>] [-
    Location <string>] [-VirtualNetworkName <string>] [-AddressPrefix
    <string>] [-SubnetName <string>] [-SubnetAddressPrefix <string>] [-
    PublicIpAddressName <string>] [-DomainNameLabel <string>] [-
    AllocationMethod <string>] [-SecurityGroupName <string>] [-OpenPorts
    <int[]>] [-Linux] [-Size <string>] [-AvailabilitySetName <string>] [-
    SystemAssignedIdentity] [-UserAssignedIdentity <string>] [-AsJob] [-
    DataDiskSizeInGb <int[]>] [-EnableUltraSSD] [-ProximityPlacementGroup
    <string>] [-HostId <string>] [-DefaultProfile <IAzureContextContainer>]
    [-WhatIf] [-Confirm] [<CommonParameters>]
```

Notice a familiar parameter? -AsJob! Let's see what it does in this command:

```
PS /Users/travisp/> Get-Help New-AzVM -Parameter AsJob

-AsJob <System.Management.Automation.SwitchParameter>
    Run cmdlet in the background and return a Job to track progress.

    Required?                    false
    Position?                    named
    Default value                False
    Accept pipeline input?       False
    Accept wildcard characters?  false
```

This parameter tells New-AzVM to return a Job. If we fire off that cmdlet, after we put in a username and password for the VM, we'll see that we get a Job back.

```
PS /Users/travisp/> New-AzVm -Name myawesomevm -Image UbuntuLTS  -AsJob

cmdlet New-AzVM at command pipeline position 1
Supply values for the following parameters:
Credential
User: azureuser
Password for user azureuser: ***********
```

```
Id Name                  PSJobTypeName    State    HasMoreData   Location  Command
-- ----                  -------------    -----    -----------   --------  -------
8  Long Running O... AzureLongRunni... Running  True          localhost New-AzVM
```

What makes this so awesome is that you can manage these jobs just as you would the jobs that were returned from `Start-Job` or `Start-ThreadJob`. You'll see later how we go about managing jobs, but this is an example of how custom jobs might appear. Look for the `-AsJob` parameter!

## 14.7  Getting job results

The first thing you'll probably want to do after starting a job is to check whether your job has finished. The `Get-Job` cmdlet retrieves every job currently defined by the system and shows you each one's status:

```
PS /Users/travisp/> get-job
Id Name                  PSJobTypeName    State      HasMoreData   Location    Command
-- ----                  -------------    -----      -----------   --------    -------
1  Job1                  BackgroundJob    Completed  True          localhost   gci
3  Job3                  BackgroundJob    Completed  True          localhost   gci
5  Job5                  ThreadJob        Completed  True          PowerShell  gci
8  Job8                  BackgroundJob    Completed  True          server-r2, lo...
11 MyRemoteJob           BackgroundJob    Completed  True          server-r2, lo...
13 Long Running O... AzureLongRunni... Running    True          localhost   New-AzVM
```

You can also retrieve a specific job by using its ID or its name. We suggest that you do that and pipe the results to `Format-List *`, because you've gathered some valuable information:

```
PS /Users/travisp/> get-job -id 1 | format-list *
State         : Completed
HasMoreData   : True
StatusMessage :
Location      : localhost
Command       :  gci
JobStateInfo  : Completed
Finished      : System.Threading.ManualResetEvent
InstanceId    : e1ddde9e-81e7-4b18-93c4-4c1d2a5c372c
Id            : 1
Name          : Job1
ChildJobs     : {Job2}
PSBeginTime   : 12/12/2019 7:18:58 PM
PSEndTime     : 12/12/2019 7:18:58 PM
PSJobTypeName : BackgroundJob
Output        : {}
Error         : {}
Progress      : {}
Verbose       : {}
Debug         : {}
Warning       : {}
Information   : {}
```

**TRY IT NOW**  If you're following along, keep in mind that your job IDs and names might be different from ours. Focus on the output of `Get-Job` to retrieve your job IDs and names, and substitute yours in the examples. Also keep in mind that Microsoft has expanded the job object over the last few PowerShell versions, so your output when looking at all properties might be different.

The `ChildJobs` property is one of the most important pieces of information, and we'll cover it in a moment. To retrieve the results from a job, use `Receive-Job`. But before you run this, you need to know a few things:

- You have to specify the job from which you want to receive results. You can do this by job ID or job name, or by getting jobs with `Get-Job` and piping them to `Receive-Job`.
- If you receive the results of the parent job, those results will include all output from all child jobs. Alternatively, you can choose to get the results from one or more child jobs.
- Typically, receiving the results from a job clears them out of the job output cache, so you can't get them a second time. Specify `-keep` to keep a copy of the results in memory. Or you can output the results to a CLIXML file, if you want to retain a copy to work with.
- The job results may be deserialized objects, which you learned about in chapter 13. These are snapshots from the point in time when they were generated, and they may not have any methods that you can execute. But you can pipe the job results directly to cmdlets such as `Sort-Object`, `-Format-List`, `Export-CSV`, `ConvertTo-HTML`, `Out-File`, and so on, if desired.

Here's an example:

```
PS /Users/travisp/> receive-job -id 1

    Directory: /Users/travisp


Mode                 LastWriteTime         Length Name
----                 -------------         ------ ----
d----          11/24/2019 10:53 PM                Code
d----          11/18/2019 11:23 PM                Desktop
d----           9/15/2019  9:12 AM                Documents
d----           12/8/2019 11:04 AM                Downloads
d----           9/15/2019  7:07 PM                Movies
d----           9/15/2019  9:12 AM                Music
d----           9/15/2019  6:51 PM                Pictures
d----           9/15/2019  9:12 AM                Public
```

The preceding output shows an interesting set of results. Here's a quick reminder of the command that launched this job in the first place:

```
PS /Users/travisp/> start-job -scriptblock { gci }
```

When we received the results from `Job1`, we didn't specify -keep. If we try to get those same results again, we'll get nothing, because the results are no longer cached with the job:

```
PS /Users/travisp/> receive-job -id 1
```

Here's how to force the results to stay cached in memory:

```
PS /Users/travisp/> receive-job -id 3 -keep

    Directory: /Users/travisp

Mode                 LastWriteTime         Length Name
----                 -------------         ------ ----
d----          11/24/2019 10:53 PM               Code
d----          11/18/2019 11:23 PM               Desktop
d----           9/15/2019  9:12 AM               Documents
d----           12/8/2019 11:04 AM               Downloads
d----           9/15/2019  7:07 PM               Movies
d----           9/15/2019  9:12 AM               Music
d----           9/15/2019  6:51 PM               Pictures
d----           9/15/2019  9:12 AM               Public
```

You'll eventually want to free up the memory that's being used to cache the job results, and we'll cover that in a bit. But first, let's look at a quick example of piping the job results directly to another cmdlet:

```
PS /Users/travisp> receive-job -name myremotejob | sort-object PSComputerName
   | Format-Table -groupby PSComputerName
   PSComputerName: localhost
NPM(K)    PM(M)      WS(M) CPU(s)     Id ProcessName PSComputerName
------    -----      ----- ------     -- ----------- --------------
     0        0      56.92   0.70    484 pwsh        localhost
     0        0     369.20  70.17   1244 Code        localhost
     0        0      71.92   0.20   3492 pwsh        localhost
     0        0     288.96  15.31    476 iTerm2      localhost
```

This was the job we started by using `Invoke-Command`. The cmdlet has added the `PSComputerName` property so we can keep track of which object came from which computer. Because we retrieved the results from the top-level job, this includes all of the computers we specified, which allows this command to sort them on the computer name and then create an individual table group for each computer. `Get-Job` can also keep you informed about which jobs have results remaining:

```
PS /Users/travisp> get-job
Id Name          PSJobTypeName    State      HasMoreData Location   Command
-- ----          -------------    -----      ----------- --------   -------
1  Job1          BackgroundJob    Completed  False       localhost  gci
3  Job3          BackgroundJob    Completed  True        localhost  gci
5  Job5          ThreadJob        Completed  True        PowerShell gci
8  Job8          BackgroundJob    Completed  True        server-r2, lo...
11 MyRemoteJob   BackgroundJob    Completed  False       server-r2, lo...
13 Long Running O... AzureLongRunni... Running   True        localhost  New-AzVM
```

The `HasMoreData` column will be `False` when no output is cached with that job. In the case of `Job1` and `MyRemoteJob`, we've already received those results and didn't specify `-keep` at that time.

## 14.8 *Working with child jobs*

We mentioned earlier that most jobs consist of one top-level parent job and at least one child job. Let's look at a job again:

```
PS /Users/travisp> get-job -id 1 | format-list *
State         : Completed
HasMoreData   : True
StatusMessage :
Location      : localhost
Command       :  dir
JobStateInfo  : Completed
Finished      : System.Threading.ManualResetEvent
InstanceId    : e1ddde9e-81e7-4b18-93c4-4c1d2a5c372c
Id            : 1
Name          : Job1
ChildJobs     : {Job2}
PSBeginTime   : 12/27/2019 2:34:25 PM
PSEndTime     : 12/27/2019 2:34:29 PM
PSJobTypeName : BackgroundJob
Output        : {}
Error         : {}
Progress      : {}
Verbose       : {}
Debug         : {}
Warning       : {}
Information   : {}
```

> **TRY IT NOW**   Don't follow along for this part, because if you've been following along up to now, you've already received the results of `Job1`. If you'd like to try this, start a new job by running `Start-Job -script { dir }`, and use that new job's ID instead of the ID number 1 we used in our example.

You can see that `Job1` has a child job, `Job2`. You can get it directly now that you know its name:

```
PS /Users/travisp> get-job -name job2 | format-list *
State         : Completed
StatusMessage :
HasMoreData   : True
Location      : localhost
Runspace      : System.Management.Automation.RemoteRunspace
Debugger      : System.Management.Automation.RemotingJobDebugger
IsAsync       : True
Command       :  dir
JobStateInfo  : Completed
Finished      : System.Threading.ManualResetEvent
InstanceId    : a21a91e7-549b-4be6-979d-2a896683313c
Id            : 2
```

```
Name          : Job2
ChildJobs     : {}
PSBeginTime   : 12/27/2019 2:34:25 PM
PSEndTime     : 12/27/2019 2:34:29 PM
PSJobTypeName :
Output        : {Applications, Code, Desktop, Documents, Downloads, Movies,
                ➥ Music...}
Error         : {}
Progress      : {}
Verbose       : {}
Debug         : {}
Warning       : {}
Information   : {}
```

Sometimes a job has too many child jobs to list in that form, so you may want to list them a bit differently, as follows:

```
PS /Users/travisp> get-job -id 1 | select-object -expand childjobs
Id Name              PSJobTypeName   State       HasMoreData  Location  Command
-- ----              -------------   -----       -----------  --------  -------
2  Job2                              Completed   True         localhost gci
```

This technique creates a table of the child jobs for job ID 1, and the table can be whatever length it needs to be to list them all. You can receive the results from any individual child job by specifying its name or ID with `Receive-Job`.

## 14.9 *Commands for managing jobs*

Jobs also use three more commands. For each of these, you can specify a job either by giving its ID, giving its name, or getting the job and piping it to one of these cmdlets:

- `Remove-Job`—This deletes a job, and any output still cached with it, from memory.
- `Stop-Job`—If a job seems to be stuck, this command terminates it. You can still receive whatever results were generated to that point.
- `Wait-Job`—This is useful if a script is going to start a job or jobs and you want the script to continue only when the job is done. This command forces the shell to stop and wait until the job (or jobs) is completed, and then allows the shell to continue.

For example, to remove the jobs that we've already received output from, we'd use the following command:

```
PS /Users/travisp> get-job | where { -not $_.HasMoreData } | remove-job
PS /Users/travisp> get-job
Id Name              PSJobTypeName   State       HasMoreData  Location  Command
-- ----              -------------   -----       -----------  --------  -------
3  Job3              BackgroundJob   Completed   True         localhost gci
5  Job5              ThreadJob       Completed   True         PowerShell gci
8  Job8              BackgroundJob   Completed   True         server-r2, lo...
13 Long Running O... AzureLongRunni... Completed True         localhost New-AzVM
```

Jobs can also fail, meaning that something went wrong with their execution. Consider this example:

```
PS /Users/travisp> invoke-command -command { nothing } -hostname notonline
    -asjob -jobname ThisWillFail
Id Name              PSJobTypeName   State       HasMoreData  Location   Command
-- ----              -------------   -----       -----------  --------   -------
11 ThisWillFail      BackgroundJob   Failed      False        notonline  nothing
```

Here, we started a job with a bogus command and targeted a nonexistent computer. The job immediately failed, as shown in its status. We don't need to use `Stop-Job` at this point; the job isn't running. But we can get a list of its child jobs:

```
PS /Users/travisp> get-job -id 11 | format-list *
State          : Failed
HasMoreData    : False
StatusMessage  :
Location       : notonline
Command        :  nothing
JobStateInfo   : Failed
Finished       : System.Threading.ManualResetEvent
InstanceId     : d5f47bf7-53db-458d-8a08-07969305820e
Id             : 11
Name           : ThisWillFail
ChildJobs      : {Job12}
PSBeginTime    : 12/27/2019 2:45:12 PM
PSEndTime      : 12/27/2019 2:45:14 PM
PSJobTypeName  : BackgroundJob
Output         : {}
Error          : {}
Progress       : {}
Verbose        : {}
Debug          : {}
Warning        : {}
Information    : {}
```

And we can then get that child job:

```
PS /Users/travisp> get-job -name job12

Id Name  PSJobTypeName  State    HasMoreData  Location   Command
-- ----  -------------  -----    -----------  --------   -------
12 Job12                Failed   False        notonline  nothing
```

As you can see, no output was created for this job, so you won't have any results to retrieve. But the job's errors are stored in the results, and you can get them by using `Receive-Job`:

```
PS /Users/travisp> receive-job -name job12
OpenError: [notonline] The background process reported an error with the
➥ following message: The SSH client session has ended with error message:
➥ ssh: Could not resolve hostname notonline: nodename nor servname provided,
➥ or not known.
```

The full error is much longer; we truncated it here to save space. You'll notice that the error includes the hostname that the error came from, [notonline]. What happens if only one of the computers can't be reached? Let's try:

```
PS /Users/travisp> invoke-command -command { nothing }
-computer notonline,server-r2 -asjob -jobname ThisWillFail
Id Name             PSJobTypeName   State      HasMoreData  Location     Command
-- ----             -------------   -----      -----------  --------     -------
13 ThisWillFail     BackgroundJob   Running    True         notonline,lo... nothing
```

After waiting for a bit, we run the following:

```
PS /Users/travisp> get-job 13
Id Name             PSJobTypeName   State      HasMoreData  Location     Command
-- ----             -------------   -----      -----------  --------     -------
13 ThisWillFail     BackgroundJob   Failed     False        notonline,lo... nothing
```

The job still fails, but let's look at the individual child jobs:

```
PS /Users/travisp> get-job -id 13 | select -expand childjobs
Id Name PSJobTypeName   State    HasMoreData  Location    Command
-- ---- -------------   -----    -----------  --------    -------
14 Job14                Failed   False        notonline   nothing
15 Job15                Failed   False        localhost   nothing
```

Okay, they both fail. We have a feeling we know why Job14 doesn't work, but what's wrong with Job15?

```
PS /Users/travisp> receive-job -name job15
Receive-Job : The term 'nothing' is not recognized as the name of a cmdlet
, function, script file, or operable program. Check the spelling of the na
me, or if a path was included, verify that the path is correct and try aga
in.
```

Ah, that's right, we told it to run a bogus command. As you can see, each child job can fail for different reasons, and PowerShell tracks each one individually.

## 14.10 Common points of confusion

Jobs are usually straightforward, but we've seen folks do one thing that causes confusion. Don't do this:

```
PS /Users/travisp> invoke-command -command { Start-Job -scriptblock { dir } }
-hostname Server-R2
```

Doing so starts up a temporary connection to Server-R2 and starts a local job. Unfortunately, that connection immediately terminates, so you have no way to reconnect and retrieve that job. In general, then, don't mix and match the three ways of starting jobs. The following is also a bad idea:

```
PS /Users/travisp> start-job -scriptblock { invoke-command -command { dir }
-hostname SERVER-R2 }
```

That's completely redundant; keep the `Invoke-Command` section and use the `-AsJob` parameter to have it run in the background.

Less confusing, but equally interesting, are the questions new users often ask about jobs. Probably the most important of these is, "Can we see jobs started by someone else?" The answer is no. Jobs and thread jobs are contained entirely within the Power-Shell process, and although you can see that another user is running PowerShell, you can't see inside that process. It's like any other application: you can see that another user is running Microsoft Word, for example, but you can't see what documents that user is editing, because those documents exist entirely inside of Word's process.

Jobs last only as long as your PowerShell session is open. After you close it, any jobs defined within it disappear. Jobs aren't defined anywhere outside PowerShell, so they depend on its process continuing to run in order to maintain themselves.

## 14.11 Lab

The following exercises should help you understand how to work with various types of jobs and tasks in PowerShell. As you work through these exercises, don't feel you have to write a one-line solution. Sometimes it's easier to break things down into separate steps.

1   Create a one-time thread job to find all the text files (`*.txt`) on the filesystem. Any task that might take a long time to complete is a great candidate for a job.
2   You realize it would be helpful to identify all text files on some of your servers. How would you run the same command from task 1 on a group of remote computers?
3   What cmdlet would you use to get the results of a job, and how would you save the results in the job queue?

## 14.12 Lab answers

```
1   Start-ThreadJob {gci / -recurse -filter '*.txt'}
2   Invoke-Command -scriptblock {gci / -recurse -filter *.txt}
    -computername (get-content computers.txt) -asjob
3   Receive-Job -id 1 -keep
```

Of course, you would use whatever job ID was applicable or the job name.

# Working with many objects, one at a time

The whole point of PowerShell is to automate administration, and that often means you'll want to perform some tasks with multiple targets. You might want to start several VMs, push to several blob storages, modify permissions of several users, and so on. In this chapter, you'll learn two distinct techniques for accomplishing these and other multiple-target tasks: batch cmdlets and object enumeration. The concepts and techniques here are the same regardless of the OS you're using.

> **NOTE** This is an extremely difficult chapter and will probably frustrate you. Please be patient—with yourself and us—and trust that we do explain everything by the end.

## 15.1 The preferred way: "Batch" cmdlets

As you've learned in several previous chapters, many PowerShell cmdlets can accept batches, or *collections*, of objects to work with. In chapter 6, for example, you learned that objects can be piped from one cmdlet to another, like this (please don't run this on any system, unless you really want to have a bad day):

```
Get-Service | Stop-Service
```

This is an example of batch management using a cmdlet. In this case, `Stop-Process` is specifically designed to accept one process object from the pipeline, and then stop it. `Set-Service`, `Start-Process`, `Move-Item`, and `Move-AdObject` are all examples of cmdlets that accept one or more input objects and then perform a task or action with each of them. PowerShell knows how to work with batches of objects and can handle them for you with a relatively simple syntax.

These *batch cmdlets* (that's our name for them—it's not an official term) are our preferred way of performing tasks. For example, let's suppose we need to change the startup type for multiple services:

```
Get-Service BITS,Spooler | Set-Service -startuptype Automatic
```

One potential downside of this approach is that cmdlets that perform an action often don't produce any output indicating that they've done their job. You won't have any visual output from either of the preceding commands, which can be disconcerting. But those cmdlets often have a -PassThru parameter, which tells them to output whatever objects they accepted as input. You could have Set-Service output the same services it modified so you can verify that they have been modified. Here's an example of using -passThru with a different cmdlet:

```
Get-ChildItem .\ | Copy-Item -Destination C:\Drivers -PassThru
```

This command retrieves all of the items in the current directory. These objects are then piped to Copy-Item, which will then copy the items to the directory C:\Drivers. Because we put the -PassThru parameter at the end, it will display on the screen what it did. If we didn't do this, then once it completed it would simply go back to our PowerShell prompt.

> **TRY IT NOW**   Copy a few files or folders from one directory to another. Try it both with and without the -PassThru parameter and note the difference.

## 15.2  *The CIM way: Invoking methods*

Before we begin, there are two things you must know:

- Windows Management Instrumentation (WMI) does not work with PowerShell 7. You must use the Common Information Model (CIM) commands, which work mostly in the same manner.
- Section 15.2 is only for those using Windows. We try our best to make sure everything we are doing in this book is cross-platform. But there are some instances where that isn't possible, and this is one of them.

Unfortunately, we don't always have cmdlets that can take whatever action we need, and that's true when it comes to the items we can manipulate through CIM. For example, consider the Win32_NetworkAdapterConfiguration CIM class. This class represents the configuration bound to a network adapter (adapters can have multiple configurations, but for now let's assume they have only one configuration apiece, which is common on client computers). Let's say that our goal is to enable DHCP on all of our computers' Intel network adapters—we don't want to enable any of the RAS or other virtual adapters.

**NOTE** We'll walk you through a brief story line meant to help you experience how folks use PowerShell. Some things may seem redundant, but bear with us—the experience itself is valuable.

We might start by trying to query the desired adapter configurations, which would allow us to get something like the following as output:

```
DHCPEnabled       : False
IPAddress         : {192.168.10.10, fe80::ec31:bd61:d42b:66f}
DefaultIPGateway  :
DNSDomain         :
ServiceName       : E1G60
Description       : Intel(R) PRO/1000 MT Network Connection
Index             : 7
DHCPEnabled       : True
IPAddress         :
DefaultIPGateway  :
DNSDomain         :
ServiceName       : E1G60
Description       : Intel(R) PRO/1000 MT Network Connection
Index             : 12
```

To achieve this output, we'd need to query the appropriate CIM object and filter it to include only configurations with *Intel* in their descriptions. The following command does that (notice that the % acts as a wildcard within the WMI filter syntax):

```
PS C:\> Get-CimInstance -ClassName Win32_NetworkAdapterConfiguration |
-Filter "description like '%intel%'" | Format-List
```

**TRY IT NOW** You're welcome to follow along with the commands we're running in this section. You may need to tweak the commands slightly to make them work. For example, if your computer doesn't have any Intel-made network adapters, you need to change the filter criteria appropriately.

Once we have those configuration objects in the pipeline, we want to enable DHCP on them (you can see that one of our adapters doesn't have DHCP enabled). We might start by looking for a cmdlet named something like *Enable-DHCP*. Unfortunately, we won't find it, because there's no such thing. There aren't any cmdlets that are capable of dealing directly with CIM objects in batches.

**TRY IT NOW** Based on what you have learned so far, what command would you use to search for a cmdlet that has *DHCP* in its name?

Our next step is to see whether the object itself has a method that's capable of enabling DHCP. To find out, we run the command `Get-CimClass` and expand into the `CimClassMethods` property:

```
PS C:\> (Get-CimClass Win32_NetworkAdapterConfiguration).CimClassMethods
```

At the top we will see a method called `EnableDHCP` (figure 15.1).

```
PS C:\Scripts> (Get-CimClass Win32_NetworkAdapterConfiguration).CimClassMethods

Name                        ReturnType Parameters
----                        ---------- ----------
EnableDHCP                      UInt32 {}
RenewDHCPLease                  UInt32 {}
RenewDHCPLeaseAll               UInt32 {}
ReleaseDHCPLease                UInt32 {}
ReleaseDHCPLeaseAll             UInt32 {}
EnableStatic                    UInt32 {IPAddress, SubnetMask}
SetGateways                     UInt32 {DefaultIPGateway, GatewayCostMetric}
EnableDNS                       UInt32 {DNSDomain, DNSDomainSuffixSearchOrder, DNSHostName, DNSServerSearchOrder}
SetDNSDomain                    UInt32 {DNSDomain}
SetDNSServerSearchOrder         UInt32 {DNSServerSearchOrder}
```

**Figure 15.1   Showing the methods available**

The next step, which a lot of PowerShell newcomers try, is to pipe the configuration objects to the method:

```
PS C:\> Get-CimInstance win32_networkadapterconfiguration -filter
"description like '%intel%'" | EnableDHCP
```

Sadly, that won't work. You can't pipe objects to a method; you can pipe only to a cmdlet. `EnableDHCP` isn't a PowerShell cmdlet. Rather, it's an action that's directly attached to the configuration object itself.

Although there's no "batch" cmdlet called `Enable-DHCP`, you can use a generic cmdlet called `Invoke-CimMethod`. This cmdlet is specially designed to accept a batch of CIM objects, such as our `Win32_NetworkAdapterConfiguration` objects, and to invoke one of the methods attached to those objects. Here's the command we run:

```
PS C:\> Get-CimInstance -ClassName Win32_NetworkAdapterConfiguration -filter
➥ "description like '%intel%'" | Invoke-CimMethod -MethodName EnableDHCP
```

You have a few things to keep in mind:

- The method name isn't followed by parentheses.
- The method name isn't case sensitive.
- `Invoke-CimMethod` can accept only one kind of WMI object at a time. In this case, we're sending it only `Win32_NetworkAdapterConfiguration` objects, which means it'll work as expected. It's okay to send it more than one object (that's the whole point, in fact), but all of the objects have to be of the same type.
- You can use `-WhatIf` and `-Confirm` with `Invoke-CimMethod`. But you can't use those when calling a method directly from an object.

The output of `Invoke-CimMethod` is very simple to understand. It gives you two things: a return value and the computer it ran on (if the computer name is blank, it ran on `localhost`).

```
ReturnValue PSComputerName
----------- --------------
         84
```

The `ReturnValue` number tells us the result of the operation. A quick search from your favorite search engine for *Win32_NetworkAdapterConfiguration* turns up the documentation page, and we can then click through to the `EnableDHCP` method to see the possible return values and their meanings. Figure 15.2 shows what we discover.

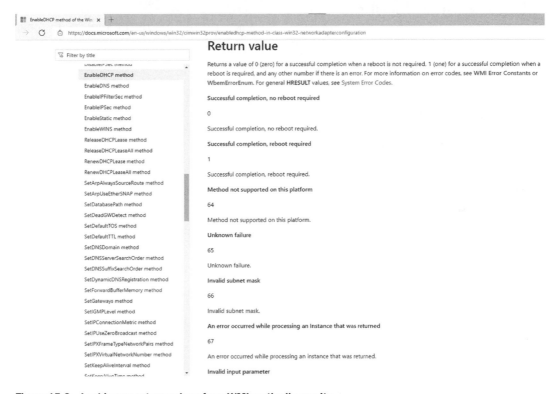

**Figure 15.2   Looking up return values for a WMI method's results**

A value of 0 means success, whereas 84 means that the IP isn't enabled on that adapter configuration and DHCP can't be enabled. But which bit of the output goes with which of our two network adapter configurations? It's difficult to tell, because the output doesn't tell you which specific configuration object produces it. That's unfortunate, but it's the way CIM works.

    `Invoke-CimMethod` works for most situations in which you have a CIM object that has a method that you want to execute. It works well when querying CIM objects from remote computers too. Our basic rule is, "If you can get to something by using `Get-CIMInstance`, then `Invoke-CimMethod` can execute its methods."

## 15.3   *The backup plan: Enumerating objects*

Unfortunately, we've run into situations where we have a cmdlet that can produce objects, but we know of no batch cmdlet to which we can pipe those objects to take some kind of action. We've also run into situations where a cmdlet doesn't take any input from the pipeline. In either case, you can still perform whatever task you want to perform, but you'll have to fall back to a more verbose-style approach of instructing the computer to enumerate the objects and perform your task against one object at a time. PowerShell offers two ways to accomplish this: one is using a cmdlet, and the other is using a scripting construct. We focus on the first technique in this chapter because it is the easiest. *You should always try to use a cmdlet over trying to script it yourself.* We save the second approach for chapter 19, which dives into PowerShell's built-in scripting language.

For our example, since we've been talking about processes in this chapter, we'll be talking about the cmdlet. Let's look at the syntax:

```
Get-Help Get-Process -Full
```

Which gets us everything . . . but skim through the section called "Id." You'll notice that some of the parameters say they accept pipeline input, but in parentheses, it says `ByPropertyName`. This means that if we pipe an object into this cmdlet and it has a property name called `Id`, for example, this cmdlet will use that:

```
-Id <System.Int32[]>
        Specifies one or more processes by process ID (PID). To specify
    ➥ multiple IDs, use commas to separate the IDs.
        To find the PID of a process, type 'Get-Process'.

        Required?                  true
        Position?                  named
        Default value              None
        Accept pipeline input?     True (ByPropertyName)
        Accept wildcard characters?  false

    -IncludeUserName <System.Management.Automation.SwitchParameter>
        Indicates that the UserName value of the Process object is returned
    ➥ with results of the command.

        Required?                  true
        Position?                  named
        Default value              False
        Accept pipeline input?     False
        Accept wildcard characters?  false
```

However, what if we just want to pipe in a list of strings that are names of the processes that we want to create? We wouldn't be able to do that because the `Name` parameter doesn't support the other type of piping: `ByValue`. Go ahead and try it. Let's take a look at the command `New-AzKeyVault`. We will put our values in an array and pipe that to the `New-AzKeyVault` command:

```
@( "vaultInt1", "vaultProd1", "vaultInt2", "vaultProd2" ) | New-AzKeyVault
```

This gives us the following less-than-ideal red text:

```
New-AzKeyVault: The input object cannot be bound to any parameters for the
➡ command either because the command does not take pipeline input or the
➡ input and its properties do not match any of the parameters that take
➡ pipeline input.
```

Let's take a deeper look into how we can still achieve our goal even when the cmdlet can't support what we are trying to do.

### 15.3.1 *Making the cmdlets work for you*

At this point, we have to make a decision. It's possible that we're running the command incorrectly, so we have to decide whether we want to spend a lot of time figuring it out. It's also possible that `New-AzKeyVault` just doesn't support what we want to do, in which case we could be spending a lot of time trying to fix something we have no control over.

We need to create a text file with a list of vault names we want to create. Our vaultsToCreate.txt looks like this:

```
vaultInt1
vaultInt2
vaultProd1
vaultProd2
```

Our usual choice in these situations is to try a different approach. We're going to ask the computer (well, the shell) to enumerate the objects (in our case, strings) one at a time, since the `New-AzKeyVault` command accepts only one object at a time, and execute `New-AzKeyVault` on the objects. To do this, we use the `ForEach-Object` cmdlet:

```
Get-Content -Path vaultsToCreate.txt | ForEach-Object { New-AzKeyVault
-ResourceGroupName manning -Location 'UK South' -Name $_ }
```

For the four resources we created, we get four results that look like this (only part of the output is shown here, as the results can be quite long):

```
Vault Name                    : vaultInt1
Resource Group Name           : manning
Location                      : Australia Central
Resource ID                   :
    /subscriptions/*****/resourceGroups/manning/providers/Microsoft.KeyVault
      ➡ /vaults/vaultInt1
Vault URI                     : https://vaultint1.vault.azure.net/
Tenant ID                     : *********
```

```
SKU                                 : Standard
Enabled For Deployment?             : False
Enabled For Template Deployment?    : False
Enabled For Disk Encryption?        : False
Soft Delete Enabled?                :
```

In the documentation, we found that if we got back a response like this, it meant success, which means we've achieved our goal. But let's look at that command in more detail.

```
Get-Content -Path vaultsToCreate.txt |
 ForEach-Object -Process {
    New-AzKeyVault -ResourceGroupName manning -Location 'UK South' -Name $_
 }
```

This command has a lot going on. The first line should make sense: we're using Get-Content to retrieve the names of the vaults that we put in a text file. We're piping those string objects to the ForEach-Object cmdlet:

- First, you see the cmdlet name: ForEach-Object.
- Next, we use the -Process parameter to specify a script block. We didn't originally type the -Process parameter name, because it's a positional parameter. But that script block—everything contained within the curly braces—is the value for the -Process parameter. We went ahead and included the parameter name when we reformatted the command for easier reading.
- ForEach-Object executes its script block once for each object that was piped into ForEach-Object. Each time the script block executes, the next piped-in object is placed into the special $_ placeholder, which you see getting passed in as the Name parameter in New-AzKeyVault.

## 15.4  *Let's speed things up*

In previous chapters, we've talked about using PowerShell jobs to run commands in parallel so that you save time. To streamline this time-saving ability, PowerShell 7 introduces a new parameter on ForEach-Object: -Parallel. It's best understood with an example using the ever-famous Measure-Command cmdlet that allows you to measure all sorts of things, but we'll be using it to time how long a script block runs. It looks like this:

```
Measure-Command {  <# The script we want to time #> }
```

So let's give it a go. First we'll try something simple using the regular ForEach-Object:

```
Get-Content -Path vaultsToCreate.txt | ForEach-Object -Process {
  Write-Output $_
  Start-Sleep 1
}
```

All this is going to do is print out each of the lines in the file and then sleep for one second per line. If we have five lines in the file, you can probably guess how long this will take to run, but let's use `Measure-Command`:

```
Measure-Command {
    Get-Content -Path vaultsToCreate.txt |
    ForEach-Object -Process {
      Write-Output $_
      Start-Sleep 1
    }
}
```

When we run that, we get the following output:

```
Days              : 0
Hours             : 0
Minutes           : 0
Seconds           : 5
Milliseconds      : 244
Ticks             : 52441549
TotalDays         : 6.06962372685185E-05
TotalHours        : 0.00145670969444444
TotalMinutes      : 0.0874025816666667
TotalSeconds      : 5.2441549
TotalMilliseconds : 5244.1549
```

Let's look specifically at the `Seconds` value, which is 5. That makes sense, right? If we have five lines in our file, and we process each line one at a time, and we sleep for 1 second each, we expect that command to run in roughly 5 seconds.

Now let's change that same command to use `Parallel` instead of `Process`:

```
Measure-Command {
    Get-Content -Path vaultsToCreate.txt |
    ForEach-Object -Parallel {
      Write-Output $_
      Start-Sleep 1
    }
}
```

Any guesses? Let's run it:

```
Days              : 0
Hours             : 0
Minutes           : 0
Seconds           : 1
Milliseconds      : 340
Ticks             : 13405417
TotalDays         : 1.55155289351852E-05
TotalHours        : 0.000372372694444444
TotalMinutes      : 0.0223423616666667
TotalSeconds      : 1.3405417
TotalMilliseconds : 1340.5417
```

One second! That's because `Parallel` does as the name implies—it runs the script blocks in parallel rather than in sequence. Since we have five items in our file and we run all of them in parallel, and we sleep for 1 second each, the whole operation takes only about 1 second. This is very useful for tasks that are long-running or in scenarios where you have a lot of smaller tasks that you'd like to batch. We can even take our existing example and use `Parallel ForEach`:

```
Get-Content -Path vaultsToCreate.txt |
 ForEach-Object -Parallel {
   New-AzKeyVault -ResourceGroupName manning -Location 'UK South' -Name $_
}
```

`Parallel` is a very strong parameter on `ForEach`, but it does have some limitations that you should be aware of. For starters, by default, `Parallel ForEach` will run only five script blocks in parallel. This is called the *throttle limit* and can be adjusted with the `ThrottleLimit` parameter. Go back to that file we've been using, and make sure it has a total of 10 lines. The difference is quite noticeable:

```
Measure-Command {
   Get-Content -Path vaultsToCreate.txt |
   ForEach-Object -Process {
     Write-Output $_
     Start-Sleep 1
   }
}
```

Without the throttle limit set, we get 2 seconds:

```
Days              : 0
Hours             : 0
Minutes           : 0
Seconds           : 2
Milliseconds      : 255
Ticks             : 22554472
TotalDays         : 2.6104712962963E-05
TotalHours        : 0.000626513111111111
TotalMinutes      : 0.0375907866666667
TotalSeconds      : 2.2554472
TotalMilliseconds : 2255.4472
```

However, if we up the throttle limit to 10, we get

```
Measure-Command {
   Get-Content -Path vaultsToCreate.txt |
   ForEach-Object -ThrottleLimit 10 -Process {
     Write-Output $_
     Start-Sleep 1
   }
}
```

The command finishes in 1 second!

```
Days                 : 0
Hours                : 0
Minutes              : 0
Seconds              : 1
Milliseconds         : 255
Ticks                : 12553654
TotalDays            : 1.45296921296296E-05
TotalHours           : 0.000348712611111111
TotalMinutes         : 0.0209227566666667
TotalSeconds         : 1.2553654
TotalMilliseconds    : 1255.3654
```

`Parallel ForEach` is a very powerful feature of PowerShell. You'll save a lot of time if you take advantage of it in the right way.

## 15.5 *Common points of confusion*

The techniques in this chapter are among the most difficult in PowerShell, and they often cause the most confusion and frustration. Let's look at some of the problems newcomers tend to run into. We provide some alternative explanations that will help you avoid the same issues.

### 15.5.1 *Which way is the right way?*

We use the terms *batch cmdlet* or *action cmdlet* to refer to any cmdlet that performs an action against a group, or collection, of objects all at once. Rather than having to instruct the computer to "go through this list of things, and perform this one action with each of those things," you can send the whole group to a cmdlet, and the cmdlet handles it.

Microsoft is getting better about providing these kinds of cmdlets with its products, but its coverage isn't 100% yet (and probably won't be for many years because of the many complex Microsoft products that exist). But when a cmdlet does exist, we prefer to use it. That said, other PowerShell developers prefer alternate ways, depending on what they learned first and what they remember most easily. All of the following have the same result:

```
                                                  Batch cmdlet       ForEach-Object calling
                                                                     the Kill() method
Get-Process -name *B* | Stop-Process        ◄──┘
Get-Process -name *B* | ForEach-Object { $_.Kill()}   ◄──┘
Get-Process -Name *B* | ForEach-Object -Parallel { Stop-Process $_ }
ForEach-Object calling Stop-Process
```

Let's look at how each approach works:

- Batch cmdlet. Here, we're using `Get-Process` to retrieve all processes with a *B* in their name, and then stop them.

- ForEach-Object calling the Kill() method. This approach is similar to the batch cmdlet, but rather than using a batch cmdlet, we're piping the processes to ForEach-Object and asking it to execute each service's Kill()
- ForEach-Object calling Stop-Process using -Parallel.

Heck, there's even a fourth approach—using PowerShell's scripting language to do the same thing. You'll find lots of ways to accomplish almost anything in PowerShell, and none of them are wrong. Some are easier than others to learn, remember, and repeat, which is why we've focused on the techniques we have, in the order that we did. Which should you use? It doesn't matter, because there's no one right way. You may even end up using a mix of these, depending on the circumstances and the capabilities that the shell can offer you for the task at hand.

### 15.5.2  *Diminishing returns of Parallel ForEach*

Remember our Parallel ForEach example? It looked like this:

```
Measure-Command {
    Get-Content -Path vaultsToCreate.txt |
    ForEach-Object -Parallel {
      Write-Output $_
      Start-Sleep 1
    }
}
```

Now let's say vaultsToCreate.txt had 100 lines in it. Should we try to set the ThrottleLimit to 100 so the operation can complete in 1 second? Let's try:

```
Measure-Command {
    Get-Content -Path vaultsToCreate.txt |
    ForEach-Object -ThrottleLimit 100 -Parallel {
      Write-Output $_
      Start-Sleep 1
    }
}
```

This gives us the output of 3 seconds. That's odd:

```
Days              : 0
Hours             : 0
Minutes           : 0
Seconds           : 3
Milliseconds      : 525
Ticks             : 35250040
TotalDays         : 4.07986574074074E-05
TotalHours        : 0.000979167777777778
TotalMinutes      : 0.0587500666666667
TotalSeconds      : 3.525004
TotalMilliseconds : 3525.004
```

Why so slow? Well, it turns out the bottleneck is your machine, which can run only so many things in parallel before it starts to slow down. This is like `Start-ThreadJob` that we saw in chapter 14. A single process can only do so many things in parallel before it starts to run slower than running them serially.

It's a strange concept, but imagine if you were working on a bunch of tasks at the same time. You'd have to constantly context switch between each of those tasks to make progress on all of them at the same time. In some cases, you reach a point where you'd be more effective if you simply waited to start a task until after you were finished with other tasks that are already in progress. We typically call this phenomenon "diminishing returns," meaning that as you attempt to do more in parallel, it becomes less worth it and could even impact results in a negative way if you're not careful.

### 15.5.3 *Method documentation*

Always remember that piping objects to `Get-Member` reveals methods:

```
Get-Process | Get-Member
```

PowerShell's built-in help system doesn't document methods objects. For example, if you get a member list for a process object, you can see that methods named `Kill` and `Start` exist:

```
TypeName: System.Diagnostics.Process
Name                     MemberType   Definition
----                     ----------   ----------
BeginErrorReadLine       Method       void BeginErrorReadLine()
BeginOutputReadLine      Method       void BeginOutputReadLine()
CancelErrorRead          Method       void CancelErrorRead()
CancelOutputRead         Method       void CancelOutputRead()
Close                    Method       void Close()
CloseMainWindow          Method       bool CloseMainWindow()
Dispose                  Method       void Dispose(), void
    IDisposable.Dispose()
Equals                   Method       bool Equals(System.Object obj)
GetHashCode              Method       int GetHashCode()
GetLifetimeService       Method       System.Object GetLifetimeService()
GetType                  Method       type GetType()
InitializeLifetimeService Method      System.Object
    InitializeLifetimeService()
Kill                     Method       void Kill(), void Kill(bool
    entireProcessTree)
Refresh                  Method       void Refresh()
Start                    Method       bool Start()
ToString                 Method       string ToString()
WaitForExit              Method       void WaitForExit(), bool
    WaitForExit(int milliseconds)
WaitForInputIdle         Method       bool WaitForInputIdle(), bool
 ➥ WaitForInputIdle(int milliseconds)
```

To find the documentation for these, focus on the `TypeName`, which in this case is `System.Diagnostics.Process`. Search for that complete type name in a search engine, and you'll usually come across the official developer documentation for that type, which will lead to the documentation for the specific method you're after.

### 15.5.4 *ForEach-Object confusion*

The `ForEach-Object` cmdlet has a punctuation-heavy syntax, and adding in a method's own syntax can create an ugly command line. We've compiled some tips for breaking any mental logjams:

- Try to use the full cmdlet name instead of its `%` or `ForEach` alias. The full name can be easier to read. If you're using someone else's example, replace aliases with the full cmdlet names.
- The script block enclosed in curly braces executes once for each object that's piped into the cmdlet.
- Within the script block, the `$_` represents the current object in the pipeline.
- Use `$_` by itself to work with the entire object you piped in; follow `$_` with a period to work with individual methods or properties.
- Method names are always followed by parentheses, even if the method doesn't require any parameters. When parameters are required, they're delimited by commas and included within the parentheses.

## 15.6  Lab

**NOTE**    For this lab, you need a machine with PowerShell 7 or higher on it.

Try to answer the following questions and complete the specified tasks. This is an important lab, because it draws on skills you've learned in many previous chapters, and you should be continuing to use and reinforce these skills as you progress through the remainder of this book:

1  What method of a `DirectoryInfo` object (produced by `Get-ChildItem`) will delete the directory?
2  What method of a `Process` object (produced by `Get-Process`) would terminate a given process?
3  Write three commands that could be used to delete all files and directories that have `deleteme` in the name, assuming that multiple files and directories have this in the name.
4  Assume you have a text list of computer names but want to display them in all uppercase. What PowerShell expression could you use?

## 15.7  Lab answers

1  Find the methods like this:

```
Get-ChildItem | Get-Member -MemberType Method
```

You should see a `Delete()` method.

2 Find the methods like this:

```
get-process | Get-Member -MemberType Method
```

You should see a `Kill()` method. You could verify by checking the MSDN documentation for this process object type. Of course, you shouldn't need to invoke the method because there is a cmdlet, `Stop-Process`, that will do the work for you.

3
```
Get-ChildItem *deleteme* | Remove-Item -Recurse -Force
Remove-Item *deleteme* -Recurse -Force
Get-ChildItem *deleteme* | foreach {$_.Delete()}
```

4
```
Get-content computers.txt | foreach {$_.ToUpper()}
```

# Variables: A place to store your stuff

We've already mentioned that PowerShell contains a scripting language, and in a few more chapters, we'll start to play with it. But once you start scripting, you may want to store your objects as variables for later use, so we'll get those out of the way in this chapter. You can use variables in many places other than long, complex scripts, so we'll also use this chapter to show you some practical ways to use them.

## 16.1 Introduction to variables

A simple way to think of a *variable* is as a box in the computer's memory that has a name. You can put whatever you want into the box: a single computer name, a collection of services, an XML document, and so on. You access the box by using its name, and when accessing it, you can put things in it or retrieve things from it. Those things stay in the box, allowing you to retrieve them over and over.

PowerShell doesn't place a lot of formality around variables. For example, you don't have to explicitly announce or declare your intention to use a variable before you do so. You can also change the types or objects of the contents of a variable: one moment you might have a single process in it, and the next moment you can store an array of computer names in it. A variable can even contain multiple different things, such as a collection of services *and* a collection of processes (although we admit that, in those cases, using the variable's contents can be tricky).

## 16.2 Storing values in variables

Everything in PowerShell—and we do mean *everything*—is treated as an object. Even a simple string of characters, such as a computer name, is considered an object. For example, piping a string to Get-Member (or its alias, gm) reveals that the

202

object is of the type `System.String` and that it has a great many methods you can work with (we're truncating the following list to save space):

```
PS > "SRV-02" | Get-Member
```

This gives you:

```
    TypeName: System.String

Name                  MemberType      Definition
----                  ----------      ----------
Clone                 Method          System.Object Clone(), System.O...
CompareTo             Method          int CompareTo(System.Object val...
Contains              Method          bool Contains(string value), bo...
CopyTo                Method          void CopyTo(int sourceIndex, ch...
EndsWith              Method          bool EndsWith(string value), bo...
EnumerateRunes        Method          System.Text.StringRuneEnumerato...
Equals                Method          bool Equals(System.Object obj),...
GetEnumerator         Method          System.CharEnumerator GetEnumer...
GetHashCode           Method          int GetHashCode(), int GetHashC...
GetPinnableReference  Method          System.Char&, System.Private.Co...
GetType               Method          type GetType()
```

> **TRY IT NOW**   Run this same command in PowerShell to see if you get the complete list of methods—and even a property—that comes with a `System.String` object.

Although that string is technically an object, you'll find that folks tend to refer to it as a simple value like everything else in the shell. That's because, in most cases, what you're concerned about is the string itself—`"SRV-02"` in the previous example—and you're less concerned about retrieving information from properties. That's different from, say, a process where the entire process object is a big, abstract data construct, and you're usually dealing with individual properties such as VM, PM, Name, CPU, ID, and so forth. A `String` is an object, but it's a much less complicated object than something like a `Process`.

PowerShell allows you to store these simple values in a variable. To do this, specify the variable, and use the equals sign operator—the *assignment* operator—followed by whatever you want to put within the variable. Here's an example:

```
$var = "SRV-02"
```

> **TRY IT NOW**   Follow along with these examples, because then you'll be able to replicate the results we demonstrate. You should use your test server's name rather than SRV-02.

It's important to note that the dollar sign ($) isn't part of the variable's name. In our example, the variable name is var. The dollar sign is a cue to the shell that what follows is going to be a variable name and that we want to access the contents of that variable. In this case, we're setting the contents of the variable.

Let's look at some key points to keep in mind about variables and their names:

- Variable names usually contain letters, numbers, and underscores, and it's most common for them to begin with a letter or an underscore.
- Variable names can contain spaces, but the name must be enclosed in curly braces. For example, `${My Variable}` represents a variable named `My Variable`. Personally, we dislike variable names that contain spaces because they require more typing, and they're harder to read.
- Variables don't persist between shell sessions. When you close the shell, any variables you created go away.
- Variable names can be quite long—long enough that you don't need to worry about how long. Try to make variable names sensible. For example, if you'll be putting a computer name into a variable, use `computername` as the variable name. If a variable will contain a bunch of processes, then `processes` is a good variable name.
- Some folks who have experience with other scripting languages may be used to using prefixes to indicate what is stored in the variable. For example, `strComputerName` is a common type of variable name, meaning that the variable holds a string (the `str` part). PowerShell doesn't care whether you do that, but it's no longer considered a desirable practice by the PowerShell community.

To retrieve the contents of a variable, use the dollar sign followed by the variable name, as shown in the following example. Again, the dollar sign tells the shell that you want to access the *contents* of a variable; following it with the variable name tells the shell which variable you're accessing:

```
$var
```

This outputs

```
SRV-02
```

You can use a variable in place of a value in almost any situation, for example, when using `Get-Process ID`. The command might typically look like this:

```
Get-Process -Id 13481
```

This outputs

```
NPM(K)    PM(M)    WS(M)    CPU(s)      Id  SI ProcessName
------    -----    -----    ------      --  -- -----------
     0     0.00    86.21      4.12   13481 ...80 pwsh
```

You can substitute a variable for any of the values:

```
$var = "13481"

Get-Process -Id $var
```

Which gives you

```
NPM(K)    PM(M)      WS(M)     CPU(s)      Id  SI ProcessName
------    -----      -----     ------      --  -- -----------
     0     0.00      86.21       4.12   13481 ...80 pwsh
```

By the way, we realize that var is a pretty generic variable name. We'd normally use processId, but in this specific instance, we plan to reuse $var in several situations, so we decided to keep it generic. Don't let this example stop you from using more sensible variable names in real life. We may have put a string into $var to begin with, but we can change that anytime we want:

```
PS > $var = 5
PS > $var | get-member
   TypeName: System.Int32
Name          MemberType Definition
----          ---------- ----------
CompareTo     Method     int CompareTo(System.Object value), int CompareT...
Equals        Method     bool Equals(System.Object obj), bool Equals(int ...
GetHashCode   Method     int GetHashCode()
GetType       Method     type GetType()
GetTypeCode   Method     System.TypeCode GetTypeCode()
```

In the preceding example, we placed an integer into $var, and then we piped $var to Get-Member. You can see that the shell recognizes the contents of $var as a System .Int32, or a 32-bit integer.

## 16.3 *Using variables: Fun tricks with quotes*

Because we're talking about variables, this is an excellent time to cover a neat Power-Shell feature. Up to this point in the book, we've advised you to generally enclose strings within single quotation marks. The reason for that is PowerShell treats everything enclosed in single quotation marks as a literal string.

Consider the following example:

```
PS > $var = 'What does $var contain?'
PS > $var
What does $var contain?
```

Here you can see that the $var within single quotes is treated as a literal. But in double quotation marks, that's not the case. Check out the following trick:

```
PS > $computername = 'SRV-02'
PS > $phrase = "The computer name is $computername"
PS > $phrase
The computer name is SRV-02
```

We start our example by storing SRV-02 in the variable $computername. Next, we store "The computer name is $computername" in the variable $phrase. When we do this, we use double quotes. PowerShell automatically seeks out dollar signs within double quotes and replaces any variables it finds *with their contents*. Because we display the contents of $phrase, the $computername variable is replaced with SRV-02.

This replacement action happens only when the shell initially parses the string. At this point, $phrase contains "The computer name is SRV-02"—it doesn't contain the "$computername" string. We can test that by trying to change the contents of $computername to see whether $phrase updates itself:

```
PS > $computername = 'SERVER1'
PS > $phrase
The computer name is SRV-02
```

As you can see, the $phrase variable stays the same.

Another facet of this double-quotes trick is the PowerShell escape character. This character is the backtick (`), and on a US keyboard it's located on one of the upper-left keys, usually below the Esc key and often on the same key as the tilde (~) character. The problem is that, in some fonts, it's practically indistinguishable from a single quote. In fact, we usually configure our shell to use the Consolas font, because that makes distinguishing the backtick easier than when using the Lucida Console or Raster fonts.

Let's look at what this escape character does. It removes whatever special meaning might be associated with the character after it, or in some cases, it adds special meaning to the following character. We have an example of the first use:

```
PS > $computername = 'SRV-02'
PS > $phrase = "`$computername contains $computername"
PS > $phrase
$computername contains SRV-02
```

When we assign the string to $phrase, we use $computername twice. The first time, we precede the dollar sign with a backtick. Doing this takes away the dollar sign's special meaning as a variable indicator and makes it a literal dollar sign. You can see in the preceding output, on the last line, that $computername is stored in the variable. We don't use the backtick the second time, so $computername is replaced with the contents of that variable. Now let's look at an example of the second way a backtick can work:

```
PS > $phrase = "`$computername`ncontains`n$computername"
PS > $phrase
$computername
contains
SRV-02
```

Look carefully, and you'll notice we use `n twice in the phrase—once after the first `$computername` and once after `contains`. In the example, the backtick adds special meaning. Normally, *n* is a letter, but with the backtick in front of it, it becomes a carriage return and line feed (think *n* for *new line*).

Run `help about_escape` for more information, including a list of other special escape characters. You can, for example, use an escaped *t* to insert a tab, or an escaped *a* to make your computer beep (think *a* for *alert*).

## 16.4 Storing many objects in a variable

Up till now, we've been working with variables that contain a single object, and those objects have all been simple values. We've worked directly with the objects themselves, rather than with their properties or methods. Let's now try putting a bunch of objects into a single variable.

One way to do this is to use a comma-separated list, because PowerShell recognizes those lists as collections of objects:

```
PS > $computers = 'SRV-02','SERVER1','localhost'
PS > $computers
SRV-02
SERVER1
Localhost
```

Notice that we're careful in this example to put the commas outside the quotation marks. If we put them inside, we'd have a single object that includes commas and three computer names. With our method, we get three distinct objects, all of which are `String` types. As you can see, when we examine the contents of the variable, PowerShell displays each object on its own line.

### 16.4.1 Working with single objects in a variable

You can also access individual elements in the variable, one at a time. To do this, specify an index number for the object you want, in square brackets. The first object is always at index number 0, and the second is at index number 1, and so forth. You can also use an index of -1 to access the last object, -2 for the next-to-last object, and so on. Here's an example:

```
PS > $computers[0]
SRV-02
PS > $computers[1]
SERVER1
```

```
PS > $computers[-1]
localhost
PS > $computers[-2]
SERVER1
```

The variable itself has a property that lets you see how many objects are in it:

```
$computers.count
```

This results in

```
3
```

You can also access the properties and methods of the objects inside the variable as if they were properties and methods of the variable itself. This is easier to see, at first, with a variable that contains a single object:

```
PS > $computername.length
6
PS > $computername.toupper()
SRV-02
PS > $computername.tolower()
srv-02
PS > $computername.replace('02','2020')
SRV-2020
PS > $computername
SRV-02
```

In this example, we're using the `$computername` variable we created earlier in the chapter. As you may remember, that variable contains an object of the type `System .String`, and you should have seen the complete list of properties and methods of that type when you piped a string to `Get-Member` in section 16.2. We use the `Length` property, as well as the `ToUpper()`, `ToLower()`, and `Replace()` methods. In each case, we have to follow the method name with parentheses, even though neither `ToUpper()` nor `ToLower()` requires any parameters inside those parentheses. Also, none of these methods change what is in the variable—you can see that on the last line. Instead, each method creates a new `String` based on the original one, as modified by the method.

What if you want to change the contents of the variable? You can assign a new value to the variable pretty easily:

```
PS > $computers = "SRV-02"
PS > $computers
SRV-02

PS > $computers = "SRV-03"
PS > $computers
SRV-03
```

### 16.4.2  *Working with multiple objects in a variable*

When a variable contains multiple objects, the steps can get trickier. Even if every object inside the variable is of the same type, as is the case with our $computers variable, and you can call a method on every object, it might not be what you want to do. You probably want to specify which object within the variable you want and then access a property or execute a method on that specific object:

```
PS > $computers[0].tolower()
SRV-02
PS > $computers[1].replace('SERVER','CLIENT')
CLIENT1
```

Again, these methods are producing new strings, not changing the ones inside the variable. You can test that by examining the contents of the variable:

```
PS > $computers
SRV-02
SERVER1
Localhost
```

What if you want to change the contents of the variable? You assign a new value to one of the existing objects:

```
PS > $computers[1] = $computers[1].replace('SERVER','CLIENT')
PS > $computers
SRV-02
CLIENT1
Localhost
```

You can see in this example that we change the second object in the variable, rather than produce a new string.

### 16.4.3  *Other ways to work with multiple objects*

We want to show you two other options for working with the properties and methods of a bunch of objects contained in a variable. The previous examples executed methods on only a single object within the variable. If you want to run the ToLower() method on every object within the variable, and store the results back into the variable, you do something like this:

```
PS > $computers = $computers | ForEach-Object { $_.ToLower()}
PS > $computers
srv-02
client1
localhost
```

This example is a bit complicated, so let's break it down in figure 16.1. We start the pipeline with $computers =, which means the results of the pipeline will be stored in that variable. Those results overwrite whatever was in the variable previously.

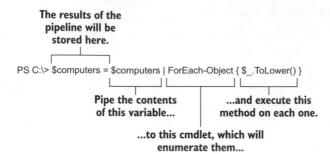

**The results of the pipeline will be stored here.**

PS C:\> $computers = $computers | ForEach-Object { $_.ToLower() }

**Pipe the contents of this variable...**

**...and execute this method on each one.**

**...to this cmdlet, which will enumerate them...**

Figure 16.1   Using `ForEach-Object` to execute a method against each object contained within a variable

The pipeline begins with `$computers` being piped to `ForEach-Object`. The cmdlet enumerates each object in the pipeline (we have three computer names, which are `string` objects) and executes its script block for each. Within the script block, the `$_` placeholder contains one piped-in object at a time, and we're executing the `ToLower()` method on each object. The new `String` objects produced by `ToLower()` are placed into the pipeline—and into the `$computers` variable.

You can do something similar with properties by using `Select-Object`. This example selects the `Length` property of each object you pipe to the cmdlet:

```
$computers | select-object length
```

This gives you

```
Length
------
     6
     7
     9
```

Because the property is numeric, PowerShell right-aligns the output.

### 16.4.4  Unrolling properties and methods in PowerShell

You *can* access properties and methods by using a variable that contains multiple objects:

```
$processes = Get-Process
$processes.Name
```

Under the hood, PowerShell "sees" that you're trying to access a property in that example. It also sees that the collection in `$processes` doesn't have a `Name` property—but the individual objects within the collection do. So it implicitly enumerates, or unrolls, the objects and grabs the `Name` property of each. This is equivalent to the following:

```
Get-Process | ForEach-Object { $_.Name }
```

And it is also equivalent to this:

```
Get-Process | Select-Object -ExpandProperty Name
```

The same thing works for methods:

```
$objects = Get-ChildItem ./*.txt -File
$objects.Refresh()
```

## 16.5 *More tricks with double quotes*

We have another cool technique you can use with double quotes, which is a somewhat conceptual extension of the variable-replacement trick. Suppose, for example, that you've put a bunch of processes into the $processes variable. Now you want to put only the name of the first one into a string:

```
$processes = Get-Process
$firstname = "$processes[0].name"
$firstname
```

This results in:

```
System.Diagnostics.Process System.Diagnostics.Process
System.Diagnostics.Process System.Diagnostics.Process
System.Diagnostics.Process System.Diagnostics.Process
System.Diagnostics.Process System.Diagnostics.Process
System.Diagnostics.Process System.Diagnostics.Process
System.Diagnostics.Process System.Diagnostics.Process
System.Diagnostics.Process System.Diagnostics.Process
System.Diagnostics.Process System.Diagnostics.Process
System.Diagnostics.Process System.Diagnostics.Process
System.Diagnostics.Process System.Diagnostics.Process
System.Diagnostics.Process System.Diagnostics.Process
System.Diagnostics.Process System.Diagnostics.Process
System.Diagnostics.Process System.Diagnostics.Process
System.Diagnostics.Process System.Diagnostics.Process
System.Diagnostics.Process System.Diagnostics.Process
System.Diagnostics.Process System.Diagnostics.Process
System.Diagnostics.Process System.Diagnostics.Process
System.Diagnostics.Process System.Diagnostics.Process
System.Diagnostics.Process System.Diagnostics.Process[0].name
```

Err, oops. The [ immediately after $processes in the example isn't normally a legal character in a variable name, which causes PowerShell to try to replace $processes. Doing this jams the name of every service into your string. The [0].name part isn't replaced at all. The solution is to put all of that into an expression:

```
$processes = Get-Process | where-object {$_.Name}
$firstname = "The first name is $($processes[0].name)"
$firstname
```

This results in

```
The first name is AccountProfileR
```

Everything within `$()` is evaluated as a normal PowerShell command, and the result is placed into the string, replacing anything that's already there. Again, this works only in double quotes. This `$()` construct is called a *subexpression*.

We have another cool trick you can do in PowerShell. Sometimes you'll want to put something more complicated into a variable and then display that variable's contents within quotation marks. In PowerShell, the shell is smart enough to enumerate all of the objects in a collection even when you refer to a single property or method, provided that all of the objects in the collection are of the same type. For example, we'll retrieve a list of processes and put them into the `$processes` variable, and then include only the process names in double quotes:

```
$processes = Get-Process | where-object {$_.Name}
$var = "Process names are $processes.name"
$var
```

This results in

```
Process names are System.Diagnostics.Process (AccountProfileR)
    System.Diagnostics.Process (accountsd) System.Diagnostics.Process
    (adprivacyd) System.Diagnostics.Process (AdvertisingExte)
    System.Diagnostics.Process (AirPlayUIAgent) System.Diagnostics.Process
    (akd) System.Diagnostics.Process (AMPArtworkAgent)
    System.Diagnostics.Process (AMPDeviceDiscov) System.Diagnostics.Process
    (AMPLibraryAgent) System.Diagnostics.Process (amsaccountsd)
    System.Diagnostics.Process (APFSUserAgent) System.Diagnostics.Process
    (AppleSpell) System.Diagnostics.Process (AppSSOAgent)
    System.Diagnostics.Process (appstoreagent) System.Diagnostics.Process
    (askpermissiond) System.Diagnostics.Process (AssetCacheLocat)
    System.Diagnostics.Process (assistantd) System.Diagnostics.Process
    (atsd) System.Diagnostics.Process (AudioComponentR)
    System.Diagnostics.Process (backgroundtaskm) System.Diagnostics.Process
    (bird)
```

We truncated the preceding output to save space, but we hope you get the idea. Obviously, this might not be the exact output you're looking for, but between this technique and the subexpressions technique we showed you earlier in this section, you should be able to get exactly what you want.

## 16.6    *Declaring a variable's type*

So far, we've put objects into variables and let PowerShell figure out what types of objects we were using. PowerShell doesn't care what kind of objects you put into the box. But you might care.

For example, suppose you have a variable that you expect to contain a number. You plan to do some arithmetic with that number, and you ask a user to input that number. Let's look at an example, which you can type directly into the command line:

```
PS > $number = Read-Host "Enter a number"
Enter a number: 100
PS > $number = $number * 10
PS > $number
100100100100100100100100100100
```

**TRY IT NOW** We haven't shown you Read-Host yet—we're saving it for the next chapter—but its operation should be obvious if you follow along with this example.

What the heck? How can 100 multiplied by 10 be 100100100100100100100100100100? What crazy new math is that?

If you're sharp-eyed, you may have spotted what's happening. PowerShell doesn't treat our input as a number; it treats it as a string. Instead of multiplying 100 by 10, PowerShell *duplicated the string* "100" *10 times*. The result, then, is the string 100, listed 10 times in a row. Oops.

We can verify that the shell is in fact treating the input as a string:

```
PS > $number = Read-Host "Enter a number"
Enter a number: 100
PS > $number | Get-Member
   TypeName: System.String
Name           MemberType          Definition
----           ----------          ----------
Clone          Method              System.Object Clone()
CompareTo      Method              int CompareTo(System.Object valu...
Contains       Method              bool Contains(string value)
```

Yep, piping $number to Get-Member confirms that the shell sees it as a System.String, not a System.Int32. There are a couple of ways to deal with this problem, and we'll show you the easiest one.

First, we tell the shell that the $number variable should contain an integer, which will force the shell to try to convert any input to a real number. We do that in the following example by specifying the desired data type, int, in square brackets immediately prior to the variable's first use:

```
PS > [int]$number = Read-Host "Enter a number"   ⟵── Forces the variable to [int]
Enter a number: 100
PS > $number | Get-Member
   TypeName: System.Int32           ⟵── Confirms that the variable is Int32
Name          MemberType Definition
----          ---------- ----------
CompareTo     Method     int CompareTo(System.Object value), int CompareT...
Equals        Method     bool Equals(System.Object obj), bool Equals(int ...
GetHashCode   Method     int GetHashCode()
GetType       Method     type GetType()
GetTypeCode   Method     System.TypeCode GetTypeCode()
```

```
ToString      Method      string ToString(), string ToString(string format...
PS > $number = $number * 10
PS > $number
1000            ⟵─── The variable was treated as a number.
```

In this example, we use [int] to force $number to contain only integers. After entering our input, we pipe $number to Get-Member to confirm that it is indeed an integer and not a string. At the end, you can see that the variable is treated as a number, and multiplication takes place.

Another benefit to using this technique is that the shell will throw an error if it can't convert the input into a number, because $number is capable of storing only integers:

```
PS > [int]$number = Read-Host "Enter a number"
Enter a number: Hello
MetadataError: Cannot convert value "Hello" to type "System.Int32". Error:
➥ "Input string was not in a correct format."
```

This is a great example of how to prevent problems down the line, because you're assured that $number will contain the exact type of data you expect it to.

You can use many object types in place of [int], but the following list includes some of the ones you'll most commonly use:

- [int]—Integer numbers
- [single] *and* [double]—Single-precision and double-precision floating numbers (numbers with a decimal portion)
- [string]—A string of characters
- [char]—Exactly one character (e.g., [char]$c = 'X')
- [xml]—An XML document; whatever string you assign to this will be parsed to make sure it contains valid XML markup (e.g., [xml]$doc = Get-Content MyXML.xml)

Specifying an object type for a variable is a great way to prevent certain tricky logic errors in more-complex scripts. As the following example shows, once you specify the object type, PowerShell enforces it until you explicitly retype the variable:

```
                              ┌─ Declares $x as an integer
PS > [int]$x = 5 ⟵──┘
PS > $x = 'Hello'   ⟵──┐ Creates an error by putting a string into $x
MetadataError: Cannot convert value "Hello" to type "System.Int32".
➥ Error: "Input string was not in a correct format."
PS > [string]$x = 'Hello'⟵┐
PS > $x | Get-Member       └─ Retypes $x as a string
   TypeName: System.String        ⟵──────────────────
Name              MemberType            Definition │ Confirms a new type of $x
----              ----------            ----------
Clone             Method                System.Object Clone()
CompareTo         Method                int CompareTo(System.Object valu...
```

You can see that we start by declaring $x as an integer and placing an integer into it. When we try to put a string into it, PowerShell throws an error because it can't convert that particular string into a number. Later we retype $x as a string, and we're able to put a string into it. We confirm that by piping the variable to Get-Member and checking its type name.

## 16.7 Commands for working with variables

We've started to use variables at this point, without formally declaring our intention to do so. PowerShell doesn't require advanced variable declaration, and you can't force it to make a declaration. (Some folks may be looking for something like Option Explicit and will be disappointed; PowerShell has something called Set-StrictMode, but it isn't exactly the same thing.) But the shell does include the following commands for working with variables:

- New-Variable
- Set-Variable
- Remove-Variable
- Get-Variable
- Clear-Variable

You don't need to use any of these except perhaps Remove-Variable, which is useful for permanently deleting a variable (you can also use the Remove-Item command within the VARIABLE: drive to delete a variable). You can perform every other function—creating new variables, reading variables, and setting variables—by using the ad hoc syntax we've used up to this point in the chapter. Using these cmdlets offers no specific advantages, in most cases, as you are forcing variable assignment until you run your script. This can be problematic for tools that provide completions as you type, such as Visual Studio Code. These complications will be more accurate if you use the normal assignment operators, because PowerShell can look at your script and predict the data style of the variable's value.

If you do decide to use these cmdlets, you give your variable name to the cmdlets' -name parameters. This is *only the variable name*—it doesn't include the dollar sign. The one time you might want to use one of these cmdlets is when working with something called an *out-of-scope* variable. Messing with out-of-scope variables is a poor practice, and we don't cover them (or much more on scope) in this book, but you can run help about_scope in the shell to learn more.

## 16.8 Variable best practices

We've mentioned most of these practices already, but this is a good time to review them quickly:

- Keep variable names meaningful but succinct. Whereas $computername is a great variable name because it's clear and concise, $c is a poor name because what it contains isn't clear. The variable name $computer_to_query_for_data is a bit long for our taste. Sure, it's meaningful, but do you want to type that over and over?

- Don't use spaces in variable names. We know you can, but it's ugly syntax.
- If a variable contains only one kind of object, declare that when you first use the variable. This can help prevent confusing logic errors. Suppose you're working in a commercial script development environment (such as Visual Studio Code). In that case, the editor software can provide code-hinting features when you tell it the type of object that a variable will contain.

## 16.9    Common points of confusion

The biggest single point of confusion we see new students struggle with is the variable name. We hope we've done an excellent job explaining it in this chapter, but always remember that the dollar sign *isn't part of the variable's name.* It's a cue to the shell that you want to access the *contents* of a variable; what follows the dollar sign is taken as the variable's name. The shell has two parsing rules that let it capture the variable name:

- If the character immediately after the dollar sign is a letter, number, or underscore, the variable name consists of all the characters following the dollar sign, up to the next white space (which might be a space, tab, or carriage return).
- If the character immediately after the dollar sign is an opening curly brace {, the variable name consists of everything after that curly brace up to, but not including, the closing curly brace }.

## 16.10  Lab

1  Create a background job that gets all processes that start with pwsh from two computers (use localhost twice if you have only one computer to experiment with).

2  When the job finishes running, receive the results of the job into a variable.

3  Display the contents of that variable.

4  Export the variable's contents to a CLIXML file.

5  Get a list of all the services currently running on your local machine and save it in a variable $processes.

6  Replace $processes with just the bits and print spooler service.

7  Display the contents of $processes.

8  Export $processes to a CSV file.

## 16.11  Lab answers

```
1  Invoke-Command {Get-Process pwsh} -computername
   localhost,$env:computername -asjob
2  $results = Receive-Job 4 -Keep
3  $results
4  $results | Export-CliXml processes.xml
5  $processes = get-service
```

```
6  $processes = get-service -name bits,spooler
7  $processes
8  $processes | export-csv -path c:\services.csv
```

## 16.12 *Further exploration*

Take a few moments and skim through some of the previous chapters in this book. Given that variables are primarily designed to store something you might use more than once, can you find a use for variables in our topics in previous chapters?

For example, in chapter 13 you learned to create connections to remote computers. In that chapter, you created, used, and closed a connection more or less in one step. Wouldn't it be useful to create the connection, store it in a variable, and use it for several commands? That's only one instance of where variables can come in handy (and we'll show you how to do that in chapter 20). See if you can find any more examples.

# Input and output 17

Up to this point in the book, we've primarily been relying on PowerShell's native ability to output tables and lists. As you start to combine commands into more complex scripts, you'll probably want to gain more precise control over what's displayed. You may also need to prompt a user for input. In this chapter, you'll learn how to collect that input and how to display whatever output you might desire.

We want to point out, however, that the contents of this chapter are useful only for scripts that interact with human eyeballs and fingertips. For scripts that run unattended, these aren't appropriate techniques, because there won't be a human being around to interact with.

## 17.1 Prompting for, and displaying, information

The way PowerShell displays and prompts for information depends on how it's being run. You see, PowerShell is built as a kind of under-the-hood engine.

What you interact with is called a *host application*. The command-line console you see when running the PowerShell executable in a terminal application is often called the *console host*. Another common host is called the *integrated host*, which is represented as the PowerShell Integrated Console supplied by the PowerShell extension for Visual Studio Code. Other non-Microsoft applications can host the shell's engine as well. In other words, you, as the user, interact with the hosting application, and it, in turn, passes your commands through to the engine. The hosting application displays the results that the engine produces.

**NOTE**  Another well-known host is in the PowerShell worker for Azure Functions. Azure Functions is Microsoft Azure's serverless offering, which is fancy talk for a service that allows you to run an arbitrary PowerShell script in the cloud without managing the underlying environment that script is running in. This host is interesting—because it's run unattended, there's no interactive element of this host, unlike the console or integrated host.

Figure 17.1 illustrates the relationship between the engine and the various hosting applications. Each hosting application is responsible for physically displaying any output the engine produces and physically collecting any input the engine requests. That means PowerShell can display output and manage input in different ways.

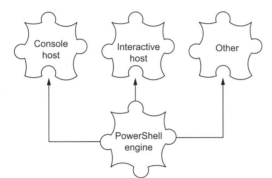

**Figure 17.1  Various applications are capable of hosting the PowerShell engine.**

We want to point out these differences because it can sometimes be confusing to newcomers. Why would one command behave one way in the command-line window but behave differently in, say, Azure Functions? It's because the hosting application determines the way in which you interact with the shell, not the PowerShell engine. The commands we're about to show you exhibit slightly different behavior depending on where you run them.

## 17.2  *Read-Host*

PowerShell's `Read-Host` cmdlet is designed to display a text prompt and then collect text input from the user. Because you saw us use this for the first time in the previous chapter, the syntax may seem familiar:

```
PS C:\> read-host "Enter a computer name"
Enter a computer name: SERVER-UBUNTU
SERVER-UBUNTU
```

This example highlights two important facts about the cmdlet:

- A colon is appended to the end of the line of text.
- Whatever the user types is returned as the result of the command (technically, it's placed into the pipeline, but more on that later).

You'll often capture the input into a variable, which looks like this:

```
PS C:\> $computername = read-host "Enter a computer name"
Enter a computer name: SERVER-UBUNTU
```

> **TRY IT NOW**   Time to start following along. At this point, you should have a valid computer name in the $computername variable. Don't use SERVER-UBUNTU unless that's the name of the computer you're working on.

## 17.3   *Write-Host*

Now that you can collect input, you'll want some way of displaying output. The Write-Host cmdlet is one way. It's not always the best way, but it's available to you, and it's important that you understand how it works.

As figure 17.2 illustrates, Write-Host runs in the pipeline like any other cmdlet, but it doesn't place anything into the pipeline. Instead, it does two things: writes a record into the "information stream" (don't worry, we'll cover this later!) and writes directly to the hosting application's screen.

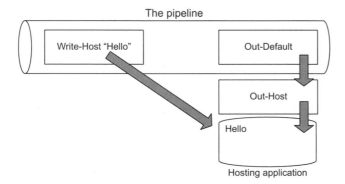

Figure 17.2   **Write-Host bypasses the pipeline and writes directly to the hosting application's display.**

Now, because Write-Host writes directly to the host app's screen, it's able to use alternate foreground and background colors through its -ForegroundColor and -BackgroundColor command-line parameters. You can see all the available colors by running get-help -command write-host.

> **TRY IT NOW**   Run Get-Help Write-Host. What colors are available for the ForegroundColor and BackgroundColor parameters? Now that we know what colors are available, let's have a little fun.

```
PS C:\> write-host "COLORFUL!" -Foreground yellow -BackgroundColor magenta
COLORFUL!
```

> **TRY IT NOW**   You'll want to run this command yourself to see the colorful results.

**NOTE** Not every application that hosts PowerShell supports alternate text colors, and not every application supports the full set of colors. When you attempt to set colors in such an application, it will usually ignore any colors it doesn't like or can't display. That's one reason we tend to avoid relying on special colors at all.

The `Write-Host` command has a bad reputation because in earlier version of PowerShell, it didn't do much. It acted as a mechanism to display information to the user via the console and didn't muddy any of the streams (yes, we know, we keep talking about these pesky things, and we will get to them, we promise). But starting in PowerShell 5, the `Write-Host` command was redesigned. It is now a wrapper for the `Write-Information` command, as it needed to be backward compatible. It still will output the text to your screen but will also put your text into the information stream so you can use it later. But `Write-Host` does have its limitations and may not always be the correct cmdlet for the job.

For example, you should never use `Write-Host` to manually format a table. You can find better ways to produce the output, using techniques that enable PowerShell itself to handle the formatting. We won't dive into those techniques in this book, because they belong more in the realm of heavy-duty scripting and tool making. However, you can check out *Learn PowerShell Scripting in a Month of Lunches* by Don Jones and Jeffery Hicks (Manning, 2017) for full coverage of those output techniques.

`Write-Host` is also not the best way to produce error messages, warnings, debugging messages, and so on—again, you can find more specific ways to do those things, and we'll cover those in this chapter. The only time you will really be using `Write-Host` is if you want to make a message on the screen with fancy colors in it.

**NOTE** We often see people using `Write-Host` to display what we call "warm and fuzzy" messages—things like "Now connecting to SERVER2," and "Testing for folder." We suggest you use the `Write-Verbose` messages instead. The reason we suggest this is because the output being sent the `Verbose` stream (which can be suppressed) as opposed to the `Information` stream.

### Above and beyond

We'll dive into `Write-Verbose` and the other `Write` cmdlets a bit more in chapter 20. But if you try `Write-Verbose` now, you might be disappointed to discover that it doesn't produce any output. Well, not by default.

If you plan to use `Write` cmdlets, the trick is to turn them on first. For example, set `$VerbosePreference="Continue"` to enable `Write-Verbose`, and `$VerbosePreference="SilentlyContinue"` to suppress its output. You'll find similar "preference" variables for `Write-Debug` (`$DebugPreference`) and `Write-Warning` (`$WarningPreference`).

> **(continued)**
> Chapter 20 includes an even cooler way to use `Write-Verbose`.
>
> It may seem *much* easier to use `Write-Host`, and if you want to, you can. But keep in mind that by using the other cmdlets, such as `Write-Verbose`, you're going to be following PowerShell's own patterns more closely, resulting in a more consistent experience.

## 17.4  *Write-Output*

Unlike `Write-Host`, `Write-Output` can send objects into the pipeline. Because it isn't writing directly to the display, it doesn't permit you to specify alternative colors or anything. In fact, `Write-Output` (or its alias, `Write`) isn't technically designed to display output at all. As we said, it sends objects into the pipeline—it's the pipeline itself that eventually displays those objects. Figure 17.3 illustrates how this works.

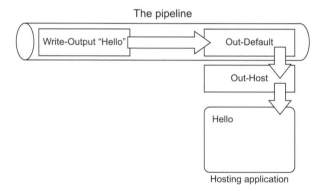

**Figure 17.3  `Write-Output` puts objects into the pipeline, which in some cases eventually results in those objects being displayed.**

Refer to chapter 11 for a quick review of how objects go from the pipeline to the screen. Let's look at the basic process:

1   `Write-Output` puts the `String` object `Hello` into the pipeline.
2   Because nothing else is in the pipeline, `Hello` travels to the end of the pipeline, where `Out-Default` always sits.
3   `Out-Default` passes the object to `Out-Host`.
4   `Out-Host` asks PowerShell's formatting system to format the object. Because in this example it's a simple `String`, the formatting system returns the text of the string.
5   `Out-Host` places the formatted result onto the screen.

The results are similar to what you'd get using `Write-Host`, but the object takes a different path to get there. That path is important, because the pipeline could contain other things. For example, consider the following command (which you're welcome to try):

```
PS C:\> write-output "Hello" | where-object { $_.length -gt 10 }
```

You don't see any output from this command, and figure 17.4 illustrates why. `Hello` is placed into the pipeline. But before it gets to `Out-Default`, it has to pass through `Where-Object`, which filters out anything having a `Length` property of less than or equal to `10`, which in this case includes our poor `Hello`. Our `Hello` gets dropped out of the pipeline, and because there's nothing left in the pipeline for `Out-Default`, there's nothing to pass to `Out-Host`, so nothing is displayed. Contrast that command with the following one:

```
PS C:\> write-host "Hello" | where-object { $_.length -gt 10 }
Hello
```

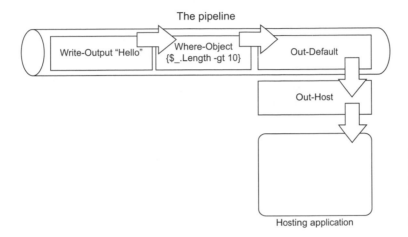

Figure 17.4
**Placing objects into the pipeline means they can be filtered out before they're displayed.**

All we've done is replace `Write-Output` with `Write-Host`. This time, `Hello` goes directly to the screen, not into the pipeline. `Where-Object` has no input and produces no output, so nothing is displayed by `Out-Default` and `Out-Host`. But because `Hello` has been written directly to the screen, we see it anyway.

`Write-Output` may seem new, but it turns out you've been using it all along. It's the shell's default cmdlet. When you tell the shell to do something that isn't a command, the shell passes whatever you typed to `Write-Output` behind the scenes.

## 17.5  *Other ways to write*

PowerShell has a few other ways to produce output. None of these write to the pipeline as `Write-Output` does; they work a bit more like `Write-Host`. But all of them produce output in a way that can be suppressed.

The shell comes with built-in configuration variables for each of these alternative output methods. When the configuration variable is set to `Continue`, the commands we're about to show you do indeed produce output. When the configuration variable is set to `SilentlyContinue`, the associated output command produces nothing. Table 17.1 contains the list of cmdlets.

**Table 17.1  Alternative output cmdlets**

| Cmdlet | Purpose | Configuration variable |
|---|---|---|
| Write-Warning | Displays warning text, in yellow by default, and preceded by the label WARNING: | $WarningPreference (Continue by default) |
| Write-Verbose | Displays additional informative text, in yellow by default, and preceded by the label VERBOSE: | $VerbosePreference (SilentlyContinue by default) |
| Write-Debug | Displays debugging text, in yellow by default, and preceded by the label DEBUG: | $DebugPreference (SilentlyContinue by default) |
| Write-Error | Produces an error message | $ErrorActionPreference (Continue by default) |
| Write-Information | Displays informational messages and allows structured data to be written to an information stream | $InformationPreference (SilentlyContinue by default) |

**NOTE**  Write-Host uses Write-Information under the hood, which means that Write-Host messages get sent to the information stream in addition to the host application. This gives us the ability to do more with Write-Host by controlling its behavior with $InformationPreference, among other things that we can do with PowerShell streams.

Write-Error works a bit differently because it writes an error to PowerShell's error stream. PowerShell also has a Write-Progress cmdlet that can display progress bars, but it works entirely differently. Feel free to read its help for more information and for examples; we don't cover it in this book.

To use any of these cmdlets, first make sure that its associated configuration variable is set to Continue. (If it's set to SilentlyContinue, which is the default for a couple of them, you won't see any output at all.) Then use the cmdlet to output a message.

**NOTE**  Some PowerShell hosting applications may display the output from these cmdlets in a different location. In Azure Functions, for example, debugging text is written to a log in Application Insights (an Azure log-reporting service) instead of a terminal window because in a serverless environment, you're not looking at a terminal; the PowerShell script is running somewhere up in the cloud. This is done for ease of debugging your scripts and so that you can see the output somewhere.

## 17.6 Lab

> **NOTE** For this lab, you need a computer running the OS of your choice with PowerShell v7 or later.

`Write-Host` and `Write-Output` can be a bit tricky to work with. See how many of these tasks you can complete, and if you get stuck, it's okay to peek at the sample answers available at the end of this chapter.

1 Use `Write-Output` to display the result of 100 multiplied by 10.
2 Use `Write-Host` to display the result of 100 multiplied by 10.
3 Prompt the user to enter a name, and then display that name in yellow text.
4 Prompt the user to enter a name, and then display that name only if it's longer than five characters. Do this all with a single PowerShell expression—don't use a variable.

That's all for this lab. Because these cmdlets are all straightforward, we want you to spend more time experimenting with them on your own. Be sure to do that—we'll offer some ideas in section 17.8.

> **TRY IT NOW** After you've completed this lab, try completing review lab 3, which you'll find in the appendix of this book.

## 17.7 Lab answers

1 `write-output (100*10)`
  or simply type the formula: `100*10`

2 Any of these approaches works:
```
$a= 100*10
Write-Host $a
Write-Host "The value of 100*10 is $a"
Write-Host (100*10)
```

3 
```
$name = Read-Host "Enter a name"
Write host $name -ForegroundColor Yellow
```

4 `Read-Host "Enter a name" | where {$_.length -gt 5}`

## 17.8 Further exploration

Spend some time getting comfortable with all of the cmdlets in this chapter. Make sure you can display `Verbose` output, and accept input. You'll be using the commands from this chapter often from here on out, so you should read their help files and even jot down quick syntax reminders for future reference.

# Sessions: *Remote control with less work*

*18*

In chapter 13, we introduced you to PowerShell's remoting features. In that chapter, you used two primary cmdlets—`Invoke-Command` and `Enter-PSSession`—to access both one-to-many and one-to-one remote control. Those two cmdlets work by creating a new remoting connection, doing whatever work you specify, and then closing that connection.

There's nothing wrong with that approach, but it can be tiring to have to continually specify computer names, credentials, alternative port numbers, and so on. In this chapter, you'll look at an easier, more reusable way to tackle remoting. You'll also learn about a third way to use remoting called *implicit remoting*, which will allow you to add proxy commands by importing a module from a remote machine into your remote session.

Anytime you need to connect to a remote computer, using either `Invoke-Command` or `Enter-PSSession`, you have to at least specify the computer's name (or names, if you're invoking a command on multiple computers). Depending on your environment, you may also have to specify alternative credentials, which means being prompted for a password. You might also need to specify alternative ports or authentication mechanisms, depending upon how your organization has configured remoting.

None of that is difficult to specify, but it can be tedious to have to repeat the process again and again. Fortunately, we know of a better way: reusable sessions.

**NOTE** The examples in this chapter can only be completed if you have another computer to connect to and if you have enabled PS remoting. Reference chapter 13 for more information.

## 18.1   *Creating and using reusable sessions*

A *session* is a persistent connection between your copy of PowerShell and a remote copy of PowerShell. When the session is active, both your computer and the remote machine devote a small amount of memory and processor time toward maintaining the connection. However, there's little network traffic involved in the connection. PowerShell maintains a list of all the sessions you've opened, and you can use those sessions to invoke commands or to enter a remote shell.

   To create a new session, use the `New-PSSession` cmdlet. Specify the computer name or hostname (or names), and, if necessary, specify an alternative username, port, authentication mechanism, and so forth. Let's also not forget that we can use SSH as opposed to WinRM by using the `-hostname` parameter. Either way, the result will be a session object, which is stored in PowerShell's memory:

```
PS C:\> new-pssession -computername srv02,dc17,print99

PS C:\> new-pssession -hostname LinuxWeb01,srv03
```

To retrieve those sessions, run `Get-PSSession`:

```
PS C:\> get-pssession
```

> **TIP**   As mentioned in chapter 13, when using the `-computername` parameter, we are using the WinRM (HTTP/HTTPS) protocol. When we use the `-hostname` parameter, we are specifying to use SSH as our communication protocol.

Although that works, we prefer to create the sessions and immediately store them in a variable to access the session later. For example, Julie has multiple web servers that she routinely reconfigures by using `Invoke-Command`. To make the process easier, she stores those sessions in a specific variable:

```
PS C:\> $iis_servers = new-pssession -computername web01,web02,web03
    ➥ -credential WebAdmin

PS C:\> $web_servers = new-pssession -hostname web04,web05,web06
    ➥ -username WebAdmin
```

Never forget that those sessions consume resources. If you close the shell, they'll close automatically, but if you're not actively using them, it's a good idea to manually close them even if you're planning to continue using the shell for other tasks so that you are not tying up resources on your machine or the remote machine.

   To close a session, use the `Remove-PSSession` cmdlet. For example, to close only the IIS sessions, use the following command:

```
PS C:\> $iis_servers | remove-pssession
```

Or, if you want to close all open sessions, use this next command:

```
PS C:\> get-pssession | remove-pssession
```

That's easy enough.

But once you get some sessions up and running, what will you do with them? For the next couple of sections, we'll assume you've created a variable named $sessions that contains at least two sessions. We'll use localhost and SRV02 (you should specify your own computer names). Using localhost isn't cheating: PowerShell starts up a real remoting session with another copy of itself. Keep in mind that this will work only if you've enabled remoting on all computers to which you're connected, so revisit chapter 13 if you haven't enabled remoting.

**TRY IT NOW**    Start to follow along and run these commands, and be sure to use valid computer names. If you have only one computer, use both its name and localhost. Hopefully, you will also have a machine running macOS or Linux that you can follow along with.

### Above and beyond

There's a cool syntax that allows you to create multiple sessions with one command and have each session assigned to a unique variable (instead of having them all lumped into one variable, as we previously did):

```
$s_server1,$s_server2 = new-pssession -computer SRV02,dc01
```

This syntax puts the session for SRV02 into $s_server1, and the session for DC01 into $s_server2, which can make it easier to use those sessions independently.

But use caution: We've seen instances where the sessions aren't created in exactly the order you specify, so $s_server1 might end up containing the session for DC01 instead of SRV02. You can display the variable's contents to see which computer it's connected to.

Here's how we'll get our sessions up and running:

```
PS C:\> $session01 = New-PSSession -computername SRV02,localhost
```

```
PS C:\> $session02 = New-PSSession -hostname linux01,linux02 -keyfilepath
➥ {path to key file}
```

Remember that we've already enabled remoting on these computers, and the Windows machines are all in the same domain. Again, revisit chapter 13 if you'd like a refresher on how to enable remoting.

## 18.2   *Enter-PSSession with session objects*

Okay, now that you know all about the reasons for using sessions, let's see how, exactly, to use them. As we hope you recall from chapter 13, the Enter-PSSession cmdlet is the one you use to engage a one-to-one remote interactive shell with a single remote computer. Rather than specifying a computer name or hostname with the cmdlet, you can specify a single session object. Because our $session01 and $session02 variables have more than one session object, we must specify one of them using an index (which you first learned to do in chapter 16):

```
PS C:\> enter-pssession -session $session010]
[SRV02]: PS C:\Users\Administrator\Documents>
```

You can see that our prompt changes to indicate that we're now controlling a remote computer. Exit-PSSession returns us to the local prompt, but the session remains open for further use:

```
[SRV02]: PS C:\Users\Administrator\Documents> exit-pssession
PS C:\>
```

What do you do if you have multiple sessions and forget the index number a particular session has? You can take the session variable and pipe it to Get-Member and examine the session object's properties. For example, when we pipe $session02 to Get-Member, we get the following output:

```
PS C:\> $session01 | gm
    TypeName: System.Management.Automation.Runspaces.PSSession

Name                   MemberType      Definition
----                   ----------      ----------
Equals                 Method          bool Equals(System.Object obj)
GetHashCode            Method          int GetHashCode()
GetType                Method          type GetType()
ToString               Method          string ToString()
ApplicationPrivateData Property        psprimitivedictionary App...
Availability           Property        System.Management.Automat...
ComputerName           Property        string ComputerName {get;}
ComputerType           Property        System.Management.Automat...
ConfigurationName      Property        string ConfigurationName {get;}
ContainerId            Property        string ContainerId {get;}
Id                     Property        int Id {get;}
InstanceId             Property        guid InstanceId {get;}
Name                   Property        string Name {get;set;}
Runspace               Property        runspace Runspace {get;}
Transport              Property        string Transport {get;}
VMId                   Property        System.Nullable[guid] VMId {get;}
VMName                 Property        string VMName {get;}
DisconnectedOn         ScriptProperty  System.Object DisconnectedOn...
ExpiresOn              ScriptProperty  System.Object ExpiresOn {get...
IdleTimeout            ScriptProperty  System.Object IdleTimeout {get=$t...
State                  ScriptProperty  System.Object State {get=$this...
```

In the preceding output, you can see that the session object has a `ComputerName` property, which means you can filter for that session:

```
PS C:\> enter-pssession -session ($sessions | where { $_.computername -eq
➥ 'SRV02' })
[SRV02]: PS C:\Users\Administrator\Documents>
```

That's awkward syntax, though. If you need to use a single session from a variable, and you can't remember which index number is which, it might be easier to forget about using the variable.

Even though you stored your session objects in the variable, they're also still stored in PowerShell's master list of open sessions. You can access them by using `Get-PSSession`:

```
PS C:\> enter-pssession -session (get-pssession -computer SRV02)
```

`Get-PSSession` retrieves the session having the computer named `SRV02` and passes it to the `-session` parameter of `Enter-PSSession`.

When we first figured out that technique, we were impressed, but it also led us to dig a bit deeper. We pulled up the full help for `Enter-PSSession` and read more closely about the `-session` parameter. Here's what we looked at:

```
-Session <System.Management.Automation.Runspaces.PSSession>
        Specifies a PowerShell session ( PSSession ) to use for the
    interactive session. This parameter takes a
        session object. You can also use the Name , InstanceID , or ID
    parameters to specify a PSSession .

        Enter a variable that contains a session object or a command that
    creates or gets a session object, such as a
        `New-PSSession` or `Get-PSSession` command. You can also pipe a
    session object to `Enter-PSSession`. You can
        submit only one PSSession by using this parameter. If you enter a
    variable that contains more than one
        PSSession , the command fails.

        When you use `Exit-PSSession` or the EXIT keyword, the interactive
    session ends, but the PSSession that you
        created remains open and available for use.
```

If you think back to chapter 9, you'll find that pipeline input information near the end of the help interesting. It tells us that the `-session` parameter can accept a `PSSession` object from the pipeline. We know that `Get-PSSession` produces `PSSession` objects, so the following syntax should also work:

```
PS C:\> Get-PSSession -ComputerName SRV02 | Enter-PSSession
[SRV02]: PS C:\Users\Administrator\Documents>
```

And it does work. We think that's a much more elegant way to retrieve a single session, even if you've stored them all in a variable.

> **TIP** Storing sessions in a variable is fine as a convenience. But keep in mind that PowerShell is already storing a list of all open sessions. Having them in a variable is useful only when you want to refer to a bunch of sessions at once, as you'll see in the next section.

## 18.3 Invoke-Command with session objects

Sessions show their usefulness with `Invoke-Command`, which you'll remember you use to send a command (or an entire script) to multiple remote computers in parallel. With our sessions in a `$session01` variable, we can easily target them all with the following command:

```
PS C:\> invoke-command -command { Get-Process } -session $session01
```

The `-session` parameter of `Invoke-Command` can also be fed with a parenthetical command, much as we've done with computer names in previous chapters. For example, the following sends a command to every session connected to a computer whose name is listed:

```
PS C:\> invoke-command -command { get-process bits } -session (get-pssession
    -computername server1,server2,server3)
```

You might expect that `Invoke-Command` would be able to receive session objects from the pipeline, as you know `Enter-PSSession` can. But a glance at the full help for `Invoke-Command` shows that it can't do that particular pipeline trick. Too bad, but the preceding example of using a parenthetical expression provides the same functionality without too difficult a syntax.

## 18.4 Implicit remoting: Importing a session

Implicit remoting, for us, is one of the coolest and most useful—possibly *the* coolest and *the* most useful—feature a command-line interface has ever had, on any operating system, ever. Yet it's barely documented in PowerShell. Sure, the necessary commands are well documented, but how they come together to form this incredible capability isn't mentioned. Fortunately, we have you covered on this one.

Let's review the scenario: You already know that Microsoft is shipping more and more modules with Windows Server and other products, but sometimes you can't install those modules on your local computer for one reason or another. The `Active-Directory` module, which shipped for the first time with Windows Server 2008 R2, is a perfect example: it exists only on domain controllers and on servers/clients with the Remote Server Administration Tools (RSAT) installed. Let's look at the entire process in a single example:

```
PS C:\> $session = new-pssession -comp SRV02
PS C:\> invoke-command -command { import-module activedirectory }
        session $session
PS C:\> import-pssession -session $session -module activedirectory -prefix rem

ModuleType Name                         ExportedCommands            Reviews the temporary
---------- ----                         ----------------            local module
Script       tmp_2b9451dc-b973-495d... {Set-ADOrganizationalUnit, Get-ADD...
```

Here is what's happening in that example:

1   We start by establishing a session with a remote computer that has the Active
    Directory module installed.

2   We tell the remote computer to import its local Active Directory module. That's
    just one example; we could have chosen to load any module. Because the ses-
    sion is still open, the module stays loaded on the remote computer.

3   We then tell our computer to import the commands from that remote session.
    We want only the commands in the Active Directory module, and when they're
    imported, we want a `rem` prefix to be added to each command's noun. That
    allows us to keep track of the remote commands more easily. It also means the
    commands won't conflict with any same-named commands already loaded into
    our shell.

4   PowerShell creates a temporary module on our computer that represents the
    remote commands. The commands aren't copied over; instead, PowerShell cre-
    ates shortcuts for them, and those shortcuts point to the remote machine.

Now we can run the Active Directory module commands or even ask for help. Instead
of running `New-ADUser`, we run `New-remADUser`, because we added that `rem` prefix to
the commands' nouns. The commands remain available until we either close the shell
or close that session with the remote computer. When we open a new shell, we have to
repeat this process to regain access to the remote commands.

   When we run these commands, they don't execute on our local machine. Instead,
they're implicitly remoted to the remote computer. It executes them for us and sends
the results to our computer.

   We can envision a world where we don't ever install administrative tools on our
computers again. What a hassle we'd avoid. Today, you need tools that can run on
your computer's operating system and talk to whatever remote server you're trying to
manage—and getting everything to match up can be impossible. In the future, you
won't do that. You'll use implicit remoting. Servers will offer their management features as another service, via Windows PowerShell.

   Now for the bad news: The results brought to your computer through implicit
remoting are all deserialized, meaning that the objects' properties are copied into an
XML file for transmission across the network. The objects you receive this way don't
have any methods. In most cases, that's not a problem, but some modules and snap-ins

produce objects that you're meant to use in a more programmatic way, and those don't lend themselves to implicit remoting. We hope you'll encounter few (if any) objects with this limitation, as a reliance on methods violates some PowerShell design practices. If you do run into such objects, you won't be able to use them through implicit remoting.

## 18.5 Using disconnected sessions

PowerShell v3 introduced two improvements to its remote control capabilities. First, sessions are much less fragile, meaning they can survive brief network hiccups and other transient interruptions. You get that benefit even if you aren't explicitly using a session object. Even if you've used `Enter-PSSession` and its `-ComputerName` parameter, you're technically still using a session under the hood, so you get the more-robust connectivity.

The other new feature introduced in v3 is one you have to explicitly use: disconnected sessions. Say you're sitting on COMPUTER1, logged in as Admin1 (who is a member of the Domain Admins group), and you create a new connection to COMPUTER2:

```
PS C:\> New-PSSession -ComputerName COMPUTER2
Id Name              ComputerName  State
-- ----------------- ------------- -----
 4 Session4          COMPUTER2     Opened
```

You can then disconnect that session. You still do this on COMPUTER1, where you're sitting, and it disengages the connection between the two computers, but it leaves the copy of PowerShell up and running on COMPUTER2. Note that you do this by specifying the session's ID number, which was displayed when you first created the session:

```
PS C:\> Disconnect-PSSession -Id 4
Id Name              ComputerName  State
-- ----------------- ------------- -----
 4 Session4          COMPUTER2     Disconnected
```

This is something you obviously need to think about—you're leaving a copy of Power-Shell running on COMPUTER2. Assigning useful idle time-out periods and so forth becomes important. In earlier versions of PowerShell, a session that you disconnected went away, so you had no cleanup. Starting with v3, it's possible to litter your environment with running sessions, which means you have to exercise a bit more responsibility.

But here's the cool part: we'll log into another computer, COMPUTER3, as the same domain admin named Admin1, and retrieve a list of sessions running on COMPUTER2:

```
PS C:\> Get-PSSession -computerName COMPUTER2
Id Name              ComputerName  State
-- ----------------- ------------- -----
 4 Session4          COMPUTER2     Disconnected
```

Neat, right? You couldn't see this session if you'd logged in as a different user, even as another administrator; you can see only the sessions you created on COMPUTER2. But now, having seen it, you can reconnect it. This will allow you to reconnect to a session that you disconnected from either intentionally or unintentionally, and you will be able to pick up right where you left your session:

```
PS C:\> Get-PSSession -computerName COMPUTER2 | Connect-PSSession
Id Name                ComputerName  State
-- ----                ------------  -----
 4 Session4            COMPUTER2     Open
```

Let's spend some time talking about managing these sessions. In PowerShell's WSMan drive, you'll find settings that can help you keep disconnected sessions under control. You can also centrally configure most of these via Group Policy. The key settings to look for include the following:

- In WSMan:\localhost\Shell:
  - IdleTimeout—Specifies the amount of time a session can be idle before it's shut down automatically. The default is about 2,000 hours (expressed in seconds), or about 84 days.
  - MaxConcurrentUsers—Specifies the number of users who can have a session open at once.
  - MaxShellRunTime—Determines the maximum amount of time a session can be open. The default is, for all practical purposes, infinite. Keep in mind that IdleTimeout can override this if the shell is sitting idle, as opposed to running commands.
  - MaxShellsPerUser—Sets a limit on the number of sessions a single user can have open at once. Multiply this by MaxConcurrentUsers to figure out the maximum possible number of sessions, for all users, on the computer.
- In WSMan:\localhost\Service:
  - MaxConnections—Sets the upper limit on incoming connections to the entire remoting infrastructure. Even if you allow a larger number of shells per user or a maximum number of users, MaxConnections is the absolute limit on incoming connections.

As an administrator, you obviously have a higher level of responsibility than a standard user. It's up to you to keep track of your sessions, particularly if you'll be disconnecting and reconnecting. Sensible time-out settings can help ensure that shell sessions don't sit around idling for long stretches of time.

## 18.6   Lab

**NOTE** For this lab, you need a Windows Server 2016, macOS, or Linux machine running PowerShell v7 or later. If you have access to only a client computer (running Windows 10 or later), you won't be able to complete tasks 6 through 9 of this lab.

To complete this lab, you should have two computers: one to remote from and another to remote to. If you have only one computer, use its computer name to remote to it. You should get a similar experience that way:

1 Close all open sessions in your shell.
2 Establish a session to a remote computer. Save the session in a variable named `$session`.
3 Use the `$session` variable to establish a one-to-one remote shell session with the remote computer. Display a list of processes and then exit.
4 Use the `$session` variable with `Invoke-Command` and list the time zone of the remote machine.
5 If you are on a Windows client, use `Get-PSSession` and `Invoke-Command` to get a list of the 20 most recent security event log entries from the remote computer.
6 If you are on a macOS or Linux client, count the number of items in the `/var` directory. *Tasks 7–10 can only be performed on a Windows machine.*
7 Use `Invoke-Command` and your `$session` variable to load the `ServerManager` module on the remote computer.
8 Import the `ServerManager` module's commands from the remote computer to your computer. Add the prefix `rem` to the imported commands' nouns.
9 Run the imported `Get-WindowsFeature` command.
10 Close the session that's in your `$session` variable.

## 18.7   Lab answers

```
1  get-pssession | Remove-PSSession
2  $session=new-pssession -computername localhost
3  enter-pssession $session
   Get-Process
   Exit
4  invoke-command -ScriptBlock { get-timezone } -Session $session
5  Invoke-Command -ScriptBlock {get-eventlog -LogName System
   -Newest 20} -Session (Get-PSSession)
   Get-ChildItem -Path /var | Measure-Object | select count
6  Invoke-Command -ScriptBlock {Import-Module ServerManager}
   -Session $session
7  Import-PSSession -Session $session -Prefix rem
   -Module ServerManager
8  Get-RemWindowsFeature
9  Remove-PSSession -Session $session
```

## 18.8   Further exploration

Take a quick inventory of your environment: What PowerShell-enabled products do you have? Exchange Server? SharePoint Server? VMware vSphere? System Center Virtual Machine Manager? These and other products all include PowerShell modules, many of which are accessible via PowerShell remoting.

# *You call this scripting?* 19

So far, you could've accomplished everything in this book by using PowerShell's command-line interface. You haven't had to write a single script. That's a big deal for us, because we see a lot of administrators initially shying away from scripting, perceiving it (rightly) as a kind of programming, and feeling (correctly) that learning it can sometimes take more time than it's worth. Hopefully, you've seen how much you can accomplish in PowerShell without having to become a programmer. But at this point, you may also be starting to feel that constantly retyping the same commands is going to become pretty tedious. You're right, so in this chapter we're going to dive into PowerShell scripting—but we're still not going to be programming. Instead, we're going to focus on scripts as little more than a way of saving our fingers from unnecessary retyping.

## 19.1 *Not programming, more like batch files*

Most system administrators have, at one point or another, created a command-line batch file (which usually has a .bat, .cmd, or .sh filename extension). These are nothing more than simple text files (that you can edit with a text editor, such as vi) containing a list of commands to be executed in a specific order. Technically, you call those commands a *script*, because like a Hollywood script, they tell the performer (your computer) exactly what to do and say, and in what order to do and say it. But batch files rarely look like programming, in part because the cmd.exe shell has a limited language that doesn't permit incredibly complicated scripts.

PowerShell scripts work similarly to Bash or sh scripts. List the commands that you want run, and the shell will execute those commands in the order specified. You can create a script by copying a command from the host window and pasting it into a text editor. We expect you'll be happier writing scripts with the VS Code PowerShell extension, or with a third-party editor of your choice.

VS Code, in fact, makes scripting practically indistinguishable from using the shell interactively. When using VS Code, you type the command or commands you want to run, and then click the Run button in the toolbar to execute those commands. Click Save, and you've created a script without having to copy and paste anything at all.

**HEADS UP**  Just a reminder that this chapter is very Windows focused as far as the examples are concerned.

## 19.2  *Making commands repeatable*

The idea behind PowerShell scripts is, first and foremost, to make it easier to run a given command over and over, without having to manually retype it every time. That being the case, we need to come up with a command that you'll want to run over and over again, and use that as an example throughout this chapter. We want to make this decently complex, so we'll start with something from CIM and add in some filtering, sorting, and other stuff.

At this point, we're going to switch to using VS Code instead of the normal console window, because VS Code will make it easier for us to migrate our command into a script. Frankly, VS Code makes it easier to type complex commands, because you get a full-screen editor instead of working on a single line within the console host. Here's our command:

```
Get-CimInstance -class Win32_LogicalDisk -computername localhost `
-filter "drivetype=3" | Sort-Object -property DeviceID |
Format-Table -property DeviceID,
@{label='FreeSpace(MB)';expression={$_.FreeSpace / 1MB -as [int]}},
@{label='Size(GB)';expression={$_.Size / 1GB -as [int]}},
@{label='%Free';expression={$_.FreeSpace / $_.Size * 100 -as [int]}}
```

**TIP**  Remember, you can use name instead of label, and either can be abbreviated to a single character, n or l. But it's easy for a lowercase *L* to look like the number 1, so be careful!

Figure 19.1 shows how we enter this into VS Code. Notice that we select the two-pane layout by using the toolbar button on the far right of the layout choices. Also notice

```
C: > Scripts > ⚡ test.ps1
  1   Get-CimInstance -ClassName Win32_LogicalDisk -ComputerName localhost -Filter "DriveType=3" |
  2      Sort-Object -Property DeviceID |  ◄
  3      Format-Table -Property DeviceID , ◄                      Continued as one
  4      @{Label='FreeSpace(MB)';Expression={$_.FreeSpace /1MB -as [int]}},   pipeline command
  5      @{Label='Size(GB)';Expression={$_.Size /1GB -as [int]}},
  6      @{Label='%Free';Expression={$_.FreeSpace / $_.Size * 100 -as [int]}}
  7   |
```

```
PROBLEMS    OUTPUT    DEBUG CONSOLE    TERMINAL

PS C:\Scripts> Get-CimInstance -ClassName Win32_LogicalDisk -ComputerName localhost -Filter "DriveType=3" |
   Sort-Object -Property DeviceID |
   Format-Table -Property DeviceID ,
   @{Label='FreeSpace(MB)';Expression={$_.FreeSpace /1MB -as [int]}},
   @{Label='Size(GB)';Expression={$_.Size /1GB -as [int]}},
   @{Label='%Free';Expression={$_.FreeSpace / $_.Size * 100 -as [int]}}

DeviceID FreeSpace(MB) Size(GB) %Free
-------- ------------- -------- -----
C:              17091      237     7
```

**Figure 19.1  Entering and running a command in VS Code using the two-pane layout**

that we format our command so that each physical line ends in either a pipe character or a comma. By doing so, we're forcing the shell to recognize these multiple lines as a single, one-line command. You could do the same thing in the console host, but this formatting is especially effective because it makes the command a lot easier to read. Also notice that we use full cmdlet names and parameter names and that we specify every parameter name rather than using positional parameters. All of that will make our script easier to read and follow, either for someone else or in the future when we might have forgotten our original intent.

We run the command by clicking the Run toolbar icon (you could also press F5) to test it, and our output shows that it's working perfectly. Here's a neat trick in VS Code: you can highlight a portion of your command and press F8 to run just the highlighted portion. Because we've formatted the command so that there's one distinct command per physical line, that makes it easy for us to test our command bit by bit. We could highlight and run the first line independently. If we were satisfied with the output, we could highlight the first and second lines and run them. If that worked as expected, we could run the whole command.

At this point, we can save the command—and we can start calling it a *script* now. We'll save it as Get-DiskInventory.ps1. We like giving scripts cmdlet-style verb-noun names. You can see how this script is starting to look and work a lot like a cmdlet, so it makes sense to give it a cmdlet-style name.

## 19.3  *Parameterizing commands*

When you think about running a command over and over, you might realize that some portion of the command will have to change from time to time. For example, suppose you want to give Get-DiskInventory.ps1 to some of your colleagues, who might be less experienced in using PowerShell. It's a complex, hard-to-type command, and they might appreciate having it bundled into an easier-to-run script. But, as written, the script runs only against the local computer. You can certainly imagine that some of your colleagues might want to get a disk inventory from one or more remote computers instead.

One option is to have them open the script and change the -computername parameter's value. But it's entirely possible that they wouldn't be comfortable doing so, and there's a chance they'll change something else and break the script entirely. It would be better to provide a formal way for them to pass in a different computer name (or a set of names). At this stage, you need to identify the things that might need to change when the command is run, and replace those things with variables.

We'll set the computer name variable to a static value for now so that we can still test the script. Here's our revised script.

> **Listing 19.1   Get-DiskInventory.ps1, with a parameterized command (Windows only)**

```
$computername = 'localhost'              ◁——— Sets a new variable
Get-CimInstance -class Win32_LogicalDisk `◁——┐
                                             └ Breaks the line with a backtick
```

```
-computername  $computername  `      ◁────  Uses a variable
-filter "drivetype=3" |
Sort-Object -property DeviceID |
Format-Table -property DeviceID,
    @{label='FreeSpace(MB)';expression={$_.FreeSpace / 1MB -as [int]}},
    @{label='Size(GB)';expression={$_.Size / 1GB -as [int]}},
    @{label='%Free';expression={$_.FreeSpace / $_.Size * 100 -as [int]}}
```

We do three things here, two of which are functional and one of which is purely cosmetic:

- We add a variable, $computername, and set it equal to localhost. We've noticed that most PowerShell commands that accept a computer name use the parameter name -computername, and we want to duplicate that convention, which is why we chose the variable name that we did.

- We replace the value for the -computername parameter with our variable. Right now, the script should run exactly the same as it did before (and we tested to make sure it does), because we put localhost into the $computername variable.

- We add a backtick after the -computername parameter and its value. This escapes, or takes away, the special meaning of the carriage return at the end of the line. That tells PowerShell that the next physical line is part of this same command. You don't need to do that when the line ends in a pipe character or a comma, but in order to fit the code within this book, we needed to break the line before the pipe character. This will work only if the backtick character is the last thing on the line!

**Listing 19.2   Get-FilePath.ps1, with a parameterized command (cross-platform)**

```
$filePath = '/usr/bin/'                        ◁────  Sets a new variable
get-childitem -path $filepath | get-filehash |  ◁─┐
Sort-Object hash | Select-Object -first 10        │ Breaks the line after a
                                                  │ pipe and uses a variable
```

We do three things here, two of which are functional and one of which is purely cosmetic:

- We add a variable, $filepath, and set it equal to /usr/bin. We've noticed that the Get-ChildItem command accepts a path parameter name -path, and we want to duplicate that convention, which is why we chose the variable name that we did.

- We replace the value for the -path parameter with our variable. Right now, the script should run exactly the same as it did before (and we tested to make sure it does), because we left the path parameter blank, and it runs in the current working directory.

- If you need to break up your command into multiple lines, the best way to do this is to put a line break after the pipe symbol. PowerShell knows that if there is nothing next to the pipe symbol, then the next line of code will be a continuation of the previous line. This can be very helpful if you have a very long pipeline.

```
Get-Process | Sort-Object   ⟵——— Shows our original command

Get-Process |               ⟵——— Breaks the command at a pipe
Sort-Object

                            | Breaks the command with a backtick
Get-Process `         ⟵————|
 | Sort-Object       Starting the line with a pipeline symbol
```

**TIP**   After you make any changes, run your script to validate it is still working. We always do that after making any kind of change to ensure we haven't introduced a random typo or other error.

## 19.4   *Creating a parameterized script*

Now that we've identified the elements of the script that might change from time to time, we need to provide a way for someone else to specify new values for those elements. We need to take that hardcoded $computername variable and turn it into an input parameter. PowerShell makes this easy.

---
**Listing 19.3   Get-DiskInventory.ps1, with an input parameter**
---

```
param (
  $computername = 'localhost'  ⟵——— Uses a param block
)
Get-CimInstance -class Win32_LogicalDisk -computername $computername `
 -filter "drivetype=3" |
 Sort-Object -property DeviceID |
 Format-Table -property DeviceID,
     @{label='FreeSpace(MB)';expression={$_.FreeSpace / 1MB -as [int]}},
     @{label='Size(GB';expression={$_.Size / 1GB -as [int]}},
     @{label='%Free';expression={$_.FreeSpace / $_.Size * 100 -as [int]}}
```

All we did was add a Param() block around our variable declaration. This defines $computername as a parameter and specifies that localhost is the default value to be used if the script is run without a computer name being specified. You don't have to provide a default value, but we like to do so when there's a reasonable value that we can think of.

   All parameters declared in this fashion are both named and positional, meaning that we can now run the script from the command line in any of these ways:

```
PS C:\> .\Get-DiskInventory.ps1 SRV-02
PS C:\> .\Get-DiskInventory.ps1 -computername SRV02
PS C:\> .\Get-DiskInventory.ps1 -comp SRV02
```

In the first instance, we use the parameter positionally, providing a value but not the parameter name. In the second and third instances, we specify the parameter name, but in the third instance we abbreviate that name in keeping with PowerShell's normal rules for parameter name abbreviation. Note that in all three cases, we have to specify a path (.\, which is the current folder) to the script, because the shell won't automatically search the current directory to find the script.

   You can specify as many parameters as you need to by separating them with commas. For example, suppose that we want to also parameterize the filter criteria. Right now, it's retrieving only logical disks of type 3, which represents fixed disks. We could change that to a parameter, as in the following listing.

**Listing 19.4   Get-DiskInventory.ps1, with an additional parameter**

```
param (
  $computername = 'localhost',
  $drivetype = 3            ⟵── Specifies an additional parameter
)
Get-CimInstance -class Win32_LogicalDisk -computername $computername `
 -filter "drivetype=$drivetype" |  ⟵┐
 Sort-Object -property DeviceID |    │ Uses a parameter
 Format-Table -property DeviceID,
     @{label='FreeSpace(MB)';expression={$_.FreeSpace / 1MB -as [int]}},
     @{label='Size(GB';expression={$_.Size / 1GB -as [int]}},
     @{label='%Free';expression={$_.FreeSpace / $_.Size * 100 -as [int]}}
```

Notice that we take advantage of PowerShell's ability to replace variables with their values inside double quotation marks (you learned about that trick in chapter 16). We can run this script in any of the three original ways, although we could also omit either parameter if we wanted to use the default value for it. Here are some permutations:

```
PS C:\> .\Get-DiskInventory.ps1 SRV1 3
PS C:\> .\Get-DiskInventory.ps1 -ComputerName SRV1 -drive 3
PS C:\> .\Get-DiskInventory.ps1 SRV1
PS C:\> .\Get-DiskInventory.ps1 -drive 3
```

In the first instance, we specify both parameters positionally, in the order in which they're declared within the `Param()` block. In the second case, we specify abbreviated parameter names for both. The third time, we omit `-drivetype` entirely, using the default value of 3. In the last instance, we leave off `-computername`, using the default value of `localhost`.

## 19.5   *Documenting your script*

Only a truly mean person would create a useful script and not tell anyone how to use it. Fortunately, PowerShell makes it easy to add help into your script, using comments. You're welcome to add typical programming-style comments to your scripts, but if you're using full cmdlet and parameter names, sometimes your script's operation will be obvious. By using a special comment syntax, however, you can provide help that mimics PowerShell's own help files. This listing shows what we've added to our script.

**Listing 19.5   Adding help to Get-DiskInventory.ps1**

```
<#
.SYNOPSIS
Get-DiskInventory retrieves logical disk information from one or
more computers.
.DESCRIPTION
Get-DiskInventory uses CIM to retrieve the Win32_LogicalDisk
instances from one or more computers. It displays each disk's
drive letter, free space, total size, and percentage of free
```

```
space.
.PARAMETER computername
The computer name, or names, to query. Default: Localhost.
.PARAMETER drivetype
The drive type to query. See Win32_LogicalDisk documentation
for values. 3 is a fixed disk, and is the default.
.EXAMPLE
Get-DiskInventory -computername SRV02 -drivetype 3
#>
param (
  $computername = 'localhost',
  $drivetype = 3
)
Get-CimInstance -class Win32_LogicalDisk -computername $computername `
 -filter "drivetype=$drivetype" |
 Sort-Object -property DeviceID |
 Format-Table -property DeviceID,
     @{label='FreeSpace(MB)';expression={$_.FreeSpace / 1MB -as [int]}},
     @{label='Size(GB';expression={$_.Size / 1GB -as [int]}},
     @{label='%Free';expression={$_.FreeSpace / $_.Size * 100 -as [int]}}
```

PowerShell ignores anything on a line that follows a # symbol, meaning that # designates a line as a comment. We can also use the <# #> block comment syntax instead, because we have several lines of comments and want to avoid starting each line with a separate # character.

Now we can drop to the normal console host and ask for help by running help .\Get-DiskInventory.ps1 (again, you have to provide a path because this is a script and not a built-in cmdlet). Figure 19.2 shows the results, which proves that PowerShell is reading those comments and creating a standard help display.

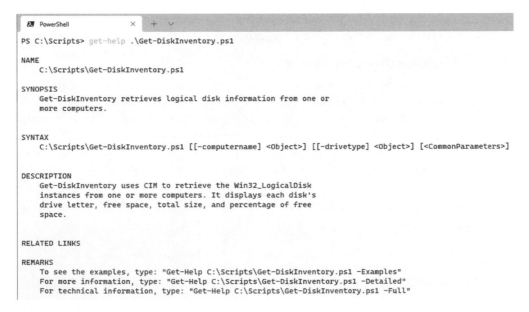

**Figure 19.2   Viewing the help by using the normal help command**

We can even run `help .\Get-DiskInventory -full` to get full help, including parameter information in our example.

These special comments are called *comment-based help*. There are several keywords in addition to `.DESCRIPTION`, `.SYNOPSIS`, and the others we've used. For a full list, run `help about_comment_based_help` in PowerShell.

## 19.6   *One script, one pipeline*

We normally tell folks that anything in a script will run exactly as if you manually typed it into the shell, or if you copied the script to the clipboard and pasted it into the shell. That's not entirely true, though. Consider this simple script:

```
Get-Process
Get-UpTime
```

Just two commands. But what happens if you were to type those commands into the shell manually, pressing Enter after each?

> **TRY IT NOW**   Run these commands on your own to see the results. They create fairly long output that won't fit well within this book or even in a screenshot.

When you run the commands individually, you're creating a new pipeline for each command. At the end of each pipeline, PowerShell looks to see what needs to be formatted and creates the tables that you undoubtedly saw. The key here is that *each command runs in a separate pipeline*. Figure 19.3 illustrates this: two completely separate commands, two individual pipelines, two formatting processes, and two different-looking sets of results.

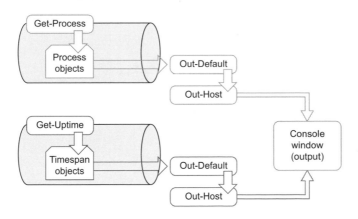

**Figure 19.3   Two commands, two pipelines, and two sets of output in a single console window**

You may think we're crazy for taking so much time to explain something that probably seems obvious, but it's important. Here's what happens when you run those two commands individually:

1   You run `Get-Process`.
2   The command places `Process` objects into the pipeline.

3   The pipeline ends in Out-Default, which picks up the objects.

4   Out-Default passes the objects to Out-Host, which calls on the formatting system to produce text output (you learned about this in chapter 11).

5   The text output appears on the screen.

6   You run Get-UpTime.

7   The command places TimeSpan objects into the pipeline.

8   The pipeline ends in Out-Default, which picks up the objects.

9   Out-Default passes the objects to Out-Host, which calls on the formatting system to produce text output.

10   The text output appears on the screen.

So you're now looking at a screen that contains the results from two commands. We want you to put those two commands into a script file. Name it Test.ps1 or something simple. Before you run the script, though, copy those two commands onto the clipboard. In your editor, you can highlight both lines of text and press Ctrl-C to get them onto the clipboard.

With those commands on the clipboard, go to the PowerShell console host and press Enter. That pastes the commands from the clipboard into the shell. They should execute exactly the same way, because the carriage returns also get pasted. Once again, you're running two distinct commands in two separate pipelines.

Now go back to your editor and run the script. Different results, right? Why is that?

In PowerShell, every command executes within a single pipeline, and that includes scripts. Within a script, any command that produces pipeline output will be writing to a single pipeline: the one that the script itself is running in. Take a look at figure 19.4.

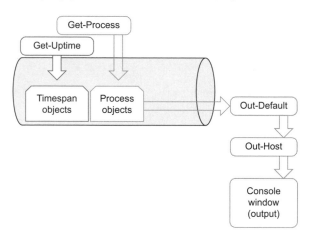

Figure 19.4   **All commands within a script run within that script's single pipeline.**

We'll try to explain what happens:

1   The script runs Get-Process.

2   The command places Process objects into the pipeline.

3   The script runs Get-UpTime.

4 The command places `TimeSpan` objects into the pipeline.

5 The pipeline ends in `Out-Default`, which picks up both kinds of objects.

6 `Out-Default` passes the objects to `Out-Host`, which calls on the formatting system to produce text output.

7 Because the `Process` objects are first, the shell's formatting system selects a format appropriate to processes. That's why they look normal. But then the shell runs into the `TimeSpan` objects. It can't produce a whole new table at this point, so it winds up producing a list.

8 The text output appears on the screen.

This different output occurs because the script writes two kinds of objects to a single pipeline. This is the important difference between putting commands into a script and running them manually: within a script, you have only one pipeline to work with. Normally, your scripts should strive to output only one kind of object so that PowerShell can produce sensible text output.

## 19.7 *A quick look at scope*

The last topic we need to visit is *scope*. Scopes are a form of container for certain types of PowerShell elements, primarily aliases, variables, and functions.

The shell itself is the top-level scope and is called the *global scope*. When you run a script, a new scope is created around that script, and it's called the *script scope*. The script scope is a subsidiary—or a *child*—of the global scope. Functions also get their own *private scope*, which we will cover later in the book.

Figure 19.5 illustrates these scope relationships, with the global scope containing its children, and those containing their own children, and so forth.

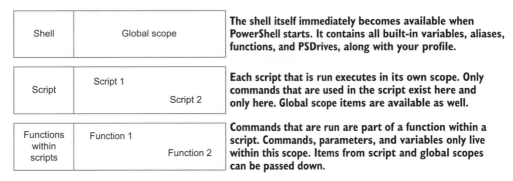

**Figure 19.5  Global, script, and function (private) scopes**

A scope lasts only as long as needed to execute whatever is in the scope. The global scope exists only while PowerShell is running, a script scope exists only while that script is running, and so forth. When whatever it is stops running, the scope vanishes, taking everything inside with it. PowerShell has specific—and sometimes confusing—rules for scoped elements, such as aliases, variables, and functions, but the main rule is this: If you try to access a scoped element, PowerShell sees whether it exists within the current scope. If it doesn't, PowerShell sees whether it exists in the current scope's parent. It continues going up the relationship tree until it gets to the global scope.

> **TIP**  To get the proper results, it's important that you follow these steps carefully and precisely.

Let's see this in action. Follow these steps:

1 Close any PowerShell or PowerShell editor windows you may have open so that you can start from scratch.
2 Open a new PowerShell window and a new VS Code window.
3 In VS Code, create a script that contains one line: `Write $x`.
4 Save the script as C:\Scope.ps1.
5 In the regular PowerShell window, run the script with C:\Scope.ps1. You shouldn't see any output. When the script runs, a new scope is created for it. The $x variable doesn't exist in that scope, so PowerShell goes to the parent scope—the global scope—to see whether $x exists there. It doesn't exist there, either, so PowerShell decides that $x is empty and writes that (meaning, nothing) as the output.
6 In the normal PowerShell window, run $x = 4. Then run C:\Scope.ps1 again. This time, you should see 4 as the output. The variable $x still isn't defined in the script scope, but PowerShell is able to find it in the global scope, so the script uses that value.
7 In VS Code, add $x = 10 to the top of the script (before the existing `Write` command), and save the script.
8 In the normal PowerShell window, run C:\Scope.ps1 again. This time, you'll see 10 as the output. That's because $x is defined within the script scope, and the shell doesn't need to look in the global scope. Now run $x in the shell. You'll see 4, proving that the value of $x within the script scope doesn't affect the value of $x within the global scope.

One important concept here is that when a scope defines a variable, alias, or function, that scope loses access to any variables, aliases, or functions having the same name in a parent scope. The locally defined element will always be the one PowerShell uses. For example, if you put `New-Alias Dir Get-Service` into a script, then within that script the alias `Dir` will run `Get-Service` instead of the usual `Get-ChildItem`. (In reality, the shell probably won't let you do that, because it protects the built-in aliases from being redefined.) By defining the alias within the script's scope, you prevent the shell from going to the parent scope and finding the normal, default `Dir`. Of course, the script's redefinition of `Dir` will last only for the execution of that script, and the default `Dir` defined in the global scope will remain unaffected.

It's easy to let this scope stuff confuse you. You can avoid confusion by never relying on anything that's in any scope other than the current one. So before you try to access a variable within a script, make sure you've already assigned it a value within that same scope. Parameters in a `Param()` block are one way to do that, and there are many other ways to put values and objects into a variable.

## 19.8 Lab

**NOTE** For this lab, you need any computer running Windows 10 or Server 2019 with PowerShell v7 or later.

The following command is for you to add to a script. You should first identify any elements that should be parameterized, such as the computer name. Your final script should define the parameter, and you should create comment-based help within the script. Run your script to test it, and use the `Help` command to make sure your comment-based help works properly. Don't forget to read the help files referenced within this chapter for more information. Here's the command:

```
Get-CimInstance -classname Win32_LogicalDisk -filter "drivetype=3" |
Where { ($_.FreeSpace / $_.Size) -lt .1 } |
Select -Property DeviceID,FreeSpace,Size
```

Here's a hint: At least two pieces of information need to be parameterized. This command is intended to list all drives that have less than a given amount of free disk space. Obviously, you won't always want to target `localhost` (we're using the PowerShell equivalent of `%computername%` in our example), and you might not want 10% (that is, .1) to be your free-space threshold. You could also choose to parameterize the drive type (which is 3 here), but for this lab, leave that hardcoded with the value 3.

## 19.9 Lab answer

```
<#
.Synopsis
Get drives based on percentage free space
.Description
This command will get all local drives that have less than the specified
➥ percentage of free space available.
.Parameter Computername
The name of the computer to check. The default is localhost.
.Parameter MinimumPercentFree
The minimum percent free diskspace. This is the threshold. The default value
➥ is 10. Enter a number between 1 and 100.
.Example
PS C:\> Get-DiskSize -minimum 20
Find all disks on the local computer with less than 20% free space.
.Example
PS C:\> Get-DiskSize -Computername SRV02 -minimum 25
Find all local disks on SRV02 with less than 25% free space.
#>
Param (
    $Computername = 'localhost',
    $MinimumPercentFree = 10
```

```
)
#Convert minimum percent free
$minpercent = $MinimumPercentFree / 100
Get-CimInstance -classname Win32_LogicalDisk -computername $computername `
    -filter "drivetype=3" |
Where { $_.FreeSpace / $_.Size -lt $minpercent } |
Select -Property DeviceID, FreeSpace, Size
```

# 20
# *Improving your parameterized script*

In the previous chapter, we left you with a pretty cool script that had been parameterized. The idea of a parameterized script is that someone else can run the script without having to worry about or mess with its contents. Script users provide input through a designated interface—parameters—and that's all they can change. In this chapter, we're going to take things a bit further.

> **HEADS UP** Just a reminder that this chapter is very Windows focused as far as the examples are concerned.

## 20.1 Starting point

Just to make sure we're on the same page, let's agree to use listing 20.1 as a starting point. This script features comment-based help, two input parameters, and a command that uses those input parameters. We've made one minor change since the previous chapter: we changed the output to be selected objects, rather than a formatted table that we used in section 19.4.

> **Listing 20.1 Starting point: Get-DiskInventory.ps1**

```
<#
.SYNOPSIS
Get-DiskInventory retrieves logical disk information from one or
more computers.
.DESCRIPTION
Get-DiskInventory uses CIM to retrieve the Win32_LogicalDisk
instances from one or more computers. It displays each disk's
drive letter, free space, total size, and percentage of free
space.
.PARAMETER computername
```

```
The computer name, or names, to query. Default: Localhost.
.PARAMETER drivetype
The drive type to query. See Win32_LogicalDisk documentation
for values. 3 is a fixed disk, and is the default.
.EXAMPLE
Get-DiskInventory -ComputerName SRV02 -drivetype 3
#>
param (
  $computername = 'localhost',
  $drivetype = 3
)
Get-CimInstance -class Win32_LogicalDisk -ComputerName $computername `
 -filter "drivetype=$drivetype" |
 Sort-Object -property DeviceID |
 Select-Object -property DeviceID,
     @{label='FreeSpace(MB)';expression={$_.FreeSpace / 1MB -as [int]}},
     @{label='Size(GB)';expression={$_.Size / 1GB -as [int]}},
     @{label='%Free';expression={$_.FreeSpace / $_.Size * 100 -as [int]}}
```

> **Notice the Select-Object as opposed to Format-Table we used in chapter 19.**

Why did we switch to `Select-Object` instead of `Format-Table`? We generally feel it's a bad idea to write a script that produces preformatted output. After all, if someone needed this data in a CSV file, and the script was outputting formatted tables, that person would be out of luck. With this revision, we can run our script this way to get a formatted table:

```
PS C:\> .\Get-DiskInventory | Format-Table
```

Or we could run it this way to get that CSV file:

```
PS C:\> .\Get-DiskInventory | Export-CSV disks.csv
```

The point is that outputting objects (which `Select-Object` does), as opposed to formatting displays, makes our script more flexible in the long run.

## 20.2  *Getting PowerShell to do the hard work*

We're going to turn on some PowerShell magic by adding just one line to our script. This technically turns our script into an *advanced script*, which enables a whole slew of useful PowerShell capabilities. The following listing shows the revision.

---

**Listing 20.2   Making Get-DiskInventory.ps1 an advanced script**

```
<#
.SYNOPSIS
Get-DiskInventory retrieves logical disk information from one or
more computers.
.DESCRIPTION
Get-DiskInventory uses WMI to retrieve the Win32_LogicalDisk
instances from one or more computers. It displays each disk's
drive letter, free space, total size, and percentage of free
space.
```

```
.PARAMETER computername
The computer name, or names, to query. Default: Localhost.
.PARAMETER drivetype
The drive type to query. See Win32_LogicalDisk documentation
for values. 3 is a fixed disk, and is the default.
.EXAMPLE
Get-DiskInventory -ComputerName SRV02 -drivetype 3
#>
[CmdletBinding()]           ⟵          The [CmdletBinding()] must be the first
param (                                line after the comment-based help;
  $computername = 'localhost',         PowerShell knows to look for it here.
  $drivetype = 3
)
Get-CimInstance -class Win32_LogicalDisk -ComputerName $computername `
 -filter "drivetype=$drivetype" |
 Sort-Object -property DeviceID |
 Select-Object -property DeviceID,
     @{name='FreeSpace(MB)';expression={$_.FreeSpace / 1MB -as [int]}},
     @{name='Size(GB)';expression={$_.Size / 1GB -as [int]}},
     @{name='%Free';expression={$_.FreeSpace / $_.Size * 100 -as [int]}}
```

As noted, it's important that the `[CmdletBinding()]` directive be the first line in the script after the comment-based help. PowerShell knows to look for it only there. With this one change, the script will continue to run normally, but we've enabled several neat features that we'll explore next.

## 20.3   *Making parameters mandatory*

From here, we could say we are all done, but that wouldn't be much fun, now, would it? Our script is in its existing form because it provides a default value for the -ComputerName parameter—and we're not sure one is really needed. We'd rather prompt for that value than rely on a hardcoded default. Fortunately, PowerShell makes it easy—again, adding just one line will do the trick, as shown in the next listing.

> **Listing 20.3   Giving Get-DiskInventory.ps1 a mandatory parameter**

```
<#
.SYNOPSIS
Get-DiskInventory retrieves logical disk information from one or
more computers.
.DESCRIPTION
Get-DiskInventory uses WMI to retrieve the Win32_LogicalDisk
instances from one or more computers. It displays each disk's
drive letter, free space, total size, and percentage of free
space.
.PARAMETER computername
The computer name, or names, to query. Default: Localhost.
.PARAMETER drivetype
The drive type to query. See Win32_LogicalDisk documentation
for values. 3 is a fixed disk, and is the default.
.EXAMPLE
```

```
Get-DiskInventory -ComputerName SRV02 -drivetype 3
#>
[CmdletBinding()]
param (
    [Parameter(Mandatory=$True)]
    [string]$computername,
    [int]$drivetype = 3
)
Get-CimInstance -class Win32_LogicalDisk -ComputerName $computername `
 -filter "drivetype=$drivetype" |
 Sort-Object -property DeviceID |
 Select-Object -property DeviceID,
     @{name='FreeSpace(MB)';expression={$_.FreeSpace / 1MB -as [int]}},
     @{name='Size(GB)';expression={$_.Size / 1GB -as [int]}},
     @{name='%Free';expression={$_.FreeSpace / $_.Size * 100 -as [int]}}
```

> The [Parameter(Mandatory=$True)] decorator will make PowerShell prompt for a computer name if whoever runs this script forgets to provide one.

---

### Above and beyond

When someone runs your script but doesn't provide a mandatory parameter, PowerShell will prompt them for it. There are two ways to make PowerShell's prompt more meaningful to that user.

First, use a good parameter name. Prompting someone to fill in *comp* isn't as helpful as prompting them to provide a computerName, so try to use parameter names that are descriptive and consistent with what other PowerShell commands use.

You can also add a help message:

```
[Parameter(Mandatory=$True,HelpMessage="Enter a computer name to query")
```

Some PowerShell hosts will display that help message as part of the prompt, making it even clearer to the user, but not every host application will use this attribute, so don't be dismayed if you don't see it all the time as you're testing. We like including it anyway, when we're writing something intended to be used by other people. It never hurts. But for brevity, we'll omit HelpMessage from our running example in this chapter.

---

Just that one *decorator*, [Parameter(Mandatory=$True)], will make PowerShell prompt for a computer name if whoever runs this script forgets to provide one. To help Power-Shell even further, we've given both of our parameters a data type: [string] for -ComputerName, and [int] (which means *integer*) for -drivetype.

Adding these kinds of attributes to parameters can become confusing, so let's examine the Param() block syntax more closely—look at figure 20.1.

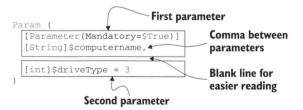

Figure 20.1  Breaking down the Param() block syntax

Here are the important things to notice:

- All of the parameters are enclosed within the `Param()` block's parentheses.

- A single parameter can include multiple decorators, which can be either strung out on one line or placed on separate lines, as we've done in figure 20.1. We think multiple lines are more readable—but the important bit is that they all go together. Here, the `Mandatory` attribute modifies only `-ComputerName`; it has no effect at all on `-drivetype`.

- Each parameter name except the last one is followed by a comma.

- For better readability, we also like to put a blank line between parameters. We think it helps to visually separate them better, making the `Param()` block less confusing.

- We define each parameter as if it were a variable `$computername` and `$drive-type`, but someone who runs this script will treat them as normal PowerShell command-line parameters, such as `-ComputerName` and `-drivetype`.

> **TRY IT NOW**  Try saving the script in listing 20.3 and running it in the shell. Don't specify a `-ComputerName` parameter, and see how PowerShell prompts you for that information.

## 20.4 *Adding parameter aliases*

Is *computername* the first thing that comes to mind when you think about computer names? Possibly not. We used `-ComputerName` as our parameter name because it's consistent with the way other PowerShell commands are written. Look at `Get-Service`, `Get-CimInstance`, `Get-Process`, and others, and you'll see a `-ComputerName` parameter on them all. So we went with that.

But if something like `-host` comes more easily to your mind, you can add that as an alternative name, or alias, for the parameter. It's just another decorator, as shown in the following listing. Don't use `-hostname`, however, as that indicates an SSH connection when using PowerShell Remoting.

---

**Listing 20.4   Adding a parameter alias to Get-DiskInventory.ps1**

```
<#
.SYNOPSIS
Get-DiskInventory retrieves logical disk information from one or
more computers.
.DESCRIPTION
Get-DiskInventory uses WMI to retrieve the Win32_LogicalDisk
instances from one or more computers. It displays each disk's
drive letter, free space, total size, and percentage of free
space.
.PARAMETER computername
The computer name, or names, to query. Default: Localhost.
.PARAMETER drivetype
The drive type to query. See Win32_LogicalDisk documentation
for values. 3 is a fixed disk, and is the default.
```

```
.EXAMPLE
Get-DiskInventory -ComputerName SRV02 -drivetype 3
#>
[CmdletBinding()]
param (
  [Parameter(Mandatory=$True)]
  [Alias('host')]              ◄──────
  [string]$computername,
  [int]$drivetype = 3
)
Get-CimInstance -class Win32_LogicalDisk -ComputerName $computername `
 -filter "drivetype=$drivetype" |
 Sort-Object -property DeviceID |
 Select-Object -property DeviceID,
     @{name='FreeSpace(MB)';expression={$_.FreeSpace / 1MB -as [int]}},
     @{name='Size(GB)';expression={$_.Size / 1GB -as [int]}},
     @{name='%Free';expression={$_.FreeSpace / $_.Size * 100 -as [int]}}
```

**This addition is part of the -ComputerName parameter; it has no effect on -drivetype.**

With this minor change, we can now run this:

```
PS C:\> .\Get-DiskInventory -host SRV02
```

> **NOTE** Remember, you have to type only enough of a parameter name for PowerShell to understand which parameter you mean. In this case, -host was enough for PowerShell to identify -hostname. We could also have typed the full thing.

Again, this new addition is part of the -ComputerName parameter; it has no effect on -drivetype. The -ComputerName parameter's definition now occupies three lines of text, although we could also have strung everything together on one line:

```
[Parameter(Mandatory=$True)][Alias('hostname')][string]$computername,
```

We just think that's a lot harder to read.

## 20.5  Validating parameter input

Let's play with the -drivetype parameter a little bit. According to the MSDN documentation for the Win32_LogicalDisk WMI class (do a search for the class name, and one of the top results will be the documentation), drive type 3 is a local hard disk. Type 2 is a removable disk, which should also have a size and free space measurement. Drive types 1, 4, 5, and 6 are less interesting (does anyone use RAM drives, type 6, anymore?), and in some cases they might not have an amount of free space (type 5, for optical disks). So we'd like to prevent anyone from using those types when they run our script. This listing shows the minor change we need to make.

> **Listing 20.5   Adding parameter validation to Get-DiskInventory.ps1**

```
<#
.SYNOPSIS
Get-DiskInventory retrieves logical disk information from one or
```

```
more computers.
.DESCRIPTION
Get-DiskInventory uses WMI to retrieve the Win32_LogicalDisk
instances from one or more computers. It displays each disk's
drive letter, free space, total size, and percentage of free
space.
.PARAMETER computername
The computer name, or names, to query. Default: Localhost.
.PARAMETER drivetype
The drive type to query. See Win32_LogicalDisk documentation
for values. 3 is a fixed disk, and is the default.
.EXAMPLE
Get-DiskInventory -ComputerName SRV02 -drivetype 3
#>
[CmdletBinding()]
param (
  [Parameter(Mandatory=$True)]
  [Alias('hostname')]
  [string]$computername,
  [ValidateSet(2,3)]          <──
  [int]$drivetype = 3
)
Get-CimInstance -class Win32_LogicalDisk -ComputerName $computername `
 -filter "drivetype=$drivetype" |
 Sort-Object -property DeviceID |
 Select-Object -property DeviceID,
     @{name='FreeSpace(MB)';expression={$_.FreeSpace / 1MB -as [int]}},
     @{name='Size(GB)';expression={$_.Size / 1GB -as [int]}},
     @{name='%Free';expression={$_.FreeSpace / $_.Size * 100 -as [int]}}
```

**We add [ValidateSet(2,3)] to the script to tell PowerShell that only two values, 2 and 3, are accepted by our -drivetype parameter and that 3 is the default.**

There are a bunch of other validation techniques you can add to a parameter, and when it makes sense to do so, you can add more than one to the same parameter. Run `help about_functions_advanced_parameters` for a full list. We'll stick with `ValidateSet()` for now.

**TRY IT NOW**  Save this script and run it again. Try specifying `-drivetype 5` and see what PowerShell does.

## 20.6  *Adding the warm and fuzzies with verbose output*

In chapter 17, we mentioned how we prefer to use `Write-Verbose` over `Write-Host` for producing the step-by-step progress information that some folks like to see their scripts produce. Now's the time for a real example. We've added a few verbose output messages in the following listing.

**Listing 20.6  Adding verbose output to Get-DiskInventory.ps1**

```
<#
.SYNOPSIS
Get-DiskInventory retrieves logical disk information from one or
more computers.
.DESCRIPTION
```

```
Get-DiskInventory uses WMI to retrieve the Win32_LogicalDisk
instances from one or more computers. It displays each disk's
drive letter, free space, total size, and percentage of free
space.
.PARAMETER computername
The computer name, or names, to query. Default: Localhost.
.PARAMETER drivetype
The drive type to query. See Win32_LogicalDisk documentation
for values. 3 is a fixed disk, and is the default.
.EXAMPLE
Get-DiskInventory -ComputerName SRV02 -drivetype 3
#>
[CmdletBinding()]
param (
  [Parameter(Mandatory=$True)]
  [Alias('hostname')]
  [string]$computername,
  [ValidateSet(2,3)]
  [int]$drivetype = 3
)
Write-Verbose "Connecting to $computername"
Write-Verbose "Looking for drive type $drivetype"
Get-CimInstance -class Win32_LogicalDisk -ComputerName $computername `
 -filter "drivetype=$drivetype" |
 Sort-Object -property DeviceID |
 Select-Object -property DeviceID,
     @{name='FreeSpace(MB)';expression={$_.FreeSpace / 1MB -as [int]}},
     @{name='Size(GB)';expression={$_.Size / 1GB -as [int]}},
     @{name='%Free';expression={$_.FreeSpace / $_.Size * 100 -as [int]}}
Write-Verbose "Finished running command"
```

**Adds in three verbose output messages**

Now try running this script in two ways. This first attempt shouldn't display any of the verbose output:

```
PS C:\> .\Get-DiskInventory -ComputerName localhost
```

Now for a second attempt, where we want the verbose output displayed:

```
PS C:\> .\Get-DiskInventory -ComputerName localhost -verbose
```

**TRY IT NOW**   This is a lot cooler when you see it for yourself. Run the script as we've shown here, and see the differences for yourself.

How cool is that? When you want verbose output (pointed out in code listing 20.6), you can get it—and you don't have to code the -Verbose parameter at all! It comes for free when you add [Cmdlet-Binding()]. And a really neat part is that it will also activate verbose output for every command that your script contains! So any commands you use that are designed to produce verbose output will do so "automagically." This technique makes it easy to turn the verbose output on and off, making it a lot more flexible than Write-Host. And you don't have to mess around with the $Verbose-Preference variable to make the output show up onscreen.

Also, notice in the verbose output how we made use of PowerShell's double quotation mark trick: by including a variable ($computername) within double quotes, the output is able to include the contents of the variable so we can see what PowerShell is up to.

## 20.7 Lab

This lab requires you to recall some of what you learned in chapter 19, because you'll be taking the following command, parameterizing it, and turning it into a script—just as you did for the lab in chapter 19. But this time we also want you to make the -ComputerName parameter mandatory and give it a host alias. Have your script display verbose output before and after it runs this command too. Remember, you have to parameterize the computer name—but that's the only thing you have to parameterize in this case.

Be sure to run the command as is before you start modifying it, to make sure it works on your system:

```
Get-CimInstance win32_networkadapter -ComputerName localhost |
 where { $_.PhysicalAdapter } |
 select MACAddress,AdapterType,DeviceID,Name,Speed
```

To reiterate, here's your complete task list:

- Make sure the command runs as is before modifying it.
- Parameterize the computer name.
- Make the computer name parameter mandatory.
- Give the computer name parameter an alias, hostname.
- Add comment-based help with at least one example of how to use the script.
- Add verbose output before and after the modified command.
- Save the script as Get-PhysicalAdapters.ps1.

## 20.8 Lab answer

```
<#
.Synopsis
Get physical network adapters
.Description
Display all physical adapters from the Win32_NetworkAdapter class.
.Parameter Computername
The name of the computer to check.
.Example
PS C:\> c:\scripts\Get-PhysicalAdapters -computer SERVER01
#>
[cmdletbinding()]
Param (
[Parameter(Mandatory=$True,HelpMessage="Enter a computername to query")]
[alias('host')]
[string]$Computername
)
```

```
Write-Verbose "Getting physical network adapters from $computername"
Get-CimInstance -class win32_networkadapter -computername $computername |
 where { $_.PhysicalAdapter } |
 select MACAddress,AdapterType,DeviceID,Name,Speed
Write-Verbose "Script finished."
```

**Above and beyond**

Take what you have learned so far and modify the script we made in chapter 19, Get-FilePath.ps1 (listing 19.2) and

- Make it an advanced function.
- Add mandatory parameters.
- Add verbose output.
- Adapt the formatting to make exporting to a CSV easier.

# Using regular expressions to parse text files

Regular expressions are one of those awkward topics. We often have students ask us to explain them, only to realize—halfway through the conversation—that they didn't need regular expressions at all. A *regex*, as a regular expression is sometimes known, is useful in text parsing, which is something you end up doing a lot of in UNIX and Linux operating systems. In PowerShell, you tend to do less text parsing—and you tend to need regexes less often. That said, we certainly know of times when, in PowerShell, you need to parse textual content such as a log file. That's how we cover regular expressions in this chapter: as a tool to parse text files.

Don't get us wrong: there's much more you can do with regular expressions, and we cover a few of those things at the end of this chapter. But to make sure you have a good expectation up front, let's be clear that we don't cover regular expressions comprehensively or exhaustively in this book. Regular expressions can get *incredibly* complicated. They're an entire technology unto themselves. We'll get you started, and try to do so in a way that's immediately applicable to many production environments, and then we'll give you some pointers for digging deeper on your own, if that's your need.

Our goal with this chapter is to introduce you to regex syntax in a simplified fashion and show you how PowerShell can use regular expressions. If you want to move on to more-complicated expressions on your own, you're welcome to, and you'll know how to use those within the shell.

## 21.1 The purpose of regular expressions

A regular expression is written in a specific language, and its purpose is to define a text pattern. For example, an IPv4 address consists of one to three digits, a period, one to three more digits, a period, and so forth. A regex can define that pattern, although it would accept an invalid address like 211.193.299.299. That's the difference between recognizing a text pattern and checking for the validity of the data.

One of the biggest uses of regular expressions—and the use we cover in this chapter—is to detect specific text patterns within a larger text file, such as a log file. For example, you might write a regex to look for the specific text that represents an HTTP 500 error in a web server log file, or to look for email addresses in an SMTP server log file. In addition to detecting the text pattern, you might use the regex to capture the matched text, enabling you to extract those email addresses from the log file.

## 21.2   *A regex syntax primer*

The simplest regex is an exact string of text that you want to match. Car, for example, is technically a regex, and in PowerShell it'll match CAR, car, Car, CaR, and so on; PowerShell's default matching is case insensitive.

Certain characters, however, have special meaning within a regex, and they enable you to detect patterns of variable text. Here are some examples:

- \w matches "word characters," which means letters, numbers, and underscores, but no punctuation and no whitespace. The regex \won would match Don, Ron, and ton, with the \w standing in for any single letter, number, or underscore.
- \W matches the opposite of \w (so this is one example where PowerShell is sensitive to case), meaning it matches whitespace and punctuation—"nonword characters," in the parlance.
- \d matches any digit from 0 through 9 inclusive.
- \D matches any nondigit.
- \s matches any whitespace character, including a tab, space, or carriage return.
- \S matches any nonwhitespace character.
- . (a period) stands in for any single character.
- [abcde] matches any character in that set. The regex c[aeiou]r would match car and cur, but not caun or coir.
- [a-z] matches one or more characters in that range. You can specify multiple ranges as comma-separated lists, such as [a-f,m-z].
- [^abcde] matches one or more characters that are not in that set, meaning the regex d[^aeiou] would match dns but not don.
- ? follows another literal or special character and matches exactly one instance of that character. So, the regex ca?r would match car but would not match coir. It would also match ca because ? can also match zero instances of the preceding character.
- * matches any number of instances of the preceding character. The regex ca*r would match both cair and car. It would also match ca because * also matches zero instances of the preceding character.
- + matches one or more instances of the preceding character. You'll see this used a lot with parentheses, which create a sort of subexpression. For example, the

regex `(ca)+r` would match `cacacacar` because it matches repeating instances of the `ca` subexpression.

- `\` (backslash) is the regex escape character. Use it in front of a character that normally has special meaning in the regex syntax, to make that character a literal. For example, the regex `\.` would match a literal period character, rather than allowing the period to stand in for any single character, as it normally does. To match a literal backslash, escape it with a backslash: `\\`.

- `{2}` matches exactly that many instances of the preceding character. For example, `\d{1}` matches exactly one digit. Use `{2,}` to match two or more, and use `{1,3}` to match at least one, but no more than three.

- `^` matches the beginning of the string. For example, the regex `c.r` would match `car` as well as `pteranocar`. But the regex `^c.r` would match `car` but would not match `pteranocar` because the `^` makes the matching occur at the beginning of the string. This is a different use of `^` than in the previous example, where it was used with square brackets, `[]`, to indicate a negative match.

- `$` matches the end of the string. For example, the regex `.icks` would match `hicks` and `sticks` (the match would technically be on `ticks` in that example), and would also match `Dickson`. But the regex `.icks$` would not match `Dickson` because the `$` indicates that the string should reach its end after the s.

There you have it—a whirlwind look at the basic regex syntax. As we wrote earlier, there's a lot more where that came from, but this is enough to get some basic work done. Let's look at some example regular expressions:

- `\d{1,3}\.\d{1,3}\.\d{1,3}\.\d{1,3}` matches the pattern of an IPv4 address, although it'll accept illegal data like `432.567.875.000`, as well as legal data like `192.169.15.12`.

- `\\\\\w+(\\\w+)+` matches a Universal Naming Convention (UNC) path. All the backslashes make that regex hard to read—which is one reason it's important to test and tweak your regular expressions before you rely on them in a production task.

- `\w{1}\.\w+@company\.com` matches a specific type of email address: first initial, a period, last name, and then `@company.com`. For example, `sam.smith@company.com` would be a valid match. You do have to be a bit careful with these. For example, `Samuel.smith@company.com.org` or `Smith@company.com.net` would also be a valid match. The regex is fine with there being extra text before and after the matched portion. That's where the `^` and `$` anchors come into play in many situations.

**NOTE** You'll find more about basic regex syntax by running `help about_regular_expressions` in PowerShell. At the end of this chapter, we provide some additional resources for further exploration.

## 21.3   *Using regex with -Match*

PowerShell includes a comparison operator, -Match, and a case-sensitive cousin, -CMatch, that work with regular expressions. Here are some examples:

```
PS C:\> "car" -match "c[aeiou]r"
True
PS C:\> "caaar" -match "c[aeiou]r"
False
PS C:\> "caaar" -match "c[aeiou]+r"
True
PS C:\> "cjinr" -match "c[aeiou]+r"
False
PS C:\> "cear" -match "c[aeiou]r"
False
```

Although it has many uses, we're primarily going to rely on -Match to test regular expressions and make sure they're working properly. As you can see, its left-hand operand is whatever string you're testing, and the right-hand operand is the regular expression. If there's a match, it outputs True; if not, you get False.

> **TRY IT NOW**   This is a good time to take a break from reading and try using the -Match operator. Run through some of the examples we just mentioned, and make sure you're comfortable using the -Match operator in the shell.

## 21.4   *Using regex with Select-String*

Now we reach the real meat of this chapter. We're going to use some web server log files as examples, because they're exactly the kind of pure-text file that a regex is designed to deal with. It'd be nice if we could read these logs into PowerShell in a more object-oriented fashion but, well, we can't. So a regex it is.

Let's start by scanning through the log files to look for any 40*x* errors. These are often File Not Found and similar, and we want to be able to generate a report of the bad files for our organization's web developers. The log files contain a single line for each HTTP request, and each line is broken into space-delimited fields. We have some files that contain 401 and so forth as part of their filename—for example, error401.html—and we don't want those to be included in our results. We specify a regex such as \s40[0-9]\s because that specifies a space on either side of the 40*x* error code. It should find all errors from 400 through 409 inclusive. Here's our command:

```
PS C:\logfiles> get-childitem -filter *.log -recurse |
 select-string -pattern "\s40[0-9]\s" |
 format-table Filename,LineNumber,Line -wrap
```

Notice that we change to the C:\LogFiles directory to run this command. We start by asking PowerShell to get all files matching the *.log filename pattern and to recurse subdirectories. That ensures that all of our log files are included in the output. Then we use Select-String and give it our regex as a pattern. The result of the command is a `MatchInfo` object; we use `Format-Table` to create a display that includes the file-name, the line number, and the line of text that contains our match. This can be easily redirected to a file and given to our web developers.

> **NOTE**   You may have noticed that we used `Format-Table`. We did this for two reasons. The first is because we wanted to wrap the text on the screen, and the second is because we are simply making the screen look cleaner, and we aren't outputting any of the information.

Next, we want to scan the files for all access by Gecko-based web browsers. Our developers tell us they've been having some problems with customers accessing the sites using those browsers, and they want to see which files in particular are being requested. They think they've narrowed the problem down to browsers running under Windows NT 10.0, meaning we're looking for user-agent strings that look something like this:

```
(Windows+NT+10.0;+WOW64;+rv:11.0)+Gecko
```

Our developers have stressed that the 64-bit thing isn't specific, so they don't want the log results limited to just `WOW64` user-agent strings. We come up with this regex: `10\.0;[\w\W]+\+Gecko`. Let's break that down:

- `10\.0;`—This is 10.0. Notice that we escaped the period to make it a literal character rather than the single-character wildcard that a period normally indicates.
- `[\w\W]+`—This is one or more word or nonword characters (in other words, anything).
- `\+Gecko`—This is a literal +, then *Gecko*.

Here's the command to find matching lines from the log files, along with the first couple of lines of output:

```
PS C:\logfiles> get-childitem -filter *.log -recurse |
Select-string -pattern "10\.0;[\w\W]+\+Gecko"
W3SVC1\u_ex120420.log:14:2012-04-20 21:45:04 10.211.55.30 GET
    /MyApp1/Testpage.asp - 80 - 10.211.55.29
    Mozilla/5.0+(Windows+NT+10.0;+WOW64;+rv:11.0)+Gecko/20100101+Firefox/11.
    0 200 0 0 1125
W3SVC1\u_ex120420.log:15:2012-04-20 21:45:04 10.211.55.30 GET /TestPage.asp -
    80 - 10.211.55.29
    Mozilla/5.0+(Windows+NT+10.0;+WOW64;+rv:11.0)+Gecko/20100101+Firefox/11.
    0 200 0 0 1 109
```

We left the output in its default format this time, rather than sending it to a format cmdlet.

As a final example, let's turn from IIS log files to the Windows Security log. Event log entries include a `Message` property, which contains detailed information about the event. Unfortunately, this information is formatted for easy human reading, not for easy computer-based parsing. We'd like to look for all events with ID 4624, which indicates an account logon (that number may differ in different versions of Windows; our example is from Windows Server 2008 R2). But we want to see only those events related to logons for accounts starting with WIN, which relates to computer accounts in our domain and whose account names end in TM20$ through TM40$, which are the specific computers we're interested in. A regex for this might look something like `WIN[\W\w]+TM[234][0-9]\$`. Notice how we need to escape the final dollar sign so that it isn't interpreted as an end-of-string anchor. We need to include `[\W\w]` (nonword and word characters) because it's possible for our account names to include a hyphen, which wouldn't match the `\w` word character class. Here's our command:

```
PS C:\> get-eventlog -LogName security | where { $_.eventid -eq 4624 } |
select -ExpandProperty message | select-string -pattern
"WIN[\W\w]+TM[234][0-9]\$"
```

We start by using `Where-Object` to keep only events with ID 4624. We then expand the contents of the `Message` property into a plain string and pipe it to `Select-String`. Note that this will output the matching message text; if our goal was to output the entire matching event, we would have taken a different approach:

```
PS C:\> get-eventlog -LogName security | where { $_.eventid -eq 4624 -and
➥ $_.message -match "WIN[\W\w]+TM[234][0-9]\$" }
```

Here, rather than outputting the contents of the `Message` property, we simply look for records where the `Message` property contains text matching our regex—and then output the entire event object. It's all about what you're after in terms of output.

## 21.5  Lab

**NOTE**  For this lab, you need any computer running PowerShell v7 or later.

Make no mistake about it, regular expressions can make your head spin, so don't try to create complex regexes right off the bat—start simple. Here are a few exercises to ease you into it. Use regular expressions and operators to complete the following:

1  Get all files in your Windows or /usr directory that have a two-digit number as part of the name.
2  Find all modules loaded on your computer that are from Microsoft, and display the name, version number, author, and company name. (Hint: Pipe `Get-module` to `Get-Member` to discover property names.)
3  In the Windows Update log, you want to display only the lines where the agent began installing files. You may need to open the file in Notepad to figure out what string you need to select. You may need to run `Get-WindowsUpdateLog`, and the corresponding log will be placed on your desktop.

   For Linux, find your history log and display the lines where you installed packages.

4 Using the `Get-DNSClientCache` cmdlet, display all listings in which the `Data` property is an IPv4 address.

5 If you are on a Linux (or Windows) machine, find the lines of the HOSTS file that contain IPV4 addresses.

## 21.6 Lab answers

1 
```
Get-ChildItem c:\windows | where {$_.name -match "\d{2}"}
- Get-ChildItem /usr | where {$_.name -match "\d{2}"}
```
2 
```
get-module | where {$_.companyname -match "^Microsoft"} |
Select Name,Version,Author,Company
```
3 
```
get-content C:\Windows\WindowsUpdate.log |
Select-string "[\w+\W+]Installing Update"
Get-content ./apt/history.log | select-string "[\w+\W+]Installing"
```
4 You could get by with a pattern that starts with one to three numbers followed by a literal period, like this:

```
get-dnsclientcache | where { $_.data -match "^\d{1,3}\." }
```

Or you could match an entire IPv4 address string:

```
get-dnsclientcache | where
{ $_.data -match "^\d{1,3}\.\d{1,3}\.\d{1,3}\.\d{1,3}"}
```
5 
```
gc /etc/hosts | where {$_ -match "^\d{1,3}\.\d{1,3}\.\d{1,3}\.\d{1,3}"}
```

## 21.7 Further exploration

You'll find regular expressions used in other places in PowerShell, and many of them involve shell elements that we don't cover in this book. Here are some examples:

- The `Switch` scripting construct includes a parameter that lets it compare a value to one or more regular expressions.

- Advanced scripts and functions (script cmdlets) can utilize a regular expression–based input-validation tool to help prevent invalid parameter values.

- The `-Match` operator (which we covered briefly in this chapter) tests for string matches against a regular expression, and—something we didn't share earlier—captures matched strings to an automatic `$matches` collection.

PowerShell utilizes industry-standard regex syntax, and if you're interested in learning more, we recommend *Mastering Regular Expressions* by Jeffrey E. F. Friedl (O'Reilly, 2006). A gazillion other regex books are out there, some of which are specific to Windows and .NET (and thus PowerShell), some of which focus on building a regex for specific situations, and so forth. Browse your favorite online bookstore and see if any books look appealing to you and your specific needs.

We also use a free online regex repository, http://RegExLib.com, which has numerous regex examples for a variety of purposes (phone numbers, email addresses, IP addresses, you name it). We've also found ourselves using http://RegExTester.com, a website that lets you interactively test regular expressions to get them dialed in exactly the way you need.

# 22

## *Using someone else's script*

Much as we hope you'll be able to construct your own PowerShell commands and scripts from scratch, we also realize that you'll rely heavily on the internet for examples. Whether you're repurposing examples from someone's blog, or tweaking a script you've found in an online script repository, being able to reuse someone else's PowerShell script is an important core skill. In this chapter, we'll walk you through the process we use to understand someone else's script and make it our own.

> **THANKS** Credit goes to Brett Miller, who provided us with the script we use in this chapter. We deliberately asked him for a less-than-perfect script that doesn't necessarily reflect all of the best practices we normally like to see. And in some instances, we *worsened* this script to make this chapter better reflect the real world. We truly appreciate his contribution to this learning exercise!

Note that we've also selected these scripts specifically because they use advanced PowerShell features that we haven't taught you. Again, we think that's realistic: you're going to run across stuff that looks unfamiliar, and part of this exercise is about how to quickly figure out what the script is doing, even if you aren't fully trained on every technique the script uses.

## 22.1 *The script*

This is a true real-world scenario that most of our students have been through. They have a problem, go the internet, find a script that does what they need to do. It's important that you understand what is happening. The following listing shows the complete script, which is entitled Get-AdExistence.ps1. This script is designed to work with Microsoft's AD cmdlets. This will only work on a Windows-based computer. If you do not have access to a Windows machine with Active Directory installed, you can still follow along with us, as we will be going through this script piece by piece.

**Listing 22.1  Get-AdExistence.Ps1**

```
<#
.Synopsis
   Checks if computer account exists for computer names provided
.DESCRIPTION
   Checks if computer account exists for computer names provided
.EXAMPLE
   Get-ADExistence $computers
.EXAMPLE
   Get-ADExistence "computer1","computer2"
#>
function Get-ADExistence{
    [CmdletBinding()]
    Param(
        # single or array of machine names
        [Parameter(Mandatory=$true,
                   ValueFromPipeline=$true,
                   ValueFromPipelineByPropertyName=$true,
                   HelpMessage="Enter one or multiple computer names")]
        [String[]]$Computers
     )
    Begin{}
    Process {
        foreach ($computer in $computers) {
            try {
                $comp = get-adcomputer $computer -ErrorAction stop
                $properties = @{computername = $computer
                                Enabled = $comp.enabled
                                InAD = 'Yes'}
            }
            catch {
                $properties = @{computername = $computer
                                Enabled = 'Fat Chance'
                                InAD = 'No'}
            }
            finally {
                $obj = New-Object -TypeName psobject -Property $properties
                Write-Output $obj
            }
        } #End foreach

    } #End Process
    End{}
} #End Function
```

### 22.1.1 *Parameter block*

First up is a parameter block, which you learned to create in chapter 19:

```
Param(
        # single or array of machine names
        [Parameter(Mandatory=$true,
                 ValueFromPipeline=$true,
        [String[]]$Computers
    )
```

This parameter block looks a bit different, but it appears to be defining a `-Computers` parameter that can accept an array, and it's mandatory. Fair enough. When you run this, you'll need to provide this information. The next couple of lines are more mysterious:

```
Begin{}
Process
```

We haven't gone into process blocks yet, but for now just know this is where the meat of the script belongs. We go over this more in detail in the *Learn Scripting in a Month of Lunches* (Manning, 2017).

### 22.1.2 *Process block*

We haven't covered `Try Catch` yet, but it is coming, don't worry. For now, just know that you will `Try` to do the thing, and if that doesn't work you will `CATCH` the error it throws. Next we see two variables, `$comp` and `$properties`.

```
foreach ($computer in $computers) {
        try {
            $comp = get-adcomputer $computer
            $properties = @{computername = $computer
                            Enabled = $comp.enabled
                            InAD = 'Yes'}
        }
        catch {
            $properties = @{computername = $computer
                            Enabled = 'Fat Chance'
                            InAD = 'No'}
        }
```

`$Comp` is running an Active Directory command to see if the computer exists, and if it does, it will store the AD information in the `$comp` variable. `$Properties` is a hash table that we have created that stores some information that we need that includes the ComputerName, Enabled, and if it's in AD or not.

The remainder of our script takes our hash table that we created and turns that into a PS custom object, then writes it to the screen with `Write-Output`.

```
finally {
        $obj = New-Object -TypeName psobject -Property $properties
        Write-Output $obj
    }
```

> **Above and beyond**
> What would we need to change to write this to a text file or a CSV file?

## 22.2 *It's a line-by-line examination*

The process in the previous section is a line-by-line analysis of the script, and that's the process we suggest you follow. As you progress through each line, do the following:

- Identify variables, try to figure out what they'll contain, and write that down on a piece of paper. Because variables are often passed to command parameters, having a handy reference of what you think each variable contains will help you predict what each command will do.
- When you run across new commands, read their help and try to understand what they're doing. For Get- commands, try running them—plugging in any values that the script passes in variables to parameters—to see what output is produced.
- When you run across unfamiliar elements, such as if or [environment], consider running short code snippets inside a virtual machine to see what those snippets do (using a VM helps protect your production environment). Search for those keywords in help (using wildcards) to learn more.

Above all, don't skip a single line. Don't think, "Well, I don't know what that does, so I'll just keep going." Stop and find out what each line does, or what you think it does. That helps you figure out where you need to tweak the script to meet your specific needs.

## 22.3 *Lab*

Listing 22.2 shows a complete script. See if you can figure out what it does and how to use it. Can you predict any errors that this might cause? What might you need to do in order to use this in your environment?

Note that this script should run as is (you may have to run it as administrator to access the security log), but if it doesn't run on your system, can you track down the cause of the problem? Keep in mind that you've seen most of these commands, and for the ones you haven't, there are the PowerShell help files. Those files' examples include every technique shown in this script.

**Listing 22.2 Get-LastOn.ps1**

```
function get-LastOn {
    <#
    .DESCRIPTION
    Tell me the most recent event log entries for logon or logoff.
    .BUGS
```

```
Blank 'computer' column
.EXAMPLE
get-LastOn -computername server1 | Sort-Object time -Descending |
Sort-Object id -unique | format-table -AutoSize -Wrap
ID               Domain          Computer Time
--               ------          -------- ----
LOCAL SERVICE    NT AUTHORITY             4/3/2020 11:16:39 AM
NETWORK SERVICE  NT AUTHORITY             4/3/2020 11:16:39 AM
SYSTEM           NT AUTHORITY             4/3/2020 11:16:02 AM
Sorting -unique will ensure only one line per user ID, the most recent.
Needs more testing
.EXAMPLE
PS C:\Users\administrator> get-LastOn -computername server1 -newest 10000
 -maxIDs 10000 | Sort-Object time -Descending |
 Sort-Object id -unique | format-table -AutoSize -Wrap
ID               Domain          Computer Time
--               ------          -------- ----
Administrator    USS                      4/11/2020 10:44:57 PM
ANONYMOUS LOGON  NT AUTHORITY             4/3/2020 8:19:07 AM
LOCAL SERVICE    NT AUTHORITY             10/19/2019 10:17:22 AM
NETWORK SERVICE  NT AUTHORITY             4/4/2020 8:24:09 AM
student          WIN7                     4/11/2020 4:16:55 PM
SYSTEM           NT AUTHORITY             10/18/2019 7:53:56 PM
USSDC$           USS                      4/11/2020 9:38:05 AM
WIN7$            USS                      10/19/2019 3:25:30 AM
PS C:\Users\administrator>
.EXAMPLE
get-LastOn -newest 1000 -maxIDs 20
Only examines the last 1000 lines of the event log
.EXAMPLE
get-LastOn -computername server1| Sort-Object time -Descending |
Sort-Object id -unique | format-table -AutoSize -Wrap
#>
param (
        [string]$ComputerName = 'localhost',
        [int]$MaxEvents = 5000,
        [int]$maxIDs = 5,
        [int]$logonEventNum = 4624,
        [int]$logoffEventNum = 4647
    )
    $eventsAndIDs = Get-WinEvent -LogName security -MaxEvents $MaxEvents
➥ -ComputerName $ComputerName |
    Where-Object {$_.id -eq $logonEventNum -or `
    $_.instanceid -eq  $logoffEventNum} |
    Select-Object -Last $maxIDs -Property TimeCreated,MachineName,Message
    foreach ($event in $eventsAndIDs) {
        $id = ($event |
        parseEventLogMessage |
        where-Object {$_.fieldName -eq "Account Name"}  |
        Select-Object -last 1).fieldValue
        $domain = ($event |
        parseEventLogMessage |
        where-Object {$_.fieldName -eq "Account Domain"}  |
        Select-Object -last 1).fieldValue
        $props = @{'Time'=$event.TimeCreated;
```

```
                    'Computer'=$ComputerName;
                    'ID'=$id
                    'Domain'=$domain}
               $output_obj = New-Object -TypeName PSObject -Property $props
               write-output $output_obj
         }
     }
     function parseEventLogMessage()
     {
         [CmdletBinding()]
         param (
             [parameter(ValueFromPipeline=$True,Mandatory=$True)]
             [string]$Message
         )
         $eachLineArray = $Message -split "`n"
         foreach ($oneLine in $eachLineArray) {
             write-verbose "line:_$oneLine_"
             $fieldName,$fieldValue = $oneLine -split ":", 2
                 try {
                     $fieldName = $fieldName.trim()
                     $fieldValue = $fieldValue.trim()
                 }
                 catch {
                     $fieldName = ""
                 }
                 if ($fieldName -ne "" -and $fieldValue -ne "" )
                 {
                 $props = @{'fieldName'="$fieldName";
                         'fieldValue'=$fieldValue}
                 $output_obj = New-Object -TypeName PSObject -Property $props
                 Write-Output $output_obj
                 }
         }
     }
Get-LastOn
```

## 22.4  Lab answer

The script file seems to define two functions that won't do anything until called. At
the end of the script is a command, Get-LastOn, which is the same name as one of the
functions, so we can assume that's what is executed. Looking at that function, you can
see that it has numerous parameter defaults, which explains why nothing else needs to
be called. The comment-based help also explains what the function does. The first
part of this function is using Get-WinEvent:

```
$eventsAndIDs = Get-WinEvent -LogName security -MaxEvents $MaxEvents |
  Where-Object { $_.id -eq $logonEventNum -or $_.id -eq $logoffEventNum } |
  Select-Object -Last $maxIDs -Property TimeCreated, MachineName, Message
```

If this were a new cmdlet, we'd look at help and examples. The expression seems to be
returning a user-defined maximum of events. After looking at the help for Get-
WinEvent, we see that the parameter -MaxEvents will return the maximum number of

events sorted from newest to oldest. Therefore, our variable of $MaxEvents comes from a parameter and has a default value of 5000. These event logs are then filtered by Where-Object, looking for two event log values (event IDs of 4627 and 4647), also from the parameter.

Next it looks like something is done with each event log in the foreach loop. Here's a potential pitfall: In the foreach loop, it looks like other variables are getting set. The first one is taking the event object and piping it to something called parseEventmessage. This doesn't look like a cmdlet name, but we did see it as one of the functions. Jumping to it, we can see that it takes a message as a parameter and splits each one into an array. We might need to research the -Split operator.

Each line in the array is processed by another foreach loop. It looks like lines are split again, and there is a try/catch block to handle errors. Again, we might need to read up on that to see how it works. Finally, there is an if statement, where it appears that if the split-up strings are not empty, then a variable called $props is created as a hash table or associative array. This function would be much easier to decipher if the author had included some comments. Anyway, the parsing function ends by calling New-Object, another cmdlet to read up on.

This function's output is then passed to the calling function. It looks like the same process is repeated to get $domain.

Oh, look, another hash table and New-Object, but by now we should understand what the function is doing. This is the final output from the function and hence the script.

# *Adding logic and loops*

Looping (or going through a list of objects one at a time) is a fundamental concept in any language, and PowerShell is no exception. There will come a time when you will need to execute a block of code numerous times. PowerShell is well equipped to handle this for you.

## 23.1 Foreach and Foreach-Object

This section may be a bit confusing, as there is a difference between `Foreach` and `Foreach-Object`. Take a look at figure 23.1 for a visual representation of how `Foreach` works.

### 23.1.1 Foreach

Probably the most common form of looping is the `Foreach` command. `Foreach` allows you to iterate through a series of values in a collection of items, such as an array. The syntax of a `Foreach` command is

```
Foreach (p
temporary variable IN collection object)
{Do Something}
```

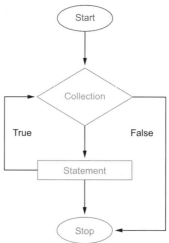

**Figure 23.1  Diagram of how Foreach works**

The process block (the part surrounded by {} ) will execute as many times as the number of collection objects. Let's look at the following command and break it down:

```
PS C:\Scripts> $array = 1..10
PS C:\Scripts> foreach ($a in $array) {Write-output $a}
```

First, we made a variable called $array that will contain an array of numbers from 1 to 10. Next, we are making a temporary variable ($a) and assigning it to the current item in the collection that we are working with. The variable is available only inside the script block and will change as we iterate through the array.

Finally, the script block represented by the curly braces { } will output $a to the screen (figure 23.2).

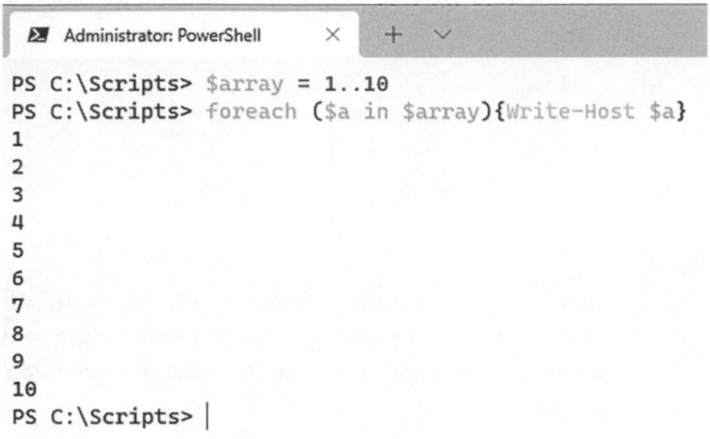

```
PS C:\Scripts> $array = 1..10
PS C:\Scripts> foreach ($a in $array){Write-Host $a}
1
2
3
4
5
6
7
8
9
10
PS C:\Scripts> |
```

Figure 23.2   Writing the output of an array using foreach

### 23.1.2 *Foreach-Object*

The Foreach-Object cmdlet performs an operation defined in a script block on each item in the input collection objects. Most frequently, the Foreach-Object is called via the pipeline.

> **TIP**    Use Foreach if you are looping through multiple objects, and use Foreach-Object if you are using it in the pipeline.

Let's look at the command Get-ChildItem | ForEach-Object {$_.name}. First, we are running the command Get-ChildItem and sending the objects down the pipeline to the Foreach-Object cmdlet.

Next, we are saying for every item received from Get-ChildItem, run the command $_.name (figure 23.3). If you recall from earlier in the text, $_ is simply the current object in the pipeline. By using $_.Name, we are taking the name property from the object and displaying it on the screen.

For both the Foreach and Foreach-Object cmdlets, the commands are executed sequentially, meaning it will take item[0], run the commands you have specified, followed by the following item[1], and so on until the input collection is empty. Usually this isn't a problem, but eventually, if you have a lot of commands in the process block or your input collection is enormous, you can see where executing these one at a time would impact your script's run time.

```
PS /mnt/c/Users/James> Get-ChildItem | Foreach-Object {$_.Name}
3D Objects
AppData
Application Data
Contacts
Cookies
Creative Cloud Files
Documents
Downloads
Favorites
```

**Figure 23.3   This shows how to use `foreach-object` with the pipeline.**

Hopefully, before you started diving into the chapter, you used the help feature to look at all the parameters available for `Foreach-Object`.

**TRY IT NOW**   Run `get-help Foreach-Object` and review the results.

### Above and beyond

The `%` is also an alias for the `ForEach-Object` command. The command from earlier could have been written

```
Get-ChildItem | %{$_.name}
```

which would have yielded the same results. But let's remember that it is always best to use full cmdlet names.

### 23.1.3  *Foreach-Object -Parallel*

As we mentioned before, the main drawback with the `Foreach-Object` command has been that it runs sequentially. There have been a few community-driven modules to help enable a parallel feature for the `Foreach-Object` command. With the introduction of PowerShell 7 (preview 3), a new `-Parallel` parameter was added to the `Foreach-Object` command. Instead of the command(s) being run sequentially, we can now run the same commands on most or all of our input objects at the same time. For example, suppose you are creating 1,000 new users in Active Directory. You could run the command

```
import-csv c:\scripts\newusers.csv |
ForEach-Object {New-aduser -Name $_.Name }
```

which would run the `New-Aduser` command 1,000 times sequentially. Or you can run the command with the `Parallel` parameter:

```
import-csv c:\scripts\newusers.csv |
ForEach-Object -Parallel {New-aduser -Name $_.Name }
```

The following command takes an array of numbers (1–5) and pipes it to a traditional Foreach-Object command, writes the output to the screen, and sleeps for 2 seconds (figure 23.4).

```
1..5 | ForEach-Object {Write-Output $_; start-sleep -Seconds 2}
```

```
PS C:\Scripts> 1..5 | ForEach-Object {Write-Output $_;Start-Sleep -Seconds 2}
1
2
3
4
5
PS C:\Scripts> |
```

Figure 23.4  **Takes an array, pipes to Foreach-Object, then runs a second command**

We can see by using the measure-command cmdlet that this will take 10 seconds to complete.

```
PS C:\Scripts> measure-command {1..5 | ForEach-Object {Write-Output "$_";
➡ start-sleep -Seconds 2}}

Days              : 0
Hours             : 0
Minutes           : 0
Seconds           : 10
Milliseconds      : 47
Ticks             : 100471368
TotalDays         : 0.000116286305555556
TotalHours        : 0.00279087133333333
TotalMinutes      : 0.16745228
TotalSeconds      : 10.0471368
TotalMilliseconds : 10047.1368
```

When we add the -parallel parameter, we will execute what is inside the command block on all the numbers in the array at once.

```
1..5 | ForEach-Object -parallel {Write-Output "$_"; start-sleep -Seconds 2}
```

By using the parallel parameter, we decreased our run time from 10 seconds to 2 seconds.

```
PS C:\Scripts> measure-command {1..5 | ForEach-Object -parallel {Write-Output
➡ "$_"; start-sleep -Seconds 2}}

Days              : 0
Hours             : 0
Minutes           : 0
Seconds           : 2
Milliseconds      : 70
Ticks             : 20702383
```

```
TotalDays          : 2.39610914351852E-05
TotalHours         : 0.000575066194444444
TotalMinutes       : 0.0345039716666667
TotalSeconds       : 2.0702383
TotalMilliseconds  : 2070.2383
```

Because each script block is running simultaneously, the order in which the results are returned to the screen cannot be guaranteed. There is also a throttle limit or the maximum number of script blocks that can be run in parallel at once that we need to make sure you know about—the default is 5. In our example, we had only 5 items in our input collection, so all 5 script blocks were running simultaneously. However, if we change our example from 5 items to 10 items, we will notice the run time changes from 2 seconds to 4 seconds. We can, however, change the throttle limit to a higher one by using the -throttlelimit parameter.

```
1..10 | ForEach-Object -parallel {Write-Output "$_"; start-sleep -Seconds 2}
➥ -ThrottleLimit 10
```

**TRY IT NOW** Change the array to 10 items; then use the measure-command cmdlet to see how long it takes to execute.

There is, however, a limitation with the parallel feature. In order to run each script block simultaneously, a new runspace is created. This can lead to significant performance degradation if the script blocks you are running are resource intensive.

## 23.2 *While*

If you have done any kind of scripting or programming before, then a while loop should not be new concept to you. A while loop is an iterative loop, or it will run until the terminating condition is satisfied. Like the Foreach loop we just talked about, the while loop has a script block, where you can put your commands to be executed (figure 23.5). The basic syntax is as follows: While (condition) {commands}.

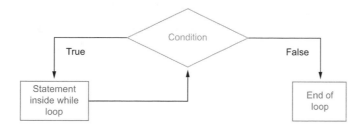

**Figure 23.5  Diagram showing how a while loop works**

- *Condition*—A Boolean ($True or $False) statement. The loop will execute while the condition is True and will terminate when the condition is False. Example: While ($n -ne 10).
- *Commands*—Simple or complex commands that you want to execute while the condition is True.

Here is a quick example:

```
$n=1
While ($n -le 10){Write-Output $n; $n++}
```

We can also start adding logic operators such as -and and -or into our condition statement:

```
While ($date.day -ne 25 -and $date.month -ne 12)
{Write-Host "Its not Christmas Yet"}
```

> **TIP**  If you were to run the above command, it would run indefinitely unless you happened to run it on 25-December. Use Ctrl-C to break the execution.

## 23.3   Do While

As we mentioned before, the while loop will execute only while the condition is true. But what if you wanted to execute the loop at least once regardless of whether the condition was true or not? That is where the Do While loop comes into play.

With Do {commands} While (condition), notice that the script block and condition block are reversed. This will allow us to execute the script block at least one time, then evaluate our condition to see if we need to repeat the loop:

```
$date = get-date

do {
    Write-Output "Checking if the month is December"
    $date = $date.AddMonths(1)
} while ($date.Month -ne 12 )
```

## 23.4   Lab

1  Find a directory that has a lot of items in it. Use a Foreach loop and count the number of characters in each filename.

   – Do the same, but this time use the -parallel parameter.

2  Start the notepad process (or text editor of your choice); then write a do while loop that will display the following text until the process is closed: $process is open.

## 23.5   Lab answers

```
1  $items = Get-ChildItem SOMEWHERE YOU |CHOSE
   foreach ($i in $items){Write-Output "The character length of $i is
   ➥ "($i).Length}
2  start-process notepad
   $Process - "notepad"
   do {
       Write-Host "$process is open"
   } while ((get-process).name -contains "notepad")
```

# Handling errors

*24*

In this chapter, we'll focus on how to capture, deal with, log, and otherwise handle errors the tool may encounter.

> **NOTE** PowerShell.org offers a free e-book called *The Big Book of PowerShell Error Handling*, which dives into this topic from a more technical reference perspective, at https://devopscollective.org/ebooks/. We recommend checking it out once you've completed this tutorial-focused chapter.

Before we get started, there are two variables that we need to get comfortable with. The first is the $Error automation variable. This contains an array of error objects that have occurred in your current session, with the most recent error object showing up at $Error[0]. By default, all errors will be put into this variable. You can change this behavior by setting your ErrorAction common parameter to Ignore. You can get more information about automatic variables by running get-help about_automatic_variables.

The second built-in variable that you can use is the common parameter variable ErrorVariable. This is an object that you can send errors to, so you can use them at a later time if needed (e.g., for writing to a log file):

```
New-PsSession -ComputerName SRV01 -ErrorVariable a
```

ErrorVariable will only hold the most recent error unless you add a + (plus) sign in front of it:

```
New-PsSession -ComputerName SRV01 -ErrorVariable +a
```

> **NOTE**   We did not use the $ in front of the error variable because it is not needed here.

## 24.1   *Understanding errors and exceptions*

PowerShell defines two broad types of bad situations: an *error* and an *exception*. Because most PowerShell commands are designed to deal with multiple things at once, and because in many cases a problem with one thing doesn't mean you want to stop dealing with all the other things, PowerShell tries to err on the side of "just keep going." So, often, when something goes wrong in a command, PowerShell will emit an *error* and keep going (figure 24.1). For example:

```
Get-Service -Name BITS,Nobody,WinRM
```

```
PS C:\Scripts> get-service -Name Bits,Nobody,Winrm
Get-Service: Cannot find any service with service name 'Nobody'.

Status   Name             DisplayName
------   ----             -----------
Running  Bits             Background Intelligent Transfer Servi…
Running  Winrm            Windows Remote Management (WS-Managem…

PS C:\Scripts>
```

**Figure 24.1   `Get-Service` with a service that doesn't exist**

The service `Nobody` doesn't exist, so PowerShell will emit an *error* on that second item. But by default, PowerShell will *keep going* and process the third item in the list. When PowerShell is in this keep-going mode, *you can't have your code respond to the problem condition.* If you want to do something about the problem, you have to change PowerShell's default response to this kind of *nonterminating error*.

At a global level, PowerShell defines an `$ErrorActionPreference` variable, which tells PowerShell what to do in the event of a nonterminating error—that is, this variable tells PowerShell what to do when a problem comes up, but PowerShell is able to keep going. The default value for this variable is `Continue`. Here are the options:

- `Break`—Enter the debugger when an error occurs or when an exception is raised.
- `Continue` *(default)*—Displays the error message and continues executing.
- `Ignore`—Suppresses the error message and continues to execute the command. The `Ignore` value is intended for per-command use, not for use as a saved preference. `Ignore` isn't a valid value for the `$ErrorActionPreference` variable.
- `Inquire`—Displays the error message and asks you whether you want to continue.

- SilentlyContinue—No effect. The error message isn't displayed, and execution continues without interruption.
- Stop—Displays the error message and stops executing. In addition to the error generated, the Stop value generates an ActionPreferenceStopException object to the error stream.
- Suspend—Automatically suspends a workflow job to allow for further investigation. After investigation, the workflow can be resumed. The Suspend value is intended for per-command use, not for use as a saved preference. Suspend isn't a valid value for the $ErrorActionPreference variable.

Rather than changing $ErrorActionPreference globally, you'll typically want to specify a behavior on a per-command basis. You can do this using the -ErrorAction common parameter, which exists on every PowerShell command—even the ones you write yourself that include [CmdletBinding()]. For example, try running these commands, and note the different behaviors:

```
Get-Service -Name Foo,BITS,Nobody,WinRM -ErrorAction Continue
Get-Service -Name BITS,Nobody,WinRM -ErrorAction SilentlyContinue
Get-Service -Name BITS,Nobody,WinRM -ErrorAction Inquire
Get-Service -Name BITS,Nobody,WinRM -ErrorAction Ignore
Get-Service -Name BITS,Nobody,WinRM -ErrorAction Stop
```

The thing to remember is that *you can't handle exceptions in your code unless PowerShell actually generates an exception.* Most commands *won't* generate an exception unless you run them with the Stop error action. One of the biggest mistakes people make is forgetting to add -EA Stop to a command where they want to handle the problem (-EA is short for -ErrorAction).

## 24.2 *Bad handling*

We see people engage in two fundamentally bad practices. These aren't *always* bad, but they're *usually* bad, so we want to bring them to your attention.

First up is globally setting the preference variable right at the top of a script or function:

```
$ErrorActionPreference='SilentlyContinue'
```

In the olden days of VBScript, people used On Error Resume Next. This is essentially saying, "I don't want to know if anything is wrong with my code." People do this in a misguided attempt to suppress possible errors that they know won't matter. For example, attempting to delete a file that doesn't exist will cause an error—but you probably don't care, because mission accomplished either way, right? But to suppress that unwanted error, you should be using -EA SilentlyContinue on the Remove-Item command, not globally suppressing *all* errors in your script.

The other bad practice is a bit more subtle and can come up in the same situation. Suppose you *do* run Remove-Item with -EA SilentlyContinue, and then suppose you try to delete a file that does exist but that you don't have permission to delete. You'll suppress the error and wonder why the file still exists.

Before you start suppressing errors, make sure you've thought it through. Nothing is more vexing than spending hours debugging a script because you suppressed an error message that would have told you where the problem was. We can't tell you how often this comes up in forum questions.

## 24.3   *Two reasons for exception handling*

There are two broad reasons to handle exceptions in your code. (Notice that we're using their official name, *exceptions*, to differentiate them from the nonhandleable *errors* that we wrote about previously.)

Reason one is that you plan to run your tool out of your view. Perhaps it's a scheduled task, or maybe you're writing tools that will be used by remote customers. In either case, you want to make sure you have evidence for any problems that occur, to help you with debugging. In this scenario, you might globally set $ErrorActionPreference to Stop at the top of your script, and wrap the entire script in an error-handling construct. That way, any errors, even unanticipated ones, can be trapped and logged for diagnostic purposes. Although this is a valid scenario, it isn't the one we're going to focus on in this book.

We'll focus on reason two—you're running a command *where you can anticipate a certain kind of problem occurring*, and you want to actively deal with that problem. This might be a failure to connect to a computer, a failure to log on to something, or another scenario along those lines. Let's dig into that.

## 24.4   *Handling exceptions*

Suppose you are building a script that connects to remote machines. You can anticipate the New-PSSession command running into problems: a computer might be offline or nonexistent, or the computer might not work with the protocol you've selected. You want to catch those conditions and, depending on the parameters you ran with, log the failed computer name to a text file and/or try again using the other protocol. You'll start by focusing on the command that could cause the problem and make sure it'll generate a *terminating exception* if it runs into trouble. Change this:

```
$computer = 'Srv01'
Write-Verbose "Connecting to $computer"
$session = New-PSSession -ComputerName $computer
```

to this:

```
$computer = 'Srv01'
Write-Verbose "Connecting to $computer"
$session = New-PSSession -ComputerName $computer -ErrorAction Stop
```

But what if we want to run this command on multiple computers? We have two options. The first option is to put multiple computer names into the $computer variable. After all, it does accept an array of strings.

```
$computer = 'Srv01','DC01','Web02'
Write-Verbose "Connecting to $computer"
$session = New-PSSession -ComputerName $computer -ErrorAction Stop
```

Here is where you will need to make some personal decisions. Do you want to let your script continue to run if an error occurs and capture the error for later use, or do you want your script to stop running immediately? A lot of this will depend on what you are trying to accomplish. If you are attempting to connect to five remote computers to run a command, is it okay if it runs on only four of them, and you log the error that the fifth computer could not be contacted, or do you need the command to run on either all five or none of them?

You have two options here. The first option is to wrap your command in a foreach loop. That way ErrorAction is set each time the command is executed. If you have one failure, the rest of the sessions will still be created. This, however, negates the fact that New-PSSession computername parameter can take an array of objects as its input:

```
foreach ($computer in $computername) {
        Write-Verbose "Connecting to $computer"
     $session = New-PSSession -ComputerName $Computer -ErrorAction Stop
       }
```

The second option is to tell PowerShell to continue and put the error in the Error-Variable common parameter (don't forget to append the + symbol to the existing variable data):

```
$computer = 'Srv01','DC01','Web02'
   $session = New-PSSession -ComputerName $Computer -ErrorVariable a
```

Make sure you understand why this design principle is so important! As we mentioned before, we do not want to suppress useful errors if we can help it.

> **TRY IT NOW** Using what you have learned so far in this chapter and in previous chapters, get the state of the spooler service and the print service. Make sure to log your errors.

Just changing the error action to Stop isn't enough, though. You also need to wrap your code in a Try/Catch construct. If an exception occurs in the Try block, then all the subsequent code in the Try block will be skipped, and the Catch block will execute instead:

```
try { blahfoo }
catch { Write-Warning "Warning: An error occurred." }
```

Here's what's happening: within the Catch block, you take the opportunity to write out a warning message for the benefit of the user. They can suppress warnings by adding -Warning-Action SilentlyContinue when running the command. This is some complex logic—go through it a few times, and make sure you understand it!

## 24.5   *Handling exceptions for noncommands*

What if you're running something—like a .NET Framework method—that doesn't have an -ErrorAction parameter? In *most* cases, you can run it in a Try block as is, because *most* of these methods will throw trappable, terminating exceptions if something goes wrong. The nonterminating exception thing is unique to PowerShell commands like functions and cmdlets.

But you *still* may have instances when you need to do this:

```
Try {
    $ErrorActionPreference = "Stop"
    # run something that doesn't have -ErrorAction
    $ErrorActionPreference = "Continue"
} Catch {
    # ...
}
```

This is your error handling of last resort. Basically, you're temporarily modifying $ErrorActionPreference for the duration of the one command (or whatever) for which you want to catch an exception. This isn't a common situation in our experience, but we figured we'd point it out.

## 24.6   *Going further with exception handling*

It's possible to have multiple Catch blocks after a given Try block, with each Catch dealing with a specific type of exception. For example, if a file deletion failed, you could react differently for a File Not Found or an Access Denied situation. To do this, you'll need to know the .NET Framework type name of each exception you want to call out separately. *The Big Book of PowerShell Error Handling* has a list of common ones and advice for figuring these out (e.g., generating the error on your own in an experiment, and then figuring out what the exception type name was). Broadly, the syntax looks like this:

```
Try {
    # something here generates an exception
} Catch [Exception.Type.One] {
    # deal with that exception here
} Catch [Exception.Type.Two] {
    # deal with the other exception here
} Catch {
    # deal with anything else here
} Finally {
    # run something else
}
```

Also shown in that example is the optional `Finally` block, which will always run after the `Try` or the `Catch`, whether or not an exception occurs.

> **Deprecated exception handling**
>
> You may, in your internet travels, run across a `Trap` construct in PowerShell. This dates back to v1, when the PowerShell team frankly didn't have time to get `Try/Catch` working, and `Trap` was the best short-term fix they could come up with. `Trap` is *deprecated*, meaning it's left in the product for backward compatibility, but you're not intended to use it in newly written code. For that reason, we're not covering it here. It *does* have some uses in global, "I want to catch and log any possible error" situations, but `Try/Catch` is considered a more structured, professional approach to exception handling, and we recommend that you stick with it.

## 24.7  Lab

Using what you have learned so far, do the following:

- Create a function that will get the uptime on remote machines. Make sure you are using the built-in commands in PowerShell 7 and not .NET methods.
- Make sure the function can accept input for multiple machines.
- Include error-handling methods that we discussed in this chapter such as `Try/ Catch` and error actions.

> **Above and beyond**
>
> Take what you have learned so far about remoting and make your function work regardless of the operating system. Here is a hint: There are three built-in variables that may prove useful:
>
> ```
> $IsMacOS
> $IsLinux
> $IsWindows
> ```

Here are some key things to remember:

- `$Error` contains all the error messages in your session.
- `ErrorVariable` can be used to store errors as well (append the + sign to it).
- `Try/Catch` is your friend, but only with nonterminating errors.

## 24.8  Lab answer

```
Function Get-PCUpTime {
    param (
        [string[]]$ComputerName = 'localhost'
    )
```

```
try {
    foreach ($computer in $computerName) {
        If ($computer -eq "localhost") {
            Get-Uptime
        }
        Else { Invoke-command -ComputerName $computer -ScriptBlock
        ➥ { Get-Uptime } -ErrorAction Stop}
    }
}
catch {
    Write-Error "Cannot connect To $computer"
}
}
```

# Debugging techniques

In the previous chapter, we talked about how to handle bad situations (errors and exceptions) but specifically the bad situations that you were expecting. There's another type of bad situation that can happen as your scripts become more and more complex. These situations, that we've alluded to already, are called *bugs*. These are the side effects of a long night scripting, or lack of coffee in the morning. In other words, they're the side effects of us being human. We all make mistakes, and this chapter will be focused on some techniques on how to find and squash the bugs in your scripts.

> **NOTE** We'll be diving into some of the features that the PowerShell extension for Visual Studio Code has to offer, so if you need a refresher on how to get set up, be sure to go back to chapter 2 and follow the steps there.

## 25.1 Output everything

Without diving too deep into Azure Pipelines concepts, the script in listing 25.1 will get details about published artifacts we care about and download them to the Temp drive. If you've never heard the term *artifact* before, it's basically a file that has been published somewhere other tools can download it. Additionally, you'll notice some environment variables in the script (prefixed with $env:). This is because the script was written to be run inside of Azure Pipelines where these artifacts exist.

Let's start with something familiar from chapter 17 where we talked about the different output streams. The different streams are tools in your toolbox for understanding what your code is doing and when it's doing it. Thoughtful placing of Write-* statements can make it easy to find the bug in your scripts and get you back on track. We won't cover this topic too much since we already dedicated chapter 17 to input and output, but the following listing provides an example of when something like Write-Debug would come in handy.

```
$BUILDS_API_URL =
➥ "$env:SYSTEM_COLLECTIONURI$env:SYSTEM_TEAMPROJECT/_apis/build/builds/
➥ $env:BUILD_BUILDID"

function Get-PipelineArtifact {
    param($Name)
    try {
        Write-Debug "Getting pipeline artifact for: $Name"
        $res = Invoke-RestMethod "$BUILDS_API_URL)artifacts?api-version=6.0"
        ➥ -Headers @{
            Authorization = "Bearer $env:SYSTEM_ACCESSTOKEN"
        } -MaximumRetryCount 5 -RetryIntervalSec 1

        if (!$res) {
            Write-Debug 'We did not receive a response from the Azure
            ➥ Pipelines builds API.'
            return
        }

        $res.value | Where-Object { $_.name -Like $Name }
    } catch {
        Write-Warning $_
    }
}

# Determine which stages we care about
$stages = @(
    if ($env:VSCODE_BUILD_STAGE_WINDOWS -eq 'True') { 'Windows' }
    if ($env:VSCODE_BUILD_STAGE_LINUX -eq 'True') { 'Linux' }
    if ($env:VSCODE_BUILD_STAGE_OSX -eq 'True') { 'macOS' }
)
Write-Debug "Running on the following stages: $stages"

Write-Host 'Starting...' -ForegroundColor Green
$stages | ForEach-Object {
    $artifacts = Get-PipelineArtifact -Name "vscode-$_"

    foreach ($artifact in $artifacts) {
        $artifactName = $artifact.name
        $artifactUrl = $artifact.resource.downloadUrl
        Write-Debug "Downloading artifact from $artifactUrl to
    Temp:/$artifactName.zip"
        Invoke-RestMethod $artifactUrl -OutFile "Temp:/$artifactName.zip"
        ➥ -Headers @{
            Authorization = "Bearer $env:SYSTEM_ACCESSTOKEN"
        } -MaximumRetryCount 5 -RetryIntervalSec 1  | Out-Null

        Expand-Archive -Path "Temp:/$artifactName.zip" -DestinationPath
        ➥ 'Temp:/' | Out-Null
    }
}
Write-Host 'Done!' -ForegroundColor Green
```

Now, let's say you run this script and it doesn't work the way you are expecting it to work. One of the simplest ways to debug a script is to run the script, asking it to show the debug stream. Let's do a comparison.

Running the script normally produces

```
PS > ./publishing.ps1
Starting...
Done!
PS >
```

This is not very informative. However, all we have to do is set our debug preference to `Continue`, and we can see the contents of the debug stream:

```
PS > $DebugPreference = 'Continue'
PS > ./publishing.ps1
Starting...
DEBUG: Running on the following stages: Windows Linux
DEBUG: Getting pipeline artifact for: vscode-Windows
DEBUG: Downloading artifact from <redacted> to Temp:/vscode-windows-
➥ release.zip
DEBUG: Getting pipeline artifact for: vscode-Linux
DEBUG: Downloading artifact from <redacted> to Temp:/vscode-linux-release.zip
Done!
```

This is more useful information. It ran for Windows and Linux . . . but wait, wasn't it supposed to also run for macOS?

```
$stages = @(
    if ($env:VSCODE_BUILD_STAGE_WINDOWS -eq 'True') { 'Windows' }
    if ($env:VSCODE_BUILD_STAGE_LINUX -eq 'True') { 'Linux' }
    if ($env:VSCODE_BUILD_STAGE_OSX -eq 'True') { 'macOS' }
)
```

Do you see the bug? I'll wait a second. Got it? A few years ago, Apple changed the name of their operating system from OSX to macOS, and it looks like the script wasn't completely updated properly because it's still referencing `VSCODE_BUILD_STAGE_OSX` instead of `VSCODE_BUILD_STAGE_MACOS`. That first debug statement says that it's running only Windows and Linux, so that's our hint that something is wrong around there.

Debugging like this is often used in an environment that can't be made interactive. Azure Pipelines and GitHub Actions are great examples of environments like this where you don't have the ability to remote into the container or VM that your script is running in, so your only debugging option is to leverage PowerShell's streams to give you as much information as possible. This type of debugging is also useful if you have the ability to run scripts on your local machine or in a container/VM that you have access to, but there are complementary solutions as well that we'll get into now.

## 25.2 One line at a time

Debugging using PowerShell's streams is "debugging the past," as you are looking at what has already happened. Debugging this way is useful but can be tedious because you have to wait to see what shows up in these streams before you take action. If you don't have enough information in the debug stream, you have to make a change to add more information to the debug stream, which requires you to run your script over and over again. If you're trying to debug an issue that happens only 30 minutes into your script running, that means any change you make (even if it's just to get more information) will take 30 minutes to verify. Thankfully, the PowerShell team has several ways to cut down on the time spent debugging. The first of these tactics is what we like to call *F8 debugging* or *line-by-line debugging*.

The premise is simple. Let's take a large script and run it line by line in our console. It sounds like it could be tedious to copy and paste each line, but the PowerShell extension for VS Code streamlines this experience. Let's start with a basic script to demonstrate:

```
Write-Host 'hello'
$processName = 'pwsh'
Get-Process $processName
```

Go ahead and create a test.ps1 file with the code above, and open it in VS Code. Next, click on the first line (the `Write-Host`) so that the cursor is on line 1 (figure 25.1).

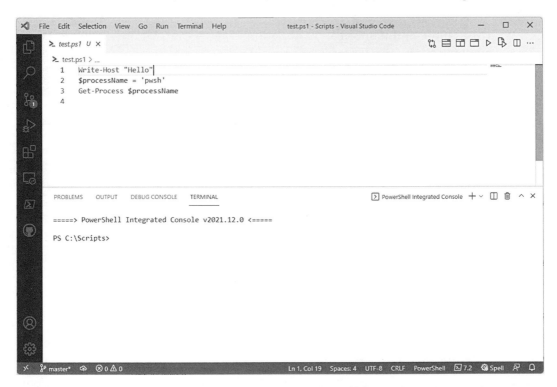

**Figure 25.1   Visual Studio Code with our script. The Run and Run Selection buttons in the top-right corner are highlighted.**

We highlight two buttons in the screen's top-right corner. If you hover over these, they say Run and Run Selection (F8), respectively. The Run button will run your entire script, but we'll come back to why that button is special. For now, let's focus on the other one. In fact, with the cursor on line 1, let's click the Run Selection (F8) button and see what happens. The PowerShell extension will take the current line your cursor is on and run that snippet in the PowerShell Integrated Console in figure 25.2.

**Figure 25.2** Visual Studio Code with our script. It runs only what is highlighted.

The Run Selection button will run any snippet that you have selected, as shown in figure 25.2, or it will run the current line if you have nothing selected. Select some of the lines and click the Run Selection button. You'll notice that it will run exactly what you've selected.

**TRY IT NOW** If you haven't done so yet, run the last two lines (either by selecting both of them or one at a time), and you'll see something similar to the following output:

```
PS > $processName = 'pwsh'
Get-Process $processName

NPM(K)    PM(M)      WS(M)     CPU(s)      Id  SI ProcessName
------    -----      -----     ------      --  -- -----------
     0     0.00      40.48      17.77    5286 ...85 pwsh
     0     0.00      11.27      11.49   29257 ...57 pwsh
     0     0.00      13.94       3.32   32501 ...01 pwsh
     0     0.00     131.63     461.71   35051 ...51 pwsh
     0     0.00     121.53      19.31   35996 ...96 pwsh
```

Here is where it gets interesting. Click inside of the PowerShell Integrated Console, and then run $processName in it. You'll see that the value we set in our script has persisted inside of the PowerShell Integrated Console. This means that we can run a script line by line and see the entire state of the script as it's happening, giving us more visibility into exactly what our script is doing. This means that we can debug our script faster because we are able to get an overview of what's happening and when it's happening *as it's happening*.

> **NOTE**   We call this *F8 debugging* because Run Selection is bound to the F8 key in VS Code, so you can just press F8 instead of having to click the button in the top right.

You were able to see the value of the variable $processName in your console, but you can take this a step further and set the value to something else whenever you'd like. For example, set $processName to code* in your console (figure 25.3), and then use Run Selection to run line 3 (the Get-Process).

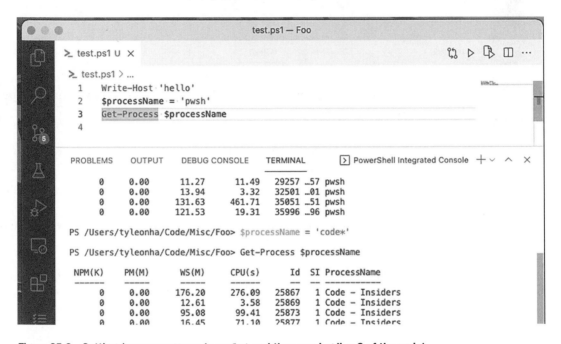

Figure 25.3   Setting **$processName** to **code*** and then running line 3 of the script

Notice that the output is no longer the result of pwsh but instead is the result of code*. This blurs the line between the script in your editor and your console, which can be very useful when you want to see if your script handles different inputs correctly. With that said, keep track of any changes you make because you don't want a manually set variable to cause other issues in your script. If your PowerShell Integrated Console is ever in a bad state and you want to restart it, open the Command Palette using Ctrl+Shift+P on Windows or Linux or Cmd+Shift+P on macOS and type PowerShell: Restart Current Session and run that. This will give you a clean slate (a fresh PowerShell instance) that you can use.

The preceding example is simple, and the strategy itself is simple. Here's the usual workflow that we use:

1 If your script has parameters, set the values to those in the PowerShell Integrated Console ahead of time to simulate running the script with those parameter values.

2 Select the first line or part of your script that you are fairly certain doesn't have the issue in it; then press F8.

3 Dig around. Run the important variables in the console to see what their values are. You can also run functions in the console that you use to see what they return.

4 Select the next line and press F8. Repeat 3 or go to 5.

5 Found what looks off? Make the change to the script you think needs to be made and go back to number 1.

By adopting this strategy, you will gain confidence in debugging your PowerShell scripts and those of others as well (as we talked about in chapter 23). This is a necessary skill in any workplace because when push comes to shove, you will have scripts break and you will have to roll up your sleeves and fix them.

## 25.3   *Hey, script, stop right there . . . with breakpoints*

F8 debugging is sufficient for debugging scripts interactively, and you could stop here in this chapter and do well for yourself. But we want to really prepare you for what you might see in the real world. To do that, we want to talk about a third type of debugging, which we call *breakpoint debugging*. Breakpoint debugging is popularized by our friends, the software developers/engineers. They have been using this type of debugging for many years, and the PowerShell team made it possible to use breakpoint debugging in PowerShell—which is a unique feature for a shell to have (Bash, cmd, Zsh, etc., don't have breakpoint debugging capabilities).

So what's it all about? Well, at a high level, the way breakpoint debugging works is you'll run your script "with debugging" (VS Code jargon); this tells VS Code which lines in your script you want to stop at for further inspection (these stopping points are called *breakpoints*). We want to be clear: you were already doing this in the previous section with F8 debugging, where you ran a selection up to the part you want to investigate, only this time it's even more integrated into VS Code. Okay, let's look at how to set breakpoints and how it works in VS Code.

As shown in figure 25.4, when you put your cursor over a line number (let's do line number 3), a faded red dot appears in the "gutter" of VS Code (it's always between the line numbers and the activity bar on the left). If you click on that red dot, it becomes solid and no longer disappears when you hover away from it. Congratulations, you've just set your very first breakpoint! Let's put that breakpoint to the test. Remember the Run button that is next to the Run Selection button? Well, that button runs your script "with debugging," which means breakpoints will be stopped at if they are set. Let's try it. Click the Run button in the top right, or press the F5 key, which is bound to Run.

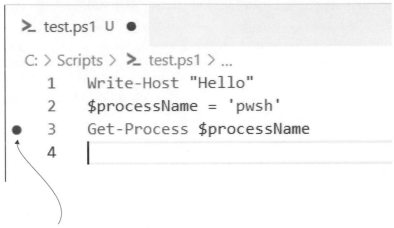

**Click this to place a breakpoint.**

**Figure 25.4    Place a breakpoint by clicking on the faded red dot next to the line number.**

Figure 25.5 gives an overview of what you see when you start debugging a script. At the top of the screen, you see a set of buttons that control how you would like to proceed in the debugging process.

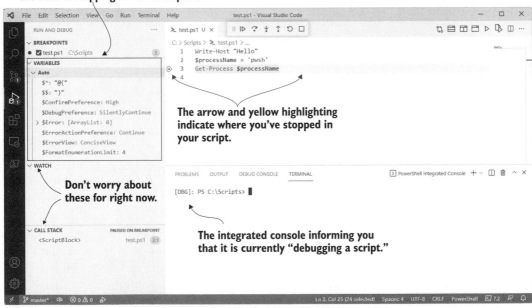

**Figure 25.5    When your script stops at a breakpoint, VS Code displays useful information for debugging your script. This includes indicating where you've stopped in your script, a list of all your breakpoints, a list of variables that are currently set, and more.**

Here's what each of those buttons does:

Ⅰ▷ *Resume*—Hits "play" on the script to continue running the script

↻ *Step over*—Runs the current highlighted line and stops on the line right after

↺ *Restart*—Stops running the script and starts it over again from the beginning

▫ *Stop*—Stops running the script and exits the debug experience

Don't worry about the buttons ⇅ ⇅ for now. They are part of the concept of the call stack, which is a bit more advanced than where we want to take this book. This also means that we will not cover the Call Stack view. We also will not be covering the Watch view, because it's not necessary to learn (and frankly we rarely use the feature), so we'll leave it as an exercise for you to research if you like.

> **TRY IT NOW**   This is a perfect opportunity for you to play around with all the different UI elements we've called out so far. Run (with debugging) a simple script that sets some variables and runs a few simple cmdlets like `Get-Process` or `Get-ChildItem`.

Going forward in this book, continue to leverage F8 and breakpoint debugging so you can improve your skills. We promise you it's like riding a bike. Once you get the hang of it, you'll keep that knowledge with you forever. Your ability to find problems in your scripts and ability to iterate on a script will be a lot better than someone without this foundational knowledge.

## 25.4   *Lab*

Practice makes perfect when it comes to debugging. There are two parts of the lab for this chapter. Go back to the script you looked at in chapter 22's lab. Modify it and add better logging so that you can more easily understand what the script is doing.

Make sure that you add logging that shows on the screen only when you want to see debug logging but otherwise does not pollute the screen if don't want to see debug logging. Revisit every script you've written in this book so far. Try debugging using

- F8 debugging
- Breakpoint debugging

# Tips, tricks, and techniques

We're nearing the end of your month of lunches, so we'd like to share a few random extra tips and techniques to round out your education.

## 26.1 Profiles, prompts, and colors: Customizing the shell

Every PowerShell session starts out the same: the same aliases, the same PSDrives, the same colors, and so forth. Why not customize the shell a little bit more?

### 26.1.1 PowerShell profiles

We've explained before that there's a difference between a PowerShell hosting application and the PowerShell engine itself. A hosting application, such as the console or the VS Code, is a way for you to send commands to the PowerShell engine. The engine executes your commands, and the hosting application is responsible for displaying the results. The hosting application is also responsible for loading and running *profile scripts* each time the shell starts.

These profile scripts can be used to customize the PowerShell environment by loading modules, changing to a different starting directory, defining functions that you'll want to use, and so forth. For example, here is the profile script that Sarah uses on her computer:

```
Import-Module ActiveDirectory
Import-Module DBATools
cd c:\
```

The profile loads the two modules that Sarah uses the most, and it changes to the root of her C: drive, which is where Sarah likes to begin working. You can put any commands you like into your profile.

**NOTE** You might think there's no need to load the Active Directory module, because PowerShell will implicitly load it as soon as Sarah tries to use one of the commands in that module. But that particular module also maps an `AD:` PSDrive, and Sarah likes to have that available as soon as the shell starts.

There's no default profile, and the exact profile script that you create will depend on how you want it to work. Details are available if you run `help about_profiles`, but you mainly need to consider whether you'll be working in multiple different hosting applications. For example, we tend to switch back and forth between the regular console, Windows Terminal, and VS Code. We like to have the same profile running for all three, so we have to be careful to create the right profile script file in the right location. We also have to be careful about what goes into that profile, as some commands that tweak console-specific settings such as colors can cause errors in VS Code or Windows Terminal. Here are the files that the console host tries to load, and the order in which it tries to load them:

1. `$pshome\profile.ps1`—This will execute for all users of the computer, no matter which host they're using (remember that `$pshome` is predefined within PowerShell and contains the path of the PowerShell installation folder).

2. `$pshome\Microsoft.PowerShell_profile.ps1`—This will execute for all users of the computer if they're using the console host.

3. `$pshome/Microsoft.VSCode_profile.ps1`—If you are using the VS Code with the PowerShell extension, this script will be executed instead.

4. `$home\Documents\WindowsPowerShell\profile.ps1`—This will execute only for the current user (because it lives under the user's home directory), no matter which host they're using.

5. `$home\Documents\WindowsPowerShell\Microsoft.PowerShell_profile.ps1`—This will execute for the current user if they're using the console host. If they're using VS Code with the PowerShell extension, the `$home\Documents\Windows-PowerShell\Microsoft.VSCode_profile.ps1` script will be executed instead.

If one or more of these scripts doesn't exist, there's no problem. The hosting application will simply skip it and move on to the next one.

On 64-bit systems, there are variations for both 32- and 64-bit scripts, because there are separate 32- and 64-bit versions of PowerShell itself. You won't always want the same commands run in the 64-bit shell as you do in the 32-bit shell—that is, some modules and other extensions are available for only one or the other architecture, so you wouldn't want a 32-bit profile trying to load a 64-bit module into the 32-bit shell, because it won't work.

**TRY IT NOW** Run `$Profile | Format-List -force` and list out all your profiles.

Note that the documentation in `about_profiles` is different from what we've listed here, and our experience is that the preceding list is correct. Here are a few more points about that list:

- `$pshome` is a built-in PowerShell variable that contains the installation folder for PowerShell itself; on most systems, that's in C:\Program Files\PowerShell\7.
- `$home` is another built-in variable that points to the current user's profile folder (such as C:\Users\Sarah).
- We've used *Documents* to refer to the Documents folder, but on some versions of Windows it will be *My Documents*.
- We've written "no matter which host they're using," but that technically isn't true. It's true of hosting applications (e.g., VS Code) written by Microsoft, but there's no way to force the authors of non-Microsoft hosting applications to follow these rules.

Because we want the same shell extensions to load whether we're using the console host or the VS Code, we chose to customize $home\Documents\WindowsPowerShell\ profile.ps1, because that profile is run for both of the Microsoft-supplied hosting applications.

**TRY IT NOW**   Take your profile for a test drive by creating one or more profile scripts for yourself. Even if all you put in them is a simple message, such as `Write-Output "It Worked"`, this is a good way to see the different files in action. Remember that you have to close the shell (or VS Code) and reopen it to see the profile scripts run.

Keep in mind that profile scripts are scripts and are subject to your shell's current execution policy. If your execution policy is `Restricted`, your profile won't run; if your policy is `AllSigned`, your profile must be signed. Chapter 4 discussed the execution policy.

**TIP**   In VS Code, you can run the command `code $profile` and it will open the VS Code profile. Similarly, in the console, you can run `notepad $profile` and it will open your console-specific profile.

### 26.1.2   *Customizing the prompt*

The PowerShell prompt—the `PS C:\>` that you've seen through much of this book—is generated by a built-in function called `Prompt`. If you want to customize the prompt, you can replace that function. Defining a new `Prompt` function is something that can be done in your profile script so that your change takes effect each time you open the shell. Here's the default prompt:

```
function prompt
{
    $(if (test-path variable:/PSDebugContext) { '[DBG]: ' }
    else { '' }) + 'PS ' + $(Get-Location) `
    + $(if ($nestedpromptlevel -ge 1) { '>>' }) + '> '
}
```

This prompt first tests to see whether the $DebugContext variable is defined in the shell's VARIABLE: drive. If it is, this function adds [DBG]: to the start of the prompt. Otherwise, the prompt is defined as PS along with the current location, which is returned by the Get-Location cmdlet. If the shell is in a nested prompt, as defined by the built-in $nestedpromptlevel variable, the prompt will have >> added to it.

Here's an alternative prompt function. You could enter this directly into any profile script to make it the standard prompt for your shell sessions:

```
function prompt {
 $time = (Get-Date).ToShortTimeString()
 "$time [$env:COMPUTERNAME]:> "
}
```

This alternative prompt displays the current time, followed by the current computer name (which is contained within square brackets):

```
6:07 PM [CLIENT01]:>
```

Note that this uses PowerShell's special behavior with double quotation marks, in which the shell will replace variables (such as $time) with their contents.

One of the most useful pieces of code to add to your profile is to change the title bar of your PowerShell Windows:

```
$host.UI.RawUI.WindowTitle = "$env:username"
```

### 26.1.3 *Tweaking colors*

In previous chapters, we mentioned how stressed out we can get when a long series of error messages scrolls by in the shell. Sarah always struggled in English class when she was a kid, and seeing all that red text reminds her of the essays she'd get back from Ms. Hansen, all marked up with a red pen. Yuck. Fortunately, PowerShell gives you the ability to modify most of the default colors it uses (figure 26.1).

The default text foreground and background colors can be modified by clicking the control box in the upper-left corner of PowerShell's window. From there, select Properties, and then select the Colors tab.

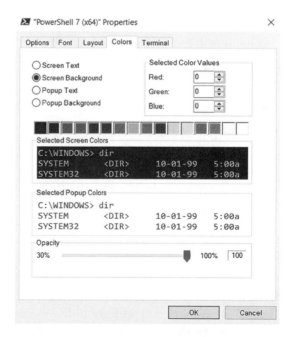

**Figure 26.1  Configuring the default shell screen colors**

Modifying the colors of errors, warnings, and other messages is a bit trickier and requires you to run a command. But you could put this command into your profile so that it executes each time you open the shell. Here's how to change the error message foreground color to green, which we find a lot more soothing:

```
(Get-Host).PrivateData.ErrorForegroundColor = "green"
```

You can change colors for the following settings:

- ErrorForegroundColor
- ErrorBackgroundColor
- WarningForegroundColor
- WarningBackgroundColor
- DebugForegroundColor
- DebugBackgroundColor
- VerboseForegroundColor
- VerboseBackgroundColor
- ProgressForegroundColor
- ProgressBackgroundColor

And here are some of the colors you can choose:

- Red
- Yellow
- Black
- White
- Green
- Cyan
- Magenta
- Blue

There are also dark versions of most of these colors: DarkRed, DarkYellow, DarkGreen, DarkCyan, DarkBlue, and so on.

## 26.2    *Operators: -as, -is, -replace, -join, -split, -contains, -in*

These additional operators are useful in a variety of situations. They let you work with data types, collections, and strings.

### 26.2.1    *-as and -is*

The -as operator produces a new object in an attempt to convert an existing object into a different type. For example, if you have a number that contains a decimal (perhaps from the result of a division operation), you can drop the decimal portion by converting, or *casting*, the number to an integer:

```
1000 / 3 -as [int]
```

The object to be converted comes first, then the -as operator, and then, in square brackets, the type you want to convert to. Types can include [string], [xml], [int], [single], [double], [datetime], and others, although those are probably the ones you'll use the most. Technically, this example of converting to an integer will round the fractional number to an integer, rather than just truncating the fractional portion of the number.

The -is operator works similarly: it's designed to return True or False if an object is of a particular type or not. Here are a few one-line examples:

```
123.45 -is [int]
"SRV02" -is [string]
$True -is [bool]
(Get-Date) -is [datetime]
```

**TRY IT NOW**   Try running each of these one-line commands in the shell to see the results.

### 26.2.2  -replace

The -replace operator uses regex and is designed to locate all occurrences of one string within another and replace those occurrences with a third string:

```
PS C:\> "192.168.34.12" -replace "34","15"
192.168.15.12
```

The source string comes first, followed by the -replace operator. Then you provide the string you want to search for within the source, followed by a comma and the string you want to use in place of the search string. In the preceding example, we replace 34 with 15.

This is not to be confused with the string replace() method, which is a static text replace. While they work similarly, they are very different.

### 26.2.3  -join and -split

The -join and -split operators are designed to convert arrays to delimited lists, and vice versa. For example, suppose you create an array with five elements:

```
PS C:\> $array = "one","two","three","four","five"
PS C:\> $array
one
two
three
four
five
```

This works because PowerShell automatically treats a comma-separated list as an array. Now, let's say you want to join this array together into a pipe-delimited string. You can do that with -join:

```
PS C:\> $array -join "|"
one|two|three|four|five
```

Saving that result into a variable will let you reuse it, or even pipe it out to a file:

```
PS C:\> $string = $array -join "|"
PS C:\> $string
one|two|three|four|five
PS C:\> $string | out-file data.dat
```

The -split operator does the opposite: it takes a delimited string and makes an array from it. For example, suppose you have a tab-delimited file containing one line and four columns. Displaying the contents of the file might look like this:

```
PS C:\> gc computers.tdf
Server1 Windows East    Managed
```

Keep in mind that gc is an alias for Get-Content.

You can use the -split operator to break that into four individual array elements:

```
PS C:\> $array = (gc computers.tdf) -split "`t"
PS C:\> $array
Server1
Windows
East
Managed
```

Notice the use of the escape character, a backtick, and a *t* (`t) to define the tab character. This has to be in double quotes so that the escape character will be recognized. The resulting array has four elements, and you can access them individually by using their index numbers:

```
PS C:\> $array[0]
Server1
```

### 26.2.4   *-contains and -in*

The -contains operator causes much confusion for PowerShell newcomers. You'll see folks try to do this:

```
PS C:\> 'this' -contains '*his*'
False
```

In fact, they mean to use the -like operator instead:

```
. PS C:\> 'this' -like '*his*'
True
```

The -like operator is designed for wildcard string comparisons. The -contains operator is used to test whether a given object exists within a collection. For example, create a collection of string objects, and then test whether a given string is in that collection:

```
PS C:\> $collection = 'abc','def','ghi','jkl'
PS C:\> $collection -contains 'abc'
True
PS C:\> $collection -contains 'xyz'
False
```

The -in operator does the same thing, but it flips the order of the operands so that the collection goes on the right and the test object on the left:

```
PS C:\> $collection = 'abc','def','ghi','jkl'
PS C:\> 'abc' -in $collection
True
PS C:\> 'xyz' -in $collection
False
```

## 26.3 *String manipulation*

Suppose you have a string of text, and you need to convert it to all uppercase letters. Or perhaps you need to get the last three characters from the string. How would you do it?

In PowerShell, strings are objects, and they come with a great many methods. Remember that a method is a way of telling the object to do something, usually to itself, and that you can discover the available methods by piping the object to gm:

```
PS C:\> "Hello" | get-member
   TypeName: System.String

Name            MemberType    Definition
----            ----------    ----------
Clone           Method        System.Object Clone()
CompareTo       Method        int CompareTo(System.Object value...
Contains        Method        bool Contains(string value)
CopyTo          Method        System.Void CopyTo(int sourceInde...
EndsWith        Method        bool EndsWith(string value), bool...
Equals          Method        bool Equals(System.Object obj), b...
GetEnumerator   Method        System.CharEnumerator GetEnumerat...
GetHashCode     Method        int GetHashCode()
GetType         Method        type GetType()
GetTypeCode     Method        System.TypeCode GetTypeCode()
IndexOf         Method        int IndexOf(char value), int Inde...
IndexOfAny      Method        int IndexOfAny(char[] anyOf), int...
Insert          Method        string Insert(int startIndex, str...
IsNormalized    Method        bool IsNormalized(), bool IsNorma...
LastIndexOf     Method        int LastIndexOf(char value), int ...
LastIndexOfAny  Method        int LastIndexOfAny(char[] anyOf),...
Normalize       Method        string Normalize(), string Normal...
PadLeft         Method        string PadLeft(int totalWidth), s...
PadRight        Method        string PadRight(int totalWidth), ...
Remove          Method        string Remove(int startIndex, int...
Replace         Method        string Replace(char oldChar, char...
```

```
Split               Method              string[] Split(Params char[] sepa...
StartsWith          Method              bool StartsWith(string value), bo...
Substring           Method              string Substring(int startIndex),...
ToCharArray         Method              char[] ToCharArray(), char[] ToCh...
ToLower             Method              string ToLower(), string ToLower(...
ToLowerInvariant    Method              string ToLowerInvariant()
ToString            Method              string ToString(), string ToStrin...
ToUpper             Method              string ToUpper(), string ToUpper(...
ToUpperInvariant    Method              string ToUpperInvariant()
Trim                Method              string Trim(Params char[] trimCha...
TrimEnd             Method              string TrimEnd(Params char[] trim...
TrimStart           Method              string TrimStart(Params char[] tr...
Chars               ParameterizedProperty char Chars(int index) {get;}
Length              Property            System.Int32 Length {get;}
```

Some of the more useful `String` methods include the following:

- `IndexOf()`—Tells you the location of a given character within the string:

```
PS C:\> "SRV02".IndexOf("-")
6
```

- `Split()`, `Join()`, *and* `Replace()`—Operate similarly to the `-split`, `-join`, and `-replace` operators we described in the previous section. We tend to use the PowerShell operators rather than the `String` methods.

- `ToLower()` *and* `ToUpper()`—Convert the case of a string:

```
PS C:\> $computername = "SERVER17"
PS C:\> $computername.tolower()
server17
```

- `Trim()`—Removes whitespace from both ends of a string.
- `TrimStart()` and `TrimEnd()`—Remove whitespace from the beginning or end of a string, respectively:

```
PS C:\> $username = "    Sarah "
PS C:\> $username.Trim()
Sarah
```

All of these `String` methods are great ways to manipulate and modify `String` objects. Note that all of these methods can be used with a variable that contains a string—as in the `ToLower()` and `Trim()` examples—or they can be used directly with a static string, as in the `IndexOf()` example.

## 26.4  *Date manipulation*

Like `String` objects, `Date` (or `DateTime`, if you prefer) objects come with a great many methods that allow date and time manipulation and calculation:

```
PS C:\> get-date | get-member
   TypeName: System.DateTime
Name                     MemberType     Definition
----                     ----------     ----------
Add                      Method         System.DateTime Add(System.TimeSpan ...
AddDays                  Method         System.DateTime AddDays(double value)
AddHours                 Method         System.DateTime AddHours(double value)
AddMilliseconds          Method         System.DateTime AddMilliseconds(doub...
AddMinutes               Method         System.DateTime AddMinutes(double va...
AddMonths                Method         System.DateTime AddMonths(int months)
AddSeconds               Method         System.DateTime AddSeconds(double va...
AddTicks                 Method         System.DateTime AddTicks(long value)
AddYears                 Method         System.DateTime AddYears(int value)
CompareTo                Method         int CompareTo(System.Object value), ...
Equals                   Method         bool Equals(System.Object value), bo...
GetDateTimeFormats       Method         string[] GetDateTimeFormats(), strin...
GetHashCode              Method         int GetHashCode()
GetType                  Method         type GetType()
GetTypeCode              Method         System.TypeCode GetTypeCode()
IsDaylightSavingTime     Method         bool IsDaylightSavingTime()
Subtract                 Method         System.TimeSpan Subtract(System.Date...
ToBinary                 Method         long ToBinary()
ToFileTime               Method         long ToFileTime()
ToFileTimeUtc            Method         long ToFileTimeUtc()
ToLocalTime              Method         System.DateTime ToLocalTime()
ToLongDateString         Method         string ToLongDateString()
ToLongTimeString         Method         string ToLongTimeString()
ToOADate                 Method         double ToOADate()
ToShortDateString        Method         string ToShortDateString()
ToShortTimeString        Method         string ToShortTimeString()
ToString                 Method         string ToString(), string ToString(s...
ToUniversalTime          Method         System.DateTime ToUniversalTime()
DisplayHint              NoteProperty   Microsoft.PowerShell.Commands.Displa...
Date                     Property       System.DateTime Date {get;}
Day                      Property       System.Int32 Day {get;}
DayOfWeek                Property       System.DayOfWeek DayOfWeek {get;}
DayOfYear                Property       System.Int32 DayOfYear {get;}
Hour                     Property       System.Int32 Hour {get;}
Kind                     Property       System.DateTimeKind Kind {get;}
Millisecond              Property       System.Int32 Millisecond {get;}
Minute                   Property       System.Int32 Minute {get;}
Month                    Property       System.Int32 Month {get;}
Second                   Property       System.Int32 Second {get;}
Ticks                    Property       System.Int64 Ticks {get;}
TimeOfDay                Property       System.TimeSpan TimeOfDay {get;}
Year                     Property       System.Int32 Year {get;}
DateTime                 ScriptProperty System.Object DateTime {get=if ((& {...
```

Note that the properties enable you to access just a portion of a DateTime, such as the day, year, or month:

```
PS C:\> (get-date).month
10
```

The methods enable two things: calculations and conversions to other formats. For example, to get the date for 90 days ago, we like to use `AddDays()` with a negative number:

```
PS C:\> $today = get-date
PS C:\> $90daysago = $today.adddays(-90)
PS C:\> $90daysago
Saturday, March 13, 2021 11:26:08 AM
```

The methods whose names start with `To` are designed to provide dates and times in an alternative format, such as a short date string:

```
PS C:\> $90daysago.toshortdatestring()
3/13/2021
```

These methods all use your computer's current regional settings to determine the correct way of formatting dates and times.

## 26.5 *Dealing with WMI dates*

While WMI isn't available in PowerShell 7, we know some of you are still using Windows PowerShell 5.1, so we want to share a tidbit of knowledge about how WMI tends to store date and time information in difficult-to-use strings. For example, the `Win32_OperatingSystem` class tracks the last time a computer was started, and the date and time information looks like this:

```
PS C:\> get-wmiobject win32_operatingsystem | select lastbootuptime
lastbootuptime
--------------
20101021210207.793534-420
```

PowerShell's designers knew you wouldn't be able to easily use this information, so they added a pair of conversion methods to every WMI object. Pipe any WMI object to `gm` and you can see those methods at or near the end:

```
PS C:\> get-wmiobject win32_operatingsystem | gm
   TypeName: System.Management.ManagementObject#root\cimv2\Win32_OperatingS
ystem
Name                                MemberType   Definition
----                                ----------   ----------
Reboot                              Method       System.Management...
SetDateTime                         Method       System.Management...
Shutdown                            Method       System.Management...
Win32Shutdown                       Method       System.Management...
Win32ShutdownTracker                Method       System.Management...
BootDevice                          Property     System.String Boo...
...
PSStatus                            PropertySet  PSStatus {Status,...
ConvertFromDateTime                 ScriptMethod System.Object Con...
ConvertToDateTime                   ScriptMethod System.Object Con...
```

We cut out most of the middle of this output so that you can easily find the Convert-FromDateTime() and ConvertToDateTime() methods. In this case, what you start with is a WMI date and time, and you want to convert that to a normal date and time, so you do it like this:

```
PS C:\> $os = get-wmiobject win32_operatingsystem
PS C:\> $os.ConvertToDateTime($os.lastbootuptime)
Thursday, October 20, 2015 9:02:07 PM
```

If you want to make that date and time information part of a normal table, you can use Select-Object or Format-Table to create custom, calculated columns and properties:

```
PS C:\> get-wmiobject win32_operatingsystem | select BuildNumber,__SERVER,
[CA]@{l='LastBootTime';e={$_.ConvertToDateTime($_.LastBootupTime)}}
BuildNumber             __SERVER               LastBootTime
-----------             --------               ------------
7600                    SRV02                  10/20/2015 9:02:07 PM
```

Dates are less of a hassle if you're using the CIM commands, because they automatically translate most date/time values into something human readable.

## 26.6　*Setting default parameter values*

Most PowerShell commands have at least a few parameters that include default values. For example, run Dir by itself and it defaults to the current path, without you having to specify a -Path parameter.

Defaults are stored in a special built-in variable named $PSDefaultParameterValues. The variable is empty each time you open a new shell window, and it's meant to be populated with a hash table (which you could do in a profile script, to have your defaults always in effect).

For example, let's say you want to create a new credential object containing a username and password, and have that credential automatically apply to all commands that have a -Credential parameter:

```
PS C:\> $credential = Get-Credential -UserName Administrator
-Message "Enter Admin credential"
PS C:\> $PSDefaultParameterValues.Add('*:Credential',$credential)
```

Or, you might want to force only the Invoke-Command cmdlet to prompt for a credential each time it's run. In this case, rather than assigning a default value, you'd assign a script block that executes the Get-Credential command:

```
PS C:\> $PSDefaultParameterValues.Add('Invoke-Command:Credential',
(Get-Credential -Message 'Enter administrator credential'
-UserName Administrator}))
```

You can see that the basic format for the Add() method's first argument is <-cmdlet>:<parameter>, and <cmdlet> and can accept wildcards such as *. The second argument for the `Add()` method is either the value you want to make the default, or a script block that executes another command or commands.

You can always examine `$PSDefaultParameterValues` to see what it contains:

```
PS C:\> $PSDefaultParameterValues
Name                               Value
----                               -----
*:Credential                       System.Management.Automation.PSCredenti
Invoke-Command:Credential          Get-Credential -Message 'Enter administ
```

You can learn more about this feature by reading the shell's `about_parameters_default_values` help file.

---

**Above and beyond**

PowerShell variables are controlled by something called *scope*. We offered a brief introduction to scope in chapter 16, and it is something that plays into these default parameter values.

If you set `$PSDefaultParameterValues` at the command line, it'll apply to all scripts and commands run within that shell session. But if you set `$-PSDefaultParameter-Values` within a script, it'll apply only to things done by that script. That's a useful technique, because it means you can start a script with a bunch of defaults, and they won't apply to other scripts, or to the shell in general.

This concept of "what happens in the script, stays in the script" is the heart of scope. You can read more about scope in the shell's `about_scope` help file, if you'd like to explore further on your own.

---

## 26.7  *Playing with script blocks*

Script blocks are a key part of PowerShell, and you've been using them quite a bit:

- The `-FilterScript` parameter of `Where-Object` takes a script block.
- The `-Process` parameter of `ForEach-Object` takes a script block.
- The hash table used to create custom properties with `Select-Object`, or custom columns with `Format-Table`, accepts a script block as the value of the `E`, or `Expression`, key.
- Default parameter values, as described in the previous section, can be set to a script block.
- Some remoting and job-related commands, including `Invoke-Command` and `Start-Job`, accept script blocks on their `-ScriptBlock` parameter.

So what is a script block? In general, it's anything surrounded by curly brackets {}, with the exception of hash tables, which use curly brackets but are preceded by the @ symbol. You can even enter a script block right from the command line and assign it to a variable. You can then use the call operator, `&`, to run the block:

```
PS C:\> $block = {
Get-process | sort -Property vm -Descending | select -first 10 }
PS C:\> &$block
Handles  NPM(K)    PM(K)     WS(K)  VM(M)    CPU(s)      Id ProcessName
-------  ------    -----     -----  -----    ------      -- -----------
    680      42    14772     13576   1387      3.84     404 svchost
    454      26    68368     75116    626      1.28    1912 powershell
    396      37   179136     99252    623      8.45    2700 powershell
    497      29    15104      6048    615      0.41    2500 SearchIndexer
    260      20     4088      8328    356      0.08    3044 taskhost
    550      47    16716     13180    344      1.25    1128 svchost
   1091      55    19712     35036    311      1.81    3056 explorer
    454      31    56660     15216    182     45.94    1596 MsMpEng
    163      17    62808     27132    162      0.94    2692 dwm
    584      29     7752      8832    159      1.27     892 svchost
```

You can do quite a bit more with script blocks. If you'd like to explore the possibilities on your own, read the shell's `about_script_blocks` help file.

## 26.8 *More tips, tricks, and techniques*

As we said at the outset of this chapter, this is an overview of some random little things that we want to show you but that did not fit neatly into one of the previous chapters. Of course, you'll continue to pick up tips and tricks with the shell as you learn more about it and gain more experience with it.

You can check out our Twitter feeds too—@TylerLeonhardt, @TravisPlunk, and @PSJamesP—where we routinely share tips and techniques that we discover and find useful. And don't forget the forums at PowerShell.org. Sometimes, learning bit by bit can be an easy way to become more proficient in a technology, so consider these and any other sources you run across as a way to incrementally and continually improve your PowerShell expertise.

# *Never the end*

*27*

We've come to nearly the end of this book, but it's hardly the end of your Power-Shell exploration. There's a lot more in the shell to learn, and based on what you've learned in this book, you'll be able to teach yourself much of it. This short chapter will help point you in the right direction.

## 27.1 Ideas for further exploration

First of all, if you are a database administrator, either by trade or by accident, we highly suggest you investigate dbatools, which is a free PowerShell module with over 500 commands that can safely and quickly automate all the tasks you need to do all the time. Like the PowerShell community, the dbatools community is inviting and engaging; you can learn more about them and the module at https://dbatools.io. The team behind dbatools has also written *Learn dbatools in a Month of Lunches* and you can read a free chapter from that book at http://mng.bz/4jED.

This book has focused on the skills and techniques that you need to be an effective PowerShell tool *user*. In other words, you should be able to start accomplishing tasks using all of the thousands of commands that are available for PowerShell, whether your needs relate to Windows, Microsoft 365, SharePoint, or something else.

Your next step is to start combining commands to create automated, multistep processes, and to do so in a way that produces packaged, ready-to-use tools for other people. We call that *tool making*, although it's more of a really long script or function, and it's the topic of its own complete book, *Learn PowerShell Scripting in a Month of Lunches*, by Don Jones and Jeffery Hicks (Manning, 2017). But even with what you've learned in this book, you can produce parameterized scripts that contain as many commands as you need to complete a task—that's the beginning of tool making. What else does tool making involve?

- PowerShell's simplified scripting language
- Scope
- Functions, and the ability to build multiple tools into a single script file
- Error handling
- Writing help
- Debugging
- Custom formatting views
- Custom type extensions
- Script and manifest modules
- Using databases
- Workflows
- Pipeline troubleshooting
- Complex object hierarchies
- Globalization and localization
- Proxy functions
- Constrained remoting and delegated administration
- Using .NET

There's lots more too. If you get interested enough and have the right background skills, you may even be a part of PowerShell's third audience: software developers. A whole set of techniques and technologies exists around developing for PowerShell, using PowerShell during development, and more. It's a big product!

## 27.2 *"Now that I've read the book, where do I start?"*

The best thing to do now is pick a task. Choose something in your production world that you personally find repetitive, and automate it using the shell. Yes, it may take longer to learn how to script it out, but the second time you need it, your work will already be done for you. You'll almost certainly run across things that you don't know how to do, and that's the perfect place to start learning. Here are some of the things we've seen other administrators tackle:

- Write a script that changes the password that a service uses to log in, and have it target multiple computers running that service. (You could do this in a single command.)
- Write a script that automates new user provisioning, including creating user accounts, mailboxes, and home directories.
- Write a script that manages Exchange or M635 mailboxes in some way—perhaps getting reports on the largest mailboxes, or creating charge-back reports based on mailbox sizes.

The biggest thing to remember is to *not overthink it*. One PowerShell developer once met an administrator who struggled for weeks to write a robust file-copying script in PowerShell so that he could deploy content across a web server farm. "Why not just use xcopy or robocopy?" he asked. The administrator stared at him for a minute and then laughed. He'd gotten so wrapped up in "doing it in PowerShell" that he forgot that PowerShell can use all of the excellent utilities that are already out there.

## 27.3   *Other resources you'll grow to love*

We spend a lot of time working with, writing about, and teaching PowerShell. Ask our families—sometimes we barely shut up about it long enough to eat dinner. That means we've accumulated a lot of online resources that we use daily and that we recommend to all of our students. Hopefully they'll provide you with a good starting point as well:

- https://powershell.org—This should be your first stop. You'll find everything from Q&A forums to free e-books, free webinars, live educational events, and a lot more. It's a central gathering place for a big chunk of the PowerShell community, including a podcast that's run for years and years.
- https://youtube.com/powershellorg—PowerShell.org's YouTube channel has tons of free PowerShell videos, including sessions recorded at the PowerShell + DevOps Global Summit.
- https://jdhitsolutions.com—This is Jeff Hick's all-purpose scripting and Power-Shell blog.
- https://devopscollective.org—This is the parent organization for Power-Shell.org, focused on the bigger-picture DevOps approach to IT management.

Students often ask if there are any other PowerShell books that we recommend. Two are *Learn PowerShell Scripting in a Month of Lunches* by Don Jones and Jeffery Hicks (Manning, 2017) and *PowerShell in Depth, Second Edition,* by Don Jones, Jeffery Hicks, and Richard Siddaway (Manning, 2014). *Windows PowerShell in Action, Third Edition* (Manning, 2017), is a comprehensive look at the language by one of its designers, Bruce Payette, along with Richard Siddaway, a Microsoft MVP. We also recommend *PowerShell Deep Dives* by Jeffery Hicks, Richard Siddaway, Oisin Grehan, and Aleksandar Nikolic (Manning, 2013), a collection of deep technical articles authored by PowerShell MVPs (proceeds from the book benefit the Save the Children charity, so please buy three copies). Finally, if you're a fan of video training, there are plenty of PowerShell videos at http://Pluralsight.com. And Tyler has a video introduction to PowerShell, "How to Navigate the PowerShell Help System," originally recorded for Twitch, now available for free at http://mng.bz/QW6R.

# *appendix*
# *PowerShell cheat sheet*

This is our opportunity to assemble a lot of the little *gotchas* into a single place. If you're ever having trouble remembering what something is or does, flip to this appendix first.

## A.1 Punctuation

PowerShell is full of punctuation, and much of it has a different meaning in the help files than it does in the shell itself. Here's what it all means within the shell:

- *Backtick* (`` ` ``)—PowerShell's escape character. It removes the special meaning of any character that follows it. For example, a space is normally a separator, which is why `cd c:\Program Files` generates an error. Escaping the space, `` cd c:\Program` Files ``, removes that special meaning and forces the space to be treated as a literal, so the command works.

- *Tilde* (~)—When the tilde is used as part of a path, it represents the current user's home directory, as defined in the `UserProfile` environment variable.

- *Parentheses* ( )—These are used in a couple of ways:
  - Just as in math, parentheses define the order of execution. PowerShell executes parenthetical commands first, from the innermost parentheses to the outermost. This is a good way to run a command and have its output feed the parameter of another command: `Get-Service -computerName (Get-Content c:\computernames.txt)`.
  - Parentheses also enclose the parameters of a method, and they must be included even if the method doesn't require any parameters: `$mystring.replace('ship','spaceship')` for example, or `Delete()`.

- *Square brackets* []—These have two main uses in the shell:
  - They contain the index number when you want to refer to a single object within an array or collection: `$services[2]` gets the third object from `$services` (indexes are always zero-based).

313

- They contain a data type when you're casting a piece of data as a specific type. For example, `$myresult / 3 -as [int]` casts the result as a whole number (integer), and `[xml]$data = Get-Content data.xml` will read the contents of `Data.xml` and attempt to parse it as a valid XML document.
- *Curly braces* `{}`—Also called *curly brackets*, these have three uses:
  - They contain blocks of executable code or commands, called *script blocks*. These are often fed to parameters that expect a script block or a filter block: `Get-Service | Where-Object { $_.Status -eq 'Running' }`.
  - They contain the key-value pairs that make up a new hash table. The opening brace is always preceded by an `@` sign. In the following example, we use braces both to enclose the hash table key-value pairs (of which there are two) and to enclose an expression script block, which is the value for the second key, e: `$hashtable = @{l='Label';e={expression}}`.
  - When a variable name contains spaces or other characters normally illegal in a variable name, braces must surround the name: `${My Variable}`.
- *Single quotation marks* (`'`)—These contain string values. PowerShell doesn't look for the escape character, nor does it look for variables, inside single quotes.
- *Double quotation marks* (`"`)—These contain string values. PowerShell looks for escape characters and the `$` character inside double quotes. Escape characters are processed, the characters following a `$` symbol (alphanumeric characters) are taken as a variable name, and the contents of that variable are substituted. For example, if the variable `$one` contains the value `World`, then `$two = "Hello $one `n"` will contain `Hello World` and a carriage return (`` `n `` is a carriage return).
- *Dollar sign* (`$`)—This tells the shell that the following alphanumeric characters represent a variable name. This can be tricky when working with cmdlets that manage variables. Supposing that `$one` contains the value `two`, then `New-Variable -name $one -value 'Hello'` will create a new variable named `two`, with the value `Hello`, because the dollar sign tells the shell that you want to use the contents of `$one`. In contrast, `New-Variable -name one -value 'Hello'` would create a new variable, `$one`.
- *Percent sign* (`%`)—This is an alias for the `ForEach-Object` cmdlet. It's also the modulus operator, returning the remainder from a division operation.
- *Question mark* (`?`)—This is an alias for the `Where-Object` cmdlet.
- *Right angle bracket* (`>`)—This is a sort of alias for the `Out-File` cmdlet. It's not technically a true alias, but it does provide for cmd.exe-style file redirection: `dir > files.txt`.
- *Math operators* (`+`, `-`, `*`, `/`, *and* `%`)—These function as standard arithmetic operators. Note that `+` is also used for string concatenation.
- *Dash, or hyphen* (`-`)—This precedes both parameter names and many operators, such as `-computerName` or `-eq`. It also separates the verb and noun components of a cmdlet name, as in `Get-Content`, and serves as the subtraction arithmetic operator.

- *At sign* (@)—This sign has four uses in the shell:
  - It precedes a hash table's opening curly brace (see curly braces in this list).
  - When used before parentheses, it encloses a comma-separated list of values that form an array: `$array = @(1,2,3,4)`. Both the @ sign and the parentheses are optional, because the shell will normally treat any comma-separated list as an array anyway.
  - It denotes a here-string, which is a block of literal string text. A here-string starts with `@"` and ends with `"@`, and the closing mark must be on the beginning of a new line. Run `help about_quoting_rules` for more information and examples. Here-strings can also be defined using single quotes.
  - It is PowerShell's splat operator. If you construct a hash table in which the keys match parameter names, and those values' keys are the parameters' values, then you can splat the hash table to a cmdlet. Run `help about_splatting` to learn more.
- *Ampersand* (&)—This is PowerShell's invocation operator, instructing the shell to treat something as a command and to run it. For example, `$a = "Dir"` places the string `Dir` into the variable `$a`. Then `& $a` will run the `Dir` command.
- *Semicolon* (;)—This is used to separate two independent PowerShell commands that are included on a single line: `Dir ; Get-Process` will run `Dir` and then `Get-Process`. The results are sent to a single pipeline, but the results of `Dir` aren't piped to `Get-Process`.
- *Pound sign, or hash tag* (#)—This is used as a comment character. Any characters following #, to the next carriage return, are ignored by the shell. The angle brackets (< and >) are used as part of the tags that define a block comment: Use `<#` to start a block comment and `#>` to end one. Everything within the block comment will be ignored by the shell.
- *Equals sign* (=)—This is the assignment operator, used to assign a value to a variable: `$one = 1`. It isn't used for quality comparisons; use `-eq` instead. Note that the equals sign can be used in conjunction with a math operator: `$var +=5` will add 5 to whatever is currently in `$var`.
- *Pipe* (|)—This is used to convey the output of one cmdlet to the input of another. The second cmdlet (the one receiving the output) uses pipeline parameter binding to determine which parameter or parameters will receive the piped-in objects. Chapters 6 and 10 have discussions of this process.
- *Forward or backward slash* (/, \)—These are used as division operators in mathematical expressions; either the forward slash (/) or backslash (\) can be used as a path separator in file paths: C:\Windows is the same as C:\Windows. The backslash is also used as an escape character in WMI filter criteria and in regular expressions.
- *Period* (.)—This has three main uses:

- It's used to indicate that you want to access a member, such as a property or method, or an object: `$_.Status` will access the `Status` property of whatever object is in the `$_` placeholder.
- It's used to dot-source a script, meaning that the script will be run within the current scope, and anything defined by that script will remain defined after the script completes: `. c:\myscript.ps1`.
- Two dots (`..`) form the range operator, which is discussed later in this appendix. You will also see two dots used to refer to the parent folder in the filesystem, such as in the `..\` path.

- *Comma* (`,`)—Outside quotation marks, the comma separates the items in a list or array: `"One",2,"Three",4`. It can be used to pass multiple static values to a parameter that can accept them: `Get-Process -computername Server1, Server2,Server3`.

- *Colon* (`:`)—The colon (technically, two colons) is used to access static members of a class; this gets into .NET Framework programming concepts; `[-datetime]::now` is an example (although you could achieve that same task by running `Get-Date`).

- *Exclamation point* (`!`)—This is an alias for the `-not` Boolean operator.

We think the only piece of punctuation on a US keyboard that PowerShell doesn't actively use for something is the caret (`^`), although those do get used in regular expressions.

## A.2   *Help file*

Punctuation within the help file takes on slightly different meanings:

- *Square brackets* `[]`—When square brackets surround any text, it indicates that the text is optional. That might include an entire parameter (`[-Name <string>]`), or it might indicate that a parameter is positional and that the name is optional (`[-Name] <string>`). It can also indicate both that a parameter is optional and, if used, can be used positionally (`[[-Name] <string>]`). If you're in any doubt, it's always legal to use the parameter name.

- *Adjacent square brackets* `[]`—These indicate that a parameter can accept multiple values (`<string[]>` instead of `<string>`).

- *Angle brackets* `< >`—These surround data types, indicating what kind of value or object a parameter expects: `<string>`, `<int>`, `<process>`, and so forth.

Always take the time to read the full help (add `-full` to the `help` command), because it provides maximum detail as well as, in most cases, usage examples.

## A.3   *Operators*

PowerShell doesn't use the traditional comparison operators found in most programming languages. Instead, it uses these:

- -eq—Equality (-ceq for case-sensitive string comparisons).
- -ne—Inequality (-cne for case-sensitive string comparisons).
- -ge—Greater than or equal to (-cge for case-sensitive string comparisons).
- -le—Less than or equal to (-cle for case-sensitive string comparisons).
- -gt—Greater than (-cgt for case-sensitive string comparisons).
- -lt—Less than (-clt for case-sensitive string comparisons).
- -contains—Returns True if the specified collection contains the object specified ($collection -contains $object); -notcontains is the reverse.
- -in—Returns True if the specified object is in the specified collection ($object -in $collection); -notin is the reverse.

Logical operators are used to combine multiple comparisons:

- -not—Reverses True and False (the ! symbol is an alias for this operator).
- -and—Both subexpressions must be True for the entire expression to be True.
- -or—Either subexpression can be True for the entire expression to be True.

In addition, there are operators that perform specific functions:

- -join—Joins the elements of an array into a delimited string.
- -split—Splits a delimited string into an array.
- -replace—Replaces occurrences of one string with another.
- -is—Returns True if an item is of the specified type ($one -is [int]).
- -as—Casts the item as the specified type ($one -as [int]).
- ..—Is a range operator; 1..10 returns 10 objects, 1 through 10.
- -f—Is the format operator, replacing placeholders with values: "{0}, {1}" -f "Hello","World".

## A.4  *Custom property and column syntax*

In several chapters, we showed you how to define custom properties by using Select-Object, or custom columns and list entries by using Format-Table and -Format-List, respectively. Here's that hash table syntax—you do this for each custom property or column:

```
@{label='Column_or_Property_Name';expression={Value_expression}}
```

Both of the keys, Label and Expression, can be abbreviated as l and e, respectively (be sure to type a lowercase *L* and not the number 1; you could also use n for Name, in place of the lowercase *L*):

```
@{n='Column_or_Property_Name';e={Value_expression}}
```

Within the expression, the $_ placeholder can be used to refer to the current object (such as the current table row, or the object to which you're adding a custom property):

```
@{n='ComputerName';e={$_.Name}}
```

Both `Select-Object` and the `Format-` cmdlets look for the n (or name or label or l) key and the e key; the `Format-` cmdlets can also use `width` and `align` (those are for `-Format-Table` only) and `formatstring`. Read the help for `Format-Table` for examples.

## A.5    *Pipeline parameter input*

In chapter 10, you learned that there are two types of parameter binding: `ByValue` and `ByPropertyName`. `ByValue` occurs first, and `ByPropertyName` occurs only if `ByValue` doesn't work.

For `ByValue`, the shell looks at the type of the object that's piped in. You can discover that type name by piping the object to `gm` yourself. The shell then looks to see whether any of the cmdlet's parameters accept that type of input and are configured to accept pipeline input `ByValue`. It's not possible for a cmdlet to have two parameters binding the same data type in this fashion. In other words, you shouldn't see a cmdlet that has two parameters, each of which accepts <string> input and both of which accept pipeline input `ByValue`.

If `ByValue` doesn't work, the shell switches to `ByPropertyName`. Here it looks at the properties of the piped-in object and attempts to find parameters with the exact same names that can accept pipeline input `ByPropertyName`. If the piped-in object has properties `Name`, `Status`, and `ID`, the shell will look to see whether the cmdlet has parameters named `Name`, `Status`, and `ID`. Those parameters must also be tagged as accepting pipeline input `ByPropertyName`, which you can see when reading the full help (add `-full` to the `help` command).

Let's look at how PowerShell does this. For this example, we'll refer to the *first cmdlet* and *second cmdlet*, assuming you have a command that looks something like `Get-Service | Stop-Service` or `Get-Service | Stop-Process`. PowerShell follows this process:

1  What is the `TypeName` of the objects produced by the first cmdlet? You can pipe the results of the cmdlet to `Get-Member` on your own to see this. For multipart type names such as `System.Diagnostics.Process`, remember just that last bit: `Process`.

2  Do any parameters of the second cmdlet accept the kind of object produced by the first cmdlet (read the full help for the second cmdlet to determine this: `help <cmdlet name> -full`)? If so, do they also accept that input from the pipeline using the `ByValue` technique? This is shown in the help file's detailed information for each parameter.

3  If the answer to step 2 is yes, then the entire object produced by the first cmdlet will be attached to the parameter identified in step 2. You're finished—do not continue to step 4. But if the answer to step 2 is no, continue to step 4.

4  Consider the objects produced by the first cmdlet. What properties do those objects have? You can see this, again, by piping the first cmdlet's output to `Get-Member`.

5  Consider the parameters of the second cmdlet (you'll need to read the full help again). Are there any parameters that (a) have the same name as one of the properties from step 4, and (b) accept pipeline input using the `ByPropertyName` technique?

If any parameters meet the criteria in step 5, the properties' values will be attached to the same-named parameters, and the second cmdlet will run. If there are no matches between property names and `ByPropertyName`-enabled parameters, the second cmdlet will run with no pipeline input.

Keep in mind that you can always manually enter parameters and values on any command. Doing so will prevent that parameter from accepting pipeline input in any way, even if it would normally have done so.

## A.6   *When to use $_*

This is probably one of the most confusing things about the shell: when is the `$_` placeholder permitted? As we learned earlier, the `$_` is a placeholder for the next object in the pipeline.

This placeholder works only when the shell is explicitly looking for it and is prepared to fill it in with something. Generally speaking, that happens only within a script block that's dealing with pipeline input, in which case the `$_` placeholder will contain one pipeline input object at a time. You'll run across this in a few places:

- In the filtering script block used by `Where-Object`:

```
Get-Service | Where-Object {$_.Status -eq 'Running' }
```

- In the script blocks passed to `ForEach-Object`, such as the main `Process` script block typically used with the cmdlet:

```
Get-CimInstance -class Win32_Service -filter "name='mssqlserver'" |
ForEach-Object -process { $_.ChangeStartMode('Automatic') }
```

- In the `Process` script block of a filtering function or an advanced function. *Learn PowerShell Toolmaking in a Month of Lunches* by Don Jones and Jeffery Hicks (Manning, 2012), discusses these.
- In the expression of a hash table that's being used to create a custom property or table column.

In every one of those cases, `$_` occurs only within the curly braces of a script block. That's a good rule to remember for figuring out when it's okay to use `$_`.

# *index*

## RELATED MANNING TITLES

### Learn PowerShell Scripting in a Month of Lunches
by Don Jones and Jeffery Hicks

ISBN 9781617295096
352 pages, $44.99
November 2017

### Learn Azure in a Month of Lunches, Second Edition
by Iain Foulds

ISBN 9781617297625
368 pages, $49.99
June 2020

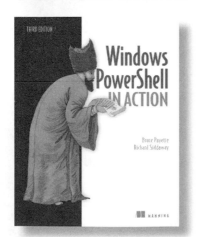

### Windows PowerShell in Action, Third Edition
by Bruce Payette and Richard Siddaway

ISBN 9781633430297
904 pages, $59.99
September 2017

*For ordering information go to www.manning.com*